How to
Master Skills for the
TOEFL iBT

新托福考试专项进阶
——中级听力

Listening

Intermediate

Will Link | Monika N. Kushwaha | Michael Kato | E2K

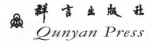

群言出版社
Qunyan Press

图书在版编目(CIP)数据

新托福考试专项进阶. 中级听力 ／（美）林克（Link，
W.），（美）库瓦哈（Kushwaha, M.N.）编著 .— 北京：
群言出版社，2009（2014.9重印）
  ISBN 978-7-80080-983-5

  I. ①新… II. ①林… ②库… III. ①英语—听说教学—高等
教育—自学参考资料 IV. ①H310.41

  中国版本图书馆CIP数据核字（2009）第027383号

版权登记：图字01—2008—3946号

How to Master Skills for the TOEFL iBT Listening Intermediate + 1MP3
Copyright © 2007, Darakwon Press
Chinese language translation rights © 2009
by Qunyan Press
Chinese language translation rights arranged with Darakwon Press

责任编辑　张　茜
封面设计　大愚设计+贾臻臻
出版发行　群言出版社(Qunyan Press)

地　　址　北京市东城区东厂胡同北巷1号（100006）
网　　站　www.qypublish.com
电子信箱　bj62605588@163.com　qunyancbs@126.com
总 编 办　010-62605588　65265404　65138815
发 行 部　010-62605019　62263345　65220236
经　　销　全国新华书店
读者服务　010-62418641　65265404　65263345
法律顾问　北京市君泰律师事务所

印　　刷　北京四季青印刷厂
版　　次　2009年8月第1版　2014年9月第13次印刷
开　　本　880×1230　1/16
印　　张　21.5
字　　数　296千字
书　　号　ISBN 978-7-80080-983-5
定　　价　45.00元

Contents

Contents(Answer Book)

Introduction

A. Information on the TOEFL® iBT

The Format of the TOEFL® iBT

Section	Number of Questions	Timing	Score
Reading	• **3~5 Passages** – approximately 700 words each – 12~14 questions per passage	60~100 min.	30 points
Listening	• **2~3 Conversations** – 12~25 exchanges each (3 min.) – 5 questions per conversation • **4~6 Lectures** – 500~800 words each (3~5 min.) – 6 questions per lecture	60~90 min.	30 points
BREAK		10 min.	
Speaking	• **2 Independent Tasks** (preparation: 15 sec. / response: 45 sec.) ❶ 1 personal experience ❷ 1 personal choice/opinion • **2 Integrated Tasks:** Read-Listen-Speak (preparation: 30 sec. / response: 60 sec.) ❶ 1 campus situation topic – reading: 75~100 words (45 sec.) – conversation: 150~180 words (60~80 sec.) ❷ 1 academic course topic – reading: 75~100 words (45 sec.) – lecture: 150~220 words (60~90 sec.) • **2 Integrated Tasks:** Listen-Speak (preparation: 20 sec. / response: 60 sec.) ❶ 1 campus situation topic – conversation: 180~220 words (60~90 sec.) ❷ 1 academic course topic – lecture: 230~280 words (90~120 sec.)	20 min.	30 points
Writing	• **1 Integrated Task:** Read-Listen-Write (20 min.) – reading: 230~300 words (3 min.) – lecture: 230~300 words (2 min.) – a summary of 150~225 words • **1 Independent Task** (30 min.) – a minimum 300-word essay	50 min.	30 points

B. Information on the Listening Section

The Listening section of the TOEFL® iBT measures test takers' ability to understand spoken English in English-speaking colleges and universities. This section has 2~3 conversations that are 12~25 exchanges (about 3 minutes) long and 4~6 lectures that are 500~800 words (3~5 minutes) long. Each conversation is followed by 5 questions and each lecture by 6 questions. Therefore, test takers have to answer 34 to 51 questions in total. The time allotted to the Listening section is 60 to 90 minutes, including the time spent listening to the conversations and lectures and answering the questions.

1. Types of Listening Passages

(1) Conversations
  _ Between a student and a professor or a teaching assistant during office hours
  _ Between a student with a person related to school services such as a librarian, housing director, bookstore employee, etc.

(2) Lectures
  _ Monologue lectures delivered by a professor unilaterally
  _ Interactive lectures with one or two students asking questions or making comments
  * One lecture may be spoken with a British or Australian accent.

2. Types of Questions

Basic Comprehension Questions

(1) Listening for Main Ideas _ This type of question asks you to identify the overall topic or main idea of a lecture or conversation.

(2) Listening for Main Purpose _ This type of question asks you why the speakers are having a conversation or why a lecture is given.

(3) Listening for Major Details _ This type of question asks you to understand specific details or facts from a conversation or lecture.

Pragmatic Understanding Questions

(4) Understanding the Function of What Is Said
  _ This type of question asks you why a speaker mentions some point in the conversation or lecture.
  _ This involves replaying part of the listening passage.

(5) Understanding the Speaker's Attitude
  _ This type of question asks you what a speaker's feelings, opinions, or degree of certainty is about some issue, idea, or person.
  _ This may involve replaying part of the listening passage.

Connecting Information Questions

(6) Understanding Organization _ This type of question asks you how the listening passage is organized or how two portions of the listening passage are related to each other.

(7) Connecting Content _ This type of question asks you to classify or sequence information in a different way from the way it was presented in the listening passage.

(8) Making Inferences _ This type of question asks you to draw a conclusion based on information given in the listening passage.

How to Use This Book

How to Master Skills for the TOEFL® iBT Listening Intermediate is designed to be used either as a textbook for a TOEFL® iBT listening preparation course or as a tool for individual learners who are preparing for the TOEFL® test on their own. With a total of 8 units, this book is organized to prepare you for the test with a comprehensive understanding of the test and thorough analysis of every question type. Each unit consists of 6 parts and provides a step-by-step program that provides question-solving strategies and the development of test-taking abilities. At the back of the book is a practice test of the Listening section of the TOEFL® iBT.

❶ Overview

This part is designed to prepare you for the type of question the unit covers. You will be given a full description of the question type and its application in the passage. You also will be given some useful tips as well as an illustrated introduction and sample.

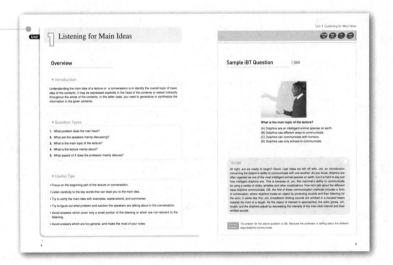

❷ Basic Drill

The purpose of this part is for you to make sure you understand the new types of questions that were described in the overview. In this part, you will be given a chance to confirm your understanding of the question types in short lectures and conversations before starting on the practice exercises.

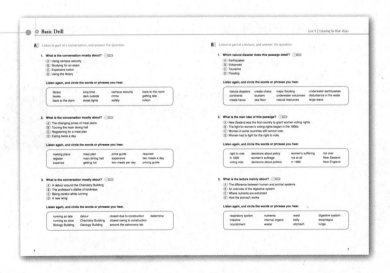

❸ Conversation & Lecture Practice

This part is the practical exercise section where you can actually practice and improve your ability to solve questions. With a total of 8 conversations and lectures, you will be able to confirm your understanding of the question types and master skills presented in each unit. A graphic organizer will be given to help you understand the material, and definitions of difficult words will also be given to help you solve the questions.

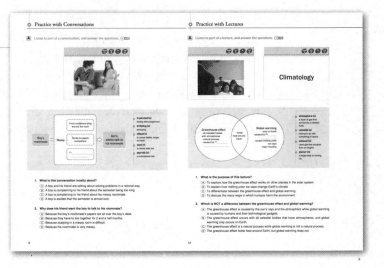

❹ Integrated Listening & Speaking

The TOEFL iBT is different from previous tests in that it is more integrated than ever. So in this part, you will be given a chance to experience the iBT style study by linking your listening skills with your speaking skills. Listen to the lectures and the summaries of the conversations again, and answer the questions. But remember! This time you have to say the answers. There is no writing.

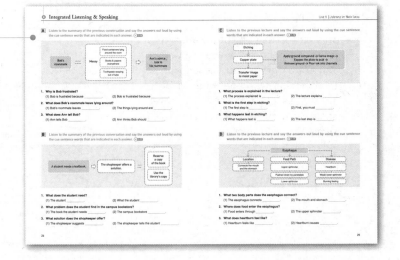

❺ Mini TOEFL iBT

This part will give you a chance to experience an actual TOEFL iBT test. You will be given two passages with 5 or 6 questions each. The topics are similar to those on the actual test, as are the questions.

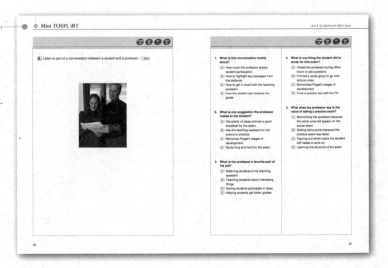

❻ Vocabulary Review

This part offers you a chance to review some of the words and phrases you need to remember after finishing each unit. Vocabulary words for each unit are also provided at the back of the book to help you prepare for each unit.

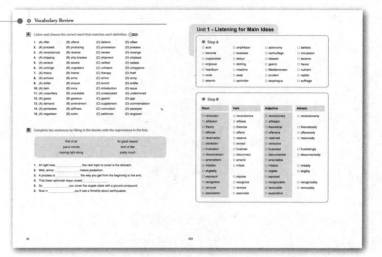

❼ Actual Test

This part offers a full practice test that is modeled on the Listening section of the TOEFL® iBT. This will familiarize you with the actual test format of the TOEFL® iBT.

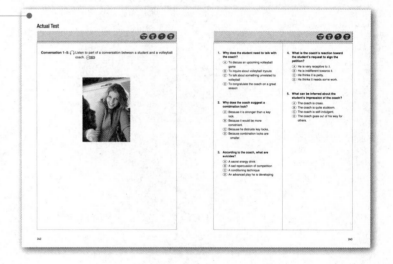

PART

Basic Comprehension

Basic comprehension of the listening passage is tested in three ways: listening for the main ideas, listening for main purpose, and listening for major details. Listening for the main ideas is to identify the overall topic of the contents. Listening for the main purpose is to search for the reason behind the contents. For questions about major details, you must understand and remember explicit details or facts from a lecture or conversation.

Unit 1

Listening for Main Ideas

1 Listening for Main Ideas

Overview

■ Introduction

Understanding the main idea of a lecture or a conversation is to identify the overall topic or basic idea of the contents. It may be expressed explicitly in the head of the contents or stated indirectly throughout the whole of the contents. In the latter case, you need to generalize or synthesize the information in the given contents.

■ Question Types

1. What problem does the man have?

2. What are the speakers mainly discussing?

3. What is the main topic of the lecture?

4. What is the lecture mainly about?

5. What aspect of X does the professor mainly discuss?

■ Useful Tips

• Focus on the beginning part of the lecture or conversation.

• Listen carefully to the key words that can lead you to the main idea.

• Try to verify the main idea with examples, explanations, and summaries.

• Try to figure out what problem and solution the speakers are talking about in the conversation.

• Avoid answers which cover only a small portion of the listening or which are not relevant to the listening.

• Avoid answers which are too general, and make the most of your notes.

Sample iBT Question

What is the main topic of the lecture?

(A) Dolphins are an intelligent animal species on earth.
(B) Dolphins use different ways to communicate.
(C) Dolphins can communicate with humans.
(D) Dolphins use only echoes to communicate.

Script

All right, are we ready to begin? Good. Last class we left off with, um, an introduction concerning the dolphin's ability to communicate with one another. As you know, dolphins are often regarded as one of the most intelligent animal species on earth, but it is hard to say just how intelligent dolphins are. This is because of, um, this mammal's ability to communicate by using a variety of clicks, whistles and other vocalizations. Now let's talk about the different ways dolphins communicate. OK, the first of these communication methods includes a form of echolocation; where dolphins locate an object by producing sounds and then listening for the echo. It works like this: um, broadband clicking sounds are emitted in a focused beam towards the front of a target. As the object of interest is approached, the echo grows, um, louder; and the dolphins adjust by decreasing the intensity of the inter-click interval and their emitted sounds.

Correct Answer The answer for the above question is (B). Because the professor is talking about the different ways dolphins communicate.

Basic Drill

1. **What is the conversation mostly about?** (o) 1-02
   - (A) Using campus security
   - (B) Studying for an exam
   - (C) Expensive tuition
   - (D) Using the library

   Listen again, and circle the words or phrases you hear.

library	long time	campus security	back to the room
books	dark outside	crime	getting late
back to the dorm	street lights	safety	tuition

2. **What is the conversation mostly about?** (o) 1-03
   - (A) The changing prices of meal plans
   - (B) Touring the main dining hall
   - (C) Registering for a meal plan
   - (D) Eating twice a day

   Listen again, and circle the words or phrases you hear.

making plans	meal plan	price guide	required
register	main dining hall	expensive	two meals a day
expense	getting full	two meals per day	pricing guide

3. **What is the conversation mostly about?** (o) 1-04
   - (A) A detour around the Chemistry Building
   - (B) The professor's dislike of tardiness
   - (C) Being careful while running
   - (D) A new wing

   Listen again, and circle the words or phrases you hear.

running so late	detour	closed due to construction	determine
running so slow	Chemistry Building	closed owing to construction	
Biology Building	Geology Building	around the astronomy lab	

B   Listen to part of a lecture, and answer the question.

1.   **Which natural disaster does this passage detail?** 〔◎ 1-05〕

   Ⓐ Earthquakes
   Ⓑ Volcanoes
   Ⓒ Tsunamis
   Ⓓ Flooding

Listen again, and circle the words or phrases you hear.

natural disasters	create chaos	major flooding	underwater earthquakes
continents	tsunami	underwater volcanoes	disturbance in the water
create havoc	sea floor	natural resources	large wave

2.   **What is the main idea of this passage?** 〔◎ 1-06〕

   Ⓐ New Zealand was the first country to grant women voting rights.
   Ⓑ The fight for women's voting rights began in the 1800s.
   Ⓒ Women in some countries still cannot vote.
   Ⓓ Women had to fight for the right to vote.

Listen again, and circle the words or phrases you hear.

right to vote	decisions about policy	women's suffering	not over
in 1829	women's suffrage	not at all	New Zealand
voting riots	decisions about politics	in 1892	New England

3.   **What is the lecture mainly about?** 〔◎ 1-07〕

   Ⓐ The difference between human and animal systems
   Ⓑ An overview of the digestive system
   Ⓒ Where nutrients are extracted
   Ⓓ How the stomach works

Listen again, and circle the words or phrases you hear.

respiratory system	nutrients	waist	digestive system
intestine	internal organs	belly	esophagus
nourishment	waste	stomach	lungs

Practice with Conversations

A Listen to part of a conversation, and answer the questions. 🔘 1-08

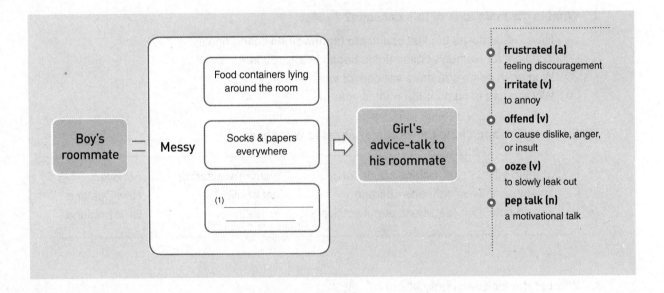

Boy's roommate — Messy

Food containers lying around the room

Socks & papers everywhere

(1) _____

Girl's advice-talk to his roommate

frustrated (a)
feeling discouragement

irritate (v)
to annoy

offend (v)
to cause dislike, anger, or insult

ooze (v)
to slowly leak out

pep talk (n)
a motivational talk

1. **What is this conversation mostly about?**

   Ⓐ A boy and his friend are talking about solving problems in a rational way.

   Ⓑ A boy is complaining to his friend about the semester being too long.

   Ⓒ A boy is complaining to his friend about his messy roommate.

   Ⓓ A boy is excited that the semester is almost over.

2. **Why does his friend want the boy to talk to his roommate?**

   Ⓐ Because the boy's roommate's papers are all over the boy's desk.

   Ⓑ Because they have to live together for 2 and a half months.

   Ⓒ Because studying in a messy room is difficult.

   Ⓓ Because his roommate is very messy.

3. Listen again, and fill in the blanks.

> **W:** So how are things going with your roommate?
>
> **M:** Oh man, he's still really _____. I can't wait till the semester is over.
>
> **W:** But Bob, the semester won't be over for _____! You have to figure out how, you know, _____. Yeah, you have to talk to him.
>
> **M:** Yeah, but I don't know what to say. I mean, I don't want to hurt his feelings or _____ him or anything. But, seriously, if he doesn't get rid of those pizza boxes, I think I'm _____.
>
> **W:** See, this is why _____. Because, you're obviously _____. I mean, I don't think it's _____ not to want empty food containers lying around the room. I mean, they could attract cockroaches. That's so gross!
>
> **M:** And it's not just the pizza boxes, which, believe me, are bad enough! His socks are everywhere, his papers are all over my desk, and his _____ _____. He won't even put a cap on it! I really think it's _____. I mean, I don't want to get sick.
>
> **W:** Oh, man! That's really _____. You could definitely get sick from that. It's _____. You just have to _____. Just be calm, and tell him that you don't appreciate his mess. Oh! You could even suggest that the two of you _____. If he has to clean up his own mess, maybe he won't make one!
>
> **M:** Yeah, I suppose I could _____. I really appreciate the suggestions. I mean, I guess I really do have to figure something out because we're not even _____.
>
> **W:** Hey, don't mention it. And if you _____ or anything, you can always ask. I'm happy to be of assistance.

4. Complete the following summary.

Bob is _____ because his roommate is _____. His roommate leaves food containers, socks, papers, and toothpaste _____. Bob is concerned that because of the _____, he might get sick. The woman convinces Bob to _____. She says it is important because Bob has to live with his roommate for another two and a half months. The woman suggests that Bob and his roommate _____ together once a week. Bob appreciates the woman's help.

unhygienic room	frustrated
clean the room	talk to his roommate
very messy	lying around

B Listen to part of a conversation, and answer the questions. 🎧 1-09

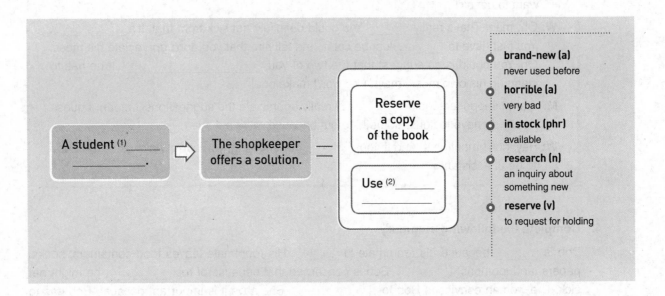

A student (1)_____ _____.

⇨ The shopkeeper offers a solution.

Reserve a copy of the book

Use (2)_____ _____

- **brand-new (a)** never used before
- **horrible (a)** very bad
- **in stock (phr)** available
- **research (n)** an inquiry about something new
- **reserve (v)** to request for holding

1. **What is this conversation mostly about?**

   Ⓐ A student needs a textbook that the store does not have in stock.
   Ⓑ The shopkeeper thinks the student should have come yesterday.
   Ⓒ A student needs help reserving a textbook.
   Ⓓ A student needs help finding the library.

2. **What does the shopkeeper tell the student to do while he waits for his textbook?**

   Ⓐ Borrow a classmate's textbook and photocopy the chapters
   Ⓑ Look for the textbook in the store's computer database
   Ⓒ Come back in a week to buy the textbook
   Ⓓ Check out the textbook at the library

3. Listen again, and fill in the blanks.

M1: Hey, how's it going? Welcome back to school. Can I help you with anything?

M2: Yeah, actually, I hope so. I was looking for this book that I need for my, um, my _____ _____. The professor really wants us to _____ now and _____, and I can't seem to find it on the shelves.

M1: All right, well let me see if I can help you with that. What's the name of the book? Oh, and if you have the author, that would probably be really helpful, too.

M2: Okay, hold on. I have to find where I wrote it down. Okay, got it. The title of the book is *Methods of Educational Research*. And the author is, um, Wiersma.

M1: All right, let me _____ to see if we have any in stock. Um, Wiersma, did you say? And *Methods of Educational Research*?

M2: Yeah, that was it.

M1: Wow, those _____. We actually had _____ come in yesterday – fifty textbooks – and _____.

M2: Oh, no! I knew I should have come by yesterday. I just got so _____. Are you _____?

M1: Hmm… Yes, I think we're going to get another shipment in, _____. But it's going to be _____. I think just twenty books or so.

M2: Oh, man! I need to have two chapters read by next week already. I don't know what I'm going to do. What a horrible way to start out this semester!

M1: Well, I have a suggestion. You could put your name down _____ that'll be in, and in the meantime, maybe you could check the library to see if they have a copy on reserve. But if you're going to do that, you should probably do it quickly because I'm sure a lot more students are going to be in your position, you know.

M2: Yeah, I guess I'll try that. Um, okay, so where do I _____?

M1: We can do that right here. But remember, you have to _____, or you'll lose your reservation, and it'll go to someone else.

M2: All right, thanks. Thanks for all your help.

4. Complete the following summary.

A student is _____ at the campus bookstore. The shopkeeper informs him that the textbook is _____. He says a new _____ in a week. The student panics because his professor has already _____ of reading from the book. The shopkeeper _____. He thinks the student should see if the book is on reserve at the library. That way, the student can do his reading without _____ while he waits for the new shipment of textbooks.

out of stock	getting behind	assigned several chapters
shipment will arrive	looking for a book	makes a suggestion

Listen to part of a conversation, and answer the questions. 🔊 1-10

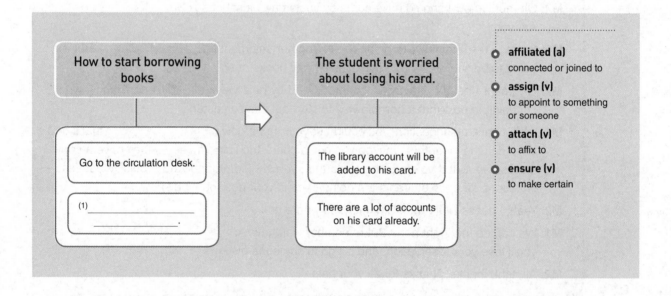

How to start borrowing books

Go to the circulation desk.

(1) _____
_____ .

The student is worried about losing his card.

The library account will be added to his card.

There are a lot of accounts on his card already.

○ **affiliated (a)**
  connected or joined to
○ **assign (v)**
  to appoint to something or someone
○ **attach (v)**
  to affix to
○ **ensure (v)**
  to make certain

1. What is this conversation mostly about?

    Ⓐ The librarian is telling the student how to start borrowing books.
    Ⓑ The librarian tells the student how to get to the circulation desk.
    Ⓒ The student tries to figure out where he left his library card.
    Ⓓ The student is talking about the many uses for his ID card.

2. Why is the student worried about losing his ID card?

    Ⓐ Because he thinks that someone will steal his money if he loses it.
    Ⓑ Because he will not be able to check out library books without it.
    Ⓒ Because there are a lot of accounts on his card.
    Ⓓ Because it will be very difficult to replace.

3. Listen again, and fill in the blanks.

W: All first-year students are required to do a _____ with a librarian or a _____ their first semester. So welcome!

M: Thank you.

W: Okay, so the first thing I'm going to do is _____ from the _____ . Okay, so what you need to do first is make sure your _____ is registered at the front desk. The _____ will, um, scan your card, and then assign you a kind of, well, _____ every time you _____ a book.

M: But why is that attached to my student ID card? I mean, couldn't I _____? That's how things were at my public library back home.

W: Well no, it's really important that your library card has a _____ of you on it for, um, _____ . See, only students and professors and people _____ _____ from this library. So by attaching a barcode to your student ID, we're pretty much ensuring that you _____ . Plus, since your ID already has your picture on it, we don't, um, we don't have to worry about anyone else using your ID and taking out books.

M: Okay, I guess I can understand that. It's just a little weird to me to have one card for everything here. I mean, it already has my _____ and a _____ on it, not to mention, it _____.

W: Well, that's kind of a good thing. You _____.

M: Well, it's kind of bad, too. If I lose it, I can't do anything. I guess I have to be really careful.

W: I guess you do. It's not so hard. Don't worry.

M: Thanks. Okay, so the first thing I have to do before I can borrow books is, um, _____ _____?

W: That's right! Once you do that, you can start borrowing books!

4. Complete the following summary.

A librarian is _____ to the book borrowing process. She tells him the first step is to _____ to his student identification card. She says that it is important that he has photo identification when borrowing books because only people _____ the university are allowed to borrow books. The student worries about having another _____ his ID card because it already _____, meal plan, and dorm entrance. He's afraid he will lose it. The librarian _____ that he will be fine.

account attached to	get a barcode attached
affiliated with	holds his money accounts
reassures him	orienting a student

D Listen to part of a conversation, and answer the questions. ⊙ 1-11

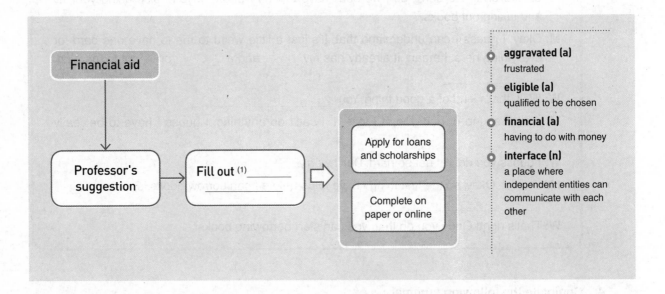

Financial aid

Professor's suggestion → Fill out (1)_____ ⟹

Apply for loans and scholarships

Complete on paper or online

aggravated (a)
frustrated

eligible (a)
qualified to be chosen

financial (a)
having to do with money

interface (n)
a place where independent entities can communicate with each other

1. **What is this conversation mostly about?**

   Ⓐ The student asks the professor about financial aid information.
   Ⓑ The student and professor compare loans and scholarships.
   Ⓒ The student and professor discuss various loan options.
   Ⓓ The professor recommends the student for a scholarship.

2. **Why does the professor tell the student to fill out the financial aid form?**

   Ⓐ Because that is the first step in getting a loan or a scholarship.
   Ⓑ Because the departmental scholarship is very competitive.
   Ⓒ Because that is the only way to transfer to another school.
   Ⓓ Because it is easier to fill it out online than on paper.

3. **Listen again, and fill in the blanks.**

> **W:** Hi, Professor. I was wondering if I could _____.
>
> **M:** Of course, that's what I do. What can I do for you?
>
> **W:** Well, I was going over my _____, and I'm really _____ because, well, I just don't think I'm going to _____ to stay at this university for more than a year. And I really would _____. I mean, I love it here.
>
> **M:** Okay, well I'm sure we can figure something out. Um, have you _____ yet?
>
> **W:** No, I don't think so.
>
> **M:** All right, then that's your first task. That form will help to _____ and, um, _____. Actually, I'm certain that you have to complete that form even if you're going for a _____.
>
> **W:** Oh, wow. So where can I get it? And who do I turn it into? And what kind of information do they ask for?
>
> **M:** Wow, that's a lot of questions. I'm pretty sure you can _____. That is where you should return it as well. Oh! Actually, I think the Financial Assistance Office has _____ so that you can complete the form via the Internet.
>
> **W:** Really? Wow, that's _____!
>
> **M:** Yes, it really is. Um, just find the site for the university's Financial Assistance Office, and you can probably _____ from there.
>
> **W:** I think I'll do that right now. Wait, do you know what kind of information I'll need to fill out the form?
>
> **M:** Um, I think it _____ to fill out the form with _____. That should have all the information you'll need.
>
> **W:** Okay, great. I have a copy of that in my room.
>
> **M:** Oh! And if you get the form in within the next couple of days, _____ _____ we're awarding for next semester. We have both need- and merit-based scholarships available.
>
> **W:** That's excellent! Thank you so much.

4. **Complete the following summary.**

A student asks a professor for advice about _____. Her professor tells her that in order to _____ or a scholarship, she must _____ the financial aid form. The form can be found at the financial aid office or online. The professor _____ to fill out the form as soon as possible. He says this because there are _____ the following semester. The student is very _____ her professor's help and advice.

urges her	get a loan	departmental scholarships available for
receiving financial aid	fill out	grateful for

Practice with Lectures

A Listen to part of a lecture, and answer the questions. 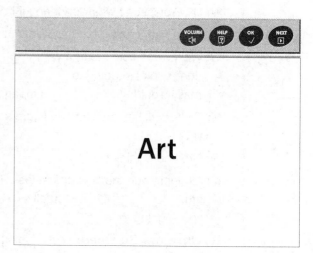 **1-12**

Art

Etching

↓

Copper plate → Apply ground compound → (1)_____ →
Expose the plate to acid →
(2)_____ → Pour ink into channels

↓

Transfer image to moist paper

- **acid-resistant (a)**
  unable to be broken down by acid
- **carve (v)**
  to cut into
- **engraver (n)**
  one who cuts figures, letters, or designs into wood or metal
- **moist (a)**
  damp

1. **What is the lecture mainly about?**
   - Ⓐ The components of ground compound
   - Ⓑ The process used to create an etching
   - Ⓒ Rembrandt's most popular painting
   - Ⓓ Rembrandt's life

2. **How is the image burned into the copper plate?**
   - Ⓐ The image is transferred to the copper plate by the ground compound.
   - Ⓑ Acid is used to carve the image onto the plate.
   - Ⓒ Ink creates the image on the copperplate.
   - Ⓓ The image is carved onto moist paper.

3. Listen again, and fill in the blanks.

> **M1:** All right class, so now we've talked about Rembrandt and his life and a bit about his work. He was _____. The thing is though, that stuff isn't what made him most famous. Rembrandt pretty much _____. We talked a little bit about that technique before, remember? So, who can tell me what etching is?
>
> **W:** Doesn't it involve _____?
>
> **M1:** That's right. Good job. The artist usually has a copper plate that he or she coats or covers _____. Um, this stuff is usually made of beeswax and resin, and this substance is called, um, bitumen. Altogether, it's _____. So what the artist does is _____, all that stuff that I just mentioned, and he carves a design through it with a sharp tool. You have to _____, actually, because you want to get through the ground to uncover the copper underneath. Then the artist _____, and the parts that are uncovered by the ground get eaten away, and _____ into those areas, creating channels. So who knows what's done with the metal plates afterwards?
>
> **M2:** They're used to make prints, right?
>
> **M1:** Absolutely. Great job. Yes, after the ground compound is removed, _____ into the parts that have been eaten away. These channels hold ink really well actually. And then _____, and you _____. Rembrandt was a genius when it came to etchings. I think that after a while, etchings were all he did. Um, let's see, does anyone recognize this etching?
>
> **M2:** I know that one. It's in a museum in Washington, D.C. Um, I think it's called "Woman and Arrow."
>
> **M1:** Pretty close. It's called "The Woman with the Arrow." Rembrandt created this etching in, hmm, 1661, I think. Yes, it was 1661.

4. Complete the following summary.

Etchings are created by covering a copper plate with a _____. Then, the artist _____ into the compound until the copper plate is exposed underneath. Next, the artist _____ over the compound. The parts of the copper plate that are covered with the compound _____. The other parts get _____ by the acid. This creates channels. The artist removes the compound and pours ink into the channels. Finally, the plate is pressed _____. This creates a print.

remain untouched	ground compound	onto moist paper
eaten away	pours acid	cuts an image

B Listen to part of a lecture, and answer the questions. 🔊 1-13

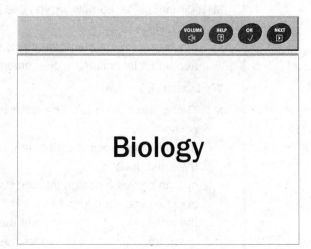

Biology

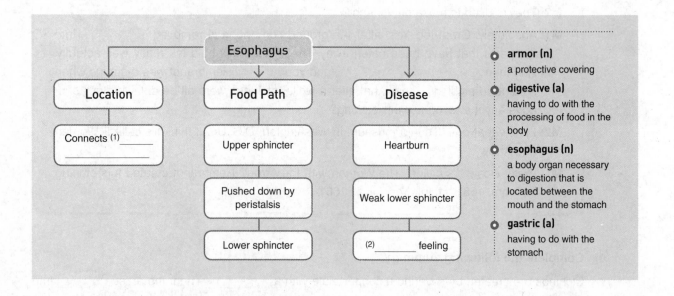

Esophagus

Location → Connects (1) _____ _____

Food Path →
Upper sphincter
↓
Pushed down by peristalsis
↓
Lower sphincter

Disease →
Heartburn
↓
Weak lower sphincter
↓
(2) _____ feeling

- **armor (n)** a protective covering
- **digestive (a)** having to do with the processing of food in the body
- **esophagus (n)** a body organ necessary to digestion that is located between the mouth and the stomach
- **gastric (a)** having to do with the stomach

1. **What is this lecture mostly about?**
   - (A) The reason people get heartburn
   - (B) An overview of the esophagus
   - (C) The location of the esophagus
   - (D) The process of peristalsis

2. **Why do people experience heartburn?**
   - (A) Because the esophagus gets blocked during peristalsis.
   - (B) Because the heart is located near the esophagus.
   - (C) Because the lower sphincter gets weak.
   - (D) Because they have a burning feeling.

3. Listen again, and fill in the blanks.

> After food is swallowed, the _____. The esophagus is basically a
> long tube. It pretty much _____. At the top of the esophagus
> is the, um, the upper _____ which is a ring-like muscle. This stays closed most of the
> time, for good reason. See, after you swallow, _____ to let the food in. Then,
> it closes right away so that the food doesn't come back out.
> Um, so once food is let into the esophagus, a process starts that's called, um, peristalsis,
> the wave-like _____. During peristalsis, the muscles in the esophagus push the
> food down the tube. Picture a toothpaste tube. To get toothpaste out of the tube, you
> have to squeeze from _____. That's what peristalsis is like, except that there's
> _____ from the top of the tube to the bottom. The food is pushed in front of the
> wave till it reaches the bottom of the esophagus. At the bottom of the, um, the esophagus,
> is the lower sphincter. When food gets to that point, the lower sphincter _____
> the stomach. Then it closes up really fast so that the acids from the stomach can't get into
> the esophagus.
> And speaking of acid getting into the esophagus, those acids are what _____
> _____. Heartburn doesn't actually have anything to do with the heart. Actually,
> um, heartburn takes place in the esophagus. It's what happens when the lower
> sphincter gets weak. Gastric acids from the stomach enter the esophagus. They cause a
> _____ feeling. See, these acids don't cause problems in the stomach because
> the stomach has, um, well it has _____, that keeps it from getting hurt. The
> esophagus doesn't have that kind of lining or armor, so gastric acids can really harm it.

4. Complete the following summary.

After food _____, digestion goes on in the esophagus. The esophagus is a long tube that
_____ the mouth and the stomach. Food _____ through the upper sphincter. Then, the
food is _____ the esophagus by a process called peristalsis. Peristalsis happens when the
_____ food down the tube. Food _____ through the lower sphincter. If the lower
sphincter is weak, you can get heartburn.

| enters the esophagus | muscles squeeze | pushed through |
| leaves the esophagus | leaves the mouth | connects |

Listen to part of a lecture, and answer the questions. 🔘 1-14

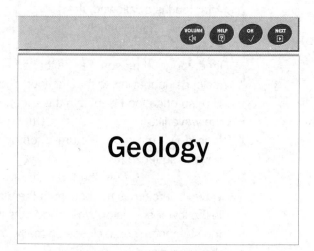

Geology

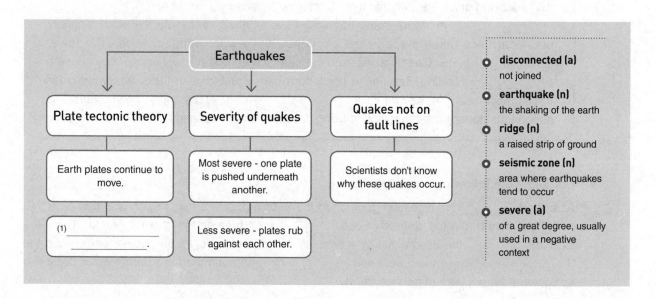

Earthquakes

Plate tectonic theory

Earth plates continue to move.

(1) _____
_____.

Severity of quakes

Most severe - one plate is pushed underneath another.

Less severe - plates rub against each other.

Quakes not on fault lines

Scientists don't know why these quakes occur.

- **disconnected (a)**
  not joined
- **earthquake (n)**
  the shaking of the earth
- **ridge (n)**
  a raised strip of ground
- **seismic zone (n)**
  area where earthquakes tend to occur
- **severe (a)**
  of a great degree, usually used in a negative context

1. **What is this lecture mostly about?**
   - (A) Earthquakes that do not occur on fault lines
   - (B) The severity of earthquakes
   - (C) The plate tectonic theory
   - (D) The causes of earthquakes

2. **Why do the most severe earthquakes occur?**
   - (A) Because one plate gets pushed under another.
   - (B) Because one plate rubs against another.
   - (C) Because the fault line gets agitated.
   - (D) Scientists do not know.

3. Listen again, and fill in the blanks.

> **M1:** The next chapter in our book _____. Um, well, I hope you've all read this chapter because I will be _____ today. Okay, to begin, the authors talk about the plate tectonic _____ as a pretty widely accepted explanation for earthquakes. Who can tell me what this theory states? Yes, go on…
>
> **W:** I think the _____ theory was that the earth's _____ that are kind of disconnected. I think they move against each other.
>
> **M1:** Very good. All right, so yes, the earth's surface is _____. Um, it's made up of these plates that move against each other. The worst earthquakes tend to happen where _____. These quakes start really deep in the _____. Other quakes, um, less severe quakes, happen where the plates slide against each other. Okay, so how many _____ are there?
>
> **M2:** Three.
>
> **M1:** And what are they?
>
> **M2:** Um, one lies around the _____. I think another is called the, um, the _____. I'm pretty sure that one _____ and then across Asia. And the third, the third one is in the ocean, _____.
>
> **M1:** Excellent. Okay, so does anyone have questions about p_____?
>
> **W:** Well, what about earthquakes that don't happen in these zones? I mean, aren't there ever earthquakes that, um, that _____?
>
> **M1:** Great question. Yes, I think that sometimes earthquakes do happen away from, um, seismic zones. These ones are tough to figure out though. So, quakes that don't occur along plate boundaries are called, um, _____. I don't think that scientists have figured out the causes for those yet, but I think that they do agree that, um, there's a lot of, um, _____ where these quakes happen.

4. Complete the following summary.

One theory about why earthquakes happen is called the _____. The earth's surface is _____ that move against each other. The most severe quakes happen when one plate gets _____ another one. Less severe quakes happen when plates _____. Scientists don't really know what causes them. There are three _____ on the earth. But sometimes earthquakes happen away from the seismic zones due to _____.

rub against each other	plate tectonic theory
major earthquake zones	pushed underneath
made up of plates	ground stress

D Listen to part of a lecture, and answer the questions. 🔊 1-15

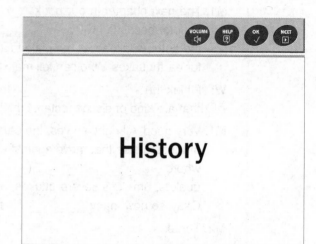

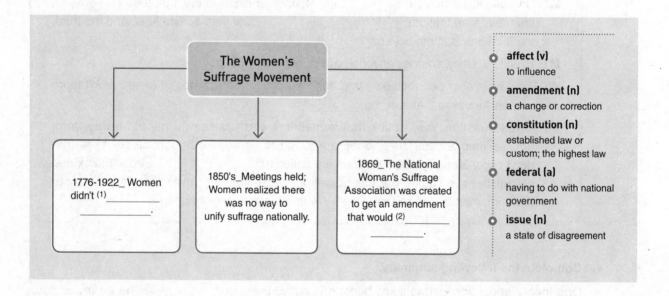

The Women's Suffrage Movement

1776-1922_ Women didn't (1) _____ _____.

1850's_Meetings held; Women realized there was no way to unify suffrage nationally.

1869_The National Woman's Suffrage Association was created to get an amendment that would (2) _____ _____.

affect (v)
to influence

amendment (n)
a change or correction

constitution (n)
established law or custom; the highest law

federal (a)
having to do with national government

issue (n)
a state of disagreement

1. **What is this lecture mostly about?**

   Ⓐ A constitutional amendment giving women the right to vote
   Ⓑ The history of the American women's suffrage movement
   Ⓒ The National Woman Suffrage Association
   Ⓓ The anti-slavery movement

2. **Why was the National Woman's Suffrage Association created?**

   Ⓐ To get an amendment to the Constitution that would give women the right to vote
   Ⓑ To tell people that governments in ancient civilizations were unfair to women
   Ⓒ To make the government put anti-slavery laws into effect
   Ⓓ To help women get the right to vote in individual states

3. Listen again, and fill in the blanks.

A thing to note about _____ in this country is that women were fighting, um, I guess you could say it was a _____. Oh, by the way, suffrage means _____. There had been a long history of women not having the right to vote. Even in the earliest democracies, in ancient Greece and Rome, women couldn't vote. And experts say that these times gave us the best thoughts and ideas of all time.

Anyway, let's just say that women had _____ before they could vote. Right. Um, so women in Great Britain and the United States fought for the right to vote during the _____. Women in_____ for this _____. However, we're just going to look at American women and what they did. So the women's suffrage movement started in the U.S. around the same time as _____. Um, that would have been during the, um, the _____. Right. So this is what happened. A group of really active women _____. And while they were doing this, they found that _____.

So these women realized that something wasn't right about how women were treated. So this is what they did. They held a couple of, um, meetings in different parts of the country _____. Now, the problem was that there was no way of giving women the right to vote nationally. Now, states could give this right to women. But, that would only _____ women in that state. Because of this, these women believed that it was _____, or change, to the Constitution to give women the right to vote. This would, um, give women the right to vote _____. So what they did was start a group called the National Woman's Suffrage Association. The purpose of the, um, the NWSA was _____.

4. Complete the following summary.

There is a long history of _____ for women. In the mid-1800s, American women started _____ their right to vote. This started during the _____. While women were fighting for rights for others, they realized that they did not have many rights themselves. American women _____ what to do. They realized that the only way that all American women would get the right to vote would be to _____ to the Constitution. So, they _____ for that purpose.

push for an amendment	started meeting about
a lack of voting rights	anti-slavery movement
fighting for	created the National Woman's Suffrage Association

Integrated Listening & Speaking

A Listen to the summary of the previous conversation and say the answers out loud by using the cue sentence words that are indicated in each answer. ⊙ 1-16

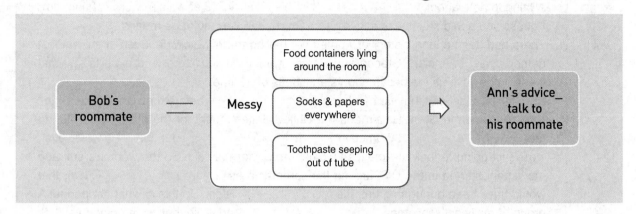

1. **Why is Bob frustrated?**

    (1) Bob is frustrated because _____. (2) Bob is frustrated because _____.

2. **What does Bob's roommate leave lying around?**

    (1) Bob's roommate leaves _____. (2) The things lying around are _____.

3. **What does Ann tell Bob?**

    (1) Ann tells Bob _____. (2) Ann thinks Bob should _____.

B Listen to the summary of the previous conversation and say the answers out loud by using the cue sentence words that are indicated in each answer. ⊙ 1-17

1. **What does the student need?**

    (1) The student _____. (2) What the student _____.

2. **What problem does the student find in the campus bookstore?**

    (1) The book the student needs _____. (2) The campus bookstore _____.

3. **What solution does the shopkeeper offer?**

    (1) The shopkeeper suggests _____. (2) The shopkeeper tells the student _____.

C Listen to the previous lecture and say the answers out loud by using the cue sentence words that are indicated in each answer. ⊙ 1-18

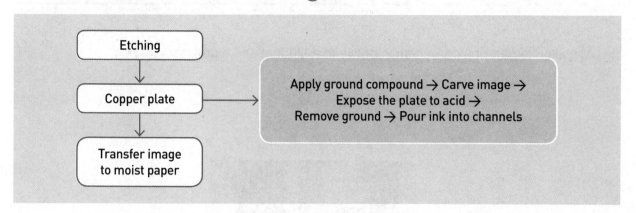

1. **What process is explained in the lecture?**

    (1) The process explained is _____.   (2) The lecture explains _____.

2. **What is the first step in etching?**

    (1) The first step is _____.   (2) First, you must _____.

3. **What happens last in etching?**

    (1) What happens last is _____.   (2) The last step is _____.

D Listen to the previous lecture and say the answers out loud by using the cue sentence words that are indicated in each answer. ⊙ 1-19

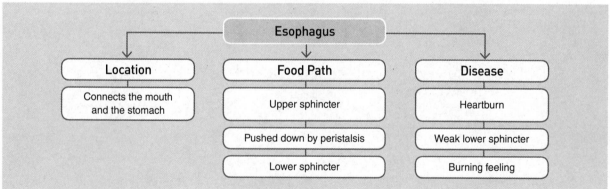

1. **What two body parts does the esophagus connect?**

    (1) The esophagus connects _____.   (2) The mouth and stomach _____.

2. **Where does food enter the esophagus?**

    (1) Food enters through _____.   (2) The upper sphincter _____.

3. **What does heartburn feel like?**

    (1) Heartburn feels like _____.   (2) Heartburn causes _____.

A Listen to part of a conversation between a student and a professor. 1-20

1. **What is this conversation mostly about?**

   (A) How much the professor enjoys student participation
   (B) How to highlight key passages from the textbook
   (C) How to get in touch with the teaching assistant
   (D) How the student can improve his grade

2. **What is one suggestion the professor makes to the student?**

   (A) Get plenty of sleep and eat a good breakfast for the exam.
   (B) Ask the teaching assistant for old exams to practice.
   (C) Memorize Piaget's stages of development.
   (D) Study long and hard for the exam.

3. **What is the professor's favorite part of his job?**

   (A) Referring students to his teaching assistant
   (B) Teaching students about interesting things
   (C) Having students participate in class
   (D) Helping students get better grades

4. **What is one thing the student did to study for this exam?**

   (A) Visited the professor during office hours to ask questions
   (B) Formed a study group to go over lecture notes
   (C) Memorized Piaget's stages of development
   (D) Took a practice test with the TA

5. **What does the professor say is the value of taking a practice exam?**

   (A) Memorizing the questions because the same ones will appear on the actual exam
   (B) Getting extra points because the practice exam was taken
   (C) Figuring out which topics the student still needs to work on
   (D) Learning the structure of the exam

B Listen to part of a lecture in a biology class. ⊙ 1-21

Biology

1. **What is this lecture mainly about?**

   Ⓐ The differences between reptiles and amphibians

   Ⓑ The ability of the horned lizard to camouflage itself

   Ⓒ A reptile called the horned lizard

   Ⓓ The scales of the horned lizard

2. **What is a horned toad?**

   Ⓐ It is really a lizard.

   Ⓑ It is an amphibian.

   Ⓒ It is a predator.

   Ⓓ It is an egg.

3. **What is camouflage?**

   Ⓐ The ability to shoot blood out of the corners of the eyes

   Ⓑ The ability to change from having gills to having lungs

   Ⓒ The ability to blend in with the surroundings

   Ⓓ The ability to puff up like a balloon

4. **According to the professor, why do people think the horned lizard is actually a toad?**

   Ⓐ Because the lizard hops around like a toad.

   Ⓑ Because the lizard is round like a toad.

   Ⓒ Because the lizard starts out as a toad.

   Ⓓ No one confuses the lizard for a toad.

5. **Listen again to part of the lecture. Then answer the question.**

   What does the professor imply when he says this? 🎧

   Ⓐ The class has already talked about the horned toad.

   Ⓑ The class has not talked about amphibians yet.

   Ⓒ The class has already covered amphibians.

   Ⓓ The class has not talked about toads yet.

6. **Which of the following is NOT a way in which a horned lizard can protect itself?**

   Ⓐ It can shoot blood out of the corners of its eyes.

   Ⓑ It can spray poison at animals who try to eat it.

   Ⓒ It can puff up and make its scales stick out.

   Ⓓ It can blend in with its surroundings.

Vocabulary Review

A Listen and choose the correct word that matches each definition. (o) **1-22**

1. (A) offer   (B) offend   (C) defend   (D) offset
2. (A) proceed   (B) producing   (C) procession   (D) process
3. (A) revolutionize   (B) reverse   (C) review   (D) revenge
4. (A) shipping   (B) ship breaker   (C) shipment   (D) shipload
5. (A) several   (B) severe   (C) settled   (D) sedate
6. (A) unhinge   (B) ungrateful   (C) unheard   (D) unhygienic
7. (A) theory   (B) theme   (C) therapy   (D) theft
8. (A) armoire   (B) arms   (C) armor   (D) army
9. (A) entail   (B) ensure   (C) enrich   (D) entitle
10. (A) item   (B) irony   (C) introduction   (D) issue
11. (A) unsanitary   (B) unsuitable   (C) unsaturated   (D) undermined
12. (A) gassy   (B) gaseous   (C) gastric   (D) gap
13. (A) demand   (B) amendment   (C) supplement   (D) commendation
14. (A) peristalsis   (B) stiffness   (C) convulsion   (D) paralysis
15. (A) negotiator   (B) suitor   (C) petitioner   (D) engraver

B Complete the sentences by filling in the blanks with the expressions in the box.

first of all	for good reason
just a minute	kind of like
moving right along	pretty much

1. All right now, _____, the next topic to cover is the stomach.
2. Well, armor _____ means protection.
3. A process is _____ the way you get from the beginning to the end.
4. That lower sphincter stays closed _____.
5. So _____, you cover the copper plate with a ground compound.
6. Now in _____, you'll see a filmstrip about earthquakes.

Listening for Main Purpose

Unit 2

_____

Listening for Main Purpose

2 Listening for Main Purpose

Overview

■ Introduction

Understanding the purpose of a lecture or a conversation is being able to identify the reason behind the contents. This type of question easily occurs with conversations rather than lectures. As in the main idea, the purpose may be expressed explicitly in the beginning of the contents or stated indirectly and spread throughout the contents. In the latter, you need to generalize or synthesize information in the given contents.

■ Question Types

1. Why does the student visit the professor?

2. Why does the student visit the registrar's office?

3. Why did the professor ask to see the student?

4. Why does the professor explain X?

■ Useful Tips

• Focus on the reason behind the lecture or conversation.

• Listen carefully to the end of casual talks.

• Try to verify the purpose with the following solution.

• Avoid answers that cover only a small portion of the listening or which are not relevant to the listening.

• Avoid answers that are too general, and make the most of your notes.

Sample iBT Question

Why did the student visit the manager?

(A) Because she wants to pay her phone bill
(B) Because she wants to complain about the bad phone line
(C) Because she doesn't want to pay her phone bill
(D) Because she wants her phone turned back on

Script

W: Hi Mr. Shanks. I'm Marcy Walker, from room 322. I have a problem. My phone line is dead. I can't call my parents. I can't access the Internet. What should I do? Can you help me get the phone turned back on?

M: Okay Marcy, I know why your telephone line was shut off. It's because you didn't pay your bill for the last two months. It's not up to me whether your phone gets shut off or not. It's up to the phone company.

W: Yeah, it's a real pain in the neck. I didn't pay my bill on time because I spent the money reserved for the phone bill in my budget on shopping and drinking.

M: That was not very smart. Now you are going to have to pay your bill, as well as a late fee of 2%. Then you'll have to fill out a reconnection form and wait for the service technician to schedule an appointment to reconnect your line.

Correct Answer The answer for the above question is (D). The reason that the female student is visiting the manager is that she wants her phone turned back on. Then she can use the Internet and make phone calls to her parents.

Basic Drill

A Listen to part of a conversation, and answer the question.

1. **What is the purpose of the conversation?** (o) 1-24

    (A) To discuss where to look for part-time job listings
    (B) To write advertisements for the classifieds section
    (C) To go over which companies are hiring
    (D) To review a newspaper section

    Listen again, and circle the words or phrases you hear.

part-time job	expenses	week or so	expensive
calculation	knight	advertisements	full-time job
extra cash	exactly	classifieds	campus

2. **What is the purpose of this conversation?** (o) 1-25

    (A) To ask the student for a graduate school letter of recommendation
    (B) To negotiate the cost of extra tutoring sessions
    (C) To get help with how to learn difficult material
    (D) To figure out how to get to the learning center

    Listen again, and circle the words or phrases you hear.

advice	test book	material	tactics
suggestion	difficult	key words	methods
learning center	complicated	ideas	cost

3. **What is the purpose of this conversation?** (o) 1-26

    (A) To figure out a schedule for studying for a history exam
    (B) To inquire about the changing schedule of library hours
    (C) To explore the campus for good places to study
    (D) To discuss the merits of studying at the library

    Listen again, and circle the words or phrases you hear.

quiet	library's hours	sleep	big history exam
student center	regular hours	chapters	convenient
exam	studying time	units	furniture

B Listen to part of a lecture, and answer the question.

1. **What is the purpose of this lecture?** ⊙ 1-27

   Ⓐ To explore how quickly computers become obsolete
   Ⓑ To discuss how technology harms the environment
   Ⓒ To investigate how technology is useful to humans
   Ⓓ To argue the positive aspects of new technologies

   Listen again, and circle the words or phrases you hear.

pollution	environment	computers	humans
harmful	smoke	recycle	garbage heaps
landfall	smog	not recyclable	waste

2. **What is the purpose of this lecture?** ⊙ 1-28

   Ⓐ To judge whether or not big businesses should give to the poor
   Ⓑ To examine the dispute about the 'trickle-down effect' theory
   Ⓒ To devalue government regulation of big businesses
   Ⓓ To support the taxation of big businesses

   Listen again, and circle the words or phrases you hear.

big businesses	professors	definitely	financial
sub-par	trickle-down	regulation	regulate
government	taxes	economic theorists	allowable

3. **What is the purpose of this lecture?** ⊙ 1-29

   Ⓐ To discuss how the film industry changed after the advent of the talkies
   Ⓑ To introduce the techniques used to bring sound to the film industry
   Ⓒ To argue the merits of physical comedy versus spoken comedy
   Ⓓ To review the timeline of Charlie Chaplin's career

   Listen again, and circle the words or phrases you hear.

silent comedy	popularity	speaking parts	talkies
industry	fame	silent films	acting
character roles	famous	comedic	actors

Practice with Conversations

Listen to part of a conversation, and answer the questions. 🔊 1-30

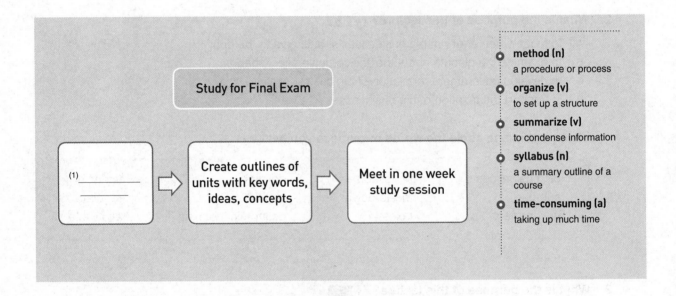

Study for Final Exam

(1) _____ _____

Create outlines of units with key words, ideas, concepts

Meet in one week study session

method (n)
a procedure or process

organize (v)
to set up a structure

summarize (v)
to condense information

syllabus (n)
a summary outline of a course

time-consuming (a)
taking up much time

1. **What is the purpose of this conversation?**
   - (A) To determine a method for studying for the final exam
   - (B) To figure out how to create a unit summary
   - (C) To go over class notes and fill in the holes
   - (D) To organize multiple exam study sessions

2. **Which of the following statements is NOT TRUE about the students' preparation method?**
   - (A) They will summarize the units from the textbook.
   - (B) They will have a study session before the exam.
   - (C) They will ask the professor for help.
   - (D) They will review their class notes.

3. **Listen again, and fill in the blanks.**

M1: Wow, that final is going to cover a lot of material. We should probably start studying soon.

M2: Yeah, we need to figure out the best way to cover all this stuff in two weeks.

M1: Yeah, we definitely _____. How many units do we have to cover?

M2: Um… okay. Let me check my syllabus. Okay, so _____, we have to cover ten units worth of material from the textbook plus class notes.

M1: Well, the class notes are easy. We'll go over _____ and just fill in any blanks we might have.

M2: Yeah, that's a good plan. I didn't miss any classes this semester. Did you?

M1: I missed one _____ because I was sick. But I got the notes from someone the week after, so I have all the notes.

M2: Okay, so we've got class notes covered. Now we just have _____.

M1: Yeah, so that's going to _____ bit. Have you read all the units yet?

M2: Yeah, I have. You?

M1: Yeah. Okay, so I've got an idea. We'll each _____. You know, we'll make an outline for each of them with key words, definitions, ideas, and such.

M2: Yeah, that sounds good. All right, so how's this? I'll do the first five units, and you take the second five units.

M1: Sounds good to me. And we should _____ by next week so that we can have a week to go over the stuff.

M2: Yeah definitely. We'll do a couple of study sessions next week.

M1: Right, and hopefully, that'll be enough. Anyway, I'm going _____. I'll see you later!

4. **Complete the following summary.**

Two students are discussing _____ for studying for their final exam. According to the syllabus, they must go over ten _____ and all their class notes. Since they both have all the class notes, they will just look over them _____ they may have. They will also _____ they have to study in half. Each student will _____ five units within one week's time. Then they will meet _____ and class notes together.

| to fill in any holes | the best method | split the units |
| to go over the units | units of material | summarize and outline |

B Listen to part of a conversation, and answer the questions.  1-31

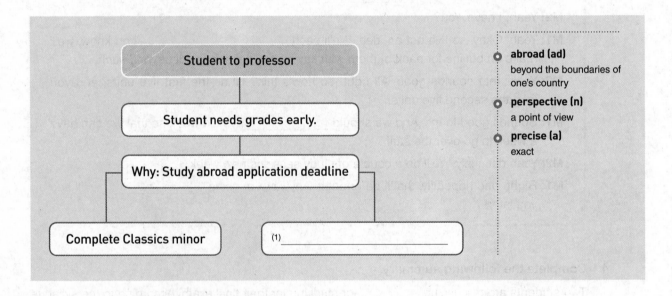

Student to professor

Student needs grades early.

Why: Study abroad application deadline

Complete Classics minor

(1) _____

abroad (ad)
beyond the boundaries of one's country

perspective (n)
a point of view

precise (a)
exact

1. **What is the purpose of this conversation?**

   (A) To ask a professor if the student can have his grades early
   (B) To organize the logistics of finishing his Finance major
   (C) To inquire about applying for a study abroad program
   (D) To explore the topography of Rome

2. **Why does the student want to study abroad?**

   (A) To obtain a letter of recommendation from the professor
   (B) To find out his class grade early
   (C) To complete his Classics minor
   (D) To complete his Finance major

3. **Listen again, and fill in the blanks.**

> **W:** Hi. Can I help you?
>
> **M:** Hi, Professor. My name is John Smith. I was wondering if I could ask you something.
>
> **W:** Of course, John. What can I do for you?
>
> **M:** All right, well I know _____. And I know generally professors don't have to get the final grades in _____. But the thing is, I've applied for a study abroad position that starts in four weeks, and I need to have all my grades in really early to be accepted _____. So I was wondering if you'd be able to _____ so I can complete the application process on time.
>
> **W:** Hm… Okay, so when is the application deadline?
>
> **M:** A week and a half from today. Three days after the final exam to be precise.
>
> **W:** And _____ is this?
>
> **M:** I'm doing a Classics program in Rome. If I'm there for a semester, it'll take care of my Classics minor.
>
> **W:** Wow, that sounds so exciting. So you're taking care of your minor first? And then you'll finish your major?
>
> **M:** Yes. I'm already a little ahead on the Finance major, so I can afford to take a semester just focusing on the minor. Plus, it's a great way to travel and _____.
>
> **W:** I absolutely agree. I think all students should do a study abroad program. Anyway, back to your question. I'll make _____ and copy that to my teaching assistant. And one of us will make sure to grade your exam first and get the grades to the registrar.
>
> **M:** Thank you so much. I really _____.
>
> **W:** No problem. Glad to help. Good luck on the exam and in Rome!
>
> **M:** Thanks!

4. **Complete the following summary.**

A student asks his professor _____. The student is applying for _____ in Classics in Rome. He needs his professor _____ early so that he may meet the application deadline. The professor is very pleased that her student is _____ to go abroad. The student is excited about _____ and gaining a new perspective. The professor says she will make a note and _____ to get the student's grades to the registrar early.

to turn in his grade	for a favor	a study abroad program
learning new things	inform her teaching assistant	taking an opportunity

Listen to part of a conversation, and answer the questions. 🎧 1-32

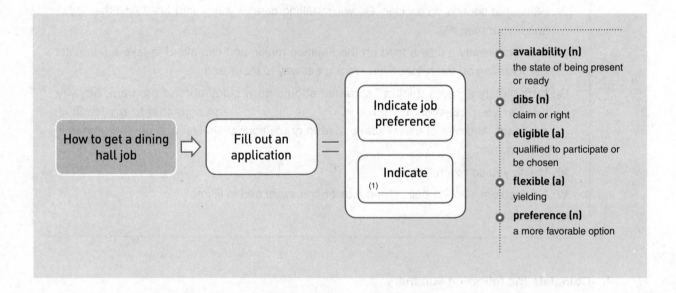

How to get a dining hall job ⇒ **Fill out an application** — Indicate job preference / Indicate (1) _____

- **availability (n)**
  the state of being present or ready
- **dibs (n)**
  claim or right
- **eligible (a)**
  qualified to participate or be chosen
- **flexible (a)**
  yielding
- **preference (n)**
  a more favorable option

1. **What is the purpose of this conversation?**
   - (A) To talk about the various food services positions at the dining hall
   - (B) To discuss the merits of working as a server versus a cook
   - (C) To review a dining hall applicant's hours of availability
   - (D) To inquire about getting a job at the dining hall

2. **Which of the following is NOT TRUE about the conversation?**
   - (A) The application process includes marking hours of availability.
   - (B) The application process includes indicating job preference.
   - (C) The position involves being able to manage a kitchen staff.
   - (D) The student is interested in working at the dining hall.

3. **Listen again, and fill in the blanks.**

> **M:** Can I help you?
>
> **W:** Yes, I heard that there are _____ at the dining hall. Do you still have openings?
>
> **M:** Yes, we do. Are you looking for a job?
>
> **W:** Yes, I am.
>
> **M:** Okay, well the way things work around here is that students who _____ work study usually have first dibs at the jobs. After that, we start hiring people who _____ work study. Are you eligible for work study?
>
> **W:** Yes, I am. The Financial Aid Office actually sent me here. They said you might be hiring dining hall staff and that this would probably be _____ to work around my classes.
>
> **M:** Well, we definitely work around the students' class schedules around here. So, I'm going to give you an application to fill out. You just have to let me know _____ here in terms of _____ cook, serve, clean, work the register, or whatever. You rank the different positions in your order of preference. Oh, and you also need to let us know what your availability is. You know, what days and hours can you work? Then we'll match up your preferences and _____.
>
> **W:** Oh, okay.
>
> **M:** So if you want, you can just take a seat at one of the tables and fill out the application right away.
>
> **W:** Ok great. Oh, how long after I turn in the application will I find out if I'm going to be hired?
>
> **M:** Oh, you'll probably be hired if _____ what we need. You'll probably get a call in a week.
>
> **W:** Oh okay, thanks! All right, I'm going to fill out the application. I'll turn it in _____ I'm done.

4. **Complete the following summary.**

A student is _____ open job positions at the dining hall. A cafeteria worker tells her that the dining hall _____ and asks if she is eligible for work study. The cafeteria worker says that work study students will be hired first. The student confirms that _____. The cafeteria worker tells the student that she will need _____ and indicate her position preferences and _____. Then, the dining hall staff will match their need with the student's preferences and availability. The student will find out if _____ in a week.

she has a job	to fill out an application	hours of availability
is still hiring	she is eligible	inquiring about

D   Listen to part of a conversation, and answer the questions.

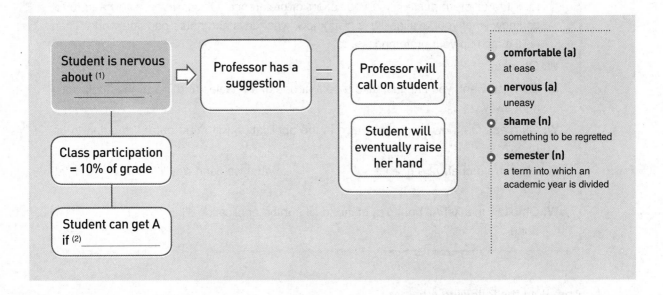

Student is nervous about (1)_____ _____

Class participation = 10% of grade

Student can get A if (2)_____

Professor has a suggestion

Professor will call on student

Student will eventually raise her hand

comfortable (a)
at ease

nervous (a)
uneasy

shame (n)
something to be regretted

semester (n)
a term into which an academic year is divided

1. **What is the purpose of this conversation?**

   Ⓐ The student and professor are discussing ways in which to calm nervousness.
   Ⓑ The professor is encouraging his student to participate more in class.
   Ⓒ The student is asking for advice about bringing up her grade.
   Ⓓ The professor wants the student to study harder for exams.

2. **Indicate whether the following statements are true or false:**

The professor thinks the student needs to study harder for her exams.	
The student is really nervous about talking in front of the class.	
The student can get an A in class if she participates more.	
The student needs help with a presentation for class.	

3. **Listen again, and fill in the blanks.**

> **W:** Hi, Professor. You wanted to see me?
>
> **M:** Yes, I did. Well remember how _____, you came to me and asked for my advice on getting your grade in my class up?
>
> **W:** Yes, I do. And I want to thank you again for your advice.
>
> **M:** Not a problem. You've done pretty well so far. Your exam scores _____. The only thing that hasn't really gotten better is your class participation. I'm kind of surprised about that. It's a really easy way to get an extra ten percent _____.
>
> **W:** Oh, well I've tried, Professor. I just get really nervous saying stuff in front of the class.
>
> **M:** Why is that?
>
> **W:** I just really don't want to sound stupid _____.
>
> **M:** Oh, no one's going to think you're stupid. You really do understand the material, you know. It shows _____. You're doing really well in the class otherwise. Besides, we've got such a small class.
>
> **W:** I know. I just can't seem to bring myself _____.
>
> **M:** Well, this isn't usually my style, but if you'd like, I can call on you at first a couple of times. And then maybe after you answer _____, you'll be more comfortable raising your hand.
>
> **W:** Well, I guess. I mean, we could try it.
>
> **M:** Well, that's really _____. You see, if you participate, you might be able to bring your grade up to an A by the time the semester's over.
>
> **W:** Oh, wow. I didn't know I was so close.
>
> **M:** Well, you really are. It would be a shame if this was _____.
>
> **W:** Ok, well, I'm really going to try. I promise.

4. **Complete the following summary.**

A professor talks to his student about _____ in class. He tells the student that she is doing really well, and the student's grades _____. The only thing the student has not improved in is class participation. The student feels really nervous about speaking _____. The professor suggests that he will call on the student first _____. Then, when she is more comfortable talking in front of the class, she can volunteer answers _____. The professor finally tells the student that if she participates more, she can probably _____ in the class.

get an A	have improved a lot	on her own
a couple of times	in front of the class	participating more

Practice with Lectures

A Listen to part of a lecture, and answer the questions. 🔘 1-34

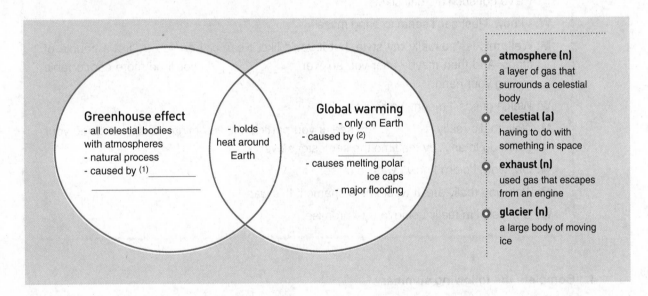

Greenhouse effect
- all celestial bodies with atmospheres
- natural process
- caused by (1)_____
_____

- holds heat around Earth

Global warming
- only on Earth
- caused by (2)_____
_____
- causes melting polar ice caps
- major flooding

- **atmosphere (n)** a layer of gas that surrounds a celestial body
- **celestial (a)** having to do with something in space
- **exhaust (n)** used gas that escapes from an engine
- **glacier (n)** a large body of moving ice

1. **What is the purpose of this lecture?**

   (A) To explore how the greenhouse effect works on other planets in the solar system

   (B) To explain how melting polar ice caps change Earth's climate

   (C) To differentiate between the greenhouse effect and global warming

   (D) To discuss the many ways in which humans harm the environment

2. **Which is NOT a difference between the greenhouse effect and global warming?**

   (A) The greenhouse effect is caused by the sun's rays and the atmosphere while global warming is caused by humans and their technological gadgets.

   (B) The greenhouse effect occurs with all celestial bodies that have atmospheres, and global warming only occurs on Earth.

   (C) The greenhouse effect is a natural process while global warming is not a natural process.

   (D) The greenhouse effect holds heat around Earth, but global warming does not.

3. Listen again, and fill in the blanks.

Many people may not realize it, but the greenhouse effect and global warming are _____ _____. The greenhouse effect is something that happens with all celestial bodies – planets, moons, and such – that have an atmosphere. Anyway, back to the greenhouse effect. The greenhouse effect is a process that happens when the sun's heat _____ _____. The sun's rays warm the earth, and the atmosphere keeps the heat in, just like a greenhouse. It's a very natural thing, and in most cases, the planet system knows _____. Anyway, like I said, it's a pretty natural process.

Now all this _____ when humans, um, add stuff to Earth's atmosphere. That's when global warming, which is not a natural process, happens. See, what happens is that people create, um, things _____. For example, cars. We drive cars all the time. So we drive our cars, and our cars burn gas, and this exhaust is pretty hot. And the atmosphere keeps this heat _____. Plus, all of our machinery and our factories and stuff, they all produce heat. So all this stuff creates what scientists are calling global warming. Earth's surface and atmosphere just _____.

Now global warming has many _____, but I think one of the biggest problems with global warming is _____. See, our planet has huge chunks of ice at both of its poles. And when global warming happens, um, the overall temperature of the planet increases. And what this does is it _____. So when ice melts, it turns into water, which goes into our oceans. And that causes the level of water to rise. And this could also _____.

4. Complete the following summary.

The greenhouse effect is _____. All celestial bodies with atmospheres experience the greenhouse effect. The sun's rays warm the planet. The atmosphere keeps this heat around the planet. In contrast, global warming is a problem _____. The problem occurs when people start creating things _____. Global warming causes the _____ of Earth to increase, which _____. Most notably, global warming causes polar ice caps and glaciers to melt. This raises the _____, which can cause flooding.

has negative effects	overall temperature	caused by man
that produce extra heat	water level of the oceans	a natural occurrence

B Listen to part of a lecture, and answer the questions. 🔊 1-35

Economics

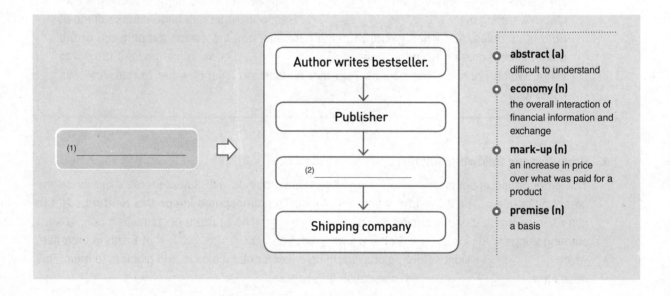

(1) _____ ➡

Author writes bestseller.
↓
Publisher
↓
(2) _____
↓
Shipping company

○ **abstract (a)**
  difficult to understand
○ **economy (n)**
  the overall interaction of financial information and exchange
○ **mark-up (n)**
  an increase in price over what was paid for a product
○ **premise (n)**
  a basis

1. **What is the purpose of this lecture?**

   Ⓐ To discuss the fairness of publishers making more money than authors
   Ⓑ To review the debates surrounding the trickle-down effect
   Ⓒ To give an example of the trickle-down effect
   Ⓓ To explore the process of writing a bestseller

2. **Indicate whether the following statements are true or false.**

Shipping companies would not benefit from the sales of a bestseller.	
There is much debate about the validity of the trickle-down effect.	
The sales of a bestselling novel affect more than just the author.	
The trickle-down effect is a geological theory.	

3. Listen again, and fill in the blanks.

M1: The next topic we have to discuss is _____ . Now this is a theory that has been highly debated _____ . It's pretty complicated, but maybe we can figure it out together. Now, who can define the trickle-down effect? Yes?

W1: Okay, so I'm not sure about this, but I think _____ is that by large businesses doing well and making profits, everybody else does well, too. I mean, because the businesses spread their profits _____ .

M1: Absolutely right. Now, it is still quite an abstract concept. So we're going to use an example that isn't _____ , but it'll help us _____ . Okay. So let's say we have an author. This author writes a bestselling novel. Of course, the author will make a lot of money. But who else makes money? Any ideas?

M2: Um… the publishing company?

M1: Definitely. The publishing company will also make _____ because it will be printing many copies of the book. All right, who else will make money?

W2: The booksellers will definitely make money off of a best-seller. They charge _____ , right?

M1: Right again. If a book is in high demand, and most best-sellers are, the booksellers can make a profit because of _____ . They pay a certain amount of money to the publishing house for the books. Then, they charge the customer more. That way, they're making a profit. Let's see. Another industry that would stand to gain _____ writing a bestseller is _____ . The books have to get from the publishing house _____ . So, shipping companies would get business from that and profit. Anyway, are there any questions about this?

4. Complete the following summary.

The trickle-down effect is a _____ . It involves the profits of one business positively _____ and individuals in the economy. An example of how this theory works can be an author who writes a _____ . The author will absolutely make money off _____ . Other companies who will _____ are the publishers, the booksellers, and the shippers.

profit from the book	of the book	affecting connecting businesses
bestselling novel	debated economic theory	

C Listen to part of a lecture, and answer the questions. 🔊 1-36

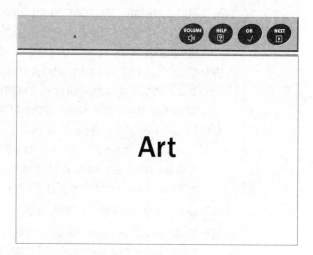

Art

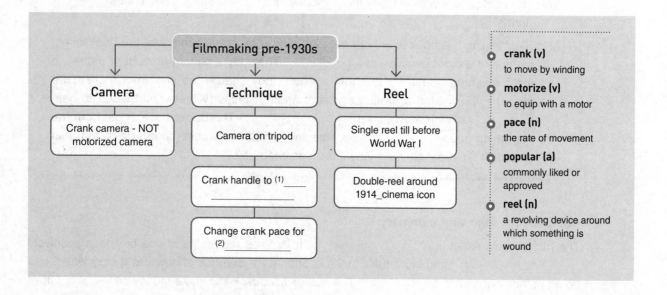

1. **What is the purpose of this lecture?**

   Ⓐ To talk about the merits of crank cameras versus motorized cameras
   Ⓑ To explore the historical era in which Vaudeville took place
   Ⓒ To discuss filmmaking techniques before the 1930s
   Ⓓ To explain how to advance film on a crank camera

2. **How were special effects created before the 1930s?**

   Ⓐ The cameraman would change the pace at which he was advancing the film.
   Ⓑ The cameraman would change the height of the tripod the camera was on.
   Ⓒ The cameraman would add another reel onto the camera.
   Ⓓ The cameraman would add a motor to the camera.

3. Listen again, and fill in the blanks.

So today, we're going to talk about how _____ before the 1930s. So before the 1930s, most filmmaking was done using what they called crank cameras. See, there were two types of _____. There were motorized cameras and crank cameras. When using crank cameras, you had to _____. Motorized cameras would forward the film automatically. But the motors on these cameras were so big and bulky that they were really hard _____. So instead, filmmakers used _____.

Anyway, how these crank cameras worked was the cameraman would either hold the camera or have the camera _____. Women didn't make films during this era, so we can correctly call the person holding the camera a cameraman. The cameraman would _____ at the scene he was trying to record. Then, he would crank the handle on the camera _____. Now, this process could be _____. The cameraman had to crank the handle at a uniform pace so that the movie didn't seem rushed or delayed, which took lots of practice. But, once the cameraman had mastered this skill, he could _____ to make special effects. For example, the experienced cameraman could decrease the number of cranks _____. This would make the actions on film look _____.

Also, for a good part of this time, films were shot _____. This meant most films were pretty short – fifteen to twenty minutes, usually. Then, right before the First World War – which started in 1914, remember – filmmakers pioneered _____. This allowed for much longer films. This is also where the icon of the double-reel camera that we see everywhere comes from.

4. Complete the following summary.

Filmmaking _____ was very different from filmmaking today. During that time, there were _____ – motorized cameras and crank cameras. Filmmakers generally used crank cameras because they were _____. The cameraman would turn the handle on a crank camera _____. This was difficult and took a lot of practice. When the cameraman had mastered this skill he could _____ to make special effects. Also, during most of this era, films were shot _____. Then, just before 1914, the double-reel process was introduced. This is where the double-reel film icon comes from.

to advance the film	on a single reel	two types of cameras
easier to carry	alter the pace	before the 1930s

D Listen to part of a lecture, and answer the questions. 🔘 1-37

Music

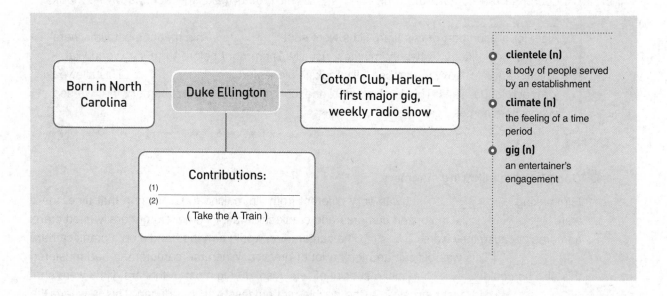

Born in North Carolina

Duke Ellington

Cotton Club, Harlem_ first major gig, weekly radio show

Contributions:
(1) _____
(2) _____
(Take the A Train)

- **clientele (n)**
  a body of people served by an establishment
- **climate (n)**
  the feeling of a time period
- **gig (n)**
  an entertainer's engagement

1. **What is the purpose of this lecture?**

    Ⓐ To discuss the process by which one traveled with a jazz band

    Ⓑ To scrutinize the geography of Harlem in New York City

    Ⓒ To explore the life and contributions of Duke Ellington

    Ⓓ To talk about the cost of music lessons

2. **Where did Duke Ellington play his first major gig?**

    Ⓐ Harlem, New York City

    Ⓑ North Carolina

    Ⓒ On the A train

    Ⓓ Europe

3. Listen again, and fill in the blanks.

> **W1:** All right class, now that we know a little bit _____, we're going to talk about some jazz musicians. Personally, I think there's no better place to start than with _____, Duke Ellington. He was born in North Carolina, but he didn't become famous till he moved to… does anyone know?
>
> **M:** New York City! He played in Harlem, right?
>
> **W1:** That's right! Duke Ellington got his first New York City gig _____ in Harlem. Harlem was _____ and musicians back then. Anyway, that's where Duke Ellington started to be well-known. So yeah, after his first gig at the Cotton Club, Duke Ellington got _____. And that spread his music everywhere. So then, a bunch of famous clientele started to go to the Cotton Club as well. This made the Cotton Club the most famous jazz club in Harlem. Anyway, the Duke made _____ jazz. First of all, he brought jazz music to all corners of the world. His band traveled everywhere, to all continents. Secondly, he wrote and _____ _____. Can anyone name any famous Duke Ellington songs?
>
> **W2:** Um… "Take the A Train."
>
> **W1:** That's right! "Take the A Train" is probably _____. It's a song about the subway line you take in New York City to get up to Harlem and the Cotton Club. Some of the Duke's other _____ are "Rockin' in Rhythm," "Satin Doll," "New Orleans," and "Crescendo in Blue."

4. Complete the following summary.

Duke Ellington was a famous _____ from the early twentieth century. He was born in North Carolina in the late 1800s, which was where he started _____. He got _____ in New York City at the Cotton Club. This gig made him _____. It also made the Cotton Club the most famous jazz club in Harlem. The Duke and his band traveled _____, including Europe and Asia. One of his most famous songs is called "Take the A Train."

famous	jazz musician	taking music lessons
all around the world	his first big gig	

51

Integrated Listening & Speaking

A Listen to the summary of the previous conversation and say the answers out loud by using the cue sentence words that are indicated in each answer. (o) **1-38**

```
                        ┌─────────────────────────┐
                        │   Study for Final Exam  │
                        └─────────────────────────┘

┌──────────────────┐      ┌───────────────────────┐      ┌──────────────────┐
│                  │  ⇨   │ Create outlines of    │  ⇨   │ Meet in one week │
│ Review class notes│      │ units with            │      │ study session    │
│                  │      │ key words, ideas,     │      │                  │
│                  │      │ concepts              │      │                  │
└──────────────────┘      └───────────────────────┘      └──────────────────┘
```

1. **What are they talking about?**

   (1) The purpose of this conversation is _____.　(2) Two students have _____.

2. **What information will the final exam cover?**

   (1) The final exam will cover _____.　(2) The information on the final exam _____.

3. **What will the students' outlines include?**

   (1) The students' outlines will include _____.　(2) The students will include _____.

B Listen to the summary of the previous conversation and say the answers out loud by using the cue sentence words that are indicated in each answer. (o) **1-39**

```
                                                      ┌──────────────────┐
                                                      │ Indicate job     │
                                                      │ preference       │
┌─────────────────────────┐    ┌────────────────────┐ └──────────────────┘
│ How to get a dining hall│ ⇨  │ Fill out an        │ =
│ job                     │    │ application        │ ┌──────────────────┐
└─────────────────────────┘    └────────────────────┘ │ Indicate         │
                                                      │ availability     │
                                                      └──────────────────┘
```

1. **What are they talking about?**

   (1) The purpose of this conversation is _____.　(2) The student has _____.

2. **What types of jobs might the student have at the dining hall?**

   (1) The student could work as _____.　(2) The jobs at the dining hall include _____.

3. **When will the student find out if she has a job?**

   (1) The student will find out _____.　(2) The dining hall staff will _____.

C Listen to the previous lecture and say the answers out loud by using the cue sentence words that are indicated in each answer. 🔊 1-40

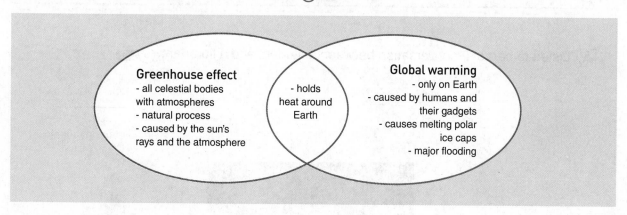

1. **What is this lecture about?**

    (1) The purpose of this lecture is _____.   (2) The topic of this lecture is _____.

2. **What causes the greenhouse effect?**

    (1) The greenhouse effect is caused by _____.   (2) What causes the greenhouse effect is _____.

3. **What is one negative effect of global warming?**

    (1) A negative effect of global warming is _____.   (2) A bad thing that happens _____.

D Listen to the previous lecture and say the answers out loud by using the cue sentence words that are indicated in each answer. 🔊 1-41

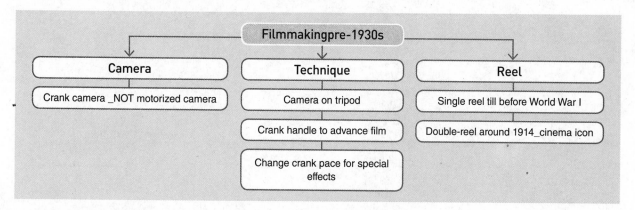

1. **What is the professor talking about in this lecture?**

    (1) The purpose of the lecture is _____.   (2) The lecture is about _____.

2. **Why didn't early filmmakers use motorized cameras?**

    (1) Filmmakers didn't use _____.   (2) Filmmakers preferred _____.

3. **How did cameramen create special effects?**

    (1) Cameramen created special effects by _____.   (2) Special effects were created by _____.

Mini TOEFL iBT

A Listen to part of a conversation between a student and a librarian. 1-42

1. **What is the purpose of this conversation?**

   Ⓐ To recall a book that someone else has borrowed from the library

   Ⓑ To understand the process of setting up an online library account

   Ⓒ To discuss the amount of time that a student can borrow a book

   Ⓓ To learn the layout of the different parts of the library

2. **Why does the librarian explain the renewal process to the student?**

   Ⓐ Because the student might need his books for more than four weeks.

   Ⓑ Because the student is having trouble finding the circulation desk.

   Ⓒ Because the student is concerned about his books being recalled.

   Ⓓ Because the student does not want to pay late fees for his books.

3. **Why does the recall process concern the student?**

   Ⓐ Because his roommate may also need the books.

   Ⓑ Because he may still need the books being recalled.

   Ⓒ Because he does not want to turn his books in late.

   Ⓓ Because he may not check his email in time.

4. **What does the librarian mean when she says someone can recall a book?**

   Ⓐ Someone can request the book from a library across the country.

   Ⓑ Someone can request that a book be turned back in.

   Ⓒ Someone can bring the book back in to the library.

   Ⓓ Someone can remember the contents of the book.

5. **Listen again to part of the conversation. Then answer the question.** 🎧

   What is the librarian referring to when she says this? 🎧

   Ⓐ Students hardly ever need to renew their books.

   Ⓑ Students hardly ever use the library's website.

   Ⓒ Fees are hardly ever charged to students.

   Ⓓ Books are hardly ever recalled.

B Listen to part of a lecture in a biology class. 2-01

Biology

1. **What is the purpose of this lecture?**

   (A) To talk about how insects and spiders are rich in nutrients

   (B) To discuss a plant called the Venus Flytrap

   (C) To explore the workings of all carnivorous plants

   (D) To review the effects of rainfall on plant life

2. **Why does the professor say that flytraps live in nutrient-poor swamplands?**

   (A) To explain the meaning of the words "Venus Flytrap"

   (B) To explain the flytrap's digestive process

   (C) To explain why flytraps need to eat bugs

   (D) To explain why flytraps live in colonies

3. **What is the purpose of the flytrap's trigger hairs?**

   (A) To inform the plant that food is sitting on the leaves

   (B) To begin the digestion process of the flytrap's prey

   (C) To absorb nutrients from the flytrap's prey

   (D) To protect the flytrap from the rain

4. **According to the lecture, what are two things that the Venus Flytrap gets from bugs that it DOES NOT get from the soil? Click on 2 answers.**

   (A) Nitrogen

   (B) Minerals

   (C) Oxygen

   (D) Topsoil

5. **Listen again to part of the lecture. Then answer the question.**

   What does the professor imply when he says this?

   (A) Flytraps are found everywhere in the Carolinas but the swamplands.

   (B) Flytraps are not found anywhere else in the world.

   (C) Flytraps are found everywhere but the Carolinas.

   (D) Flytraps are found all over the world.

6. **According to the professor, why do flytraps eat bugs?**

   (A) Because the soil where they grow has way too many nutrients for the plants.

   (B) Because the soil where they grow does not have enough nutrients.

   (C) Because the plants do not get enough sun where they grow.

   (D) Because the traps are not big enough to eat larger animals.

● Vocabulary Review

A Listen and choose the correct word that matches each definition. ◉ 2-02

1. (A) triply	(B) triangle	(C) triple	(D) tripod
2. (A) method	(B) mechanic	(C) manual	(D) manufacture
3. (A) concrete	(B) abstinent	(C) abstract	(D) actual
4. (A) preach	(B) vague	(C) process	(D) precise
5. (A) global	(B) celestial	(C) scope	(D) celadon
6. (A) dips	(B) dibble	(C) dibs	(D) divot
7. (A) abroad	(B) abroach	(C) abrupt	(D) internal
8. (A) glacis	(B) glace	(C) glabrous	(D) glacier
9. (A) syllable	(B) schedule	(C) syllabus	(D) system
10. (A) profit	(B) proficiency	(C) profile	(D) premiere
11. (A) preference	(B) precision	(C) preview	(D) presidency
12. (A) section	(B) sector	(C) semester	(D) sanction
13. (A) class	(B) clientele	(C) category	(D) compartment
14. (A) shame	(B) comfort	(C) exuberance	(D) hilarity
15. (A) connected	(B) underestimated	(C) eligible	(D) fragile

B Complete the sentences by filling in the blanks with the expressions in the box.

anyway	but I digress
I guess	it's just like
not exactly	on the contrary

1. That isn't the way I usually do things, but _____ it would be okay this time.

2. It's kind of hard to explain an abstraction, but _____ something based on an idea

3. People think global warming and the greenhouse effect are the same thing. _____, they're quite different.

4. _____, back to what we were discussing.

5. That was the way things were back a long time ago, _____. We were talking about how things are now.

6. So, even though global warming and the greenhouse effect employ similar processes, they're _____ the same thing.

Unit 3

Listening for Major Details

3 Listening for Major Details

Overview

▪ Introduction

In detail questions, you must understand and remember explicit details or facts from a lecture or conversation. These details are typically related to the main idea of the text by giving examples and elaborating on a topic or many other supporting statements. Questions are mostly asked about major details from the conversation or lecture, not minor ones.

▪ Question Types

1. According to the professor, what is one way that X can affect Y?

2. What are X?

3. What resulted from the invention of the X?

4. According to the professor, what is the main problem with the X theory?

▪ Useful Tips

• No question type needs note taking more than detail questions. Make most of your notes about details.

• Listen carefully to the major details of the conversation or lecture, not the minor ones.

• The answer to the detail question is mostly written in paraphrased sentence form from the text.

• If you are not sure of the correct response, decide which one of the choices is the most consistent with the main idea of the conversation or lecture.

Sample iBT Question

According to the professor, what can sunlight do to water?

(A) It can oxygenate water.
(B) It can kill any kind of small living things.
(C) It can boil water.
(D) It can disinfect water.

Script

M1: Sure. Boiling water on a portable stove or fire will kill most bacteria and viruses. Another option is to just be sure you carry a portable pump filter. But in this case, you have to disinfect the water with a third method. Who can tell me what a third might be?

M2: How about electricity?

M1: No, actually, I was thinking of a couple of chemicals. One is iodine which kills many, but not all, of the most common, uh, pathogens in natural fresh water sources. Second, used only in emergency situations, is chlorine based bleach. Just add two drops of 5% bleach per quart of clear water and let it stand, uh, covered, for about an hour. Alright, now that is three so far. Anyone like to take a stab at the last option?

W: Uh, sunshine?

M1: Bonus points for whoever said that in the back row. Yes, sunlight is another valid option. We call it solar purification. Water is placed in a transparent plastic bottle, which is oxygenated by shaking. It is placed for six hours in full sun, which raises the temperature and gives an extended dose of solar radiation, killing any microbes that may be present.

 The correct answer to the above question is (B). The word microbe means a very small living thing.

A   Listen to part of a conversation, and answer the question.

1.   **Where is the student's purse?** ○ 2-04

    Ⓐ Her purse is in the lunch room.
    Ⓑ She left it in a taxi.
    Ⓒ She lost it.
    Ⓓ It is in her room.

Listen again, and circle the words or phrases you hear.

problem	kidding	door	entrance
passport	building	follow	roommate
forgot	locked	credit cards	excuse me

2.   **What is the topic of the student's paper?** ○ 2-05

    Ⓐ Graduate school
    Ⓑ Political science
    Ⓒ American federalism
    Ⓓ Politics Magazine

Listen again, and circle the words or phrases you hear.

good points	newspaper	paper	advanced degree
published	exam	federalism	grade
graduate	editor	homework	scholarship

3.   **Why does the student say he will miss orientation?** ○ 2-06

    Ⓐ He will go on a business trip.
    Ⓑ He needs to fix his schedule and learn about his professors.
    Ⓒ He knows orientation is not important.
    Ⓓ He wants to go to New York with a friend.

Listen again, and circle the words or phrases you hear.

roommate	nine o'clock	teachers	mandatory
schedule	clubs	cancel	room assignment
professors	business trip	library	orientation

B Listen to part of a lecture, and answer the question.

1. **According to the lecture, what did Kennedy agree to in secret?** Ⓞ 2-07
   - Ⓐ He agreed not to invade Cuba.
   - Ⓑ He agreed to invade Cuba.
   - Ⓒ He agreed to put Soviet missiles only 90 miles from American territory.
   - Ⓓ He agreed to have the American missiles withdrawn from Turkey.

   Listen again, and circle the words or phrases you hear.

Cold War	nuclear	disadvantage	tension
tank	promise	committee	Russia
Caribbean	bomb	Turkey	blockade

2. **What event made the Empire State Building the tallest building in New York?** Ⓞ 2-08
   - Ⓐ It is the most famous building in America
   - Ⓑ The New York City Zoning Law of 1916
   - Ⓒ The collapse of the World Trade Center
   - Ⓓ The docking of airships

   Listen again, and circle the words or phrases you hear.

wonder	taller	transition	market
sky scraper	shadows	Boston	airplane
building	collapse	business	design

3. **According to the lecture, what are two examples of Latin immigrants' contributions to American culture?** Ⓞ 2-09
   - Ⓐ Chinese food is popular, and many Americans can speak Spanish.
   - Ⓑ Many cities hold parades and celebrate St. Patrick's Day.
   - Ⓒ Many pubs have a Mexican theme, and Mexican food is very popular.
   - Ⓓ Many Americans can speak Spanish, and Mexican food is very popular.

   Listen again, and circle the words or phrases you hear.

border patrol	foreign	Mexican	St. Patrick's Day
immigration	security	pubs	movies
immigrants	melting pot	culture	German

Practice with Conversations

A Listen to part of a conversation, and answer the questions. 2-10

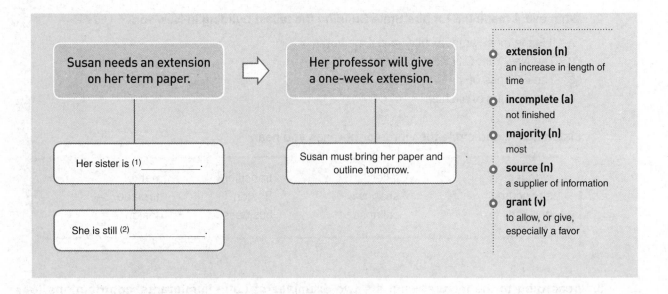

| Susan needs an extension on her term paper. | ⇒ | Her professor will give a one-week extension. |

| Her sister is (1)_____. | | Susan must bring her paper and outline tomorrow. |

| She is still (2)_____. |

- **extension (n)**
  an increase in length of time
- **incomplete (a)**
  not finished
- **majority (n)**
  most
- **source (n)**
  a supplier of information
- **grant (v)**
  to allow, or give, especially a favor

1. **What reason does the student give for needing an extension?**

　　Ⓐ She is missing a lot of information.
　　Ⓑ She has not started writing it yet.
　　Ⓒ The paper is too hard to write.
　　Ⓓ Her sister is getting married.

2. **What has caused the delay in the student's paper?**

　　Ⓐ Her outline was never approved by her professor.
　　Ⓑ Two sources she requested have not arrived yet.
　　Ⓒ Things are very busy with her sister's wedding.
　　Ⓓ She has not had time to write the paper.

3. **Listen again, and fill in the blanks.**

> **W1:** Hi, Susan. You wanted to speak to me about something?
>
> **W2:** Yes, I was wondering if I could talk to you about the _____ due in two weeks.
>
> **W1:** Sure. What's up?
>
> **W2:** My sister is _____, and I'm the maid of honor, so this week is a little crazy. I was wondering if I could have an _____.
>
> **W1:** Well, how much do you have done already? With a paper this size, I would expect that you would have the majority of it taken care of by now.
>
> **W2:** Well, I have taken care of most of it. The _____ has been in two of my sources. I needed to request them from a library across the state, and it's just taken a really long time for them to get here. I requested the books _____. And they're really important to my paper. I just feel that it would be incomplete without those sources.
>
> **W1:** So when do you expect the sources _____?
>
> **W2:** Well, according to the library, they should be here tomorrow. But I won't get time to go through them until next week.
>
> **W1:** Well, if you turn in _____ and your paper as it is tomorrow in class, I can grant you a _____.
>
> **W2:** Thanks so much! But there is a problem.
>
> **W1:** Oh really? What is that?
>
> **W2:** Well, tomorrow I must meet _____. I am going to leave at 6 AM, so I will miss all my classes tomorrow. What can I do?
>
> **W1:** How about this… why don't you slip your paper and the outline _____ before you leave? The building _____. Can you leave after that?
>
> **W2:** Yeah, I can do that. Thanks.

4. **Complete the following summary.**

Susan asks her professor for an extension on her _____. Her sister is _____, and she won't have time to _____ before the deadline. The professor wonders how much work the student has done so far. Susan tells her that the paper is _____, but she is waiting for _____ from the library to finish. The professor tells her to bring what she has and an outline _____ to class, and she will get a one-week extension.

finish the paper	mostly written
for the paper	term paper
getting married	two more books

B Listen to part of a conversation, and answer the questions. 🔘 2-11

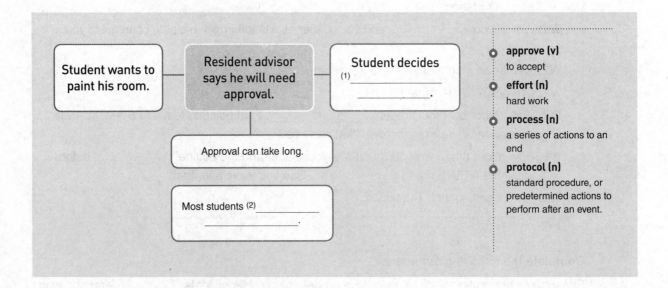

Student wants to paint his room.	Resident advisor says he will need approval.	Student decides (1) _____ _____ .

Approval can take long.

Most students (2) _____ _____ .

approve (v)
to accept

effort (n)
hard work

process (n)
a series of actions to an end

protocol (n)
standard procedure, or predetermined actions to perform after an event.

1. **What does the student want to do in his room?**

   Ⓐ He wants to hang up posters and wall hangings.
   Ⓑ He wants to put red-tape up across the door.
   Ⓒ He wants to paint the room a different color.
   Ⓓ He wants to switch dorm rooms.

2. **What does the resident advisor think the student should do?**

   Ⓐ He thinks the student should put up posters and wall hangings.
   Ⓑ He thinks the student should put red-tape across the door.
   Ⓒ He thinks the student should switch dorm rooms.
   Ⓓ He thinks the student should paint his room.

3. **Listen again, and fill in the blanks.**

M1: Hey, _____ you a question?

M2: Sure, What's up?

M1: I was just wondering how old this dorm is.

M2: It's definitely really old. It was built the same year as the college.

M1: Well, I was wondering what the protocol is for _____. Right now it's this really gross, pale green color, and I just want to make it more livable.

M2: Well, I definitely understand your wanting _____. But you have _____ by the Housing Department. And you also have to repaint it back _____.

M1: Really? That's so much work. Why do you need to get paint approved?

M2: They just need to make sure _____. You know, lead-free and stuff.

M1: Oh, well that makes sense. How long does that process usually take?

M2: Well depending on _____, it can take up to a month.

M1: Really? That's such a long time _____.

M2: Yeah, it is. Most students just end up putting up _____. It saves a lot of time and effort. And there isn't nearly as much red-tape around that.

M1: Yeah, I can understand that. I might _____.

M2: Well it's a lot easier. It's definitely a much simpler process.

M1: Yeah, I guess I'll try that. Can I _____ with the Housing Department and then cancel later? Just in case the posters look okay. If they don't look good, then I have already started the process of the request.

M2: I don't see _____. It's a good idea. Go for it.

M1: Okay, thanks for your help.

4. **Complete the following summary.**

A student does not like the color of his _____. He _____ it a different color. His resident advisor says he must get the paint choice _____ by the Housing Department. This process can take _____. According to the resident advisor, most students just put up posters and _____ instead. The student thinks that that _____ to do.

approved	up to a month sometimes
dorm room	wall hangings
might be easier	wants to paint

C   Listen to part of a conversation, and answer the questions. ⊙ **2-12**

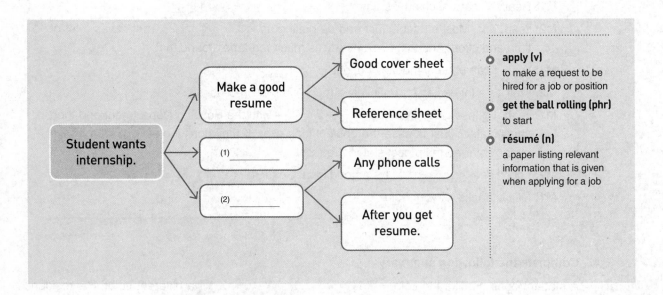

1. **According to the student, what is the purpose of a cover sheet?**

   Ⓐ A paper listing all relevant information to give to people that might be hiring.
   Ⓑ It is a list of people that can tell them why someone is a good addition.
   Ⓒ It is a way to personalize a resume and tell why someone should be hired.
   Ⓓ It tells people to come early to an interview and be polite.

2. **How does the woman know all of this information?**

   Ⓐ She has applied to many internships.
   Ⓑ Her professors told her.
   Ⓒ She went to the Career Center, and they told her.
   Ⓓ She currently has an internship.

3. Listen again, and fill in the blanks.

> **M:** Hey, can you help me?
>
> **W:** Yeah, what do you need?
>
> **M:** I am thinking about applying for some internships, but I really _____. Can you help me get the ball rolling?
>
> **W:** Yeah, have you worked _____? You need a current resume.
>
> **M:** Okay, what else?
>
> **W:** With your resume, make a cover sheet. It's basically your way of personalizing your resume and telling someone _____ and why they should choose you. Also, you should have a solid reference sheet.
>
> **M:** What is that for?
>
> **W:** You want people on there that can tell prospective employees you will be a _____. Talk to your teachers, coaches, former employers, and counselors. Ask them if you can use them on your reference sheet.
>
> **M:** That sounds great. Anything else?
>
> **W:** Oh, there is plenty. If they call for an interview and _____, call back ASAP, no matter what. That shows you care, and you never know how long they will be waiting for you. At the interview, _____, dress nicely, and be polite. You can never be too polite. Wait for them to sit, and call them sir or ma'am. All those things. At the end, _____.
>
> **M:** Wow, this seems like a lot of work.
>
> **W:** I know, but _____.
>
> **M:** Will everyone else be doing this?
>
> **W:** Well, the smart people.
>
> **M:** How do you know all this?
>
> **W:** I just came back from the Career Center, and _____. Oh my God, I almost forgot. Make follow-up calls.
>
> **M:** When?
>
> **W:** After you give them your resume, call them _____ just to confirm they got it. Ask if they need anything else, and ask when _____.

4. Complete the following summary.

A student needs help applying for an internship. Another student gives him advice. He must make a _____. With his resume, he should include a cover sheet to tell prospective employers why he would be a _____. Also, he should have a reference sheet of people _____. At an interview, he should _____ and be very polite. It is also important to _____ after he gives his resume. This shows _____. He can also check to see if they need anything else.

current resume	make follow-up calls	prospective employers can contact
good employee	he is interested	dress nicely

D Listen to part of a conversation, and answer the questions. 🔊 2-13

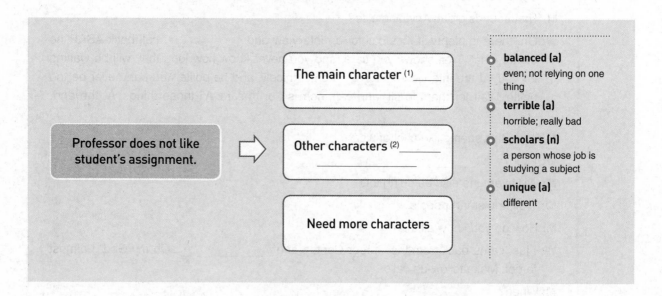

Professor does not like student's assignment.

The main character (1)_____
_____

Other characters (2)_____
_____

Need more characters

balanced (a)
even; not relying on one thing

terrible (a)
horrible; really bad

scholars (n)
a person whose job is studying a subject

unique (a)
different

1. **Why does the professor tell the student he is not writing a play?**

   Ⓐ He needs to describe more of the characters actions.
   Ⓑ He needs more characters.
   Ⓒ He is in a creative writing class.
   Ⓓ He is confused about the assignment.

2. **Why do some scholars like *The Lord of the Rings*, according to the professor?**

   Ⓐ It is a good play written like a book.
   Ⓑ The other characters talk too much.
   Ⓒ There are many characters, and they are all unique.
   Ⓓ The main character does not talk too much.

3. **Listen again, and fill in the blanks.**

> **W:** Tim, come here.
>
> **M:** Yes, ma'am?
>
> **W:** I want to talk about your assignment.
>
> **M:** Really? Did you like it?
>
> **W:** No, the story was okay, and our class is a creative writing class, but there is a lot of _____.
>
> **M:** Oh… Okay. Well, what was wrong?
>
> **W:** _____, your story was not balanced at all. Your main character _____. At times, I thought I was reading a play. Do you know why?
>
> **M:** No.
>
> **W:** I will tell you. Because in a play, the writer only writes what people say and _____ _____, and then the actors _____. Are you writing a play?
>
> **M:** No, I wasn't, I just…
>
> **W:** You just nothing. You are not writing a play. You need _____. Tell me what is going on. For example, your main character says "What a wonderful tree."
>
> **M:** It was a…
>
> **W:** Stop talking. I know it was a wonderful tree because he says so, but tell me why it was a wonderful tree. Describe it to me. Don't _____.
>
> **M:** Was there anything else?
>
> **W:** Yes, in fact there was. I don't know if your other characters talked. Just your main character. Let everyone else talk, and add a _____. This paper was terrible. Do you understand?
>
> **M:** Yes ma'am, I understand. Less talking by the main character.
>
> **W:** _____, are you listening to me? More talking _____. And more characters. Your favorite book is *The Lord of the Rings*, right? Do you know why some scholars like that book? Of course you don't. They like it because _____. And each character is unique. Make more characters, make them _____, make them talk, and have less talking by your main character. That's all.

4. **Complete the following summary.**

The professor is telling her student why his _____ assignment is not good. She tells him that the _____ is talking way too much, almost _____. He needs to describe more. She _____ tells him this. In addition, he must make his other _____. They do not talk enough. She uses the example of *The Lord of the Rings* to tell him he needs more characters and, through their words, make them _____.

characters talk more	main character	like in a play
very rudely	come to life	creative writing

Practice with Lectures

A Listen to part of a lecture, and answer the questions. 🔘 2-14

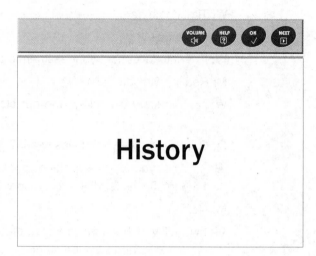

History

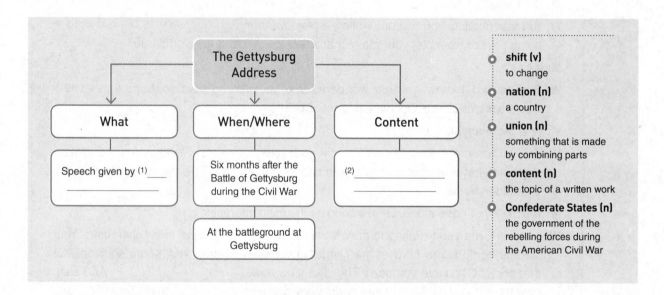

The Gettysburg Address

| What | When/Where | Content |

Speech given by (1) _____

Six months after the Battle of Gettysburg during the Civil War

(2) _____

At the battleground at Gettysburg

- **shift (v)**
  to change
- **nation (n)**
  a country
- **union (n)**
  something that is made by combining parts
- **content (n)**
  the topic of a written work
- **Confederate States (n)**
  the government of the rebelling forces during the American Civil War

1. **When did Abraham Lincoln deliver the Gettysburg Address?**
   - Ⓐ Immediately after the Battle of Gettysburg
   - Ⓑ Six months after the Battle of Gettysburg
   - Ⓒ Six months before the Civil War began
   - Ⓓ Long after the Civil War ended

2. **What was the Gettysburg Address about?**
   - Ⓐ The difference between the Union States and the Confederate States
   - Ⓑ The war between the Union States and the Confederate States
   - Ⓒ The happenings during the Battle of Gettysburg
   - Ⓓ The importance of freedom in the nation

3. Listen again, and fill in the blanks.

M1: All right, guys. Since we've been talking about _____ for a while, it's about time for us to talk about another important thing that's related to it. We're going to shift gears a bit and talk about the _____. Who can tell me who gave the Gettysburg Address?

W: That's easy! Everyone knows it was Abraham Lincoln!

M1: That's right! President Lincoln gave the Gettysburg Address. Now who can tell me when he gave this address?

M2: Didn't he _____ after the Battle of Gettysburg? I think the week after the battle, right?

M1: No, not quite. I know it makes sense that he would give the Gettysburg Address after the Battle of Gettysburg, but actually, he gave it almost half a year _____ of Gettysburg was fought. Lincoln made the speech _____ at Gettysburg. That's why it's called the Gettysburg Address. Now there are a number of reasons why this speech is famous. Probably the most important reason is _____. Lincoln spoke about the importance of freedom _____. One thing that we have to note is that _____ the United States, he called it a "nation," not a "union." Can anyone tell me why this distinction is important?

M2: Well, probably because he wanted to make it a point _____. By saying "nation," he was making a point that the Union States and the Confederate States were both part of the _____. That country was formed by the same people, and they're all basically the same people.

M1: Excellent! That's exactly right. By talking about everyone _____, he made sure to include everyone who was fighting the war. This helped motivate the North as well as welcome back the South after the war.

4. Complete the following summary.

The Gettysburg Address was a _____ given by President Abraham Lincoln. He gave this speech _____ at Gettysburg half a year _____ was fought. The Gettysburg Address is famous mostly because of its content. In this address, Lincoln talked about the importance of freedom _____. The language he used was _____. This is because he did not exclude soldiers from _____ of the war.

after that battle	famous speech	on the battleground
either side	in the nation	very important

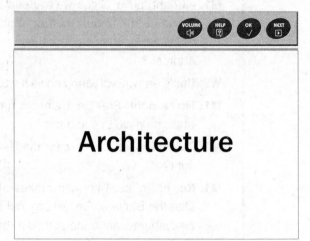

Architecture

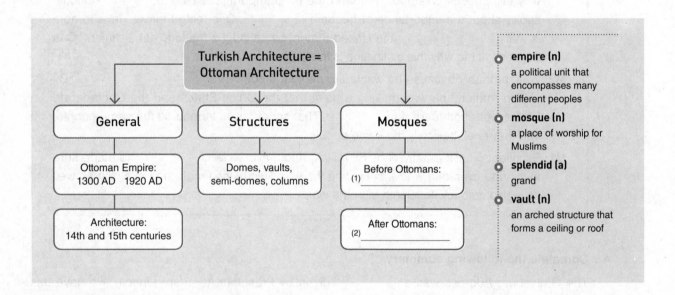

Turkish Architecture =
Ottoman Architecture

General	Structures	Mosques
Ottoman Empire: 1300 AD 1920 AD	Domes, vaults, semi-domes, columns	Before Ottomans: (1) _____
Architecture: 14th and 15th centuries		After Ottomans: (2) _____

empire (n)
a political unit that encompasses many different peoples

mosque (n)
a place of worship for Muslims

splendid (a)
grand

vault (n)
an arched structure that forms a ceiling or roof

1. **What are people usually referring to when they talk about Turkish architecture?**

   (A) Architecture from the Ottoman Empire
   (B) Architecture from present-day Turkey
   (C) Domes, vaults, and columns
   (D) Mosques in Turkey

2. **Which structures did Ottoman architecture popularize?**

   (A) Arches, vaults, and semi-domes
   (B) Domes, vaults, and semi-domes
   (C) Domes, columns, and arches
   (D) Arches, domes, and vaults

3. **Listen again, and fill in the blanks.**

> **W1:** So we're going to move forward in our discussion _____ and visit Turkey. Now, Turkey was once a part of the Ottoman Empire, so when we talk about Turkish architecture from a long time ago, we are generally _____. So who can tell me what years the _____ lasted from?
>
> **W2:** I am not sure, but didn't it start about 500 BC and fall about 500 AD?
>
> **W1:** No, you are thinking of the Roman Empire, which did play a huge role in the founding of the Ottoman Empire, but that is not correct. Anyone else?
>
> **M:** It lasted a really long time, didn't it? From about 1300 AD _____?
>
> **W1:** Yes, that's exactly right. But the architecture of the Ottoman Empire flourished during the 14th and _____. So who can tell me some of the key characteristics of Ottoman architecture?
>
> **W2:** Oh! They used a lot of domes, didn't they?
>
> **W1:** Yes, they did. They actually made _____ a really popular architectural structure. Okay, anyone else?
>
> **M:** Um... I think I read something about vaults.
>
> **W1:** Great! Vaults are very much Ottoman architectural structures. Great job, guys! So in addition to _____, the Ottomans also used a lot of semi-domes and columns. Now, if you'll remember, the Greeks originally popularized the column. But it's such a functional structure that many groups of people have used it _____. So what the Ottomans did _____ is that they used it to _____ more beautiful. Before the Ottomans, mosques were usually these big, open, dull places. But the Ottomans designed mosques to be _____. You can see examples of their mosques all around Turkey.
>
> **M:** I heard that their houses had doors _____, is that correct?
>
> **W1:** It is correct, but we will talk about that next week.

4. **Complete the following summary.**

Turkish architecture usually means Ottoman architecture. The Ottoman Empire _____ 1300 AD till 1920 AD, and its _____ flourished during the 14th and 15th centuries. The Ottomans popularized the _____ domes, vaults, and semi-domes. What the Ottomans mostly used these structures for was _____ beautiful mosques. Before the Ottomans, mosques were _____ and boring. Afterwards, they were _____.

architecture	really plain	use of
lasted from	to create	very lovely

C Listen to part of a lecture, and answer the questions. 🔊 2-16

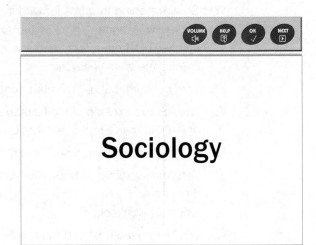

Sociology

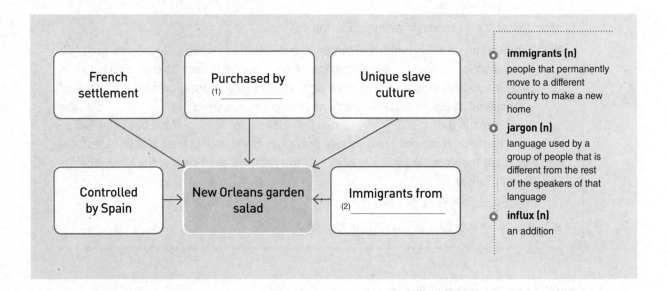

| French settlement | Purchased by (1) _____ | Unique slave culture |

| Controlled by Spain | New Orleans garden salad | Immigrants from (2) _____ |

immigrants (n)
people that permanently move to a different country to make a new home

jargon (n)
language used by a group of people that is different from the rest of the speakers of that language

influx (n)
an addition

1. **According to the professor, when did Spain control New Orleans?**
   - Ⓐ It was originally a Spanish settlement.
   - Ⓑ After the French and Indian War
   - Ⓒ Before President Jefferson bought it from Spain
   - Ⓓ After President Franco bought it from France

2. **Why is the United States a melting pot?**
   - Ⓐ All the different immigrants mix together to create something new.
   - Ⓑ It was colonized by England and Spain.
   - Ⓒ The different immigrants retain their identity but help create a new flavor.
   - Ⓓ The USA has different jargon from England.

3. **Listen again, and fill in the blanks.**

Hello, class. Last week we talked about the United States _____, where all the different immigrants mix together _____. Well, everything has exceptions, including our melting pot, right? Okay, inside the Mississippi River Valley, there is a large area that is part melting pot and part _____. In Louisiana, or more specifically, New Orleans, there have been a few _____ that are different from the rest of the United States. Unlike the rest of the United States, which was colonized by England and Spain, New Orleans was predominantly a French settlement. It also was a _____.
While the rest of the U.S. was a melting pot, mixing all its parts to create something new, New Orleans became a garden salad. Right now you are asking yourself, "What does she mean by garden salad?" A garden salad has many parts that are combined to _____. Each piece retains its _____, but combined they make something new, and hopefully better. This contrasts to the melting pot because in a melting pot, all pieces lose their identity _____.
So in New Orleans, we have a French beginning, with French culture, food, language and lifestyle. _____ is a bit of a Spanish influence, when Spain controlled the territory for about 50 years _____. After that is the American/English influence after President Jefferson _____ from France. And lastly is an influx of Latino culture from Mexico and the Caribbean.
The result now is that New Orleans has a distinct culture apart from the United States. Because of their French ancestry, they _____, such as they say "I'm making groceries," instead of our "I am grocery shopping." Again, this is because the French influence. In French, the direct translation is "to make groceries," not "to buy or go shopping."

4. **Complete the following summary.**

Most of the United States is considered a _____ because the different immigrants mix together. Inside the Mississippi River Valley, New Orleans is different from the rest of the USA. It is a _____. Its different pieces have retained their identities. New Orleans was _____ from its French beginnings. Later, Spanish, American, African, and Latin immigrants all added to the _____. One example of this difference is the jargon. The _____ has a heavy _____.

local jargon	garden salad
culture of the city	melting pot
heavily influenced	French influence

D Listen to part of a lecture, and answer the questions. 🔊 2-17

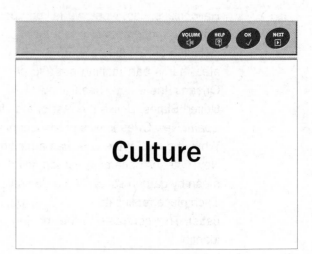

Culture

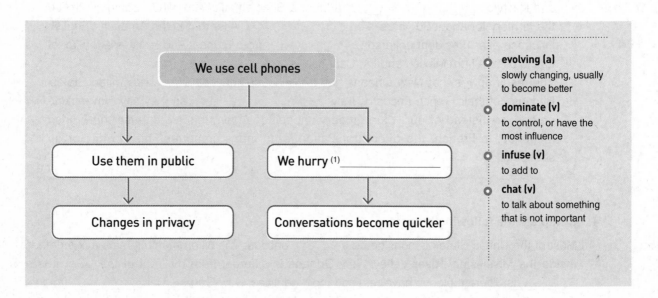

We use cell phones

Use them in public

Changes in privacy

We hurry (1)_____

Conversations become quicker

evolving (a)
slowly changing, usually to become better

dominate (v)
to control, or have the most influence

infuse (v)
to add to

chat (v)
to talk about something that is not important

1. **Why have cell phones made phone conversations faster?**

   (A) People do not like using phones in restaurants or other public places.
   (B) Cell phone conversations are considered private, so they are short in public.
   (C) Shorter conversations cost less money.
   (D) People are usually in a hurry when they use a cell phone.

2. **What would people have thought about short conversations 20 years ago?**

   (A) Short conversations are rude.
   (B) Short conversations are more efficient and save time.
   (C) Short conversations are not private.
   (D) Short conversations are okay if you are not in public.

3. **Listen again, and fill in the blanks.**

We will keep talking about the idea of a _____. I talked about how war changes a language because one culture can dominate another and infuse aspects of its language into a new language. Today, I will talk about another way a language can change. It is… can anyone guess? Technology.

My example will be, hmm, a cell phone. Cell phones have changed and are currently changing the way _____. Only 50 years ago, phone conversations were considered _____. For example, if I was at your house, and your phone rang, I would leave the room so that you could have a _____. With cell phones, people have conversations everywhere, at restaurants, on dates, umm, even on public transportation you can see people _____.

Now people are talking about what _____ in public. We will talk about work, people we hate, our relationships, and plans in front of complete strangers. The things we now talk about on the phone would have been considered _____ to say in public 50 years ago. Back then, you would be slapped by someone for talking about your boyfriend or girlfriend or a party _____.

Umm, what else? We are changing how we talk as well. We all get phone bills, so talking on the phone means _____. So, the faster you talk, the less money you use. This means we often start and end our phone conversations quickly. Before, we would take our time on the phone, ask someone how they are doing, _____ for a bit, and then get to the point. We would slowly end the conversation, often saying bye two or three times. Now, we just _____ then maybe a goodbye, and the conversation is over. That would have been so rude only 20 years ago.

4. **Complete the following summary.**

English is an _____. One way a language can evolve is through technology. Cell phones have changed _____. Cell phones allow us to speak in public places. This has changed what we _____. Many things we discuss in public were _____ and should not be spoken in public. Also, people talk quickly on cell phones to save money. This has _____. We often do not greet people the same as we did, and we end conversations _____.

how we speak	consider private
evolving language	shortened conversations
without saying "bye"	once considered private

● Integrated Listening & Speaking

A Listen to the summary of the previous conversation and say the answers out loud by using the cue sentence words that are indicated in each answer. ⊙ 2-18

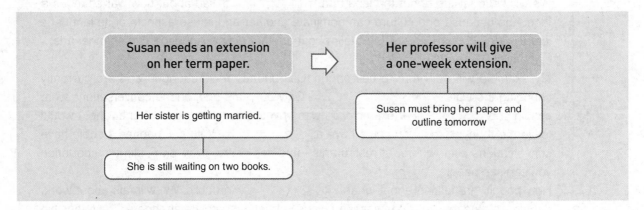

1. **Why can the student not finish her paper after she gets the sources?**

    (1) The student cannot finish _____.   (2) The student will be attending _____.

2. **What does the professor tell Susan to do?**

    (1) Susan must _____.   (2) The professor tells Susan _____.

3. **Why will the student not go to class tomorrow?**

    (1) The student will not _____.   (2) Susan will go home to _____.

B Listen to the summary of the previous conversation and say the answers out loud by using the cue sentence words that are indicated in each answer. ⊙ 2-19

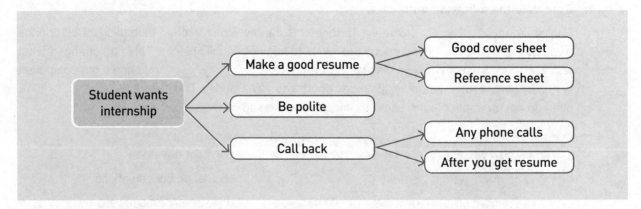

1. **Why does the female student know so much about getting an internship?**

    (1) The female student knows so much _____. (2) The female student just visited _____.

2. **Why should the student call after he drops off his resume?**

    (1) The student should call _____.   (2) To show the student is sincerely interested _____.

3. **What is the purpose of a cover sheet?**

    (1) A cover sheet _____.   (2) In order to personalize his resume, _____.

C Listen to the previous lecture and say the answers out loud by using the cue sentence words that are indicated in each answer. ⊙ 2-20

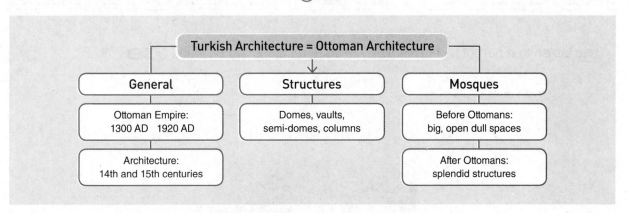

1. **What was the biggest influence on Turkish architecture?**

   (1) The biggest influence _____.   (2) The Ottoman Empire _____.

2. **When was the peak of Ottoman architecture?**

   (1) The peak of Ottoman architecture was _____.   (2) The height of architecture _____.

3. **What are some common characteristics of Turkish architecture?**

   (1) Some common characteristics _____.   (2) Domes, semi-domes, vaults, and columns _____.

D Listen to the previous lecture and say the answers out loud by using the cue sentence words that are indicated in each answer. ⊙ 2-21

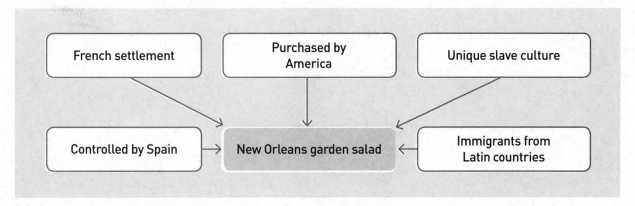

1. **Why is New Orleans considered a garden salad?**

   (1) The city has its own culture, _____.   (2) The city's culture is made of _____.

2. **What is meant by the U.S. being a melting pot?**

   (1) All of the pieces become _____.   (2) The pieces no longer have _____.

3. **Why do the people of New Orleans say "making groceries?"**

   (1) The people of New Orleans say _____.   (2) Due to their French origins, _____.

Mini TOEFL iBT

A Listen to a part of a conversation between a student and a clerk. 2-22

1. **Why does the student talk to the clerk?**

    (A) To pay a fine she got for parking her car on the wrong side of the road

    (B) To talk about car fees for having a car on campus

    (C) The student needs to buy a parking permit.

    (D) The student is not sure how much a parking permit costs.

2. **According to the conversation, when must cars be parked on alternating sides of the road?**

    (A) Cars must be parked on alternating sides of the road when the snowplows are plowing snow.

    (B) Cars must be parked on alternating sides of the road when there is snow on the ground.

    (C) Cars must be parked on alternating sides of the road every day.

    (D) Cars must be parked on alternating sides of the road during winter.

3. **How much does a one-year parking permit cost?**

    (A) A one-year parking permit costs sixty dollars.

    (B) A one-year parking permit costs thirty dollars.

    (C) A one-year parking permit costs fifty dollars.

    (D) There is no cost to for a parking permit.

4. **Listen again to part of the conversation. Then answer the question.**

    What is the student thinking when she says this?

    (A) She will park off campus.

    (B) She will bring her car home until she gets a parking permit.

    (C) She will obey the parking laws only until she gets a permit.

    (D) She will park without a permit for a few days.

5. **Why must students park on alternating sides of the road?**

    (A) To keep the roads open for buses and large cars

    (B) To create open spaces for snowplows

    (C) The clerk does not know the answer.

    (D) To force students to change the location of their cars every day

B Listen to part of a lecture in a history class. 2-23

History

1. **What is the lecture mainly about?**

   (A) The lecture answers why Europeans like feudalism.

   (B) The lecture discusses why feudalism collapsed.

   (C) The lecture detailed the advantages of feudalism.

   (D) The lecture describes what feudalism is.

2. **What did feudalism originate from?**

   (A) Feudalism originated from Roman law and Germanic tradition.

   (B) Feudalism originated from lords' needs to defend their territories.

   (C) Feudalism originated from Roman fiefs needing to be divided by European lords.

   (D) Feudalism originated because vassals needed a lord to serve.

3. **Which of the following are accurate descriptions of feudalism?**

	Yes	No
A lord would lend land to a vassal.		
A vassal would maintain the land.		
The piece of land was called a fief.		
Lords would swear allegiance to the vassal.		
There were several layers in the feudal system.		

4. **Why did feudalism collapse?**

   (A) Feudalism collapsed after vassals and lords could not agree to a value of the fiefs.

   (B) Feudalism collapsed because the lords could not afford to maintain the fiefs.

   (C) Feudalism collapsed when vassals determined they were stronger than the lords they supported.

   (D) Feudalism collapsed because lords became strong enough to maintain a standing army.

5. **What is a fief?**

   (A) A fief is the commitment a vassal pledges to his lord during times of war.

   (B) A fief is the person that works on the land and produces food.

   (C) A fief is a section of land lent by a lord to his vassal.

   (D) A fief is the person that lends land to a vassal.

6. **What did the lord gain by the feudal system?**

   (A) The lord gained a fief given to them by their vassal.

   (B) The lord gained the counsel of the vassals as well as their allegiance.

   (C) The lord gained all the income generated from the fief.

   (D) The lord gained a piece of land lent to him.

Vocabulary Review

A Listen and choose the correct word that matches each definition. ⊙ 2-24

1. (A) splendid   (B) split   (C) separate   (D) somber
2. (A) imitate   (B) immortals   (C) immigrants   (D) immediate
3. (A) premeditate   (B) premonition   (C) permanently   (D) predominantly
4. (A) janitor   (B) jeopardy   (C) jargon   (D) genocide
5. (A) evaporate   (B) evict   (C) envelope   (D) evolving
6. (A) precise   (B) penicillin   (C) point   (D) pristine
7. (A) sour   (B) source   (C) sincere   (D) century
8. (A) participle   (B) process   (C) pancreas   (D) panhandle
9. (A) rent   (B) radical   (C) resume   (D) revolution
10. (A) balanced   (B) benevolent   (C) beneficial   (D) bandwagon
11. (A) scheduler   (B) scholar   (C) schemer   (D) scoundrel
12. (A) chartering   (B) chanting   (C) chatting   (D) challenging
13. (A) extension   (B) reduction   (C) abstention   (D) contention
14. (A) gigantic   (B) huge   (C) tiny   (D) enormous
15. (A) integrate   (B) dominate   (C) personate   (D) deprecate

B Complete the sentences by filling in the blanks with the expressions in the box.

dorm room	come to life
without saying "bye"	main character
term paper	getting married

1. The Harry Potter book series is named after its _____.
2. The characters in the movie were very great. The writer made them _____.
3. I am working on my _____. It is worth 30 percent of my grade.
4. Don't be rude at the interview, don't leave _____, wait to be seated, and dress nicely.
5. _____ is what Jenny looks forward to every day. She needs to find a boyfriend soon.
6. John wants to decorate his _____ with lots of movie posters when he goes to college.

PART 2

Pragmatic Understanding

Pragmatic Understanding questions test understanding of certain features that go beyond basic comprehension. Generally, two question types test pragmatic understanding: "Function of What Is Said" and "Speaker's Attitude." "Function of What Is Said" questions test whether you can understand the underlying intentions of what is said. "Speaker's Attitude" questions test whether you can understand a speaker's attitude or opinion that has not been directly expressed. Pragmatic Understanding questions typically involve a replay of a small portion of the listening passage.

Unit 4

Understanding the Function of What Is Said

4 Understanding the Function of What Is Said

Overview

▪ Introduction

Function of What Is Said questions test whether you can understand the underlying intentions of what is said. The underlying intentions are typically hidden in the context surrounding the text of the question. Frequently, the intentions are acquired by synthesizing the entire text. This question type often involves replaying a portion of the listening passage.

▪ Question Types

1. What does the professor imply when he says this: (replay)

2. What can be inferred from the professor's response to the student? (replay)

3. What is the purpose of the woman's response? (replay)

4. Why does the student say this: (replay)

▪ Useful Tips

• Practice reading between the lines.

• Try to take notes of the context of a lecture or conversation.

• Refer to the tones the speakers are using in a conversation or lecture.

Sample iBT Question

**Listen again to part of the conversation.
Then answer the question.
What does the professor imply when he says this?**

(A) The student's answer is not exactly correct.

(B) The student's answer is correct.

(C) The student's answer is not even close.

(D) The student's answer is always off the subject.

Script

M1: They're used to make prints, right?

M2: Absolutely. Great job. Yes, after the ground compound is removed, ink is poured into the parts that have been eaten away. These channels hold ink really well actually. And then the plate is pressed onto moist paper, and you get a print. Rembrandt was a genius when it came to etchings. I think that after a while, etchings were all he did. Um, let's see, does anyone recognize this etching?

M1: I know that one. It's in a museum in Washington, D.C. Um, I think it's called "Woman and Arrow."

M2: Pretty close. It's called "The Woman with the Arrow." Rembrandt created this etching in, hmm, 1661 I think. Yes, it was 1661.

Correct Answer The answer to the above question is (A). The professor knew that the student knows the work even though he didn't say the name right.

Basic Drill

A Listen to part of a conversation, and answer the question.

1. **Why did the office worker say this?** 🎧 ⊙ 2-26
   - Ⓐ To explain why the student has a different roommate
   - Ⓑ To tell the student she must change roommates
   - Ⓒ To explain that the form is too old
   - Ⓓ To tell the student how to fill out the form

   Listen again, and circle the words or phrases you hear.

roommate	Emerson	room number	loan
class schedule	tuition	professor	class president
registration	extension	tomorrow	wrong with it

2. **Why did the professor say this?** 🎧 ⊙ 2-27
   - Ⓐ To tell the student it is okay to turn in the report late
   - Ⓑ To imply that he will be mad if the report is late
   - Ⓒ To say that the student will be penalized if the report is late
   - Ⓓ To tell the student he should apply for more scholarships

   Listen again, and circle the words or phrases you hear.

extension	part-time job	report	tomorrow
suggestion	midterm exam	policy	test material
tuition	need-based scholarship	homework	cost

3. **Why did the student say this?** 🎧 ⊙ 2-28
   - Ⓐ The mistakes are too difficult to correct.
   - Ⓑ The student thinks those are not mistakes.
   - Ⓒ The student makes the mistakes because he is in a hurry.
   - Ⓓ The student can easily correct them.

   Listen again, and circle the words or phrases you hear.

important	wrong with them	word processor	editorial
action verb	understand	grammar	proofread
common problems	study habits	librarian	printing error

B Listen to part of a lecture, and answer the question.

1. **What can be inferred from the speaker's statement when he said this?** **2-29**

   Ⓐ Tomatoes and vegetables are sweet.
   Ⓑ Vegetables are not sweet.
   Ⓒ Vegetables have no seeds in any part of the plants.
   Ⓓ Most people think tomatoes are sweet.

   Listen again, and circle the words or phrases you hear.

banana	plant	seed	medicine
juice	sweet	digest	farm
pickle	herb	eaten	root

2. **What can be inferred from the speaker's statement when she said this?** 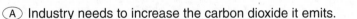 **2-30**

   Ⓐ Other weather events affect wind, rain, waves, and tides.
   Ⓑ The wind, rain, waves, tides, and other weather events do not affect the deep waters.
   Ⓒ The pycnocline affects rain.
   Ⓓ The current is created by deep waters.

   Listen again, and circle the words or phrases you hear.

pycnocline	fishing	surface	snow
salt-water	deep waters	marine	constantly
weater	shallow waters	gradual	clouds

3. **What can be inferred from the speaker's statement when he said this?** **2-31**

   Ⓐ Industry needs to increase the carbon dioxide it emits.
   Ⓑ Industry and cars are the main causes of global warming.
   Ⓒ Nothing else emits carbon dioxide.
   Ⓓ Industry is not bad for the environment.

   Listen again, and circle the words or phrases you hear.

Greenhouse gas	Mars	precipitation	average
industry	continents	extreme	blizzards
Celsius	Fahrenheit	international	emissions

Practice with Conversations

A Listen to part of a conversation, and answer the questions. ⊙ 2-32

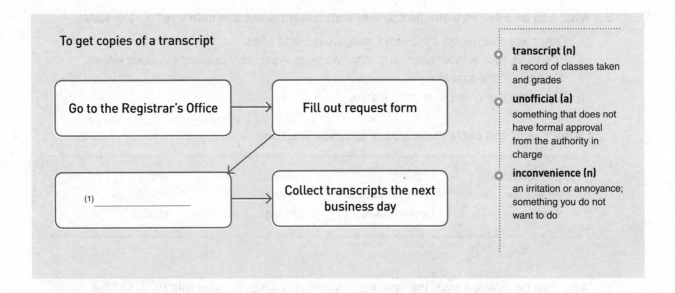

To get copies of a transcript

| Go to the Registrar's Office | → | Fill out request form |

| (1)_____ | → | Collect transcripts the next business day |

transcript (n)
a record of classes taken and grades

unofficial (a)
something that does not have formal approval from the authority in charge

inconvenience (n)
an irritation or annoyance; something you do not want to do

1. **Listen again to part of the conversation. Then answer the question.** 🎧
   Why did the student say this? 🎧
   - Ⓐ She thinks it might not be possible to get three copies.
   - Ⓑ Her friend does not like the Registrar's Office.
   - Ⓒ She thinks her friend got the wrong information.
   - Ⓓ She only needs one copy.

2. **How much money will the student need to pay for three transcripts?**
   - Ⓐ They are free.
   - Ⓑ Three dollars
   - Ⓒ Six dollars
   - Ⓓ Nine dollars

94

3. **Listen again, and fill in the blanks.**

> **M:** Boston College Registrar's Office. What may I do for you?
>
> **W:** Hello, I am currently a _____ at Boston College. I am going to _____ this summer, and I need some documents from the school.
>
> **M:** Okay, what documents do you need?
>
> **W:** I need _____, but a friend of mine said you can only get one copy at a time.
>
> **M:** Your friend is wrong. You can get as many _____ as you want, but after the first, you must _____.
>
> **W:** No problem, how much do they cost? And can you mail them to me?
>
> **M:** For the cost, that depends. Do you want _____ or unofficial ones?
>
> **W:** I need official ones.
>
> **M:** Okay, each extra one will cost three dollars. You will need to come get them though. We only mail them to alumni. I am sorry if that causes any inconveniences. I really don't know why _____. Is that okay?
>
> **W:** Sure, I can come get them. What exactly must I do?
>
> **M:** Come to the _____, fill out a form, and pay the money, and we will have them ready _____. How is that?
>
> **W:** Sure, but one more thing. What time are you guys open?
>
> **M:** Regular office hours, but we are closed during lunch _____.
>
> **W:** Okay, I will swing by tomorrow. Thanks.
>
> **M:** Sure, is there anything else I can do for you?
>
> **W:** I almost forgot! The transcripts must be in a _____ with an official school stamp on the flap. Is that a problem?
>
> **M:** No, we can do that. When you fill out the _____, write that down just to make sure you get them exactly how you want them, okay?
>
> **W:** Got it. Thanks.
>
> **M:** Goodbye.

4. **Complete the following summary.**

A graduate student at Boston College needs _____ of her transcripts. The worker at the Registrar's Office tells her that she must come to the office, _____, pay a fee of six dollars, and she can get the transcripts the next day. The student wants the transcripts _____, but the office will only mail them to alumni, not _____. The student also needs the transcripts sealed in an _____. To get that, she must _____ the request form.

three copies	mailed to her	write it on
current students	fill out a form	official envelope

B Listen to part of a conversation, and answer the questions. ⊙ 2-33

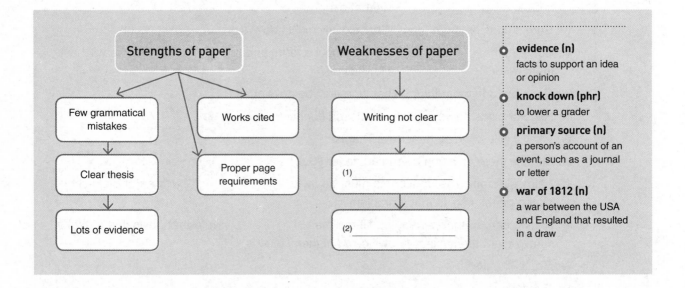

1. **Listen again to part of the conversation. Then answer the question.** 🎧
   What can be inferred when the student says this? 🎧

   Ⓐ This is a history paper, so grammatical mistakes are not significant.
   Ⓑ The student got a low grade because of the grammatical mistakes.
   Ⓒ The professor does not care about grammatical mistakes.
   Ⓓ The professor lowers grades for grammatical mistakes.

2. **Why did the student get a B?**

   Ⓐ He had too many grammatical errors.
   Ⓑ His thesis was not clear.
   Ⓒ He did not discuss the people affected by the war.
   Ⓓ He had insufficient evidence to support his thesis.

3. Listen again, and fill in the blanks.

> **M:** Hello Professor. May I talk to you? Are you busy?
>
> **W:** Go ahead.
>
> **M:** I was wondering if I could talk to you _____ on the report we just got back.
>
> **W:** Sure, is there a problem?
>
> **M:** Well, you gave me a B, but I think I deserved _____ . I thought I was going to get an A on this.
>
> **W:** Why don't you tell me why you think _____ ?
>
> **M:** Sure, first, there were only two _____ in the report, so you shouldn't have knocked me down for that. My thesis was very clear. My thesis was "England actually won the War of 1812." I supported it with a _____, I cited all my work, and I fulfilled your page requirements, so I really don't understand _____ .
>
> **W:** Yes, I remember your paper, so why do you think I gave you a B then?
>
> **M:** Honestly, that is why I am here. I really don't know.
>
> **W:** Okay, well you tell me _____ in that paper.
>
> **M:** Okay, sometimes my writing is not clear, I know that is not one of my strong points. I didn't use very many primary sources. I know you wanted us to use that, but I couldn't find a lot, and I think that is not fair if you gave me a B because I didn't have _____ _____.
>
> **W:** No, that is not it. Your paper stated that England won the War of 1812, correct?
>
> **M:** Yes.
>
> **W:** And you pointed out all the military victories and political victories they had _____ the treaty that ended the war, right?
>
> **M:** Yes.
>
> **W:** Well, the assignment was to describe how a war _____ of the countries fighting it. Did you talk about the people of Canada, America, or England?
>
> **M:** No, I didn't.
>
> **W:** Okay then, that is why you got a B. Understand?
>
> **M:** Yes, okay, bye.

4. Complete the following summary.

A student talks to a professor about his _____. He believes his paper was good, and he _____ on it. He tells the professor why his paper was good: he had _____, a clear thesis, and lots of evidence, he _____, and he wrote the appropriate length. The professor asks him the _____, which was about the War of 1812. The student did not do the assignment properly because he did not _____ affected by the war.

deserved an A	few grammatical errors	discuss the people
cited his work	details of his paper	grade on a paper

C Listen to part of a conversation, and answer the questions. 🔘 2-34

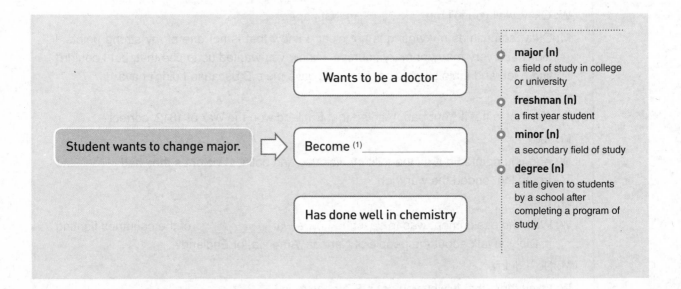

Student wants to change major. ➡️

Wants to be a doctor

Become (1) _____

Has done well in chemistry

major (n)
a field of study in college or university

freshman (n)
a first year student

minor (n)
a secondary field of study

degree (n)
a title given to students by a school after completing a program of study

1. **Listen again to part of the conversation. Then answer the question.** 🎧
   What is the student thinking when she says this? 🎧

   Ⓐ Chemistry classes are easier than history classes.
   Ⓑ She is not a good history student.
   Ⓒ She will not get good grades in her future history classes.
   Ⓓ There are not many well-paying jobs for history majors.

2. **What chemistry classes did the student already take?**

   Ⓐ The student has taken Organic Chemistry and Chemical Methods.
   Ⓑ The student had Chemical Analysis and Organic Chemistry.
   Ⓒ The student took General Chemistry and Chemical Analysis.
   Ⓓ The student took General Chemistry and Organic Chemistry.

3. Listen again, and fill in the blanks.

> **W:** Hello, Mr. Gray. I have an appointment with you now.
>
> **M:** Sure, your name is Heather, right?
>
> **W:** Yes, I want to change my major, but I was told I must _____ .
>
> **M:** You are now studying history, right?
>
> **W:** Yes, I want to change to a _____ . What do I need to do?
>
> **M:** Well, first, tell me why you want to change.
>
> **W:** When I was a freshman, I really liked history, so I decided to study it. In fact, I still like history a lot, and the professors are really good. I am sure I will keep taking history classes. But I have been _____ a lot lately, and history doesn't seem like a good major for my future.
>
> **M:** Keep going.
>
> **W:** Well, a few of my friends were talking about how much money doctors can make, so I thought about it, for a long time actually, and I decided I want to go to _____ . History won't help me _____ , but chemistry can.
>
> **M:** How long have you thought about this?
>
> **W:** Hmm, about 6 weeks. Like I said, I have thought a while about it. My cousin is in medical school, and we talked about what it would take to get in and _____ .
>
> **M:** Okay, that is good, but what will you do with your degree if you don't get into medical school?
>
> **W:** I have thought about that too. There is big demand for nurses. I also am getting a minor in education, so I _____ . Or I could be _____ until I get into medical school.
>
> **M:** Have you taken any chemistry classes?
>
> **W:** Yes, I have taken two. I got an A in General Chemistry and a B in Chemical Analysis. I actually have a note _____ .
>
> **M:** Sounds good. Let's get you changed.

4. Complete the following summary.

A student _____ to talk to her counselor. She is currently a history major, but she wants to change to become a chemistry major. She needs permission to _____ . The counselor asks her _____ to make sure she is _____ . The counselor determines the student has thought about it long enough, the change will _____ , and the student has performed well. The counselor decides the change in majors is good for the student and _____ .

some basic questions	making the right decision
change her major	made an appointment
grants her permission	help her future

D Listen to part of a conversation, and answer the questions. 🔘 2-35

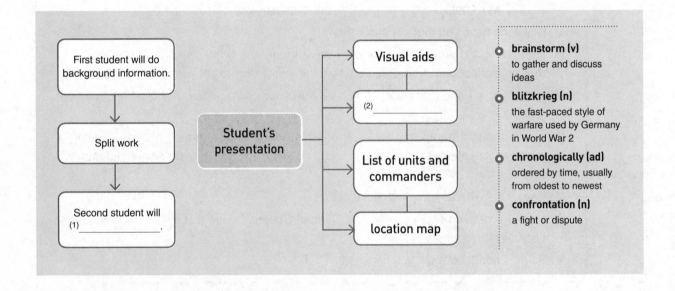

First student will do background information.

↓

Split work

↓

Second student will (1)_____ .

Student's presentation

Visual aids

(2)_____

List of units and commanders

location map

brainstorm (v)
to gather and discuss ideas

blitzkrieg (n)
the fast-paced style of warfare used by Germany in World War 2

chronologically (ad)
ordered by time, usually from oldest to newest

confrontation (n)
a fight or dispute

1. **Listen again to part of the conversation. Then answer the question. 🎧 What can be inferred from this statement?** 🎧

   Ⓐ The student always gets good grades.
   Ⓑ The student got a bad grade on a previous project.
   Ⓒ The student has an academic scholarship.
   Ⓓ The student's grades have been getting worse.

2. **What is the purpose of the third visual aid (the second map)?**

   Ⓐ To show the names of the units and their commanders.
   Ⓑ To show the terrain of Poland.
   Ⓒ To use as a battle map and show army units.
   Ⓓ To clearly show all of the important locations.

3. **Listen again, and fill in the blanks.**

> **W:** Hi John. Let's _____ now.
>
> **M:** We already decided our presentation will be on the _____ in World War 2. I think we should split it up in halves, chronologically.
>
> **W:** How about I do the prelude to the confrontation and you do the actual battles?
>
> **M:** I think the battles will be difficult for everyone to follow, so let's have some kind of _____ to help out.
>
> **W:** Good idea. This time I don't want a bad grade. Got any ideas?
>
> **M:** Yeah, we can have a battle map – a _____, with the terrain and cities. Then we can have markers to designate the German and Polish forces. As one of us talks, the other moves the pieces on the map so people can see them moving throughout the country.
>
> **W:** That's a great idea. I have another idea. We can have _____ each major unit, the individual forces in that unit, and the commanders. That way we can refer to them by their unit names or their commander, and people will understand.
>
> **M:** Oh, I like that. Then we could have one more map, too. As we move the units around, the map will become clustered, so we can have another map with the names of all the important _____ listed in big writing, so people will know where everything is.
>
> **W:** This is going to be a great project. For the background information, I think we need to cover the _____ as well as the previous German aggression in Europe.
>
> **M:** I don't know if we will have enough time. Is it that important?
>
> **W:** Yeah, it is. Poland was the first actual military conflict of the _____, so showing what had happened in the previous years will help people understand why certain events happened, like why Poland was unprepared.

4. **Complete the following summary.**

Two students are _____. They decide to _____ in half. One student will present background information, and _____ will present the German invasion of Poland. They need _____. The first visual aid will be a _____ with army units to move around the map. The second will be a list of all the units involved and their commanders. The last will be a map of Poland with the names of all the important locations _____ on it.

three visual aids	map of Poland
the other student	written very clearly
split the work	brainstorming for a project

Practice with Lectures

A   Listen to part of a lecture, and answer the questions. 2-36

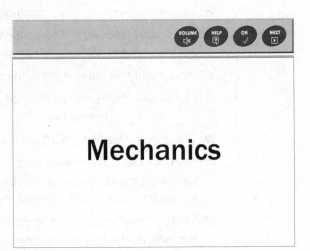

Mechanics

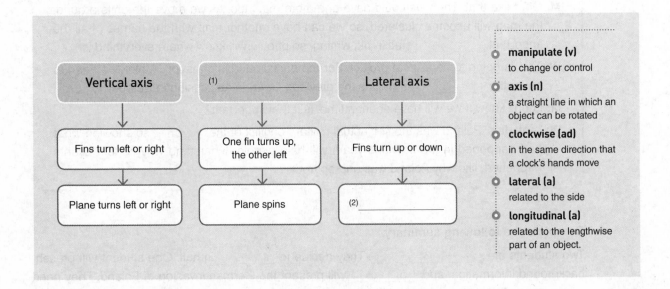

Vertical axis	(1) _____	Lateral axis
↓	↓	↓
Fins turn left or right	One fin turns up, the other left	Fins turn up or down
↓	↓	↓
Plane turns left or right	Plane spins	(2) _____

manipulate (v)
to change or control

axis (n)
a straight line in which an object can be rotated

clockwise (ad)
in the same direction that a clock's hands move

lateral (a)
related to the side

longitudinal (a)
related to the lengthwise part of an object.

1.   **Listen again to part of the lecture. Then answer the question.** 🎧
     What can be inferred from the speaker's statement when she said this? 🎧

     Ⓐ There were not many things that had to be developed for their plane.
     Ⓑ The Wright brothers could ask others for help with their airplane.
     Ⓒ There were many difficult things that had to be understood.
     Ⓓ Controlling an aircraft is very easy.

2.   **What does a turn on the vertical axis make the airplane do?**

     Ⓐ Spin
     Ⓑ Go up and down
     Ⓒ Roll
     Ⓓ Go left or right

3. Listen again, and fill in the blanks.

Hello class. Today we are going to talk about the controls of an airplane. Umm, but as you know, I like to talk a bit about the history of things. People generally credit the _____ for having accomplished the first _____. Their work is very astonishing when you consider they had to do all their own research and there was little precedence for them to look to. Even something as simple as controlling the airplane had to be imagined, tested, developed, and perfected.

Over the past 100 years, the technology of airplanes has changed, but the controls are still similar. Today, airplanes have three basic _____: turning up and down, turning left and right, and spinning. Airplanes turn by manipulating _____ that are designed in their wings. When a pilot moves the fins in the _____, they react with the air pressure to

_____.

You see, an airplane has three _____. A turn in the lateral axis can make the plane move up or down. A turn in the longitudinal axis can make the plane spin or roll. The third axis is the vertical axis. This turns the plane _____.

Each axis has its own set of fins on the aircraft. To make a turn on the lateral or vertical axis, a _____ needs only to turn the fins in the direction of the desired turn. For example, if the pilot wants to turn left, he would turn the vertical axis left. The air stream that flows around the aircraft would change, and the aircraft would turn right.

In order to turn on the _____, the pilot must do something a little different. For this axis, a turn is achieved by manipulating the fins in the same direction. To achieve a spin, the fins go in opposite directions. For example, to spin clockwise, the right fin would turn down, so the right side of the aircraft drops. The left fin would turn right, so that the left side of the aircraft would rise. With one _____, the aircraft then would perform a spin or roll.

4. Complete the following summary.

Airplanes have _____. Each axis has its own _____ built into the aircraft's wings. The fins turn and react with the _____ to enable the airplane to turn. _____ are capable. The airplane can turn up or down on the lateral axis, left or right on the vertical axis, or it can _____. For the first two types of turns, the fins turn in the direction of the _____. For a spin, the fins turn in opposite directions.

air stream	three basic turns	three axes
desired turn	set of fins	spin on the longitudinal axis

B Listen to part of a lecture, and answer the questions. 🔘 2-37

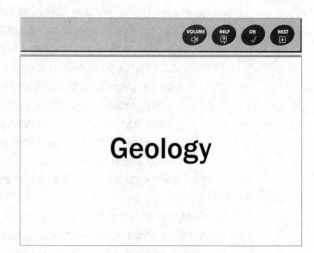

Geology

How Volcanoes Affect the Earth

	Good Effects	Bad Effects
(1)_____	Fertilizer for plants	Destroy the environment
Gases	Cool down the Earth	(2)_____
Earthquakes	Hot springs, geysers, fumaroles	

ozone (n)
a part of the atmosphere that reflects the sun's heat and radiation

albedo (n)
a part of the ozone

geysers (n)
a part of the ground that releases hot water and water vapor at different times

fumarole (n)
a hole near a volcano that emits gas and water vapor

1. **Listen again to part of the lecture. Then answer the question.** 🎧
   What did the professor mean when he said this? 🎧

   Ⓐ Your answer is not right.
   Ⓑ You will get it soon.
   Ⓒ Your answer is clearly correct.
   Ⓓ You are close to the correct answer.

2. **According to the lecture, which is NOT an effect of volcanoes?**

   Ⓐ An increase in the albedo
   Ⓑ Acid rain
   Ⓒ Geysers
   Ⓓ They warm the earth.

3. Listen again, and fill in the blanks.

> **M1:** We have studied the causes of _____. Now I want to discuss the effects volcanoes have on the Earth. We can classify the effects into _____. Can anyone take a guess what they are?
>
> **W1:** Well, I am sure one of them is _____ or is related to lava.
>
> **M1:** Yes, you are right. There are a few different kinds of _____. All of them can completely destroy the _____, but later they are very beneficial to plant life. Lava, when it is not hot, is a great fertilizer for plants. They also emit lots of ash. We will get into that tomorrow. What other categories are there besides _____?
>
> **M2:** What about other kinds of emissions, like gas? Volcanoes emit _____, right?
>
> **M1:** Yes, volcanoes emit many toxic and harmful gases, such as carbon dioxide and sulfur dioxide. Of course, not all the gases released are harmful, like _____, but others wreak havoc on our _____. When sulfur dioxide reaches the atmosphere and reacts to change into sulfuric acid, it increases the Earth's _____. What is the albedo?
>
> **W1:** The albedo reflects the _____. That reaction increases the Earth's albedo.
>
> **M1:** Yes, why?
>
> **W1:** Doesn't that mean volcanoes can actually reverse the effects of _____ and cool the Earth down?
>
> **M1:** Very good! The eruptions of the past half century have actually increased the albedo enough to cool the surface of the Earth by half of a degree Fahrenheit. But, many of the gases emitted also destroy the ozone or can _____. What other effects are there?
>
> **M2:** In the movies, all the animals run away before a volcano.
>
> **M1:** You almost got it. There are volcanic _____. There are events that occur because of volcanoes, but are not emitted from volcanoes. Any guesses?
>
> **W2:** _____. Earthquakes and volcanoes occur near faults and often accompany each other. Sometimes volcanoes cause small earthquakes.
>
> **M1:** Yes, also, there are hot springs, geysers, fumaroles, and mud pots.

4. Complete the following summary.

Volcanoes have _____ of _____. First, volcanoes produce lava. Lava can destroy or severely damage anything that _____. Later, lava works as a good fertilizer. Second, volcanoes emit _____ into the atmosphere. Some of the gases are beneficial. They can help to increase the albedo. Other gases can _____ or create acid rain. Last, there are several _____, such as geysers and earthquakes.

lies in its path	effects on the Earth	damage the ozone
three basic categories	other side effects	several gases

C   Listen to part of a lecture, and answer the questions. 🔊 2-38

Zoology

	Olympic Marmot	**Bobak Marmot**
Location in the world	Olympic Peninsula in northwest USA	(1) _____
Geography of home	Alpine meadows near mountains	Rolling grasslands and cultivated land
Defense calls	Complex; identifies kinds of predators	Simple; one call for all predators
Contact with humans	(2) _____	Humans have eaten and used as clothes.

genus (n)
a category of an animal that is more general than species

descending (a)
getting lower

trill (n)
a sound made by alternating between a high and low sound

terrain (n)
a category of land, such as desert or mountain

1. **Listen again to part of the lecture. Then answer the question.** 🎧
    What can be implied when the professor says this? 🎧

    Ⓐ Scientists do not research marmots enough.
    Ⓑ The Bobak Marmot is more intelligent than the Olympic Marmot.
    Ⓒ Studies support the idea, but scientists are not sure if their calls change with the terrain.
    Ⓓ The calls of the two marmots are identical.

2. **For what purpose have Russian people used the Bobak Marmot?**

    Ⓐ As food during times of hardship
    Ⓑ As a domesticated animal, similar to the ox, for plowing fields
    Ⓒ To watch for predators at night
    Ⓓ To protect cultivated fields

3. Listen again, and fill in the blanks.

Today, we are going to compare _____ that are the same genus. The two animals we will compare are the Olympic Marmot and the Bobak Marmot. First, they live a _____. The Olympic Marmot lives in a small area in North America. It lives on the _____ _____. Excluding Alaska, it is the northwesternmost part of the United States. Oh, yeah, and Hawaii is farther west. The Bobak Marmot's home is on the other side of the world, in the steppes of Russia and _____. Even though they are both marmots, they prefer different areas to live. The Olympic lives in the _____ near the Olympic Mountains. The Bobak is not like most marmots and lives in _____ and also has been known to live near cultivated fields.

Let's go on to defense calls. All species of marmots have calls and whistles to alert others of predators. The Olympic Marmot has much more developed calls though. Most research shows that the Bobak Marmot only has one call. This call communicates any and all forms of predators. Some studies have hinted that their call can change depending on the terrain. In flat areas, the call is slow. In rugged terrain, the calls tend to be faster.

Umm, okay the Olympic Marmot's calls are _____. Their calls are categorized into ascending, descending, flat, and trills. The different calls are used to designate the type of predator, for example a bird of prey versus a bear. The trills are believed to be used for very dangerous situations.

Olympic Marmots' natural enemies are mainly the coyote and puma, but to a lesser extent birds of prey and bobcats. Bobak Marmots' _____ are similar animals, large cats and packs of hunting canines. This may sound strange, but Bobak Marmots have been a source of _____ for many Russian people. In times of extreme hardship and famine, the Bobak Marmot has been used as food and clothing. Due to this, you can guess the Olympic Marmot is less shy around people.

4. Complete the following summary.

Two different species of the Marmot genus are the Olympic Marmot and the Bobak Marmot. The Olympic Marmot lives near the Olympic Mountains in the _____. The Bobak Marmot lives in _____ in central Asia and Russia. Both animals have calls to _____ of a predator, but the Olympic Marmots' calls are more advanced and recognize _____. The Bobak Marmot has been eaten by Russian people _____, and it has also been used as a source of _____.

Olympic Peninsula of Washington state	open grasslands
warn other marmots	different kinds of predators
during famine	fur for clothes

D Listen to part of a lecture, and answer the questions. 🔘 3-01

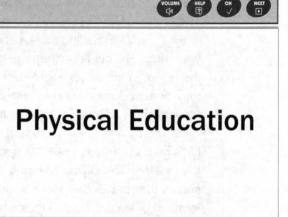

Physical Education

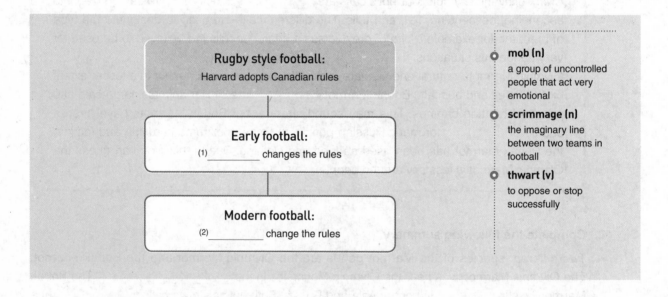

| Rugby style football: |
| Harvard adopts Canadian rules |

| Early football: |
| (1) _____ changes the rules |

| Modern football: |
| (2) _____ change the rules |

mob (n)
a group of uncontrolled people that act very emotional

scrimmage (n)
the imaginary line between two teams in football

thwart (v)
to oppose or stop successfully

1. **Listen again to part of the lecture. Then answer the question.** 🎧
    Why did the professor say this? 🎧
    Ⓐ American football is more popular in China than in America.
    Ⓑ American football is very popular in Canada.
    Ⓒ Not everyone considers football the most popular sport.
    Ⓓ Some people do not think about sports.

2. **What school played a Canadian university and changed the style of American football?**
    Ⓐ Harvard University
    Ⓑ Yale University
    Ⓒ McGill University
    Ⓓ Oxford College

3. Listen again, and fill in the blanks.

M1: Let's talk about what some people consider the most popular sport in America. Football was _____. Versions of soccer were played all over the world. The Chinese played a game called cuju over 2,200 years ago. Native Americans were playing a game like soccer before Europeans arrived in the Americas.

W: How much influence did the Native Americans have on football? Did settlers play with them?

M1: I am sure settlers and Native Americans played, but that had _____ on the development of football. Football became popular by elite _____ playing the game around the 1820s. It was mainly an unorganized version of mob style soccer. Harvard played a game _____. In 1874, McGill University of Montreal played Harvard. Harvard adopted the Canadian version of football, which was much more similar to today's football. Harvard spread that style of football to other schools, who were playing a soccer-style game.

M2: You mean Canadians were playing American-style football before Americans?

M1: Not quite. They were playing a game similar to rugby, but they did influence the development of football. By 1883, a _____ made some major changes to the game, such as reducing the number of players from 15 to 11, adding the line of scrimmage, and adding a rule if the ball is not moved five yards after three downs, the other team would gain control of the ball. This rule was created to thwart Yale's strategy of controlling the ball without attempting to score.

W: Didn't Harvard and Yale hate each other?

M1: Football _____. Harvard invented the flying wedge, which almost killed 7 Yale players in one game. 18 players were killed in 1905. This led to more changes, such as the forward pass and _____. After this, the game was pretty similar to our football today.

4. Complete the following summary.

American Football is derived from _____. In the 1820s, _____ made the sport popular, but they played a game _____. Harvard played a game more like rugby. They then played a Canadian football team and adopted the _____ of football. Harvard _____ this style to the rest of the American universities. Walter Camp changed the game even further by adding downs and the line of scrimmage and reducing the number of players. The large _____ resulted in more changes, like the forward pass and a fourth down.

similar to soccer	number of deaths	Canadian style
European soccer	passed on	American universities

● Integrated Listening & Speaking

A Listen to the summary of the previous conversation and say the answers out loud by using the cue sentence words that are indicated in each answer. ⊙ 3-02

To get copies of a transcript

Go to the Registrar's Office → Fill out request form

Pay the fee → Collect transcripts the next business day

1. **Why can't the student get her transcripts mailed?**
   (1) The student cannot get _____.   (2) The student is not an alumnus, _____.

2. **How many transcripts does the student need for her application?**
   (1) The student needs _____.   (2) The application requires _____.

3. **What must the student do to get the transcripts?**
   (1) The student must _____.   (2) After the student goes to _____.

B Listen to the summary of the previous conversation and say the answers out loud by using the cue sentence words that are indicated in each answer. ⊙ 3-03

Student wants to change major. ⇨

Wants to be a doctor

Becomes a nurse or a teacher

Has done well in chemistry

1. **Why does the student go to talk to the counselor?**
   (1) The student talks to the counselor to _____.   (2) The student has this conversation _____.

2. **What job does the student want?**
   (1) The job _____.   (2) The student _____.

3. **What is the student's current major?**
   (1) The student's _____.   (2) The student is _____.

C Listen to the previous lecture and say the answers out loud by using the cue sentence words that are indicated in each answer. (⊙ 3-04)

	Olympic Marmot	Bobak Marmot
Location in the world	Olympic Peninsula in northwest USA	Central Asia and Russia
Geography of home	Alpine meadows near mountains	Rolling grasslands and cultivated land
Defense calls	Complex; identifies kinds of predators	Simple; one call for all predators
Contact with humans	Humans have little contact.	Humans have eaten and used as clothes

1. **Where does the Olympic Marmot live?**

   (1) The Olympic Marmot lives _____.   (2) The Olympic Marmot's home is _____.

2. **What is the purpose of the marmot's calls?**

   (1) The purpose of the marmot's calls is _____.   (2) The marmot will call to other marmots _____.

3. **How did the Bobak Marmot serve people?**

   (1) The Bobak Marmot served people as _____.   (2) People used the Bobak Marmot to _____.

D Listen to the previous lecture and say the answers out loud by using the cue sentence words that are indicated in each answer. (⊙ 3-05)

How Volcanoes Affect the Earth

	Good Effects	Bad Effects
Lava	Fertilizer for plants	Destroy the environment
Gases	Cool down the Earth	Toxic gases destroy ozone
Earthquakes	Hot springs, geysers, fumaroles	Destroy buildings, kill people

1. **What do the gas emissions do to the albedo?**

   (1) The gas emissions from volcanoes _____.   (2) The albedo is increased _____.

2. **Lava at first can destroy the surrounding environment. What does the lava do next?**

   (1) Lava destroys _____.   (2) At first lava can destroy _____.

3. **What are two of the gases emitted from a volcano?**

   (1) Two of the gases emitted _____.   (2) During an eruption, volcanoes will emit _____.

A Listen to part of a conversation between a student and a professor. 3-06

1. **What is this conversation mainly about?**
   - Ⓐ The student wants the professor to write a letter of recommendation for her.
   - Ⓑ The student is telling the professor why a Nike internship is good.
   - Ⓒ The professor and student are discussing which internship is best for her.
   - Ⓓ The professor thinks the student should change her major.

2. **What is the student's major?**
   - Ⓐ The student does not have a major yet.
   - Ⓑ The student's major is journalism.
   - Ⓒ The student's major is communications.
   - Ⓓ The student will change her major from communications to marketing.

3. **Listen again to part of the conversation. Then answer the question.**

   What does the student imply when she says this?
   - Ⓐ She will ask the professor to write a letter of recommendation for her.
   - Ⓑ The student's last letter of recommendation was bad.
   - Ⓒ The student thinks the professor writes bad letters of recommendation.
   - Ⓓ The professor will not write a letter of recommendation.

4. **Listen again to part of the conversation. Then answer the question.**

   What can be inferred when the professor says this?
   - Ⓐ The student will get a good grade in the professor's class.
   - Ⓑ The student can get the Nike internship.
   - Ⓒ The student will be able to change majors.
   - Ⓓ The professor will write a good letter of recommendation for the student.

5. **According to the professor, why should the student get an internship with a newspaper or magazine and not with Nike?**
   - Ⓐ The Nike internship does not pay very well.
   - Ⓑ She should get an internship related to her major.
   - Ⓒ The professor can help her get a newspaper internship.
   - Ⓓ The Nike internship will not let her travel.

B Listen to part of a lecture in an architecture class. 3-07

Architecture

1. **What is this lecture mainly about?**

   (A) Styles of American houses 100 years ago

   (B) Why rural houses are better than city houses

   (C) The advantages of living in the country

   (D) Reasons American houses are different from the past

2. **Listen again to part of the lecture. Then answer the question.**

   What can be inferred when the student says this?

   (A) The professor will tell the answer to the student.

   (B) The student wants to talk about many reasons.

   (C) The student knows there are many reasons, but can't think of any.

   (D) The student does not believe there are many reasons.

3. **When did the nuclear family arise?**

   (A) The 20th century

   (B) The year 2000

   (C) A few hundred years ago

   (D) During the times of the Romans and Greeks

4. **Listen again to part of the lecture. Then answer the question.**

   What does the professor imply when she says this?

   (A) It's faster to build houses that look the same.

   (B) Houses are dangerous if they are built very fast.

   (C) Too many people are moving to the suburbs.

   (D) Suburban homes are too big.

5. **How did cars influence modern homes?**

   (A) Modern houses have multi-car garages.

   (B) Modern houses need gas tanks.

   (C) Designs of houses have changed to create parking places outside of the houses.

   (D) Cars make it easier to visit other people's homes, so there are guestrooms.

6. **Which of the following are reasons American homes have changed according to the dialog?**

	Yes	No
There is more space in the suburbs.		
Architectural styles have changed.		
People have more money to buy houses.		
Materials of houses have changed.		
Houses have fewer people in them.		

Vocabulary Review

A Listen and choose the correct word that matches each definition. ● 3-08

1. (A) transcribe   (B) transfer   (C) transcript   (D) transcend
2. (A) manipulating   (B) mastering   (C) mentality   (D) mediocre
3. (A) created   (B) crouton   (C) clustered   (D) catered
4. (A) precedence   (B) presents   (C) presidents   (D) participle
5. (A) tender   (B) traction   (C) tentacle   (D) terrain
6. (A) fostered   (B) freelancer   (C) freshman   (D) pharmacy
7. (A) descendent   (B) decoration   (C) desert   (D) descending
8. (A) mars   (B) mob   (C) mental   (D) mirage
9. (A) evade   (B) eventually   (C) evaporate   (D) evidence
10. (A) perfect   (B) priority   (C) penetrate   (D) participate
11. (A) chronologically   (B) cremate   (C) creation   (D) cartilage
12. (A) analogy   (B) annoyance   (C) antithesis   (D) anecdote
13. (A) decrease   (B) detriment   (C) degree   (D) diminish
14. (A) tectonic   (B) toxic   (C) titanic   (D) tiny
15. (A) genus   (B) genesis   (C) genius   (D) generosity

B Complete the sentences by filling in the blanks with the expressions in the box.

regular office hours	business days
primary sources	clockwise
background information	Native Americans

1. The bank near the river is open late. It doesn't have _____.
2. John answered first, and then the children each answered in a _____ order.
3. During the 1800s, there were many conflicts between American settlers and _____.
4. The teacher wants me to use _____, but I can't find any diaries or journals.
5. The mail usually arrives in three _____.
6. I didn't understand the situation because I didn't have enough _____.

Unit **5**

Understanding the Speaker's Attitude

5 Understanding the Speaker's Attitude

Overview

■ Introduction

Speaker's attitude questions test whether you can understand a speaker's attitude or opinion. This question asks you about the speaker's feelings, likes and dislikes, or reason behind various emotions. Also you are often asked about a speaker's degree of certainty. This question type often involves replaying a portion of the listening passage.

■ Question Types

1. What can be inferred about the student?

2. What is the professor's attitude toward X?

3. What is the professor's opinion of X?

4. What can be inferred about the student when she says this: (replay)

5. What does the woman mean when she says this: (replay)

■ Useful Tips

• Focus on the tone of voice, intonation, and the sentence stress the speakers are using in a conversation or lecture.

• Practice distinguishing between referencing and giving personal opinions.

• Avoid answers that are too far from the general tone of the lecture or conversation.

• Try to take notes on the context of the lecture or conversation.

• Pay attention to adjectives and verbs of feeling.

Sample iBT Question

Listen again to part of the conversation. Then answer the question. What can be inferred about the student when the professor says this?

(A) The student is having a hard time with her classmates.
(B) The student is going to get some handouts.
(C) The student is having difficulty recovering.
(D) The student is in trouble.

Script

W1: Well, I know you handed out the review sheets for the final exam yesterday and I was hoping to get them.

W2: Oh yeah, those review sheets. You know, I hate to tell you this, but I'm all out. I ended up giving away my master copies by accident. You'll have to get them from one of your classmates.

W1: Oh, Mrs. Lassiter, I'm begging you. The class is graded on a curve. None of my classmates want to help me. I might get a higher score than them. No one will loan me the sheets!

W2: My, you do seem to be in a predicament. Sally, I have to confess something. I was watching the game on television on Sunday, and I saw you in the crowd. You were on campus television! You didn't look very sick to me.

W1: Okay, you busted me. I was at the game. I missed class because I partied too much. You caught me in a lie. I guess I have to live with the consequences.

Correct Answer The correct answer to the above question is (D). The student is admitting that she was caught in a lie.

A Listen to part of a conversation, and answer the question.

1. What can be inferred about the student? (●) 3-10

(A) He thinks he is president of his school.
(B) He thinks his door should be fixed immediately.
(C) He wants to pay the Student Service Center extra money to fix his door.
(D) He doesn't want his door fixed.

Listen again, and circle the words or phrases you hear.

get down	Student Service Center	no problem	fill out a form
come up	really busy	differential arrangement	student center
preferential	not problematic	visit a farm	real buses

2. What is the professor's attitude toward David's problem? (●) 3-11

(A) He is sympathetic.
(B) He is angry.
(C) He is too busy to think about it.
(D) He is unsympathetic.

Listen again, and circle the words or phrases you hear.

for a second	probably not	play golf	get together
wouldn't be fair	four minutes	good weather	a big behind
golf player	will probably	go to the fair	a little behind

3. What can be inferred about the student? (●) 3-12

(A) She is a lazy student.
(B) She is finished with her project.
(C) She thinks Dr. Kline will not help her.
(D) She thinks it will be easy to make the corrections.

Listen again, and circle the words or phrases you hear.

for a moment	in that case	handed in	be the case
cite your sources	in a moment	take a book	handy things
recite your courses	between the lines	line up between	take a look

B Listen to part of a lecture, and answer the question.

1. **What is the professor's attitude toward Avram Noam Chomsky?** (o) 3-13

  (A) positive
  (B) matter-of-fact
  (C) negative
  (D) humorous

Listen again, and circle the words or phrases you hear.

living scholar	keynote speaker	significant	contributions
left wing politics	lively collar	signature copy	key intellectual figure
strong coffee	strongly criticized	right wing radical	most notably

2. **What is the professor's opinion towards the architecture of the Ottoman Empire?** (o) 3-14

  (A) He despises it.
  (B) He feels ambivalent about it.
  (C) He admires it.
  (D) He thinks it's mediocre.

Listen again, and circle the words or phrases you hear.

six hundred years	vast inner spaces	perfect harmony	nice work
seemingly weightless	surrounded Korea	six thousand years	great works
nasty thin faces	seemed baseless	perfected harmonica	surrounding areas

3. **What is the professor's opinion of the autocratic management style?** (o) 3-15

  (A) He thinks it has good and bad points.
  (B) He thinks it's the best way to manage.
  (C) He thinks it's a terrible way to manage.
  (D) He thinks the *laissez-faire* style is a better way to manage.

Listen again, and circle the words or phrases you hear.

spend some time	creating high standards	accomplish his goals
overly dependent	under confident	hot chocolate
highly creative individuals	not deliberate	all the time
score a goal	very determining	send a typewriter

Practice with Conversations

A Listen to part of a conversation, and answer the questions. 🔊 3-16

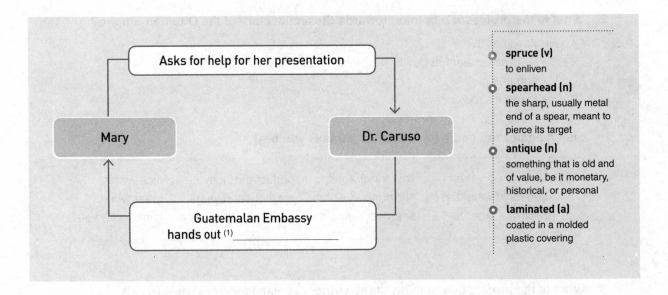

Mary

Asks for help for her presentation

Dr. Caruso

Guatemalan Embassy
hands out (1)_____

spruce (v)
to enliven

spearhead (n)
the sharp, usually metal
end of a spear, meant to
pierce its target

antique (n)
something that is old and
of value, be it monetary,
historical, or personal

laminated (a)
coated in a molded
plastic covering

1. **What can be inferred about the student?**

   Ⓐ She thinks Dr. Caruso will not help her.
   Ⓑ She thinks her project will be better with supplements from Dr. Caruso.
   Ⓒ She thinks Guatemala is a beautiful place to visit.
   Ⓓ She thinks the Guatemalan Embassy will not be helpful.

2. **What can be inferred about the deputy ambassador at the Guatemalan Embassy?**

   Ⓐ She doesn't like to help students.
   Ⓑ She wants a new job.
   Ⓒ She doesn't speak English.
   Ⓓ She is happy to help Dr. Caruso.

3. Listen again, and fill in the blanks.

W: Hi, Dr. Caruso. May I have a moment of your time?

M: Hello, Mary. Sure, what's up?

W: Well, I'm working on my _____ for my international business development class. I have to assemble a presentation as if it were a _____ tourism for Guatemala. Since you're the Professor of Latin American Studies, I was hoping you might have some _____ that I could add to my presentation to spruce it up. You know, like some posters or brochures.

M: Hmm, let me think for a second. Well, I have an ancient Aztec spearhead and some examples of Stone Age pottery and weaving. Would those _____ be of any use if I loaned them to you?

W: Uh, those sound interesting. But I was hoping for something more modern. I was thinking you might have _____, some enlarged photographs, or maybe some information about the tourism industry.

M: Aha, I see. You're doing a booth to educate people about visiting Guatemala. Okay, I can help. But I don't have the materials here. Let me give you the telephone number for the _____ downtown. I know the deputy ambassador there. I'm sure she would be happy to furnish you _____. I know they have packets of posters and brochures that they hand out for free.

W: Thank you so much. That sounds like just what I need. I'll call them right away.

M: Sure, let me just check my rolodex here for Marta's phone number. I'll call her and _____ for you. She's always very helpful when I refer students. Let me tell you _____. Last year, we took a study trip there, and two of my students lost their passports. There was a mix-up with immigration, and I called her. She got it _____.

W: Wow, it's good to have connections I guess.

M: You bet it is!

4. Complete the following summary.

Mary tells her professor that she is working on a _____ for her international business development class. She needs to make a _____ tourism to Guatemala. She asks her professor if has any _____ she could use in the presentation. He offers her some _____, but those are not what she's looking for. Then he offers to connect her with the _____. He says that they will probably have some materials for her to use. She thanks him. Then he tells her a story _____ when his friend at the Guatemalan Embassy helped him recently.

final project	campaign to increase	supplements
archeological antiques	Guatemalan Embassy	about the time

B Listen to part of a conversation, and answer the questions. 3-17

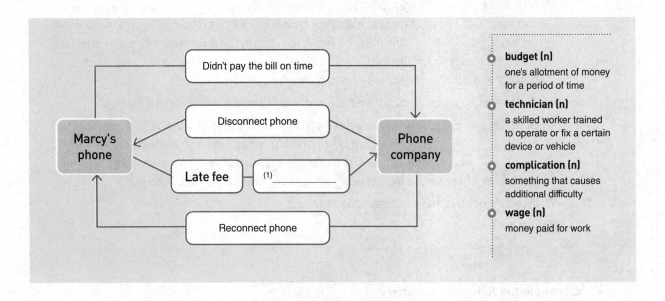

Didn't pay the bill on time

Disconnect phone

Marcy's phone

Late fee   (1)_____

Phone company

Reconnect phone

budget (n)
one's allotment of money for a period of time

technician (n)
a skilled worker trained to operate or fix a certain device or vehicle

complication (n)
something that causes additional difficulty

wage (n)
money paid for work

1. **How does the manager act toward the student?**
   Ⓐ He feels sorry that her phone was shut off.
   Ⓑ He scolds her for not paying her bill on time.
   Ⓒ He gives her money to pay her bill.
   Ⓓ He says she can never reconnect her phone.

2. **What does the student mean when she says this?** 🎧
   Ⓐ You really helped me a lot.
   Ⓑ Your job is to save people's lives.
   Ⓒ You work part-time as a lifesaver.
   Ⓓ You are not a nice person.

3. Listen again, and fill in the blanks.

> **W:** Hi, Mr. Shanks. I'm Marcy Walker from _____ 322. I have a problem. My phone line is dead. I can't call my parents. I can't access the Internet. And I need to do research for my final project. This is the worst time on Earth that this could have possibly happened to me. What should I do? Can you help me get the _____?
>
> **M:** Okay, Marcy, I know why your telephone line was _____. It's because you didn't _____ for the last two months. It's not up to me whether your _____ or not. It's up to the _____. They'll let you pay your _____ a month late. But if you are _____, they shut your phone off.
>
> **W:** Yeah, it's a real _____. I didn't pay my bill on time because I _____ reserved for the phone bill in my budget on shopping and drinking.
>
> **M:** That was not very smart. Now you are going to have to _____ as well as a late fee of 2%. Then you'll have to _____ and wait for the service technician to schedule an appointment to _____. Then you'll have to wait for him to show up here at the main desk. Then, after it's reconnected, on your next bill, you're going to have to _____. All this trouble is because you were late paying your bill. What does this complication teach you?
>
> **W:** I guess I'm going to have to get a _____ to afford all of this.
>
> **M:** Well, I'm looking for someone to _____ at night and on weekends. I can give you twenty hours a week at _____.
>
> **W:** Oh, Mr. Shanks! You're a _____. Thank you so much.
>
> **M:** Sure. You can start training tomorrow at 5 p.m.

4. Complete the following summary.

Marcy Walker tells her dorm manager that her telephone line has been _____. She is upset because she can't access the Internet or call her parents. He tells her that the phone was shut off because she didn't _____ for two months. Then he tells her she will have to pay a late fee and a _____. He scolds her for not paying her bill. She admits that she didn't pay her bill because she _____ on other things. Then the dorm manager offers her a _____ working at the front desk. He tells her she can work 20 hours per week for _____. She is happy and agrees.

shut off	pay her bill	reconnection fee
spent her money	parttime job	minimum wage

Dr. Simmons:
- had an appendectomy last summer
- is observing Fred's class next week on Tuesday

Fred:
- student teacher
- teaches (1) _____
- reads a novel and then watches the Hollywood adaptation and (2) _____
  _____

appendectomy (n)
surgery to remove an appendix from a human

shipshape (a)
in top condition

contrast (v)
to cite differences between two or more things

overambitious (a)
trying to accomplish more than one is capable of

1. **What can be inferred about the student?**

   Ⓐ He doesn't like teaching.
   Ⓑ He is not happy to see Dr. Simmons.
   Ⓒ He is a little nervous when he hears his class will be observed.
   Ⓓ He is worried about Dr. Simmons' health.

2. **Why is Fred showing Hollywood adaptations in his class?**

   Ⓐ Because he likes movies more than books.
   Ⓑ Because the students only like movies.
   Ⓒ Because he wants to make the administration angry.
   Ⓓ Because he wants students to compare and contrast movies with the original novels.

3. **Listen again, and fill in the blanks.**

> **M1:** Dr. Simmons, hi, how are you doing? I haven't seen you since last year!
>
> **M2:** Hey there, Fred. Long time no see. I'm feeling great. I had an appendectomy last summer. I was in the hospital for two weeks. That was tough. But I'm _____ now and feeling great. My body is one hundred percent shipshape! So how are you? I hear you're a _____ these days.
>
> **M1:** That's right. I'm really enjoying being on your side of the classroom. I'm teaching the _____ to Modern Literature Course.
>
> **M2:** That's what I heard. As a matter of fact, that's why I called and asked you to meet me here today. The university has assigned me to ____ your class _____, and I wanted to tell you in person.
>
> **M1:** Oh really? Did I do something wrong? Was there a complaint?
>
> **M2:** No, no, nothing of the sort. It's just _____ that the university does on all new student teachers.
>
> **M1:** Hmm, okay. I'm just surprised because I would think they would have told me about it earlier.
>
> **M2:** Well, you know, the _____ likes to use the element of surprise sometimes. They want me to observe your normal teaching style. Speaking of which, what are you teaching this semester?
>
> **M1:** I'll email you my syllabus and lesson plans before you come in. But in brief, I'm doing a _____ unit, where we read a novel and then watch the _____and discuss the difference.
>
> **M2:** That sounds really interesting. Which books and movies are you doing?
>
> **M1:** First we're reading and watching William Golding's _____. Then we're going to do Shakespeare's _____, with the Kenneth Brannaugh film adaptation. Then, if we have enough time, we'll take a look at Joseph Conrad's _____ with Francis Ford Coppala's *Apocalypse Now* for the film portion.
>
> **M2:** Wow! That's _____.
>
> **M1:** Yeah, do you think it's _____?
>
> **M2:** Maybe a little.

4. **Complete the following summary.**

Dr. Simmons and Fred meet. Dr. Simmons tells Fred that he was in the hospital for an appendectomy. He says his body is _____ now. Fred says he enjoys being a _____. Dr. Simmons tells Fred that the _____ is sending him to observe Fred's class. Dr. Simmons asks Fred about what he's teaching. Fred tells Dr. Simmons about a unit he's teaching that _____ novels and their _____. Fred asks Dr. Simmons if he thinks this syllabus is _____. Dr. Simmons says it is a little overambitious.

fully recovered	student teacher	university administration
compares and contrasts	Hollywood adaptations	overambitious

127

D Listen to part of a conversation, and answer the questions. 🔘 3-19

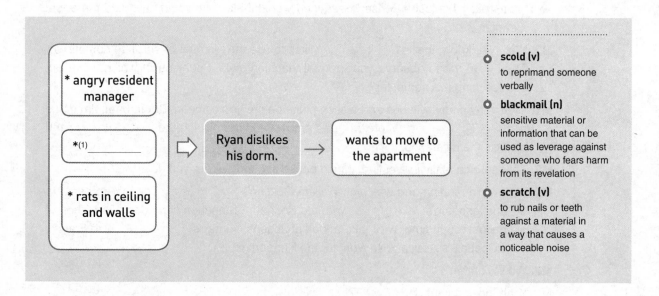

* angry resident manager

*(1) _____

* rats in ceiling and walls

Ryan dislikes his dorm.

wants to move to the apartment

scold (v)
to reprimand someone verbally

blackmail (n)
sensitive material or information that can be used as leverage against someone who fears harm from its revelation

scratch (v)
to rub nails or teeth against a material in a way that causes a noticeable noise

1. **What can be inferred about the female student?**
   - Ⓐ She thinks Ryan has another girlfriend.
   - Ⓑ She thinks Ryan should turn his music down.
   - Ⓒ She would like to move into an apartment.
   - Ⓓ She doesn't want Ryan to call her anymore.

2. **Why did the resident manager of Ryan's dormitory scold him?**
   - Ⓐ For having a dirty room
   - Ⓑ For playing music too loudly
   - Ⓒ For bringing girls into his room
   - Ⓓ For not paying his phone bill on time

3. **Listen again, and fill in the blanks.**

> **M:** Hey, Sheila. What's up sister?
>
> **W:** Oh, Ryan, I'm mad at you. Why didn't you call me yesterday like you said you would?
>
> **M:** Oh, sorry for _____. I forgot. I was busy getting _____ by the resident manager of my dorm.
>
> **W:** Really, what did you do wrong?
>
> **M:** Nothing really. Reilly, my roommate, and I were just listening to the new Slayer album. We didn't even have the stereo _____. But the walls in that old building are so thin. The pre-med students next door were trying to study. They _____ to the _____. Are the walls that thin in your building?
>
> **W:** Oh yeah, totally. But our resident manager never scolds us. That's because we live next door to her, and we hear her television _____. We have blackmail material on her. Ha ha.
>
> **M:** That's cool. I wish my resident manager would loosen up. He said if we get another noise complaint, he's going to refer us to Student Housing Services, and they're going to put us on probation.
>
> **W:** That's bad. You should get out of the dorms and _____ an apartment near campus anyways. I hate living _____. The bathrooms are so old. They look and smell like my grandmother's house.
>
> **M:** Yeah, the plumbing does seem sort of ancient. Plus I think there may be a family of rats living in the _____. I can hear them scratching _____.
>
> **W:** That's disgusting. Remind me not to visit your dorm. So what about the apartment? Have you thought about it?
>
> **M:** Yeah, I asked my dad if he would help me _____. But he said I had to spend at least one year there before he would consider helping me get an apartment.

4. **Complete the following summary.**

Sheila and Ryan meet. Sheila is mad at Ryan for _____ her. He says he didn't call her because he was busy being _____ by the resident manager of his dorm. His _____ was angry because he played music too loudly. Some students next door _____. Sheila says her resident manager never scolds her. Sheila tells Ryan he should leave the dorms and _____ an apartment. She hates living in the dorm. She thinks they are old and dirty. Ryan says he thinks there are rats living in the _____ of his dorm. But his father will not help him get an apartment.

not calling	chewed out	resident manager
called and complained	move into	ceiling and walls

Practice with Lectures

A Listen to part of a lecture, and answer the questions. 🔊 3-20

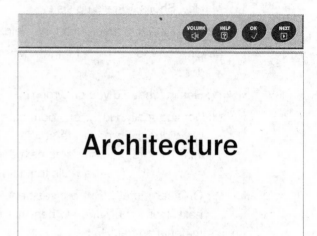

Architecture

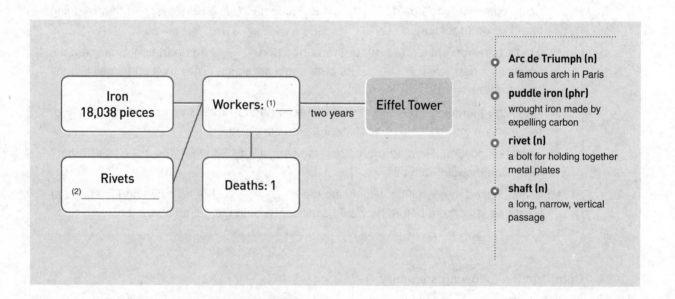

- **Arc de Triumph (n)** a famous arch in Paris
- **puddle iron (phr)** wrought iron made by expelling carbon
- **rivet (n)** a bolt for holding together metal plates
- **shaft (n)** a long, narrow, vertical passage

Iron 18,038 pieces — Workers: (1)____ — two years — Eiffel Tower

Rivets (2)____

Deaths: 1

1. **What does the student mean when she says this?**
    - (A) She thinks the Eiffel Tower is unattractive.
    - (B) She thinks the Eiffel Tower looks great.
    - (C) She thinks the Eiffel Tower was alive at one time.
    - (D) She thinks the Eiffel Tower is made from bone.

2. **How many workers died during the Eiffel Tower's construction?**
    - (A) 18,038
    - (B) 1
    - (C) 6
    - (D) 7,300

3. Listen again, and fill in the blanks.

> **W1:** Good afternoon, class. Today we are going to discuss the construction of one of the world's most _____. It's located in the middle of Paris, France.
>
> **W2:** You're talking about the Eiffel Tower, designed by Gustave Eiffel and built between 1887 and 1889.
>
> **W1:** That's absolutely correct. The Eiffel Tower today remains _____ in Paris, standing 300 meters high. The iron structure of the tower weighs a total of 7,300 tons. It took 300 workers to join together 18,038 pieces of _____ with three and a half million rivets to _____ the tower.
>
> **M:** That doesn't sound like such a big deal.
>
> **W1:** In a way, you're right. By today's standards, building that kind of structure would be quite easy. But for the time, it was _____ in the world. It _____ for over 40 years. The tower was erected to be the entrance arch for the 1898 World's Fair in Paris. Did you know that only one worker died during construction? He was killed when he fell down the elevator shaft.
>
> **W2:** Well, as famous as it is, I still think it's ugly. It looks like _____.
>
> **W1:** You wouldn't be the only one who has thought the tower was an eyesore. Many members of the French public did not _____. One famous novelist even ate his lunch at a restaurant near the tower because he felt it was the only place he could eat without having to see it.
>
> **W2:** Ha ha!
>
> **W1:** And furthermore, the city government of Paris had an agreement with Gustave Eiffel that after twenty years, rights to the tower would be theirs _____ they would tear it down. But since it proved to be _____ used for radio communications, the city allowed Eiffel's permit to _____. By that time, the tower was so _____ in French history that they could not tear it down.

4. Complete the following summary.

The Eiffel Tower was designed by Gustave Eiffel. It is still _____ in Paris. The iron structure of the tower weighs 7,300 tons. It took 300 workers to join 18,038 pieces of _____ and three and a half million rivets to ___ the tower. It _____ for tallest building in the world for over 40 years. The Eiffel Tower was the entrance arch for the 1898 World's Fair. Only one worker died during its construction. By the time the tower's permit ____, it was so _____ in French history that the government could not tear it down.

the tallest structure	puddle iron	erect
held the record	expired	firmly entrenched

B Listen to part of a lecture, and answer the questions. 🔘 3-21

Marketing

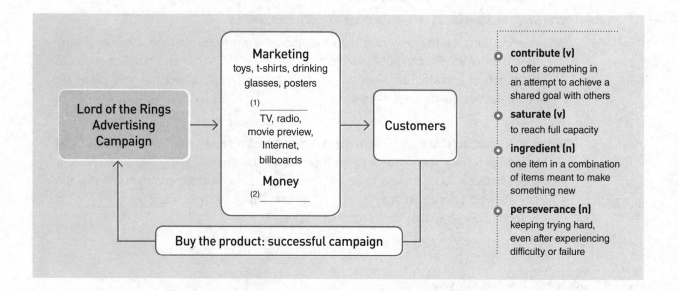

1. **What is the professor's opinion about the Lord of the Rings' advertising campaign?**

   Ⓐ He thinks it was a poor campaign.
   Ⓑ He thinks it was missing the 4 Ms.
   Ⓒ He thinks the advertising campaign for Star Wars was better.
   Ⓓ He thinks it was a very successful advertising campaign.

2. **What were the messages in The Lord of the Rings?**

   Ⓐ friendship, perseverance and the triumph of good over evil
   Ⓑ rock and roll, sex and drugs
   Ⓒ loneliness and eventual rescue
   Ⓓ friendship and loyalty between a boy and his dog

3. Listen again, and fill in the blanks.

Good afternoon, everybody. Do you remember a movie called *Lord of the Rings (LOTR)*? I'll bet you either saw it or heard about it. The reason you know about it is because it had a successful _____ around the world! To create a successful advertising campaign, you need four Ms. Those Ms stand for Marketing, Media, Money, and Message. Let's take a look at how the four Ms _____ to the huge success of *LOTR*.

First of all, the advertisers of *LOTR* had great _____. That means that aside from the actual movie, the film studio hired marketing companies to come up with many other products with the *LOTR* brand logo on them. That includes *LOTR* toys for kids, t-shirts, drinking glasses, posters, OST, and many other products. The act of putting the brand name, in this case, *LOTR*, in front of people's eyes in as many places _____ is called good marketing!

Secondly, the *LOTR* advertising campaign _____ every form of media possible. That means that there were commercials for *LOTR* on television commercials, movie previews in theaters, on the radio, and on the Internet. There were even *LOTR* billboards _____ in major American cities! Anyplace you looked, there was *LOTR*.

Thirdly, the producers of *LOTR* had the money to _____ in the various campaigns that were necessary _____. In this case, the more you invest, the higher profits you reap. If the studio couldn't afford to spend as much on advertising as they did, the movie wouldn't have been so successful. Money is an important ingredient for _____. Always!

Finally *LOTR* contained great messages. The messages in the movie were about friendship, perseverance, and the triumph of good over evil. People loved the movie and the products surrounding it because they loved the messages it portrayed. You can have the best advertising campaign on Earth, but if your product's message is bad, no one will buy it!

4. Complete the following summary.

The professor uses the movie *Lord of the Rings* as an example of a successful _____. He says that the advertisers of *LOTR* were successful because they used the four Ms. The first M is for marketing. *LOTR* employed various _____, such as selling t-shirts, posters, toys, and drinking glasses. The second M is for media. The advertisers of *LOTR* _____as many forms of media _____. The third M is for money. The producers of *LOTR* had enough money to _____ in their project. The fourth M is for message. *LOTR* had a positive message that people liked. All of these Ms _____ to success for *LOTR*.

advertising campaign	marketing strategies	saturated
as possible	invest heavily	added up

C Listen to part of a lecture, and answer the questions. 🔘 **3-22**

Climatology

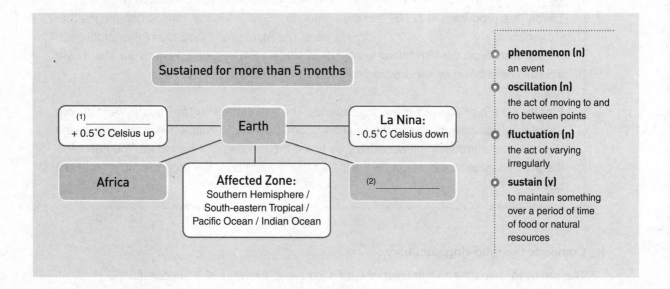

Sustained for more than 5 months

(1) _____
+ 0.5˚C Celsius up

Earth

La Nina:
- 0.5˚C Celsius down

Africa

Affected Zone:
Southern Hemisphere /
South-eastern Tropical /
Pacific Ocean / Indian Ocean

(2) _____

phenomenon (n)
an event

oscillation (n)
the act of moving to and
fro between points

fluctuation (n)
the act of varying
irregularly

sustain (v)
to maintain something
over a period of time
of food or natural
resources

1. **What is the professor's attitude toward the class?**

   Ⓐ He thinks they are all nice students.

   Ⓑ He thinks they need to pay close attention since this subject is complex.

   Ⓒ He thinks they are hard workers.

   Ⓓ He thinks this subject is easy to understand.

2. **What conditions signify a period of El Nino or La Nina?**

   Ⓐ Thunderstorms lasting five months

   Ⓑ A prolonged temperature change of 0.5˚ Celsius above or below the norm

   Ⓒ A hurricane that wipes out entire cities

   Ⓓ An earthquake, a forest fire, and a flood, all at the same time

3. Listen again, and fill in the blanks.

> Okay, class, today I'm going to provide you with overviews of the El Nino and La Nina weather phenomenon. These patterns are not easy to understand, so pay close attention. The El Nino Southern Oscillation (ENSO) is a global coupled ocean-atmosphere phenomenon. Pacific Ocean signatures such as El Nino and La Nina are _____ _____ in surface waters of the Tropical Eastern Ocean. El Nino signifies a rise of 0.5° Celsius or more and La Nina a drop of the same _____ a period longer than five months.
>
> Many of the countries _____ by ENSO events are developing nations on the continents of South America and Africa. Their economies are largely dependent on agricultural and fishing sectors as a major source of food supply, employment, and foreign exchange. New capabilities for predicting these events can have a great socio-economic impact.
>
> These episodes usually _____ every 2-7 years. They usually last one or two years. The effects of El Nino are very wide ranging. Many places experience weather that is the reverse from their normal climate. Some areas even experience terrible flooding _____ excess rainfall or forest fires _____. Aside from the drastic weather changes around the southern hemisphere, the fishing and manure industries in South America are heavily affected.
>
> In the normal Pacific pattern, equatorial winds gather. Then warm water pools towards the west. Cold water upswells along the South American coast. Since fish follow the cool _____ water, this brings them up the coast where _____. When El Nino takes effect, the warm water flows toward the South American coast. The absence of cold _____ increases warming and sends the _____ out to sea instead of along the coast. These conditions are severely damaging to local fishing industries.
>
> The causes of El Nino and La Nina _____ are still undiscovered. But many scientists are dedicating their careers to better understanding this global weather phenomenon.

4. Complete the following summary.

El Nino and La Nina signify a _____ of 0.5° Celsius higher or lower than normal for more than five months. Countries on the continents of South America and Africa are the _____ by El Nino. These episodes _____ every 2-7 years. They reverse normal climates. An example of El Nino in action is when the warm water flows towards the South American coast. The absence of cold water _____ sends the _____ out to sea. This is due to the fact that fish follow the cool _____ water. The causes of El Nino are still not fully understood by scientists.

temperature change	most affected	occur irregularly
upswelling	fish population	nutrient-rich

D Listen to part of a lecture, and answer the questions. ⊙ 3-23

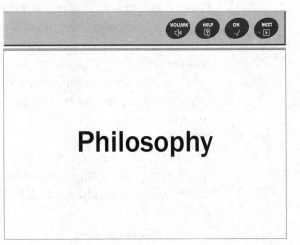

Philosophy

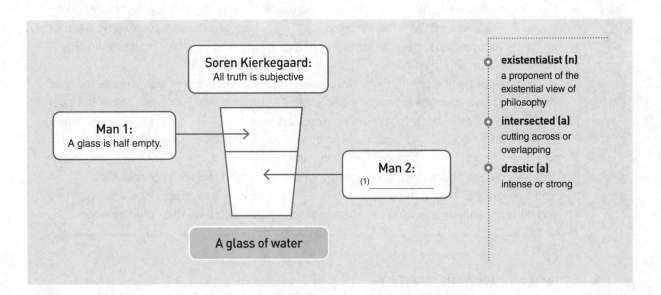

Soren Kierkegaard:
All truth is subjective

Man 1:
A glass is half empty.

Man 2:
(1) _____

A glass of water

existentialist (n)
a proponent of the existential view of philosophy

intersected (a)
cutting across or overlapping

drastic (a)
intense or strong

---

1. **Listen again to part of the lecture. Then answer the question.** 🎧
   What can be inferred when the student says this? 🎧

   (A) He agrees with the doctrine of Solipsism.
   (B) He thinks Descartes was the first existentialist.
   (C) He thinks the professor agrees with Kierkegaard.
   (D) He thinks math can prove truth about the universe.

2. **According to the professor, which two things have always gone hand in hand?**

   (A) Misery and company
   (B) Up and down
   (C) Existentialism and teen angst
   (D) Black and white

3. Listen again, and fill in the blanks.

> **M1:** Welcome, class. I'd like to start this class off with a question. Who here can tell me which great philosopher said, "I think, therefore I am"?
>
> **W:** Ooh, I've heard that before. Was it… Jean Paul Sartre?
>
> **M1:** That's a good guess, but no. This philosopher lived almost three hundred years before Jean Paul Sartre. His name is Rene Descartes. He is considered _____ _____.
>
> **M2:** Was he an existentialist?
>
> **M1:** No, he wasn't. Descartes was a _____. He was also a mathematician. His love for math and philosophy intersected. He felt math could be used to _____ about the universe. But it's interesting that you brought up the existentialists. That's an important group from modern western philosophy. Let's talk about an _____ named Soren Kierkegaard.
>
> **M2:** Why?
>
> **M1:** Soren Kierkegaard was a Danish philosopher who lived in the 1800s. He made a very important _____. He said, "All truth is subjective."
>
> **W:** Does that mean that up is down, black is white, and two plus two equals five?
>
> **M1:** No, his viewpoint was not that drastic. Kierkegaard just thought that each person experienced a different version of the truth _____ from where they were standing. For example, two men are looking at a glass of water. One man says the glass of water is half empty. The other man says the glass is half full. Their opinions seem to be conflicting. Are they? No, they are both right. Each man possesses _____. Neither one is more right or more wrong. Their truths are simply subjective. This was a precursor _____ that each person is alone in their relationship with the rest of the universe. This viewpoint, called the _____, has gotten a lot of criticism from other _____. It's accused of being selfish and egotistical.
>
> **M2:** But it makes sense to me!
>
> **M1:** Sure, existentialism and teen angst have always gone hand in hand.

4. Complete the following summary.

The professor begins the lecture with the quote, "I think, therefore I am." It is from Rene Descartes. Descartes was a _____. He was also a mathematician who believed math could be used to _____ about the universe. Soren Kierkegaard was an _____. He said, "All truth is subjective." The professor and students then discuss the meaning of truth to individual people. Kierkegaard's _____ led to the _____, that all individuals are alone with the rest of the universe. Solipsism has suffered much criticism from other _____ for being selfish and egotistical.

natural philosopher	prove truth	early existentialist
statement on truth	doctrine of Solipsism	branches of philosophy

Integrated Listening & Speaking

A Listen to the summary of the previous conversation and say the answers out loud by using the cue sentence words that are indicated in each answer. (⊙ 3-24)

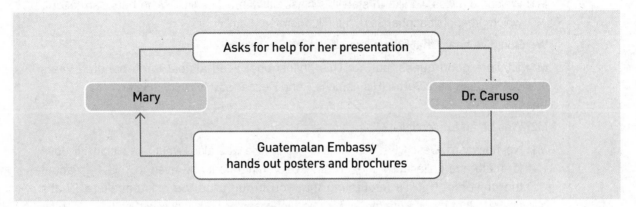

1. **What does Mary tell her professor she is doing?**

   (1) She is _____.   (2) Mary has _____.

2. **Is Mary interested in the archeological antiques he offers her?**

   (1) No, those are _____.   (2) No, the antiques are _____.

3. **What does the professor say the Guatemalan Embassy will probably do for her?**

   (1) The professor says they will have _____.   (2) He says they will _____.

B Listen to the summary of the previous conversation and say the answers out loud by using the cue sentence words that are indicated in each answer. (⊙ 3-25)

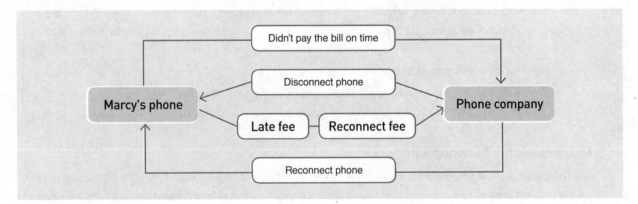

1. **What does Marcy tell her dorm manager?**

   (1) The line to _____.   (2) She tells him that _____.

2. **What does the dorm manager tell Marcy?**

   (1) He tells her it's because _____.   (2) He says the problem is that _____.

3. **What does the dorm manager offer Marcy?**

   (1) He offers her a part time job _____.   (2) He says she can have a job _____.

C Listen to the previous lecture and say the answers out loud by using the cue sentence words that are indicated in each answer. ⊙ 3-26

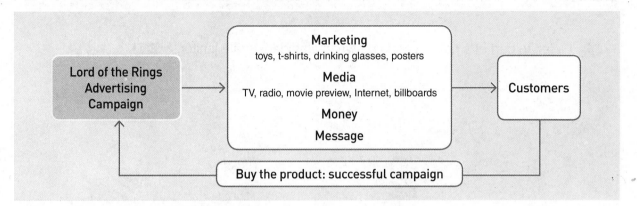

1. **What movie does the professor use as an example?**

   (1) An example of a successful _____.   (2) The Lord of the Rings is a _____.

2. **How did the advertisers use media successfully?**

   (1) They saturated _____.   (2) As many forms of _____.

3. **What kind of message did LOTR have?**

   (1) It had a _____.   (2) The message, which _____.

D Listen to the previous lecture and say the answers out loud by using the cue sentence words that are indicated in each answer. ⊙ 3-27

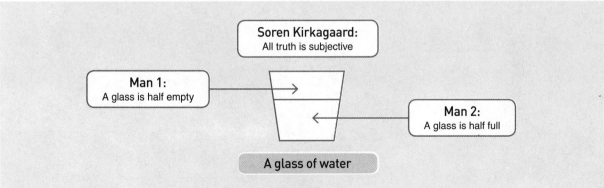

1. **What famous statement did the professor begin the lecture with?**

   (1) The professor began _____.   (2) "I think, therefore I am." is _____.

2. **What did Descartes believe about math?**

   (1) He believed that _____.   (2) The truth about the universe _____.

3. **What famous statement did Kierkegaard make?**

   (1) All truth _____.   (2) Every truth on the Earth _____.

A Listen to part of a conversation between a student and a janitor. ⊙ 3-28

1. **What is the student's problem?**

   Ⓐ Her door is broken.
   Ⓑ She doesn't like living in the dorm.
   Ⓒ Her phone was shut off.
   Ⓓ The hand dryer in her bathroom is broken.

2. **Why has the janitor been so slow to fix the hand dryer?**

   Ⓐ He's been very busy doing other things.
   Ⓑ He doesn't think hand dryers are important.
   Ⓒ He doesn't know how to fix a hand dryer.
   Ⓓ The hand dryer is too expensive to fix.

3. **Listen again to part of the conversation. Then answer the question.**

   Why does the janitor say this to the student?

   Ⓐ He thinks she is so funny.
   Ⓑ He agrees with her.
   Ⓒ He becomes angry because she is so disrespectful.
   Ⓓ He falls in love with her.

4. **Listen again to part of the conversation. Then answer the question.**

   What does the student mean when she says this?

   Ⓐ She is going to complain to the administration.
   Ⓑ She is going to give him some extra money.
   Ⓒ She is going to forget about the problem.
   Ⓓ She feels bad for being so rude.

5. **What will the janitor probably do after the conversation?**

   Ⓐ He will probably go to sleep.
   Ⓑ He will order some parts.
   Ⓒ He will probably complain about Rachel.
   Ⓓ He will probably not do anything.

B Listen to part of a lecture in an art class. 3-29

1. **What is this lecture mainly about?**

   (A) Cubist and Surrealist painters

   (B) Realist and Impressionistic painters

   (C) Realist and Cubist painters

   (D) Impressionistic and Surrealist painters

2. **What prevailing European style of painting did Carvaggio go against?**

   (A) Impressionism

   (B) Realism

   (C) Cubism

   (D) Mannerism

3. **What kind of painter was Edgar Degas?**

   (A) He was a realist and an impressionist.

   (B) He was a realist.

   (C) He was an impressionist.

   (D) He was an abstract painter.

4. **Which three realist painters are mentioned? Click on 3 answers.**

   (A) Carvaggio

   (B) Degas

   (C) Seurat

   (D) Rembrandt

5. **Listen again to part of the lecture. Then answer the question.**

   What does the professor seem to feel when she says this? 🎧

   (A) She feels angry at the students.

   (B) She feels hungry for lunch.

   (C) She feels deep admiration for Seurat's painting.

   (D) She feels ambivalent toward Seurat's painting.

6. **What does the professor's tone imply about Seurat's painting?**

   (A) It is not so good.

   (B) It is good, but not the best.

   (C) It is the worst painting ever.

   (D) It is an absolute masterpiece of impressionism.

Vocabulary Review

A Listen and choose the correct word that matches each definition. ⊙ 3-30

1. (A) notably   (B) notable   (C) note   (D) notation
2. (A) autocracy   (B) audio   (C) autocratic   (D) automobile
3. (A) sanctify   (B) sanctuary   (C) sanctimonious   (D) sanction
4. (A) hinge   (B) hinged   (C) unhinge   (D) hind
5. (A) citation   (B) recite   (C) situation   (D) cite
6. (A) problem   (B) probable   (C) probably   (D) probe
7. (A) rivets   (B) river   (C) riveted   (D) riveter
8. (A) campaigner   (B) campaign   (C) Champagne   (D) camper
9. (A) stupid   (B) sustainable   (C) stain   (D) sustain
10. (A) supplement   (B) super   (C) supple   (D) sump
11. (A) deputy   (B) departure   (C) demand   (D) default
12. (A) donation   (B) allowance   (C) budget   (D) endowment
13. (A) appendix   (B) appendage   (C) addendum   (D) appendectomy
14. (A) overambitious   (B) overflow   (C) overall   (D) overage
15. (A) scorn   (B) scold   (C) scoff   (D) spurn

B Complete the sentences by filling in the blanks with the expressions in the box.

bring out the best	between the lines	a little behind
pain in the neck	vast inner spaces	preferential treatment

1. Yeah, it's a real _____.
2. This can _____ in highly creative individuals.
3. They mastered the technique of building _____.
4. I'm afraid we can't give _____.
5. I need the extra space to write my comments _____.
6. I'm _____ on my interview project.

PART 3 Connecting Information

Connecting Information questions test your ability to integrate information from different parts of the listening passage to make inferences, to draw conclusions, to form generalizations, and to make predictions. To choose the right answer, these question types require you to make connections between or among pieces of information in the text and to identify the relationships among the ideas and details.

Unit 6

Understanding Organization

6 Understanding Organization

Overview

■ Introduction

Organization questions require you to identify the overall organization of the listening passage or the relationship between different portions of the listening passage. In the organization question, you are also asked to recognize the role of specific information such as topic changes, exemplifying, digressing, and inducing introductory and concluding remarks. This is to see whether you know how the specific part of the sentence is related to the whole content. This question type is usually shown in the lecture rather than the conversation and sometimes requires you to choose more than one answer.

■ Question Types

1. How does the professor organize the information about X that he presents to the class?

2. How is the discussion organized?

3. In what order does the speaker describe the topic?

4. Why does the professor discuss X?

5. Why does the professor mention X?

6. Why does the professor talk about X?

■ Useful Tips

• Typical types of organizations include the following patterns:
  – giving examples
  – contrasting
  – comparing
  – classifying/categorizing
  – describing causes and effects
  – explaining in chronological order

• Listen carefully for the transitions that indicate the sequence.

• Focus on the relationship between the contents led by the transitional words.

Sample iBT Question

How does the professor organize the information about the greenhouse effect that she presents to the class?

(A) chronologically

(B) from most important to least important

(C) in comparison to global warming

(D) from general to specific

Script

Many people may not realize it, but the greenhouse effect and global warming are totally different things. The greenhouse effect is something that happens with all celestial bodies – planets, moons, and such – that have an atmosphere. Anyway, back to the greenhouse effect. The greenhouse effect is a process that happens when the sun's heat enters the Earth's atmosphere. The sun's rays warm the Earth, and the atmosphere keeps the heat in, just like a greenhouse. It's a very natural thing, and in most cases, the planet system knows how to balance itself out. Anyway, like I said, it's a pretty natural process. Now all this gets messed up when humans, um, add stuff to the Earth's atmosphere. That's when global warming, which is not a natural process, happens. See what happens is that people create, um, things that create extra heat. For example, cars. We drive cars all the time. So we drive our cars, and our cars burn gas, and this exhaust is pretty hot. And the atmosphere keeps this heat around the planet. Plus, all of our machinery and our factories and stuff, they all produce heat. So all this stuff creates what scientists are calling global warming. The Earth's surface and atmosphere just keep getting hotter.

  The correct answer to the above question is (C). The teacher explains the greenhouse effect by comparing it to global warming.

Basic Drill

Listen to part of a conversation, and answer the question.

1. **Why does the professor mention majors in criminology and forensic science?** ⊙ 3-32
   - (A) Because he wants Mary to major in them
   - (B) Because he thinks they are bad subjects
   - (C) Because they are two majors that go well together
   - (D) Because he thinks society needs more forensic detectives

   Listen again, and circle the words or phrases you hear.

fine art	compliment each other	doubled over	declaration
declaring	sculpted	social science	artistically finite
double major	compliments for everyone	sculpture	scientific society

2. **What should the student do the next time he needs a book for his report?** ⊙ 3-33
   - (A) He should buy it.
   - (B) He should borrow it from a friend.
   - (C) He should reserve it.
   - (D) He should use a different book.

   Listen again, and circle the words or phrases you hear.

carded results	due in two days	wandering	water fountain
copied reservations	wondering	clerk	two weeks of duty
reservation card	waterfall	reserved a copy	cluck

3. **Why does the worker mention the bulletin board at the Student Job Center?** ⊙ 3-34
   - (A) Because he's trying to get rid of the student
   - (B) Because he doesn't want to work with this student
   - (C) Because he's trying to help this student
   - (D) Because he really wants this student to become a cashier

   Listen again, and circle the words or phrases you hear.

position is filled	I don't blame you	my cup of tea
do you have a tale	I want a cup of tea	he was looking around
might be hiring	keep looking around	what does that entail
I blame you	what position is it	we're not hiring

B   Listen to part of a lecture, and answer the question.

1.   **How does the professor organize the information about comets that she presents to the class?** ⊙ 3-35

(A) chronologically
(B) from simple to complex
(C) from complex to simple
(D) as random, general information

Listen again, and circle the words or phrases you hear.

solar system	troposphere	heavily affected
Heaven's gate	constantly changing	solar power
atmosphere	horribly afflicted	heavenly body
changeable constant	throwing up	thrown out

2.   **How is the discussion organized?** ⊙ 3-36

(A) from humorous to informative
(B) generally
(C) not seriously
(D) as a scientific hypothesis

Listen again, and circle the words or phrases you hear.

externally	eternally	nutrient molecules	semantic relation
primary decomposers	erotic	used extensively	neutral molecule
eukaryotic	primitive composer	extra use	symbiotic relationships

3.   **Why does the professor mention encoding, storage, and recall?** ⊙ 3-37

(A) Because they are his favorite aspects of memory
(B) To explain the three main stages in the retrieval of memory
(C) Because they are interesting
(D) Because the cognitive neuroscience of psychology is important

Listen again, and circle the words or phrases you hear.

traditional studies	cogent psychoanalyst	marriage between	marinated beef
listen carefully	loosen carelessly	trade students	realm of philosophy
regional philosopher	cognitive psychology	recent decades	recently decadent

Practice with Conversations

A Listen to part of a conversation, and answer the questions. ⊙ 3-38

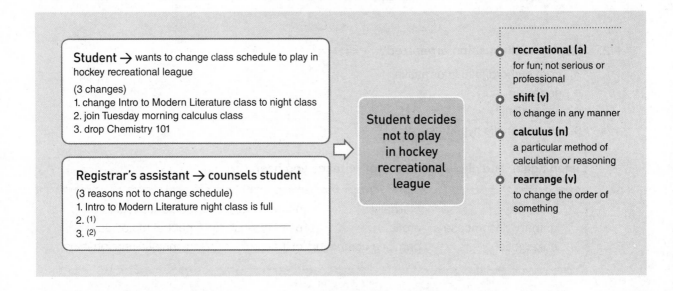

Student → wants to change class schedule to play in hockey recreational league

(3 changes)
1. change Intro to Modern Literature class to night class
2. join Tuesday morning calculus class
3. drop Chemistry 101

Registrar's assistant → counsels student

(3 reasons not to change schedule)
1. Intro to Modern Literature night class is full
2. (1) _____
3. (2) _____

Student decides not to play in hockey recreational league

- **recreational (a)**
  for fun; not serious or professional
- **shift (v)**
  to change in any manner
- **calculus (n)**
  a particular method of calculation or reasoning
- **rearrange (v)**
  to change the order of something

1. **Why does the student mention the recreational hockey league?**

   Ⓐ Because he really wants to play sports
   Ⓑ Because he hates studying
   Ⓒ Because he hates calculus
   Ⓓ Because he's explaining why he wants to change his schedule

2. **Which class is all full?**

   Ⓐ the Tuesday morning calculus class
   Ⓑ the recreational hockey league
   Ⓒ the Introduction to Modern Literature night class
   Ⓓ Chemistry 101

3. Listen again, and fill in the blanks.

M: Hi, who should I talk to about _____ for this semester?

W: You can talk to me about it. I'm the registrar's assistant.

M: All right, great. You're just the person I need to talk to. Okay, so, I want to _____ _____. So I'm going to have to shift my calculus class to Tuesday mornings, my Intro to Modern Literature course to the night class, and maybe drop Chemistry 101.

W: Hmm, that _____ a lot of rearranging. Are you sure you want to do that just to join the hockey league?

M: Oh, totally, for sure. Hockey versus Chemistry 101…Which one would you choose?

W: Do you want to graduate with a useful degree in four years?

M: Yeah, but that's not for years. I need to _____ this winter. That seems more important right now.

W: Okay, I'm looking at your schedule here, and I'm _____. First of all, the night class for Intro to Modern Literature is all full. There's no way you can get in there.

M: Oh, that stinks.

W: Well, that's just too bad. Secondly, you can transfer to the Tuesday morning calculus. But I have to warn you, it's an accelerated class. That means that they move through the book a lot faster than the low level class _____. Are you prepared _____ the increased course speed? Is calculus one of your strong suits?

M: Well no, but maybe I could…

W: Finally, about dropping Chemistry 101. Your major is Microbiology. You have to have Chemistry 101 _____ to take most of the other classes in your major. If you drop it this semester, it'll hold you up _____ in your major next semester. You could set _____ just to play recreational hockey. Do you really want to do that?

M: Hmm, I guess I'd better not. Thanks anyway.

W: No problem. Have a nice day!

4. Complete the following summary.

A student wants to change his schedule so he can join a _____. He wants to ___ his classes to different times. He also wants to ___ his Chemistry 101 class. The assistant tells him that the classes he wants to change into are either full or _____ for him. She also tells him that he _____ to graduate in four years if he drops Chemistry 101. The student _____ and decides not to play hockey.

shift	changes his mind	too advanced
recreational hockey league	might not be able	drop

B Listen to part of a conversation, and answer the questions. ⊙ 3-39

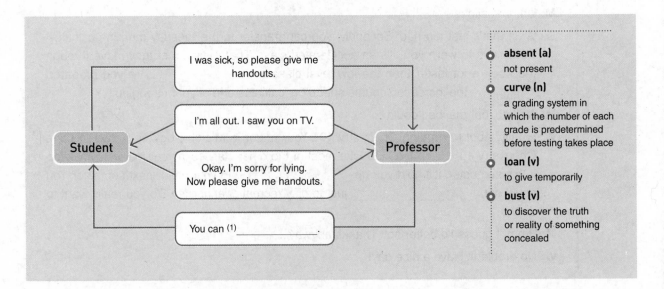

I was sick, so please give me handouts.

I'm all out. I saw you on TV.

Okay. I'm sorry for lying. Now please give me handouts.

Student

Professor

You can (1)_____.

- **absent (a)**
  not present
- **curve (n)**
  a grading system in which the number of each grade is predetermined before testing takes place
- **loan (v)**
  to give temporarily
- **bust (v)**
  to discover the truth or reality of something concealed

1. **How is the discussion organized?**
   - (A) chronologically
   - (B) in the form of a casual conversation
   - (C) as a list
   - (D) from the simple to the complex

2. **How is the class graded?**
   - (A) on a curve
   - (B) by student professors
   - (C) without letter grades
   - (D) pass or fail

3. Listen again, and fill in the blanks.

W1: Good morning, Mrs. Lassiter.

W2: Hi, Sally. You were absent yesterday. I hope you're feeling okay.

W1: Oh, uh, yeah, I'm _____ now. I was uh, oh, at home, sick in bed all weekend. Actually, that's why I was _____.

W2: Sick in bed? Oh, that's terrible. I was worried your absence _____ the big football game on Sunday and all the partying that _____ Sunday evening.

W1: Oh, Mrs. Lassiter, no way, not me. I'm not _____, football or partying.

W2: Hmm, okay. So how can I help you today?

W1: Well, I know you handed out the review sheets for the final exam yesterday, and I was hoping to get them.

W2: Oh yeah, those review sheets. You know, I hate to tell you this, but I'm all out. I ended up giving away my master copies by accident. You'll have _____ one of your classmates.

W1: Oh, Mrs. Lassiter, I'm begging you. The class is graded on a curve. None of my classmates want to help me. I might get _____. No one will loan me the sheets!

W2: My, you do seem to be in a predicament. Sally, I have to confess something. I was watching the game on television on Sunday, and I saw you in the crowd. You were on campus television! You didn't look very sick to me.

W1: Okay, you busted me. I was at the game. I missed class _____. You caught me in a lie. But now will you help me?

W2: I'll tell you again what I told you _____. You can access any of the handout sheets for this class from my website under the link that says "handouts". What do you think about that?

W1: Oh yeah. Now I remember. Okay, thanks.

4. Complete the following summary.

Sally was _____. She tells the professor she was sick all weekend. She asks for some important _____ for an _____. The professor tells her she's _____. She recommends Sally ask her classmates. Sally is upset because her classmates won't help her. The professor tells Sally that she saw her on television at the football game. Sally _____ she wasn't really sick. The professor tells her that she can get the _____ from her website online.

confesses	review sheets	absent from class
handouts	all out	upcoming exam

Listen to part of a conversation, and answer the questions. 3-40

Doug	Benny
wants to go to recreation room	the recreation room has been gutted
dislikes the Student Employment Center	knows about the change to Student Employment Center
is unhappy the recreation room has been gutted – wants to protest	thinks the protest would not be effective
doesn't think the president of the university would read the letters	suggests (1) _____
is cynical about students who protested	talks about students who (2) _____

gutted (a)
torn apart; emptied; destroyed

recruiters (n)
people who search for and actively acquire members for an organization

yuck (int)
an interjection of disgust or dislike

1. **Why does the student mention the new Student Employment Center?**

Ⓐ Because he likes it
Ⓑ Because he wants to go there
Ⓒ Because it will replace the recreation room that his friend likes
Ⓓ Because he wants to play pool

2. **Who will set up booths at the Student Employment Center?**

Ⓐ the two friends
Ⓑ students who want jobs
Ⓒ company recruiters
Ⓓ the president of the university

3. Listen again, and fill in the blanks.

> **M1:** Hey, Benny. Let's go over to the recreation room and _____ or play some video games.
>
> **M2:** Oh, Doug, haven't you heard? The recreation room is closed.
>
> **M1:** No way! Why? I love that place! I usually go there every day!
>
> **M2:** Well, you won't be going there anymore. It's been _____. They're turning it into a Student Employment Center. It's going to be a place for company recruiters _____ and for career counselors to hold resume building sessions.
>
> **M1:** Yuck, career counseling, company recruiters. That sounds like no fun! This is a total outrage. I'm going to do something about it. Do you want to help me?
>
> **M2:** What are you going to do about it? They've already closed the place. It's too late!
>
> **M1:** It's never too late. We can chain ourselves _____ so the construction workers can't go inside and tear it apart. We'll stage a protest and _____.
>
> **M2:** I don't think any of my friends would come. They're all interested in going to the career center _____ after they graduate. Maybe we should write the president of the university some angry letters.
>
> **M1:** I like that idea, but I don't think it would get anywhere. People write him angry letters all the time, and I don't think he even reads them. He has employees _____ _____ the angry letters.
>
> **M2:** I'm not so sure about that. Last year, the school administration tried _____ the benches and ash trays in Langley Park. You know, the place where everybody likes to gather and talk.
>
> **M1:** Yeah, I know about it, but I've never been there.
>
> **M2:** Yeah, well, they tried _____. All of the students who went there regularly were so upset. They held a protest. In the end, the administration didn't _____.
>
> **M1:** Sure, but I'll bet one of the protester's fathers works at the school.
>
> **M2:** Hey, don't be so cynical.

4. Complete the following summary.

Two friends meet and chat. Doug wants to go to the _____ on campus to play some games. Benny tells Doug that the recreation room has been closed. It is being changed into a _____. Doug is upset. He wants to _____. Benny doesn't think the protest _____. He wants to write angry letters to the president of the university. Doug likes the idea, but doesn't think _____. Benny tells Doug about a time when a student protest stopped the _____ from removing some benches that students liked.

administration	Student Employment Center	recreation room
would be effective	it would work	stage a protest

D Listen to part of a conversation, and answer the questions.  4-01

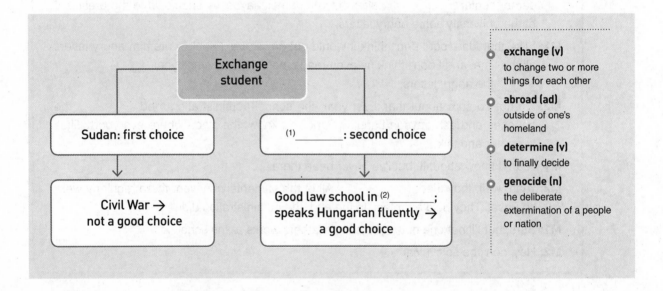

exchange (v)
to change two or more things for each other

abroad (ad)
outside of one's homeland

determine (v)
to finally decide

genocide (n)
the deliberate extermination of a people or nation

Exchange student

Sudan: first choice

(1)_____: second choice

Civil War →
not a good choice

Good law school in (2)_____;
speaks Hungarian fluently →
a good choice

1. **Why does the professor mention Hungarian exchange students studying at their school?**

    (A) Because he doesn't want Mark to go to the Sudan
    (B) Because he thinks Mark should meet them to make connections
    (C) Because he is just trying to do his job
    (D) Because Mark is not fulfilling the requirements for his major

2. **What does the professor say the student can't stop single-handedly?**

    (A) civil war
    (B) Hungarian exchange students
    (C) the school's department
    (D) genocide

3. Listen again, and fill in the blanks.

M1: Hi, Mr. Jones. May I speak with you for a few moments?

M2: Okay, Mark, how can I be of service to you today?

M1: I heard you were _____ the student exchange program for the international studies department.

M2: That's right, Mark. I am. Are you _____ studying abroad?

M1: Well, I'd never thought about it before. But I've been reading my course book and they recommend spending a semester abroad _____ majoring in international law, like me.

M2: That's absolutely correct. For students in your major, it's recommended that you spend six months to a year abroad. It prepares you _____ you'll be doing, and it helps you determine your country or region of focus. So where do you think you'd like to study?

M1: Well, I've been thinking about a few places. I've always wanted to go to the Sudan.

M2: The Sudan! Aren't they _____ a civil war? Do you really want to go there?

M1: Well, I've been reading about it, and I think I could help save some lives or something.

M2: Hmm, do you really think you can stop genocide single-handedly? I don't think that's a very realistic place for you _____. Do you have a second or third choice?

M1: Yeah, you're probably right. My parents are Hungarian. So I speak Hungarian fluently. It would be easy for me to study in Budapest _____.

M2: Now that is a much more realistic idea, Mark. I actually know of a good law school located in Budapest. We have some of their students studying here now. Maybe I could introduce you to them, and you could _____.

M1: That would be great. I'd love to make some friends that I could call if I went there. It would be nice to know some people right away.

4. Complete the following summary.

Mark is interested in _____. He talks to Mr. Jones, who is in charge of the _____. Mr. Jones asks Mark where he would like to study. Mark says he would like to study in the Sudan. Mr. Jones says it is _____ because the country is in civil war. Mark says his _____ is Budapest because he _____. Mr. Jones thinks it's a good idea. He offers to introduce Mark to some Hungarian _____ at the school.

an unrealistic idea	studying abroad	speaks Hungarian fluently
exchange students	second choice	student exchange program

Practice with Lectures

A Listen to part of a lecture, and answer the questions. ⊙ 4-02

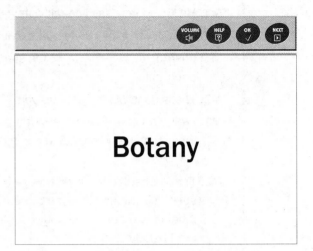

Botany

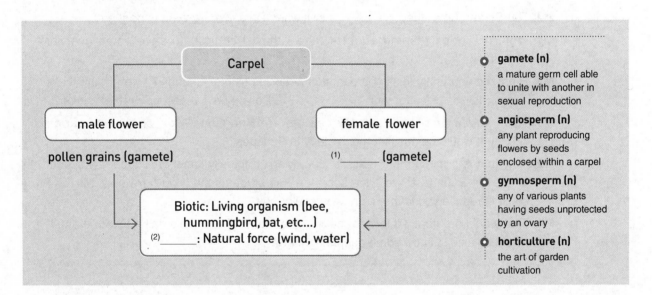

Carpel

male flower

pollen grains (gamete)

female flower

(1)_____ (gamete)

Biotic: Living organism (bee, hummingbird, bat, etc...)
(2)_____ : Natural force (wind, water)

gamete (n)
a mature germ cell able to unite with another in sexual reproduction

angiosperm (n)
any plant reproducing flowers by seeds enclosed within a carpel

gymnosperm (n)
any of various plants having seeds unprotected by an ovary

horticulture (n)
the art of garden cultivation

1. **How does the professor organize the information about the pollination process that she presents to the class?**

    Ⓐ chronologically
    Ⓑ from most important to least important
    Ⓒ separated between biotic and abiotic
    Ⓓ in the form of a funny story

2. **What is the female gamete?**

    Ⓐ the anther
    Ⓑ the wind
    Ⓒ the ovule
    Ⓓ zoophily

3. Listen again, and fill in the blanks.

Okay, class, today I want to tell you about _____. Pollination is an important step _____ seed plants. This is the name for the transfer of pollen grains to the plant carpel. The carpel is the structure _____ the ovule. The pollen grains are the male gamete, and the ovule is the female gamete. The receptive part of the carpel is called a stigma in the flowers of angiosperms and a micropyle in gymnosperms.

The study of pollination _____ many disciplines, such as botany, horticulture, entomology, and ecology. Pollination is important in horticulture because most plant fruits will not develop if the ovules are not fertilized. The pollination process as interaction between flower and vector _____ in the 18th century by Christian Konrad Sprengel.

The process of pollination requires pollinators as agents that carry or move the pollen grains _____. The various flower traits that attract different pollinators are known as pollinator syndromes.

One method of pollination common with plants is entomophily, which is pollination by insects. Bees, wasps, butterflies, and flies are just a few of the insects that usually _____ this process. Another method is called zoophily. This denotes pollination by vertebrates, such as birds or bats. The hummingbird and the honeyeater _____ this process.

Yet another method of pollination is anemophily, which is by the wind. This is common with many types of grasses and deciduous trees. In the case of aquatic plants, pollination by water is called hydrophily. All of these pollination processes _____ two categories, biotic and abiotic pollination. Biotic covers pollination by organisms, including entomophily and zoophily. This includes 80% of all pollination. Abiotic pollination covers all types _____, including anemophily and hydrophily. Of the 20% this covers, 98% is by wind and just 2% by water.

4. Complete the following summary.

Pollination is important for the _____ of seed plants. Many plants will not develop if their ovules are not fertilized. The _____ requires pollinators to _____ and carry pollen grains from the anther to the carpel. Pollination can either be _____ by biotic or abiotic means. Biotic refers to pollination by other _____. This often includes hummingbirds, bees, and bats. Abiotic _____ pollination by natural means, such as wind or water. Most pollination is biotic.

refers to	process of pollination	act as agents
carried out	living organisms	reproduction

B Listen to part of a lecture, and answer the questions. 🔘 4-03

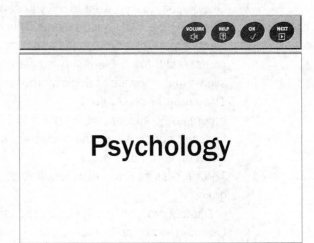

Psychology

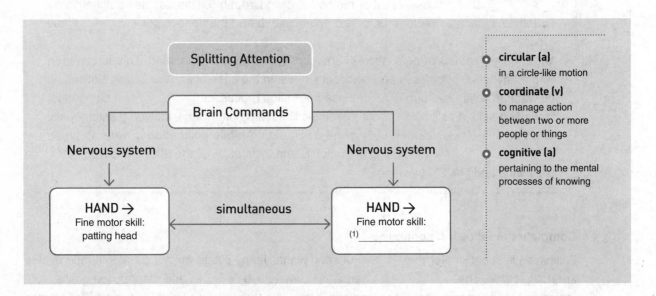

Splitting Attention

Brain Commands

Nervous system   Nervous system

HAND →   HAND →
Fine motor skill: Fine motor skill:
patting head   (1) _____
          simultaneous

○ **circular (a)**
in a circle-like motion

○ **coordinate (v)**
to manage action
between two or more
people or things

○ **cognitive (a)**
pertaining to the mental
processes of knowing

1. **Why does the professor mention patting the head and rubbing the belly at the same time?**
   - Ⓐ Because it's a cute activity
   - Ⓑ Because he wants to laugh at his students
   - Ⓒ Because this is an important ability to learn
   - Ⓓ Because it is an example of splitting attention

2. **Who was one of the first major psychologists?**
   - Ⓐ William James
   - Ⓑ Etta James
   - Ⓒ Henry James
   - Ⓓ James Joyce

3. **Listen again, and fill in the blanks.**

M1: All right class, let's get started. I'd like to begin today's class _____. With your left hand I want you to pat yourself on the head. With your right hand I want you to rub your belly with a circular motion. Can you do it?

M2: Hey, this is really difficult! I can't do it!

W: I've got it! It just takes a lot of attention. Check this out!

M1: Okay, everyone can stop now. I asked you to do this because I wanted you to notice _____ for your brain and nervous system to coordinate two different actions _____. This is called splitting your attention. Attention is the cognitive process of selectively concentrating on one thing _____. One example is listening carefully to what someone is saying _____ other conversations in the room. This is called the cocktail party effect. Attention can also be split, such as when a person drives a car and talks on a cell phone. Sometimes our attention shifts to matters _____ the external environment. This is referred to as mind wandering or "spontaneous thought."

W: But I was able to pat my head and _____ at the same time. What does that mean about me?

M1: Well, that means that you _____ splitting your attention. That reminds me of the most famous definition of attention _____, William James. He said, "Everyone knows what attention is. It is the taking possession by the mind in clear and vivid form, of one out of what seem to be several simultaneously possible objects or trains of thought. It implies _____ in order to deal effectively with others."

W: Hmm, that sounds interesting. But how is the action of rubbing my belly and patting my head _____ focusing my mind?

M1: Good question. It is linked because your cerebral cortex controls your fine motor skills, which is what those motions require.

4. **Complete the following summary.**

Coordinating the brain and nervous system to do two different actions _____ is called splitting attention. Attention is the _____ of selectively concentrating on one thing while ignoring other things. William James was one of the first _____. He defined attention as "the taking possession by the mind, in clear and vivid form, of one out of what seem to be several _____ possible objects or _____." The attention of one's mind is linked to the cerebral cortex, which controls _____.

cognitive process	simultaneous	trains of thought
at the same time	fine motor skills	major psychologists

C   Listen to part of a lecture, and answer the questions. 4-04

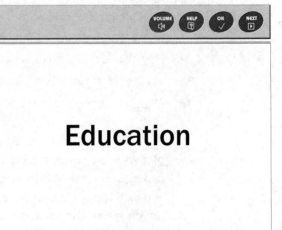

Education

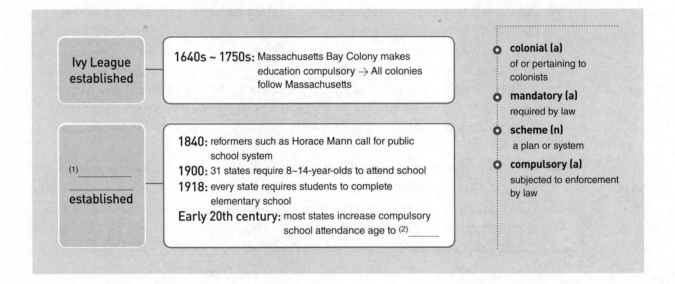

Ivy League established	**1640s ~ 1750s:** Massachusetts Bay Colony makes education compulsory → All colonies follow Massachusetts
(1) _____ established	**1840:** reformers such as Horace Mann call for public school system **1900:** 31 states require 8~14-year-olds to attend school **1918:** every state requires students to complete elementary school **Early 20th century:** most states increase compulsory school attendance age to (2) _____

- **colonial (a)** of or pertaining to colonists
- **mandatory (a)** required by law
- **scheme (n)** a plan or system
- **compulsory (a)** subjected to enforcement by law

---

1. How is the discussion organized?

ⒶⒷ in a list
Ⓑ chronologically
Ⓒ from general to specific
Ⓓ from complex to simple

2. What was the first colony to establish compulsory education?

Ⓐ the West Virginia Colony
Ⓑ the Georgia Coastal Colony
Ⓒ the Massachusetts Bay Colony
Ⓓ the New York River Colony

3. Listen again, and fill in the blanks.

Okay, everyone, today I'm going to tell you about the development of the American educational system. The first American schools opened _____. As the colonies began to develop, many began to institute mandatory education schemes. In 1642, the Massachusetts Bay Colony made "proper" education compulsory. _____ in other colonies in the 1640s and 1650s. Virtually all of the schools that opened as a result of this were private. Most of the universities which appeared between 1640 and 1750 form the contemporary Ivy League, including Harvard, Yale, Columbia, Brown, the University of Pennsylvania, and several others. After the revolution, _____ education. This made the United States have one of the highest literacy rates of the time. The school systems remained largely _____ until the 1840s. Education reformers such as Horace Mann of Massachusetts began calling for public education systems for all. He helped to create a statewide system of "common schools," _____ that everyone was entitled to the same content in education. These early efforts focused primarily on elementary education.

The common-school movement began to catch on. By 1900, 31 states required 8-to-14-year-olds to attend school. In 1918, every state required students to complete elementary school. Lessons _____ reading aloud from their texts, such as the *McGuffery Readers*, and emphasis was placed on rote memorization. Teachers often used physical punishments, such as hitting students on the knuckles _____ for incorrect answers. Secondary education progressed much more slowly, remaining the province _____ and domain of private tutors. In 1870, only 2% of 14-to-17-year-olds graduated from high school. The introduction of strict child labor laws and growing acceptance of higher education in general in the early 20th century _____ to skyrocket. Most states passed laws which increased the age for compulsory school attendance to 16.

4. Complete the following summary.

The first American schools opened during the Colonial Era. After the revolution, a _____ was placed on education. _____ remained private until the 1840s. Then _____ began calling for public education systems. They believed everyone was _____ to the same content in education. By 1900, 31 states required 8-to-14-year olds to attend school. _____ progressed more slowly. In the early 20th century, strict child labor laws and growing acceptance of higher education caused the number of high school graduates to _____.

school systems	skyrocket	educational reformers
heavier emphasis	secondary education	entitled

D Listen to part of a lecture, and answer the questions. 🔊 4-05

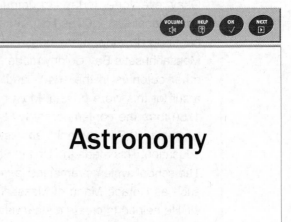

Astronomy

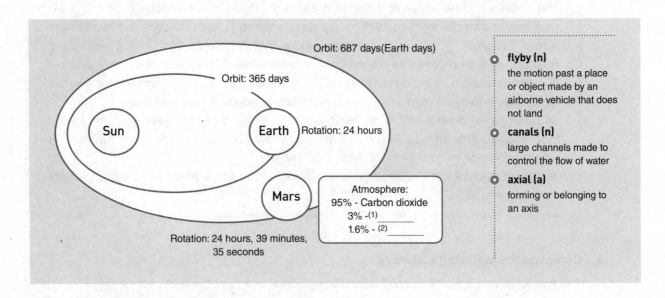

Orbit: 687 days(Earth days)

Orbit: 365 days

Sun

Earth   Rotation: 24 hours

Mars

Atmosphere:
95% - Carbon dioxide
3% - (1) _____
1.6% - (2) _____

Rotation: 24 hours, 39 minutes,
35 seconds

- **flyby (n)**
  the motion past a place or object made by an airborne vehicle that does not land
- **canals (n)**
  large channels made to control the flow of water
- **axial (a)**
  forming or belonging to an axis

1. **How does the professor discuss Mars?**

   Ⓐ as a list of statistics
   Ⓑ in an open question/answer format
   Ⓒ as an example of a hot planet
   Ⓓ in a series of anecdotes

2. **How long (in Earth days) is the Martian year?**

   Ⓐ 687 days
   Ⓑ 12 days
   Ⓒ 4,357 days
   Ⓓ 365 days

3. Listen again, and fill in the blanks.

W1: Okay everyone, today we are going to talk about _____ from the sun. It's named after Mars, the Roman god of war. Until the first flyby of Mars by Mariner 4 in 1965, it was thought that there were channels _____ on the planet's surface. People called these the Martian canals. Observations later showed that these channels do not exist. Still, of all the planets in our solar system after Earth, Mars is the most likely _____ and possibly life.

M: What about time on Mars? I heard it takes longer _____ than the Earth.

W1: Very good. That's right. Mars has a similar axial tilt to Earth, so it has similar seasonal periods. But it's further _____ and takes longer to orbit. So a Martian year is 687 Earth days long. Interestingly enough, the solar day on Mars is almost the same as Earth, being approximately 24 hours, 39 minutes, and 35 seconds.

W2: What about its atmosphere? Is it possible for humans _____ on Mars?

W1: Well, Mars has an atmosphere. But since it contains only traces of oxygen, you wouldn't want to breathe it. The Martian atmosphere is 95% carbon dioxide, 3% nitrogen and 1.6% argon. During the winter months, the atmosphere gets _____ _____ into thick slabs of dry ice.

M: But earlier, you said that it's possible for life to exist there. What kind of life could live in that kind of atmosphere?

W1: That's an interesting question. Some evidence suggests that the planet was _____ today. But whether living organisms ever existed there is still an open question. The Viking probe of the mid-1970s carried experiments designed _____ in Martian soil and had some positive results. But these were later disputed by many scientists.

4. Complete the following summary.

Mars is the 4th planet from the sun. Canals on the planet's surface that were _____ to exist do not. But Mars is still the _____ place in the solar system, besides Earth, to harbor liquid water and possibly life. Mars has _____ similar to Earth's. But its year is almost twice as long. The Martian atmosphere contains only ____ of oxygen. During the winter months, the atmosphere gets so cold that it _____ into dry ice. Whether living organisms exist on Mars is still an _____.

traces	most likely	open question
seasonal periods	once believed	condenses

Integrated Listening & Speaking

A Listen to the summary of the previous conversation and say the answers out loud by using the cue sentence words that are indicated in each answer. ⊙ 4-06

Doug	BENNY
wants to go to the recreation room	the recreation room has been gutted
dislikes the Student Employment Center	knows about the change to the Student Employment Center
is unhappy the recreation room has been gutted – wants to protest	thinks the protest would not be effective
doesn't think the president of the university would read the letters	suggests they write angry letters
is cynical about students who protested	talks about students who protested successfully last year

1. **What does Doug suggest to Benny?**

    (1) Doug suggests _____.   (2) Doug makes the suggestion _____.

2. **What does Benny tell Doug?**

    (1) Benny tells Doug some bad news about _____. (2) Benny tells Doug some bad news that _____.

3. **What does Benny suggest they do?**

    (1) Benny makes the suggestion tha _____. (2) Benny suggests that _____.

B Listen to the summary of the previous conversation and say the answers out loud by using the cue sentence words that are indicated in each answer. ⊙ 4-07

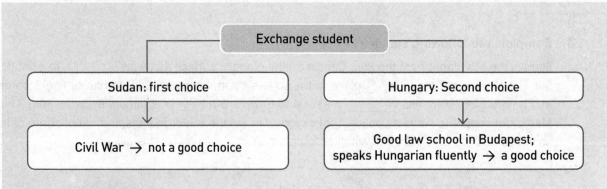

1. **Why is Mark interested in studying abroad?**

    (1) His major requires _____.   (2) It is required _____.

2. **What is Mr. Jones' job?**

    (1) Mr. Jones is in charge of _____.   (2) Mr. Jones runs _____.

3. **Why does Mark want to study in Budapest?**

    (1) His parents taught _____.   (2) He was taught _____.

C Listen to the previous lecture and say the answers out loud by using the cue sentence words that are indicated in each answer. ⊙ 4-08

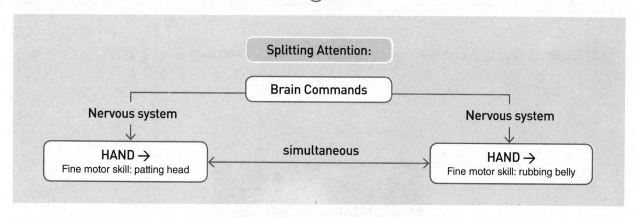

1. **How does the professor ask his students to split their attention?**

   (1) He asks them to _____.   (2) He tells them about _____.

2. **How does the professor explain attention?**

   (1) He says it's a _____.   (2) He explains that it is the _____.

3. **How is attention linked to physical actions?**

   (1) It's linked by the _____.   (2) It's linked to the _____.

D Listen to the previous lecture and say the answers out loud by using the cue sentence words that are indicated in each answer. ⊙ 4-09

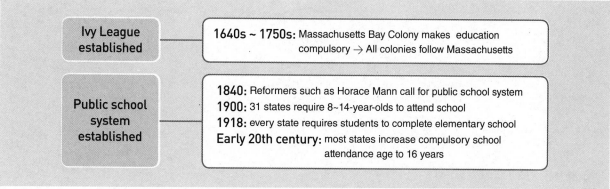

1. **How does the professor begin the lecture?**

   (1) He begins by _____.   (2) He begins with an _____.

2. **When did the U.S. put a heavier emphasis on education?**

   (1) A heavier emphasis was put _____.   (2) The U.S. put a heavier emphasis _____.

3. **What were many of the teaching methods like?**

   (1) Many of the teaching methods were _____.   (2) Many teaching methods were _____.

A Listen to part of a conversation between a student and an assistant. 4-10

1. **Why does the student go to the computer lab?**

   Ⓐ He wants to play games.
   Ⓑ He wants to visit his friend who works there.
   Ⓒ He needs to check his email quickly.
   Ⓓ He doesn't want to go to class.

2. **According to the computer lab assistant, what is required for the student to use a computer?**

   Ⓐ He has to pay money.
   Ⓑ He has to promise not to play games.
   Ⓒ He must get permission from the university president.
   Ⓓ He needs to fill out a student usage form.

3. **What is the computer lab assistant busy doing when the student first approaches him?**

   Ⓐ He is helping someone else.
   Ⓑ He is playing a computer game.
   Ⓒ He is fixing a computer.
   Ⓓ He is talking on the telephone.

4. **What are three rules of this computer lab? Click on three choices.**

   Ⓐ Students must fill out a usage card for them to keep on file.
   Ⓑ Students must not play games.
   Ⓒ Students can only use computers for 100 hours per month.
   Ⓓ Students must show their student ID card.

5. **Why does the student become frustrated and give up?**

   Ⓐ Because he doesn't have his student ID card with him.
   Ⓑ Because the assistant is too busy playing games.
   Ⓒ Because there are too many rules to follow.
   Ⓓ Because he doesn't want to go to class.

B Listen to part of a lecture in a mechanics class. 4-11

1. **How does the professor organize the information about bicycles that he presents to the class?**

   Ⓐ as a list of statistics
   Ⓑ from simple to complex information
   Ⓒ chronologically
   Ⓓ as a continuing story

2. **What are the two main points of the lecture?**

   Ⓐ Bicycles are fun to use.
   Ⓑ Bicycles are an important invention in human history.
   Ⓒ Bicycles have changed greatly since their invention.
   Ⓓ Bicycles aren't used much anymore.

3. **According to the lecture, what were the earliest versions of bicycles called?**

   Ⓐ millipedes
   Ⓑ velocipedes
   Ⓒ unicycles
   Ⓓ mountain bikes

4. **Listen again to part of the lecture. Then answer the question.**

   What does the student seem to mean when he says this? 🎧

   Ⓐ He seems to feel that bikes are strange.
   Ⓑ He seems to feel that bikes are important and influential.
   Ⓒ He seems to feel like studying bikes is a waste of time.
   Ⓓ He feels hungry and tired.

5. **What is this lecture mainly about?**

   Ⓐ the history of bicycles
   Ⓑ the history of vehicles with wheels
   Ⓒ the mechanics of bicycles
   Ⓓ the history of the human race

6. **Listen again to part of the lecture. Then answer the question.**

   What does the professor seem to imply about bicycles when he says this? 🎧

   Ⓐ This early form of bicycle was superior to bicycles of the current time.
   Ⓑ This early form of bicycle was less advanced than bicycles from the current time.
   Ⓒ This early form of bicycle would be fun to ride.
   Ⓓ He wants to buy this early form of bicycle.

Vocabulary Review

A Listen and choose the correct word that matches each definition. 🔘 **4-12**

1. (A) decimal   (B) declare   (C) declaim   (D) dare
2. (A) dude   (B) dud   (C) duke   (D) due
3. (A) misheard   (B) misery   (C) mistake   (D) misspell
4. (A) obituary   (B) object   (C) orbit   (D) omit
5. (A) symbiosis   (B) symbol   (C) symbolic   (D) simple
6. (A) real   (B) really   (C) realty   (D) realm
7. (A) disciples   (B) disks   (C) dislikes   (D) disciplines
8. (A) ignoring   (B) ignorant   (C) ignominy   (D) ingest
9. (A) privy   (B) private   (C) primate   (D) pirate
10. (A) accept   (B) accelerated (C) accented   (D) accentuated
11. (A) shield   (B) shift   (C) shilling   (D) shelter
12. (A) confess   (B) concrete   (C) contract   (D) contraband
13. (A) generosity (B) genesis   (C) genocide   (D) genetics
14. (A) wondering   (B) wasting   (C) waning   (D) wandering
15. (A) mangle   (B) mandatory   (C) manipulative (D) massively

B Complete the sentences by filling in the blanks with the expressions in the box.

an important step	checked out	new branch
spare a moment	I'll take	calling for

1. I'm so busy that I won't be able to _____ all day.
2. It's too bad that all of the copies of that new movie are _____.
3. _____ a cheeseburger, fries, a large coke, a salad, two cookies, a milkshake, three ice cream cones, and a cup of coffee.
4. Let's go to my bank's _____. It's not busy at lunchtime.
5. It was _____ in the development of medical science.
6. The parents are _____ the principal to be fired.

174

Unit 7

Connecting Content

7 Connecting Content

Overview

▪ Introduction

Connecting content questions require you to identify the relationships among ideas in a lecture or conversation. These relationships may be explicitly stated, or you may have to infer them from the words you hear. For example, you may be asked to classify items in categories, identify a sequence of events or steps in a process, or specify relationships among ideas in a dimension different from the way it was presented in the listening passage. In other connecting content questions, you may be required to make inferences about things mentioned in the listening passage and predict an outcome, draw a logical conclusion, or extrapolate some additional information.

▪ Question Types

1. What is the likely outcome of doing procedure X before procedure Y?

2. What can be inferred about X?

3. What does the professor imply about X?

▪ Useful Tips

• Pay attention to the way you format your notes.

• Focus on the category words, their characteristics, and examples.

Sample iBT Question

Order the steps in the process of the creation of glaciers.

Step	Order
Snow thaws and refreezes.	
Pressure forms glaciers.	
Granules accumulate over many years.	
Snow turns into granules.	
Snowfall covers mountainous regions.	

Script

M1: So yesterday, we started talking about how geological formations take a long time to be created. One of these formations is called the glacier. Does anyone know what a glacier is?

W: It's a lot of ice!

M1: Well, kind of. It's certainly a lot of ice, but it's a little more than just that. A glacier is like a river of ice that moves slowly. The way a glacier moves depends on the slope of the land. A glacier will move with gravity. Ok, so we have to talk about how these glaciers are formed. See what happens is snowfall covers mountainous regions. And this snow never completely melts. But, it might thaw a little bit and then refreeze a little bit. So you have this thawing and refreezing which changes the snow to granules. Then over many years, more and more snow accumulates. Can anyone guess what happens to the snow that's at the bottom of this pile?

M2: Wouldn't it get really firm? From all the pressure?

M1: Exactly! So then, over thousands of years, from lots and lots of pressure, these huge sheets of slow-moving ice form. That's how a glacier is made. The cool thing about these glaciers is that they leave imprints in the ground, kind of like fossils. So we can tell what the world was like when it was covered by glaciers back during the Ice Age.

 The right order to the steps in the process of the creation of glaciers is first, snowfall covers mountainous regions. Second, snow thaws and refreezes. Third, snow turns into granules. Fourth, granules accumulate over many years. Lastly, pressure forms glaciers.

● Basic Drill

A Listen to part of a conversation, and answer the question.

1. **What can we infer about the student's essay?** (● 4-14)
    - (A) The student's essay is in general terms.
    - (B) The student's essay is not very general.
    - (C) The student's essay supported the evidence well.
    - (D) The evidence didn't fit well in the student's essay.

    Listen again, and circle the words or phrases you hear.

describe	essay assignment	not explained	sort of
easy reassignment	can't explain	because of effects	introduction section
kind of	cause and effect	reintroduction	prescribe

2. **What is implied about the student's feelings in this conversation?** (● 4-15)
    - (A) The student is hungry and wants to eat.
    - (B) The student is trying to make a new friend.
    - (C) The student is tired of using meal tickets everyday.
    - (D) The student is angry the university is overcharging on meal plans.

    Listen again, and circle the words or phrases you hear.

misplaced	replaced	just a minute	back in cash
food voucher	back has rash	meal ticket	redundant number
just a second	student number	help you out	help them in

3. **What does the professor imply about overseas graduate programs?** (● 4-16)
    - (A) Students can easily overcome culture shock.
    - (B) Students shouldn't consider wasting their money.
    - (C) Overseas graduate students work much harder in their studies.
    - (D) Overseas programs are no different than domestic programs.

    Listen again, and circle the words or phrases you hear.

congratulate	practice experiment	more choices	overseas
a word with you	graduate students	awarded you	practical experience
broaden	less chances	overland	broken

B   Listen to part of a lecture, and answer the question.

1.   **What does the professor imply about radiocarbon dating?** (○ 4-17)

   A Radiocarbon dating is very accurate.
   B Radiocarbon dating is not very accurate.
   C Radiocarbon dating is a dirty job.
   D Radiocarbon dating should be ignored as a hoax.

   Listen again, and circle the words or phrases you hear.

only basic tools	carboniferous	contained samples	radiocarbon dating
by academics	rocky overhangs	more numerals	buy academies
increasing numbers	paper hangings	contaminated samples	some fools

2.   **What can be inferred about the relationship between apes and humans?** (○ 4-18)

   A Humans and apes are exactly the same.
   B Humans and apes should be put in separate categories.
   C The term "apes" should be changed in the dictionary.
   D Humans and apes are closely related.

   Listen again, and circle the words or phrases you hear.

still don't think	no other grapes	the other apes	not considerate
to be included	more times	still can't drink	quite apparent
quite different	not considered	increasing frequency	to be excluded

3.   **What is a possible outcome of the dolphin's ability of using echolocation?** (○ 4-19)

   A Dolphins can easily locate food.
   B Dolphins have many different eating habits.
   C Dolphins can become incredible swimmers.
   D Dolphins will become even more intelligent.

   Listen again, and circle the words or phrases you hear.

most intelligent	living in groups	to locate	variety of clicks
living in pods	relocated	vocalizations	least diligent
variety of picks	emitting calls	hitting a wall	speaking

Practice with Conversations

A Listen to part of a conversation, and answer the questions. 🔊 4-20

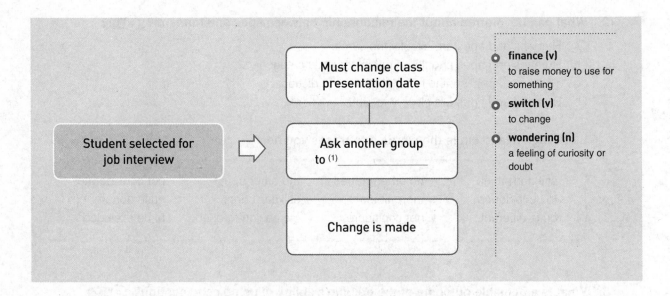

Student selected for job interview ⇨

Must change class presentation date

Ask another group to (1)_____

Change is made

finance (v)
to raise money to use for something

switch (v)
to change

wondering (n)
a feeling of curiosity or doubt

1. **What does the student imply if the presentation date is not changed?**
   - Ⓐ His group members will be happy to see him fail the course.
   - Ⓑ His group members will get angry if the date is not changed.
   - Ⓒ The student is not sure if his group's presentation will be good.
   - Ⓓ The student will attend the interview and not make the presentation.

2. **What can be inferred about the student's group reaction to the change of date?**
   - Ⓐ The group will accept the change of date.
   - Ⓑ The group will not accept the change of date.
   - Ⓒ The group will want to be graded easier for the inconvenience.
   - Ⓓ The group will be angry at the professor for changing the date.

3. Listen again, and fill in the blanks.

> **W:** Ah, yes, can I help you?
>
> **M:** Well, yes you can. I _____.
>
> **W:** What is it?
>
> **M:** Well, I just got a phone call a few minutes ago _____ for a job interview.
>
> **W:** Well, that's great news. When is the interview?
>
> **M:** Ah, that's the problem. The interview is tomorrow afternoon at three o'clock.
>
> **W:** Hey, wait a minute. You _____ at that time tomorrow.
>
> **M:** That's right. I _____ to have my group's presentation time changed to the following day. I don't want to be absent, but I have to go to the interview.
>
> **W:** Hmm, that could be a problem. Well, let's take a look at the presentation schedule. Maybe I can help.
>
> **M:** Well, this is very important to me because I really need _____.
>
> **W:** I understand. Now, let's see. Group A, hmm, they are scheduled to make their presentation two days from now. Here's what I can do. I'll call Group A's leader _____ presentation dates.
>
> **M:** Oh, that would be great!
>
> **W:** Well, this is on condition that Group A can make the change.
>
> **M:** I understand.
>
> **W:** Yes, hello. I need to ask a very big favor from your group. Would it be possible to change your presentation time to tomorrow afternoon at three o'clock? _____ _____! See you tomorrow at three o'clock then. Well, Group A can go tomorrow, so your group goes the following day.
>
> **M:** Oh, thank you so much.
>
> **W:** Just make sure you contact your group members and let them know about the change. That will be your job.
>
> **M:** No problem. I'll get on it right now. Thanks again.

4. Complete the following summary.

A student has suddenly been called for _____. The problem is he has a group class presentation at the same time as the interview. The student asks his professor if he can change the presentation time so that he can _____. The professor is willing to change the date _____ she can find another group who is willing to _____. The professor calls another group she thinks is willing to change dates. After _____, the other group is willing to change dates, and _____.

the student is thankful	change their presentation date	a job interview
communicating the problem	attend the job interview	on the condition that

181

B Listen to part of a conversation, and answer the questions. 4-21

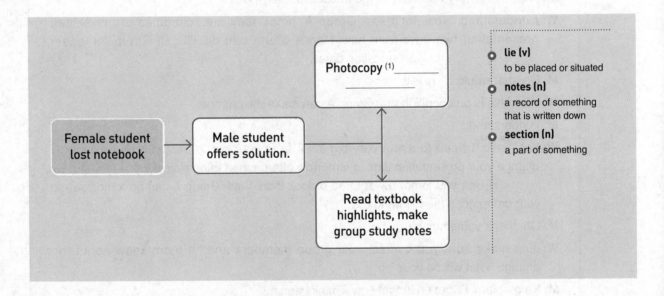

Female student lost notebook → Male student offers solution. → Photocopy (1)_____ _____

Read textbook highlights, make group study notes

- **lie (v)**
  to be placed or situated
- **notes (n)**
  a record of something that is written down
- **section (n)**
  a part of something

1. **What does the male student imply about the note taking habits of students?**

   (A) Many students make very good photocopies of their notes.
   (B) Many students highlight their textbooks on a regular basis.
   (C) Some students don't use notebooks and do very well on exams.
   (D) Many students don't highlight the important parts of their textbooks.

2. **What is the likely outcome for the female student if she follows the male student's suggestion?**

   (A) She will hope for the best when taking the test.
   (B) She will buy a new notebook as soon as possible and pass.
   (C) She will attend as many study groups as possible before the test.
   (D) She will photocopy the male student's notebook, make study notes, and pass the exam.

3. **Listen again and fill in the blanks.**

> W: All right. Are you ready to do this?
>
> M: Yeah, let's study for that history test right now because I _____ in about two hours.
>
> W: Great. Let me get my notebook out, and we'll be ready to go. Let's see, um, chemistry, biology, um, oh no. Where is my history notebook?
>
> M: Don't ask me. I have no idea.
>
> W: You've got to be kidding. I had it at _____. I thought I brought it home. Which means it _____ right now.
>
> M: Hmm, maybe it's at home then.
>
> W: No way. I don't _____ at home. My roommates tend to pick up things that are not theirs. Ah gee, I'm sure that book is lost. What am I going to do now?
>
> M: Well, I have an idea. Why don't you photocopy my notes? Then we can study and _____ on the photocopies.
>
> W: Really? I can't thank you enough. You are a lifesaver. I just can't believe I lost my book.
>
> M: No problem. There's a photocopier at the main entrance.
>
> W: Great! Say, before I do that, I have a question about how you go about studying for an exam like this one.
>
> M: Hmm, well, I got to tell you that I really look at the textbook very closely. You didn't lose your textbook, did you?
>
> W: No, ah, I've got it in my briefcase right here.
>
> M: Well, did you _____ during your readings?
>
> W: Sure, who doesn't?
>
> M: You'd be surprised. Anyways, read the highlighted sections carefully, and along _____ now, we should _____ to do well on the exam.
>
> W: You're a lifesaver.

4. **Complete the following summary.**

Two students are going to _____. One of the students has lost her notebook. She is worried that _____ study for the test. The male _____. First, the female student should _____. Then they should study together, _____ as they go along. Finally, the male _____ that she also study the highlighted sections in her textbook. The female student is grateful for all of his suggestions.

study for a test	she will not be able to
student offers a solution	student suggests
photocopy his notebook	making notations

Listen to part of a conversation, and answer the questions. ⊙ **4-22**

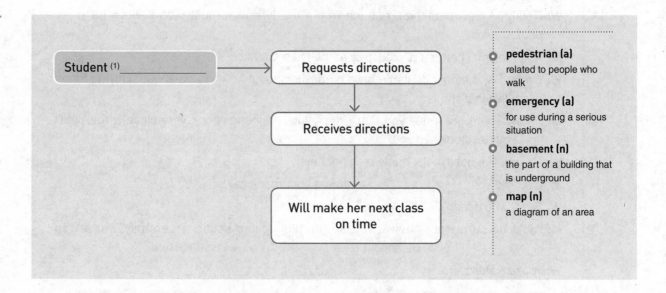

Student (1)_____ → Requests directions

Receives directions

Will make her next class on time

- **pedestrian (a)**
  related to people who walk
- **emergency (a)**
  for use during a serious situation
- **basement (n)**
  the part of a building that is underground
- **map (n)**
  a diagram of an area

1. **What does the student imply about her first week at school?**

   Ⓐ Everyone has been very helpful.
   Ⓑ This is the first time she has been lost.
   Ⓒ Everything has been going well so far.
   Ⓓ This isn't the first time she has been lost.

2. **What should be the outcome if she follows the directions correctly?**

   Ⓐ She will find the classroom in the emergency room.
   Ⓑ She will find the classroom in the chemistry building.
   Ⓒ She will find the classroom in the micro-biology building.
   Ⓓ She will find the classroom located in the basement of the hospital.

3. **Listen again, and fill in the blanks.**

> **W:** Gee, I'm so lost. Oh, excuse me, I'm looking for the main micro-biology lab. Ah, you wouldn't happen to know where it is, would you?
>
> **M:** Hmm, let me see. Well first of all, _____. This is the, ah, chemistry building.
>
> **W:** Well that figures. This is my _____, and I haven't a clue where anything is. To top it off, I'm late for yet another class. So, where exactly should I be going?
>
> **M:** Well, hmm, let's see, I'm _____ to get you from here to the university hospital.
>
> **W:** The university hospital?
>
> **M:** That's right. That's where the main micro-biology lab is located. Hey, don't ask me why. I just work here. Anyways, ah, let's get you over there. First, do you know where the university hospital is?
>
> **W:** I think so. Isn't it located on the corner of Alumni Drive and Ambassador Street?
>
> **M:** That's right. So, from here you go, umm, yes, _____, and turn left. Follow _____ until you get to Ambassador Street. Got that so far?
>
> **W:** Yeah, no problem. What do I do next?
>
> **M:** Well, when you get to Ambassador Street, turn right, and walk about 200 meters until you get to the hospital. But, ah, don't use the main entrance. You will see a driveway that _____, and this leads to the Emergency Room entrance. Following me so far?
>
> **W:** Got it. What's next?
>
> **M:** Once inside, _____. Just follow the room _____ at the basement entrance. That's it!
>
> **W:** How long a walk is it from here?
>
> **M:** Oh, maybe, um, six minutes at the most.
>
> **W:** I can't thank you enough. If I run, I should be able to make that class on time.

4. **Complete the following summary.**

A female student who is _____ is looking for a classroom but _____. She asks a university worker for directions. The worker explains she is in _____ and has about a six minute walk to the building _____. So the worker gives the student _____ to the correct building. The worker is careful to make sure the student understands the directions he is giving her. The student is very thankful for the directions as well as _____ is.

new to the university	walking directions
is hopelessly lost	she needs to get to
the wrong building	knowing where her next class

D Listen to part of a conversation, and answer the questions. 4-23

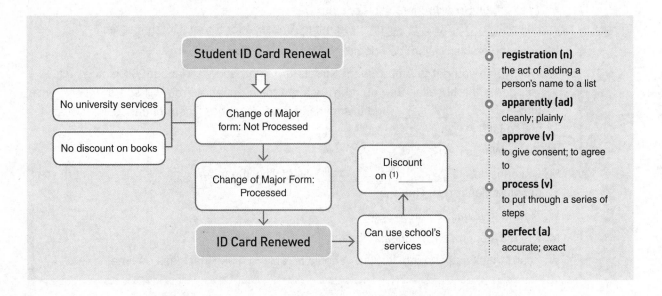

Student ID Card Renewal

No university services

No discount on books

Change of Major form: Not Processed

Change of Major Form: Processed

ID Card Renewed

Discount on (1) _____

Can use school's services

- **registration (n)**
  the act of adding a person's name to a list
- **apparently (ad)**
  cleanly; plainly
- **approve (v)**
  to give consent; to agree to
- **process (v)**
  to put through a series of steps
- **perfect (a)**
  accurate; exact

1. **What will be the student's reaction if she doesn't get an ID card?**

   (A) She might suddenly change schools.
   (B) She will wait quietly until they get around to giving her one.
   (C) She will be very upset at not being able to take advantage of school discounts.
   (D) She will ask the office worker very nicely where she can buy cheap textbooks.

2. **What is implied by the office worker?**

   (A) The student ID card was flawed.
   (B) The Change of Major Form was not processed.
   (C) The Change of Major Form was filled out incorrectly.
   (D) The student needed to present more identification to the office worker.

3. **Listen again, and fill in the blanks.**

> **W:** Hi, how are you today? I don't know if you remember me, but I was here a few days ago, um, trying to get _____.
>
> **M:** Ah, right, I remember you. I had to get some information from the Registrar's Office _____.
>
> **W:** That's right. Did you find out what the problem was?
>
> **M:** Ah, as a matter of fact, I did.
>
> **W:** Well, what was the problem? I've, um, been having a very hard time the past few days _____. Not only that, but I'm ineligible for discounts on books and supplies because I don't have a student card.
>
> **M:** Yes, and well, I'm _____ you. But, don't worry. I've got you set up with a valid student ID card.
>
> **W:** So tell me. What happened?
>
> **M:** Oh right. _____ process your *Change of Major Request Form*. Because of that error, you were not _____. You were actually listed as "withdrawn" from the school.
>
> **W:** What? Are you serious?
>
> **M:** Oh, don't worry, everything has been straightened out. The error has been corrected. Your *Change of Major Request Form* _____ along with your tuition payment which has also been processed. That being done, we then were able to issue you a new student ID card. So, here it is.
>
> **W:** _____! Am I ever glad that has been taken care of. Now I can _____, get my meal plan taken care of, and ah, oh yeah, get my parking permit.
>
> **M:** Oh, once again, I'm sorry for any problems this may have caused you.

4. **Complete the following summary.**

A student needs to get _____. Unfortunately, there was a delay, so she had to wait. This _____, including not being able to buy discounted _____ as well as not being able to use the university's student services. She is told her _____ was initially not processed, which led to her being denied a student ID card. Upon her next visit, she is told the problem _____. She is issued a new student ID card and is now entitled to _____ of having a valid ID card.

textbooks and supplies	her student ID card renewed
caused her many problems	has been corrected
Change of Major Form	all of the benefits

Practice with Lectures

A Listen to part of a lecture, and answer the questions. 🔊 4-24

Anthropology

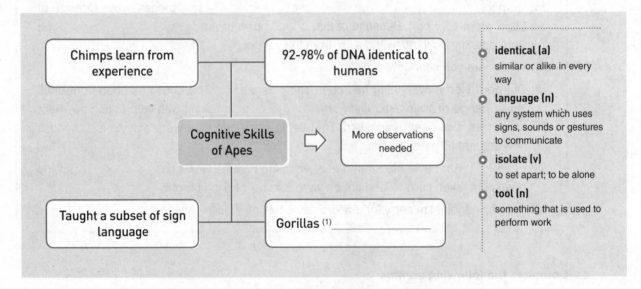

Chimps learn from experience	92-98% of DNA identical to humans

Cognitive Skills of Apes ⇨ More observations needed

Taught a subset of sign language	Gorillas (1)_____

identical (a)
similar or alike in every way

language (n)
any system which uses signs, sounds or gestures to communicate

isolate (v)
to set apart; to be alone

tool (n)
something that is used to perform work

1. **What can be implied about the students' reaction to the professor's examples?**

   Ⓐ Most of the students liked the Koko story.
   Ⓑ The students seemed very disinterested in the topic.
   Ⓒ The students were very impressed with the example given.
   Ⓓ The students felt the examples were not sufficient to make valid conclusions.

2. **In the lecture the professor talked about the similarities of the cognitive skills between apes and humans. Indicate whether each of the following is inferred by the professor about apes.**

   Click in the correct box for each phrase.

	Yes	No
Chimps learn from experience.		
Human babies learn from experience.		
Gorillas are experts at fishing.		
Chimps can make bridges in the jungle.		
Gorillas can gauge water depth crossing rivers.		

3. Listen again, and fill in the blanks.

M1: Well, let's start off this class by talking about the similarities of the cognitive skills between apes and humans. As you all know, humans and apes share many similarities, including the ability to use tools properly and imitate others.

W: Sir, can you explain how apes learn such skills?

M1: Well, ah, various studies have shown that _____ while baby humans just imitated what they were shown. This gave scientists some key information in understanding the cultural aspects of ape life and the evolutionary similarities between humans and apes.

M2: Professor, can you give us any specific examples showing how, um, humans and apes are so similar?

M1: Sure. Let's take the gorilla. With, um, with 92-98%_____, it is the next closest living relative to humans after the chimpanzee. A few individuals in captivity, such as, ah, Koko, have even been _____.

W: Well, professor, isn't _____? I mean, I haven't heard of any other situations where gorillas have shown any kind of cognitive process.

M1: Actually, there's much more evidence available to support this fact. For example, a team of scientists observed _____. A female gorilla, um, was recorded using a stick to gauge the depth of water while crossing a swamp. A second female was seen using a tree stump as a bridge and also as a support while fishing in the swamp. While this was the first such observation for a gorilla, um, for over forty years chimpanzees had been seen using tools in the wild, fishing for termites.

M2: Are you serious? You can count those examples on one hand. Surely, _____ _____ have similar cognitive skills.

M1: Well that's true, and I agree, there have not been enough observations to make any valid conclusions, and that's why several field studies are currently underway. But, let's not forget about the studies we have discussed here. We should also be realistic, um, with the numbers of studies available since it's not easy to study apes in the wild.

4. Complete the following summary.

Not long ago, humans were thought to be distinctly _____ from apes. Recent research has shown that this is not the case. For example, the _____ of apes and humans is very similar, as well as the fact that some studies of apes in the wild have shown _____ of apes being capable of learning. We now know that certain species of apes are able to use tools. What is not known is the extent of apes' _____ as well as the limit to what they can _____. Further studies are needed to answer these questions although this could be _____ to do.

learning capabilities	set apart	actually learn
conclusive evidence	DNA content	quite difficult

B Listen to part of a lecture, and answer the questions. 🔘 4-25

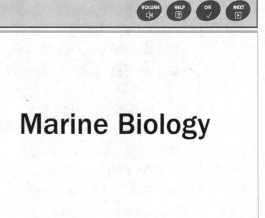

Marine Biology

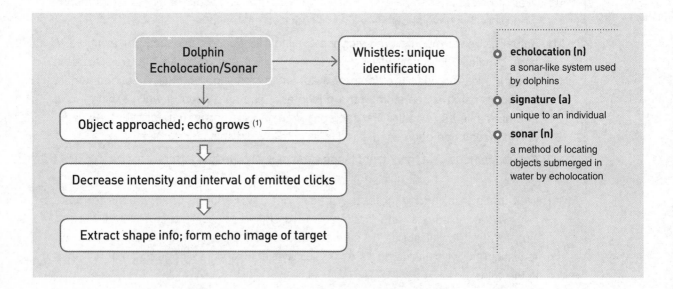

Dolphin Echolocation/Sonar → Whistles: unique identification

Object approached; echo grows (1)_____

Decrease intensity and interval of emitted clicks

Extract shape info; form echo image of target

echolocation (n)
a sonar-like system used by dolphins

signature (a)
unique to an individual

sonar (n)
a method of locating objects submerged in water by echolocation

1. **What does the professor imply about the dolphin's level of intelligence?**

   (A) It's difficult to determine just how intelligent dolphins are.
   (B) Since dolphins have no spoken language, they are not that smart.
   (C) Although they use echolocation, it doesn't make them that smart.
   (D) Dolphins and humans use different forms of communication, which makes us equal.

2. **What can we infer about why dolphins whistle?**

   (A) Dolphins use whistles as a language.
   (B) A dolphin's whistle is like a submarine's sonar.
   (C) Dolphins have a signature whistle for identifying each other.
   (D) Dolphins use body movements to communicate their whistles.

3. Listen again, and fill in the blanks.

All right, are we ready to begin? Good. Last class we left off with, um, an introduction concerning the _____ with one another. As you know, dolphins are often regarded as _____ species on Earth, but it is hard to say just how intelligent dolphins are. This is because of, um, this mammal's ability to communicate by using a variety of clicks, whistles, and other vocalizations. Now let's talk about the different ways dolphins communicate.

Okay, the first of these communication methods includes _____, where dolphins locate an object by producing sounds and then listen for the echo. It works like this: um, broadband _____ are emitted in a focused beam towards the front of a target. As the object of interest is approached, the echo grows, um, louder; and the dolphins adjust by decreasing the intensity of the inter-click interval and their emitted sounds. Anyway, we also know dolphins use different rates of click production in a, um, click train, which gives rise to the familiar barks, squeals and growls of the dolphin. A click train with a repetition rate over, um, let's see, yes, of 600 per second is called a burst pulse. Because of this process, it has been accepted by researchers that dolphins are able to form an "echoic image" of their targets. I guess you could say it's a lot like a _____.

Now let's see. Dolphins also communicate with _____. These vocal bursts are produced using six air sacs near their blow-hole, since dolphins lack vocal cords. What these vocal bursts represent is _____. Yet, each animal does have a characteristic, frequency-modulated, narrow-band _____, which is _____. In this mode of communication, um, dolphins do use about 30 distinguishable sounds. However, many researchers scoff at the idea that this is a form of dolphin language.

4. Complete the following summary.

Dolphins are considered one of the most intelligent _____ on Earth. This is because of their ability to communicate by using a _____, whistles, and other vocalizations. For example, the most _____ of communication they use is a form of echolocation, where they _____ of clicking sounds to _____. This is done much like a submarine's sonar system. They also use whistles, which are unique for each individual. The use of body movements and vocal bursts is still _____.

animal species	effective method	locate a target
variety of clicks	emit a series	not fully understood

C Listen to part of a lecture, and answer the questions. ⊙ 4-26

American Literature

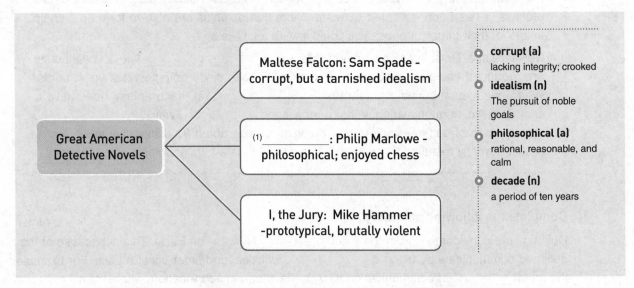

Maltese Falcon: Sam Spade -
corrupt, but a tarnished idealism

Great American
Detective Novels

(1) _____ : Philip Marlowe -
philosophical; enjoyed chess

I, the Jury: Mike Hammer
-prototypical, brutally violent

○ **corrupt (a)**
lacking integrity; crooked

○ **idealism (n)**
The pursuit of noble
goals

○ **philosophical (a)**
rational, reasonable, and
calm

○ **decade (n)**
a period of ten years

1. **What can be inferred about author Raymond Chandler?**

    Ⓐ Many readers didn't understand his complex characters.

    Ⓑ He was one of the youngest successful writers of his time.

    Ⓒ His most famous published works were written later in his life.

    Ⓓ He was a personal friend of many good writers during his successful years.

2. **In the lecture, the professor describes the greatest American detective novels. Indicate whether each of the following phrases is implied.**

Click in the correct answers in the box below.

	Yes	No
The Big Sleep was written by Philip Marlowe.		
Philip Marlowe was philosophical and liked to play chess.		
Mike Hammer was a prototypical detective.		
The main character in the *Maltese Falcon* was Sam Spade.		
The professor's favorite detective story is *The Big Sleep*.		

3. Listen again, and fill in the blanks.

Ah, now for today's lecture, we will explore some of the greatest American detective novels written by three of the best novelists of the twentieth century. My personal favorite is, well, *The Maltese Falcon*, written by the American author Samuel Dashiell Hammett. His most famous character, of course, was Sam Spade, a man who saw the, um, _____ _____ but still retained his, um, _____. Even though Spade was a tough guy, he was also a sentimentalist at heart, which makes him one of the most enduring detective characters ever created.

Well, next, um, we have American author Raymond Chandler, who based his main character, detective Philip Marlowe, initially on Hammett's Sam Spade. Marlowe first appeared in the novel *The Big Sleep*, published in, let's see, ah yes, 1939. Underneath the wisecracking tough guy public image, _____. While he was not afraid to risk physical harm, he, hmm, never became violent merely to settle scores. Chandler's treatment of the detective novel, um, _____.

His first full length book, *The Big Sleep*, was published when Chandler was, um, 51 years old while his last, *Playback*, when he was 70. Incidentally, all seven of his novels were _____ of his life. I can say that all of these novels _____ of Philip Marlowe's character, but each novel has unique qualities of narrative tone, depth, and focus that set it apart from the others.

Finally, and I just love reading this guy's work. Author Mickey Spillane who created the fictional detective Mike Hammer in the book, *I, the Jury*. Hammer is in many ways _____ _____ since he is _____, and fueled by a, um, genuine rage that never afflicts Chandler or Hammett's heroes. While other detective heroes kind of bend the law, Hammer holds it in total contempt, seeing it as nothing more than a means to an end. And, well, this is contrary to Chandler's and Hammett's characters.

4. Complete the following summary.

Some of the greatest American _____ written were created by three authors: Samuel Dashiell Hammett, Raymond Chandler, and Mickey Spillane. Each of these authors created at least one memorable detective character that has _____ for over fifty years. Characters like Sam Spade, Mike Hammer, and Philip Marlowe had many _____, yet each character has at least one _____ which _____ from all others. All three of these detective characters were characterized as tough guys, which probably makes them _____.

detective novels	major characteristic
endeared readers	sets them apart
similar attributes	so memorable

D Listen to part of a lecture, and answer the questions. 🔊 4-27

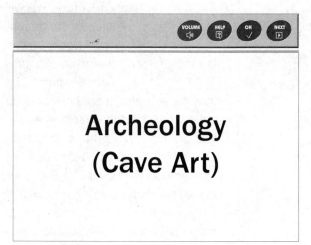

Archeology
(Cave Art)

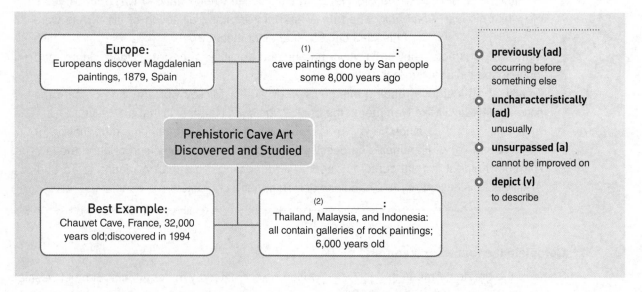

Europe:
Europeans discover Magdalenian
paintings, 1879, Spain

(1)_____:
cave paintings done by San people
some 8,000 years ago

**Prehistoric Cave Art
Discovered and Studied**

Best Example:
Chauvet Cave, France, 32,000
years old;discovered in 1994

(2)_____:
Thailand, Malaysia, and Indonesia:
all contain galleries of rock paintings;
6,000 years old

○ **previously (ad)**
occurring before
something else

○ **uncharacteristically
(ad)**
unusually

○ **unsurpassed (a)**
cannot be improved on

○ **depict (v)**
to describe

1. **What does the professor imply about cave art found outside of Europe?**

    Ⓐ Asian cave art tells us a lot about rock art galleries.
    Ⓑ African cave paintings show us how early humans looked.
    Ⓒ Those caves are not as important as the cave art found in the Chauvet Cave.
    Ⓓ Cave art found outside of Europe is more important because of its old age.

2. **In the lecture the professor describes cave paintings. Indicate whether each of the following aspects of early human culture can be inferred from cave art.**

Click in the correct answers in the box below.

	Yes	No
Humans look the same now as they did thousands of years ago.		
Cave art details many ancient dances of that time.		
Cave art details many animal species of that time.		
The most detailed cave art shows clothing styles of the time.		
Cave art shows the religious beliefs of humans at that time.		

3. **Listen again, and fill in the blanks.**

> **M1:** All right, here we go. We will begin this class with a discussion on cave paintings. _____, cave paintings were an important communication tool used by our ancestors for thousands of years. Cave paintings were relatively unknown until _____ of the Altamira Cave, in Spain, um, in 1879.
>
> **W:** Professor, could you tell us which cave has the oldest drawings?
>
> **M1:** The place with the oldest cave art is that of the Chauvet Cave in southern France. It has been _____ back to 32,000 years. The cave was named after Jean-Marie Chauvet, who discovered it on December 18, 1994.
>
> **M2:** Ah, sir, what's so special about the Chauvet Cave anyways?
>
> **M1:** Well, _____, and the quality and, hmm, quantity of paintings found in it, makes it, well, _____ that have been found with similar paintings. The walls of the Chauvet Cave are covered with predatory animals like lions, panthers, bears, owls, rhinos, and hyenas. Um, _____, there are no paintings of complete human figures. Researchers have found that the cave had been untouched for 20,000-30,000 years.
>
> **W:** Ah, Professor, are there any other caves that have been discovered with similar paintings in other parts of the world?
>
> **M1:** Oh, sure. For example, in South Africa, there are caves where the paintings are thought to have been done by the San people who settled in the area some, let's see, 8,000 years ago. The _____ and are thought _____.
>
> **M2:** Are there any other examples?
>
> **M1:** There are also rock paintings in caves in Malaysia and Indonesia. In Thailand, in the nineteenth century, there were some caves found along the Thai-Burmese border as well as other caves overlooking the Mekong River in Nakhon Sawan Province, which all contain galleries of rock paintings thought to be about 6,000 years old.

4. **Complete the following summary.**

Cave paintings were an important _____ used by our ancestors for thousands of years. Cave paintings were _____ until Europeans _____ in1879. The best example is the Chauvet Cave, which is _____ and has the _____ of cave art discovered so far. For example, the walls of the Chauvet Cave are _____ such as lions, panthers, bears, owls, rhinos, and hyenas. As is typical of most cave art, there are no paintings of complete human figures.

communication tool	best quality and quantity
first encountered them	unknown to modern man
uncharacteristically large	covered with predatory animals

Integrated Listening & Speaking

A Listen to the summary of the previous conversation and say the answers out loud by using the cue sentence words that are indicated in each answer. ⊙ 4-28

> Student selected for job interview ⟹
> - Must change class presentation date
> - Ask another group to change dates
> - Change is made

1. **What is the student's problem?**
   (1) The student's problem is that he has _____.   (2) Being suddenly called for a _____.

2. **What is the professor willing to do?**
   (1) The professor is willing _____.   (2) To change the date of the presentation, _____.

3. **What is the other group willing to do?**
   (1) The other group is willing _____.   (2) Because they are ready, _____.

B Listen to the summary of the previous conversation and say the answers out loud by using the cue sentence words that are indicated in each answer. ⊙ 4-29

> Female student lost notebook → Male student offers solution →
> - Photocopy male student's notebook
> - Read textbook highlights, make group study notes

1. **What are the two students going to do?**
   (1) The students _____.   (2) The students _____.

2. **What happened to the female student?**
   (1) The female student _____.   (2) The female student _____.

3. **What solution does the male student offer?**
   (1) The male student suggests _____.   (2) The male student tells _____.

C Listen to the previous lecture and say the answers out loud by using the cue sentence words that are indicated in each answer. ⊙ 4-30

Dolphin Echolocation/Sonar

→ Whistles: unique identification

Object approached; echo grows louder

Decrease intensity and interval of emitted clicks

Extract shape info; form echo image of target

1. **What is the dolphin's most effective method of communication?**
   (1) The most effective method of _____ .   (2) An effective method of _____ .

2. **What kind of image can dolphins form?**
   (1) Dolphins can _____ .   (2) Dolphins are able _____ .

3. **What factor accounts for the dolphin's high intelligence?**
   (1) The dolphin's intelligence can be _____ .   (2) In a display of high intelligence, _____ .

D Listen to the previous lecture and say the answers out loud by using the cue sentence words that are indicated in each answer. ⊙ 4-31

Great American Detective Novels

Maltese Falcon: Sam Spade - corrupt, but a tarnished idealism

The Big Sleep: Philip Marlow - philosophical; enjoyed chess

I, the Jury: Mike Hammer - prototypical, brutally violent

1. **What did each author create?**
   (1) Each author created _____ .   (2) At least one memorable character _____ .

2. **What was similar about each detective?**
   (1) Each detective's _____ .   (2) Similarly, each detective _____ .

3. **How many authors are mentioned in the passage?**
   (1) There are _____ .   (2) In the passage, _____ .

◉ Mini TOEFL iBT

A Listen to part of a conversation between a student and a professor. ◉ 4-32

1. **What can be implied from the student's initial request?**

   Ⓐ A student is seeking guidance for his thesis project.

   Ⓑ The student is seeking advice on how to become a TA.

   Ⓒ The professor is giving a student the school's new rules and regulations.

   Ⓓ The professor is advising the student on how to get into a tutoring program.

2. **What can be inferred about how the student feels about himself?**

   Ⓐ The student feels he is very capable.

   Ⓑ The student feels sorry for the professor.

   Ⓒ The student feels hungry and will talk later.

   Ⓓ The student feels the new rules can be a problem.

3. **What does the professor tell the student?**

   Ⓐ He tells the student all about a TA's duties.

   Ⓑ He tells the student to study hard for the TA exam.

   Ⓒ He tells the student that they don't need anymore TAs.

   Ⓓ He tells the student that TAs get low pay and no respect.

4. **According to the professor, what are some of the duties a teaching assistant performs? Choose 2 answers.**

   Ⓐ Grader

   Ⓑ Test writer

   Ⓒ Lecture writer

   Ⓓ Tutorial leader

5. **Listen again to part of the conversation. Then answer the question.** 🎧

   What does the professor imply about a teaching assistant position?

   Ⓐ The student should have more credentials.

   Ⓑ The department is not interested in hiring TAs.

   Ⓒ The department can always use bright grad students as TAs.

   Ⓓ The student should reapply when he starts the next semester.

B Listen to part of a lecture in a biology class. ⓞ 4-33

1. **What can be inferred as being the main point of this lecture?**

   (A) Polar bears' eating habits

   (B) Polar bears' running abilities

   (C) Polar bears' swimming abilities

   (D) Polar bears' fur and hibernating habits

2. **Why do polar bears hibernate?**

   (A) To digest food

   (B) To rest

   (C) To keep warm

   (D) To give birth

3. **How does the professor imply a polar bear keeps its fur from matting?**

   (A) Polar bears love to swim.

   (B) Polar bears hibernate to keep their fur from matting.

   (C) Polar bears have stiff, erect guard hairs, which keep their fur straight.

   (D) Polar bears try not to fight one another, which keeps their fur from matting.

4. **According to the lecture, where are some of the places on a polar bear's body that it can release excess heat? Click on 3 answers.**

   (A) Its toes and tail

   (B) Its muzzle and nose

   (C) Its ears and footpads

   (D) Its inner thighs and shoulders

5. **Listen again to part of the lecture. Then answer the question.**

   What does the professor imply when she says this?

   (A) The next point is cruel.

   (B) The next point is important.

   (C) The next point is a critical error.

   (D) The next point is not important.

6. **What does the professor imply about female polar bears giving birth?**

   (A) Stored body fat is important.

   (B) The cubs should often sleep.

   (C) That cubs love to live in caves.

   (D) The mother should watch the cubs carefully.

Vocabulary Review

4-34

A Listen and choose the correct word that matches each definition.

1. (A) really   (B) reel   (C) reality   (D) relate
2. (A) indent   (B) indecent   (C) identical   (D) idyllic
3. (A) clock   (B) clip   (C) chock   (D) click
4. (A) shop   (B) shape   (C) ship   (D) shave
5. (A) mountain   (B) maintain   (C) manage   (D) mainland
6. (A) recount   (B) discount   (C) encode   (D) encounter
7. (A) favor   (B) flavor   (C) flour   (D) flame
8. (A) improve   (B) disprove   (C) approve   (D) appropriate
9. (A) finance   (B) fiancé   (C) final   (D) finish
10. (A) wrote   (B) wrong   (C) wore   (D) rang
11. (A) presentation   (B) possession   (C) prescription   (D) preservation
12. (A) settlement   (B) session   (C) sesame   (D) severity
13. (A) region   (B) regeneration   (C) registration   (D) regiment
14. (A) belligerency   (B) belief   (C) belonging   (D) belie
15. (A) pedestrian   (B) pedestal   (C) pedigree   (D) peculiar

B Complete the sentences by filling in the blanks with the expressions in the box.

on one hand	wait a minute	it's a lot like
as a matter of fact	of course	been taken care of

1. You can count those examples _____.
2. I guess you could say _____ a submarine's sonar system.
3. His most famous character, _____, was Sam Spade.
4. Hey, _____! You have a class presentation tomorrow.
5. Ah, _____, I did.
6. Am I ever glad that has _____.

Unit 8

Making Inferences

8 Making Inferences

Overview

■ Introduction

Making inference questions requires you to reach a conclusion based on facts presented in the listening passage. In other words, you are to see beyond the lines in the passage and predict the outcome. The questions may be about different things from a simple process to a cause and effect to a comparison and contrast.

■ Question Types

1. What does the professor imply about X?

2. What will the student probably do next?

3. What can be inferred about X?

4. What does the professor imply when he says this: (replay)

■ Useful Tips

• While taking notes, try to add up the details from the passage to reach a conclusion.

• Make efforts to generalize about what you hear in the listening passages.

• Try to find out the meaning behind the directly stated words.

• Focus on the answers that use vocabulary not found in the listening passages.

Sample iBT Question

What can we infer about prior class sessions?

(A) Prior class sessions probably covered material needed to understand this session.

(B) Prior class sessions have nothing to do with the material currently being taught.

(C) Prior class sessions relayed information that was taught during prior semesters.

(D) Prior class sessions did not cover material that pertained to this class session.

Script .

W1: Ms. Andrews?

W2: Yes, Catherine?

W1: I have a couple of questions about class today.

W2: Ok, what can I help with?

W1: Well we went over the different Excel functions today, but some of the stuff didn't make sense to me. I think it's because this is only my second class. I think I missed something from an earlier class.

W2: Ah, right. We did cover some of the ground work for this lesson last week.

W1: That makes sense. I didn't understand how everyone already knew which formulas to enter.

W2: Of course. If you take a look at Chapter 2 in your book, I think it will help you a lot. Then, if you're still having trouble, we can tackle that later.

W1: Thanks Ms. Andrews!

The correct answer is (A). The professor mentioned about the prior lesson in the conversation. The prior lesson was about the ground work for today's lesson. So the answer is the prior class sessions probably covered material needed to understand this session.

● Basic Drill

A Listen to part of a conversation, and answer the question.

1. **What can be inferred about the student's ability?** (○ 4-36)
   - (A) The student is exceptional.
   - (B) The student doesn't apply herself.
   - (C) The student is a poor writer.
   - (D) The student is improving.

   Listen again, and circle the words or phrases you hear.

by winter	insightful	my seminar	no doubt
four winning	fight into	best writers	sore biting
quite intelligent	professorship	for writing	scholarship

2. **What does this conversation imply about the student?** (○ 4-37)
   - (A) The student is happy.
   - (B) The student is ill.
   - (C) The student has a bad attitude.
   - (D) The student is not wealthy.

   Listen again, and circle the words or phrases you hear.

are uncertain	may I	could have stayed	apprehension
can defer	haven't paid	economically	be cancelled
aid check	in the shade	without her	extension

3. **What can be inferred about the professor's character?** (○ 4-38)
   - (A) The professor is complacent.
   - (B) The professor is adamant.
   - (C) The professor is strict.
   - (D) The professor is supportive.

   Listen again, and circle the words or phrases you hear.

incident	sent around	talkative	past year
activation code	intimidated	experimental	confidence
so profound	more active	retracted it	last semester

B Listen to part of a lecture, and answer the question.

1. **What can be inferred about the human brain?** ⊙ 4-39
   Ⓐ It is an involuntary organ.
   Ⓑ It is a secondary organ.
   Ⓒ It is a primary organ.
   Ⓓ It is a vulnerable organ.

   Listen again, and circle the words or phrases you hear.

peak time	unique result	control center	sensory perception
blood loss	great deal	in the head	primary
massive number	organ of thought	beside the nerve	extremely complex

2. **What can be inferred from Chomsky's theory?** ⊙ 4-40
   Ⓐ Children are born without language basics.
   Ⓑ Children develop language only with formal instruction.
   Ⓒ Children have difficulty learning their native language.
   Ⓓ Children are born with the fundamental principles of language.

   Listen again, and circle the words or phrases you hear.

parameters	explicit subjects	requires formal	paragraphs
inquires from	faintly utter	liability	majority of
deduce	language acquisition	reduce	fully utilize

3. **What is implied about the environmental movement's membership?** ⊙ 5-01
   Ⓐ The environmental movement is well organized.
   Ⓑ The environmental movement is falling apart.
   Ⓒ The environmental movement is very diverse.
   Ⓓ The environmental movement is losing steam.

   Listen again, and circle the words or phrases you hear.

human rights	revitalize	is recognized	political movement
long lives	is represented	strong beliefs	grassy lands
public policy	naturalistic	recognition	bright lights

Practice with Conversations

A Listen to part of a conversation, and answer the questions. 🔘 5-02

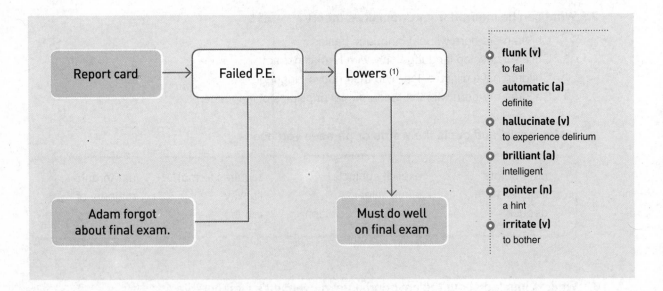

Report card → Failed P.E. → Lowers (1)_____

Adam forgot about final exam.

Must do well on final exam

- **flunk (v)**
  to fail
- **automatic (a)**
  definite
- **hallucinate (v)**
  to experience delirium
- **brilliant (a)**
  intelligent
- **pointer (n)**
  a hint
- **irritate (v)**
  to bother

1. **What does the conversation imply about the man?**
   - (A) He is not all that reliable.
   - (B) He cares greatly about his G.P.A.
   - (C) His favorite class is P.E.
   - (D) He is an outstanding student.

2. **What is implied from the conversation about the P.E. exam?**
   - (A) The exam doesn't have an effect on their final grade.
   - (B) The exam is crucial to their G.P.A.
   - (C) The exam's weight is minor toward their overall grade.
   - (D) The exam could not have been taken with their busy schedule.

3. **Listen again, and fill in the blanks.**

> **W:** Hey, Adam. Did you get your _____ in the mail yesterday?
>
> **M:** Sure did, and get this. I _____! Can you believe that? Mr. Andrews gave me an F! I can't understand why he would do this to me. I mean it is only P.E. after all! It should be an _____!
>
> **W:** You too, huh! I thought my eyes were playing tricks on me when I first looked over my report card. English, A. Biology, A minus. Statistics, A. French, B plus. P.E., F. Woah! Hang on a second! Go back. P.E., F! How did that get in there? Am I _____?
>
> **M:** Wow! Wait a minute, Gloria. You got an A minus in Biology? How'd you pull that one off?
>
> **W:** My friend is _____, so she helped me out a little bit.
>
> **M:** A little bit! What'd she do? Disguise herself as you and take the tests for you!
>
> **W:** No, she just gave me _____ to study better. Anyways, what are we going to do about this P.E. grade? It's killing my G.P.A.! Speaking of killing, my parents are going to kill me once they find out I failed the easiest course out there!
>
> **M:** Yeah, mine too! Let's think about it. We both dressed out every day, right?
>
> **W:** Right. And we both participated in the activities each day, right?
>
> **M:** Yeah, and I can't think of anything we might have _____ Mr. Andrews, can you?
>
> **W:** No, he always seemed to like us, didn't he? I haven't _____! There must be some mistake here. Some _____. I guess the best thing to do is just go over to the gym and ask him about it. What do you think?
>
> **M:** Yeah, and while we are over there we can ask him when we can _____ exam that we missed . . .
>
> **W:** Final exam? Final exam! What final! You told me there was no final! What are you talking about!
>
> **M:** Yeah, when you were _____, Mr. Andrews told us there had been a change of plans and that we would have a final exam which would count for 50% of our grade. But, it completely _____ until just now.
>
> **W:** Adam!

4. **Complete the following summary.**

Gloria and Adam are talking _____ grades. They both flunked the class, and they don't understand why. They _____ every class and believe the professor liked them a lot. When they decide to go and talk to the professor, the _____. Gloria realizes that Adam forgot to tell her about the final test they were _____ take. Because Adam forgot, they missed the test and failed the class. Once _____, Gloria becomes really _____ Adam for his mistake.

truth comes out	aggravated with	about their P.E.
supposed to	she finds this out	participated in

B   Listen to part of a conversation, and answer the questions.  5-03

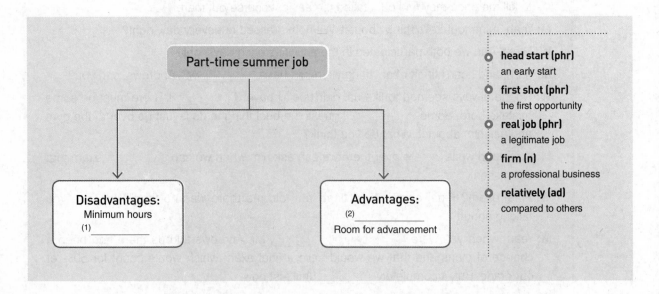

Part-time summer job

Disadvantages:
Minimum hours
(1)_____

Advantages:
(2)_____
Room for advancement

- **head start (phr)**
  an early start
- **first shot (phr)**
  the first opportunity
- **real job (phr)**
  a legitimate job
- **firm (n)**
  a professional business
- **relatively (ad)**
  compared to others

1. **What can be inferred about the student's understanding of the opportunity?**

   Ⓐ They are just looking to make easy money.

   Ⓑ They don't believe the job is challenging enough.

   Ⓒ The job could benefit them in ways other than monetarily.

   Ⓓ They would rather relax during their vacation time.

2. **What can be inferred from the professor giving these students the job opportunity?**

   Ⓐ The professor is partial to these two students.

   Ⓑ The professor is trying to be fair.

   Ⓒ The professor does not care who accepts the jobs.

   Ⓓ The professor feels any student would be a successful employee.

3. Listen again, and fill in the blanks.

W1: Okay, I've got an important job announcement to tell you about. Jeppsen Publishing is _____ two students as editorial assistants during the summer vacation. You both are my _____, so I thought I'd give you _____. This is an excellent opportunity for you to get a _____ on your future since you are both thinking about publishing as a career.

M: Uh, how much are they paying?

W1: Well, it is _____. But think about it guys. The money really isn't the issue here. What is important is the valuable experience you'll gain from working _____.

M: Yeah, I know. I expected the minimum seeing how we are just students and all, and we don't have really any professional experience. It does sound like a great job though. Jeppsen is like _____ in the country. Many people would work for them for free just to get their foot in the door.

W1: You are exactly right. This is an excellent way for you to make valuable contacts within the company _____. You never know, if they like you and, uh, you do well, who knows, they might offer you a full-time job that pays much more once you graduate from school!

W2: Oooh. It sounds really exciting! I've always wanted to work for them. Can you give us some _____ about the job? How many hours a week would we work, and what kind of duties would we have?

W1: I believe they want you to work a maximum of 25 hours a week. You'd basically be _____ your supervisor, typing up memos, and taking notes during meetings. They said you would also have a _____ the senior editors when they are editing manuscripts. Who knows? You might even get a chance to meet some famous authors!

W2: Well, this all just _____! I've already made my decision. I'm in!

M: Me too! Who knows! Maybe one of us will end up being the CEO one day!

4. Complete the following summary.

A professor is telling two students about a _____ opportunity they have been _____. The professor explains how much they will make and what the _____ will be. Most importantly, the professor _____ valuable the experience will be for the student's futures. The students are very excited about the chance and _____ what an excellent opportunity it is for them. Both students decide to accept the jobs with great _____.

summer job	chosen for	duties of the job
enthusiasm	realize	emphasizes how

C Listen to part of a conversation, and answer the questions. ⊙ 5-04

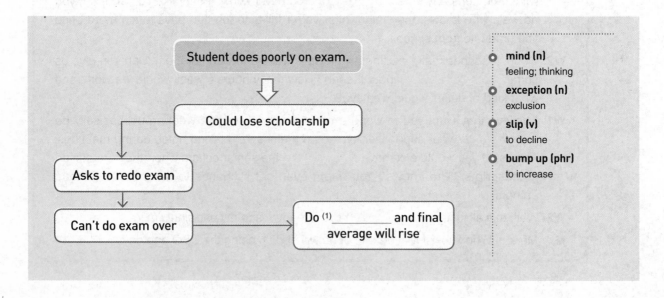

Student does poorly on exam.

⇩

Could lose scholarship

Asks to redo exam

Can't do exam over

Do (1)_____ and final average will rise

mind (n)
feeling; thinking

exception (n)
exclusion

slip (v)
to decline

bump up (phr)
to increase

1. **What can be inferred about the student's attitude?**

   Ⓐ The student displays a lot of arrogance.
   Ⓑ The student is willing to do what it takes to get good grades.
   Ⓒ The student is not very diligent.
   Ⓓ The student dislikes the professor.

2. **How could the professor be described?**

   Ⓐ Strict and without compassion
   Ⓑ Generous and easy
   Ⓒ Firm and fair
   Ⓓ Indifferent and aloof

3. Listen again, and fill in the blanks.

> **M1:** Excuse me, Mr. Adams? Do you have a minute?
>
> **M2:** Sure. What's _____?
>
> **M1:** It's about the test we had last week. I didn't do very well, and I was hoping I could _____.
>
> **M2:** A re-test, huh. You know, I don't usually allow students to take tests over unless they have a very, very good reason. Explain to me why I should _____ in your case.
>
> **M1:** Well, um, I'm afraid that _____ a C on it, I could lose my scholarship. My _____ states that I must maintain an A- average in all of my classes, and in your education class, _____.
>
> **M2:** Hmm, let's see. Uh, yes, it looks like you got a C+ on the test last week, which has brought your _____ down to a B right now. Why do you think your grade has been slipping in my class? Is the _____?
>
> **M1:** Honestly, sir, I haven't really had the time to study because of my part-time job. I've _____ as a security guard to earn some extra money, but it has really been disrupting my academics, so I quit yesterday.
>
> **M2:** Well, I _____. I know how hard it can be supporting yourself and going to school full-time, too. I'm not going to allow you to retake the test, but I am going to _____. Once you complete the essay, I'll _____ on the test to a B+. This way, uh, you'll be able to get an A- or possibly even an A in the class, depending on how you do on the final. How does that sound to you?
>
> **M1:** That sounds great! Thank you, sir, for being so understanding and giving me the opportunity to make up the extra points. I won't let you down!

4. Complete the following summary.

A student is _____ he took in the professor's class the previous week. The student is _____ with his performance and is afraid he will _____. He asks the professor if he can take it again. The professor asks the student why he believes he did so poorly. The student explains that he was too busy with a part-time job that he _____. Because of his honesty, the professor decides not to allow him to ____ the exam but to do some _____ instead.

discussing a test	not satisfied	lose his scholarship
recently quit	retake	extra credit work

D Listen to part of a conversation, and answer the questions. 🔊 5-05

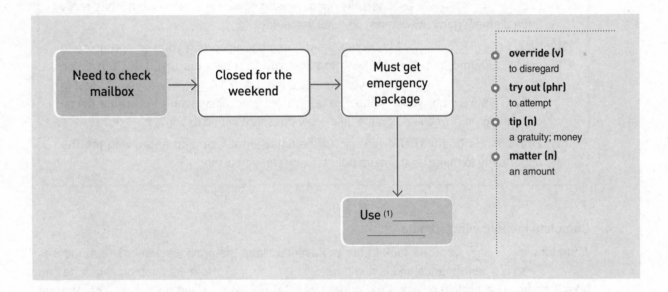

| Need to check mailbox | → | Closed for the weekend | → | Must get emergency package |

Use (1) _____ _____

- **override (v)**
  to disregard
- **try out (phr)**
  to attempt
- **tip (n)**
  a gratuity; money
- **matter (n)**
  an amount

1. **What can be inferred from the fact that the manager doesn't mention the "code" earlier?**
   - (A) The manager is willing to help her from the start.
   - (B) The manager wants to avoid the problem.
   - (C) The student is very considerate enough to understand him.
   - (D) The student doesn't want his boss to help her.

2. **How might the female student be described?**
   - (A) She is an opportunist.
   - (B) She hates birthdays.
   - (C) She is very convincing.
   - (D) She misses her father.

3. Listen again, and fill in the blanks.

> **W:** Hello, excuse me! You haven't _____, have you? I need to check my mailbox real quick.
>
> **M:** I'm sorry, miss, but yes, I've, uh, already closed up for the evening. Can't you just come back Monday morning?
>
> **W:** I could, but I'm _____ from my father today. You see, it is my birthday, and he's sent me a new digital camera, and I was hoping I could use it this weekend _____ with my friends.
>
> **M:** A new digital camera, huh. Well, uh, you see, the thing is the lock is on a timer, and it _____ and locks itself every morning and evening. It's a new type of security system they are _____. If I had a key, I'd be glad to open back up so you could get your present.
>
> **W:** Oh, no! You mean there's _____ for me to get in? I'm going to have to wait until Monday? What am I going to do? You've just got to help me out! I'm desperate!
>
> **M:** Well, there is one other way now that I think about it. I remember my manager _____ _____ an _____ in case of an emergency. It's a code I can punch in that will unlock the door. The problem is that I really hate calling my boss up and bothering him.
>
> **W:** Oh, please! I'll do anything! Couldn't I _____ or something for all your trouble? How about _____! Would that make calling your boss up a little bit easier to do? I've just got to open up that mailbox!
>
> **M:** Oh, no, no, no. I can't _____. Keep it! You need it for your beach trip this weekend! You know what? Don't worry about it. I'm going to call my boss up right now. We'll have that camera of yours in a _____!
>
> **W:** Oh, thank you so much! You are so kind!

4. Complete the following summary.

An _____ is speaking to a mailbox manager who has just _____ the office for the weekend. The student is expecting a birthday gift and hopes the manager will allow her to check her mail. Unfortunately, the door locks on an _____ and will not open up until Monday morning. The student wants to use her gift over the weekend and _____ the manager to help her. The manager finds an _____ to get inside. The student is very _____.

anxious student	locked up	electric timer
implores	alternative way	grateful

Practice with Lectures

A   Listen to part of a lecture, and answer the questions. 🎧 5-06

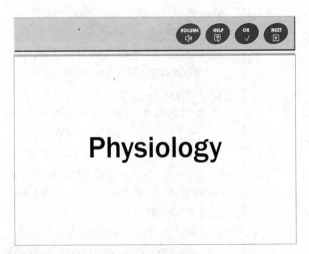

Physiology

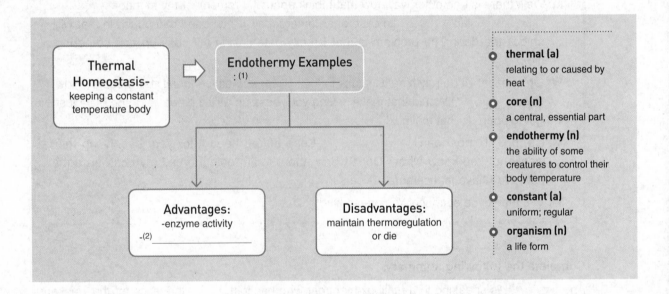

| Thermal Homeostasis- keeping a constant temperature body | ⟹ | Endothermy Examples : (1)_____ |

Advantages:
-enzyme activity
-(2)_____

Disadvantages:
maintain thermoregulation or die

- **thermal (a)**
  relating to or caused by heat
- **core (n)**
  a central, essential part
- **endothermy (n)**
  the ability of some creatures to control their body temperature
- **constant (a)**
  uniform; regular
- **organism (n)**
  a life form

1. **What can be inferred about thermal homeostasis?**

   (A) It is not vital for warm-blooded animals' survival.
   (B) It is an involuntary response by warm-blooded animals to the elements.
   (C) It is a critical defense mechanism in warm-blooded animals.
   (D) It gives warm-blooded animals an advantage over cold-blooded animals.

2. **Why does the professor use the beach example in the lecture?**

   (A) To warn the students of the dangers of sun exposure
   (B) To directly involve the students in the lesson
   (C) To scare the students into avoiding the beach
   (D) To add an abstract theory to the lecture

3. **Listen again, and fill in the blanks.**

Warm-blooded animals maintain thermal homeostasis. What I mean is they _____ _____ at a nearly constant level regardless of the temperature of the surrounding envir onment: _____. Okay. Now what we _____.

Endothermy is the ability of some creatures to control their body temperatures through internal means such as _____. You all know what I'm talking about, right? When you shiver because it's so cold in the winter or when you are sweating buckets in the summer, all your body is trying to do is maintain that constant temperature of 98.6 degrees inside.

Now, um, there are some advantages and disadvantages to all of this. The advantages are _____ and a constant body temperature, which allows warm-blooded animals to be _____. A big disadvantage is the, uh, need to maintain thermoregulation or, in other words, _____, even during inactivity, otherwise the organism will die. That's right. It _____.

_____ is one of the most important defense mechanisms in a warm-blooded organism. Is everyone following me? Sure? Great, so uh, for example, in the winter, there may not be enough food to enable an endotherm, for example, a hungry grizzly bear, to keep its _____. Um, so some animals, like our friend the grizzly, go into a controlled state of hypothermia called hibernation, or torpor. This deliberately lowers the body temperature _____. Everyone still with me? Good. Now, in hot weather, like when you were at the beach last weekend soaking up all those dangerous ultraviolet rays to make yourself look tan and pretty, endotherms _____. They may pant, sweat, lick, or seek shelter or water.

4. **Complete the following summary.**

Warm-blooded animals are able to keep their body temperatures at a _____. They use means such as _____ and sweating to do this. Another term for this _____ is endothermy. Endotherms spend a _____ of energy to maintain body temperature, and if they don't, they _____. Advantages of this regulation are increased enzyme activity and increased activity _____ situations.

could perish	constant level	in cold weather
temperature control	great amount	shivering

B Listen to part of a lecture, and answer the questions. ⊙ 5-07

Linguistics

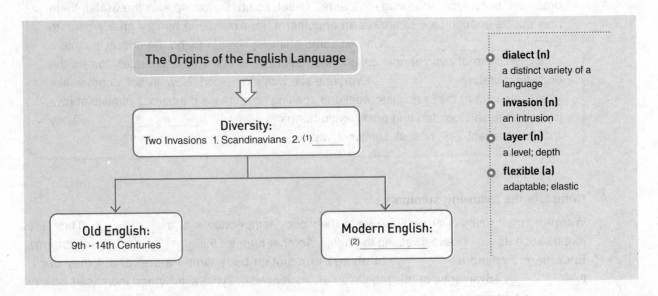

The Origins of the English Language

⬇

Diversity:
Two Invasions 1. Scandinavians 2. (1) _____

Old English:
9th - 14th Centuries

Modern English:
(2) _____

dialect (n)
a distinct variety of a language

invasion (n)
an intrusion

layer (n)
a level; depth

flexible (a)
adaptable; elastic

1. **What can be inferred about Old English from the lecture?**

   Ⓐ Old English is a diverse language.
   Ⓑ Old English is the base for many other languages.
   Ⓒ Old English is a relatively shallow language.
   Ⓓ Old English has difficult pronunciation patterns.

2. **Listen again to part of the lecture. Then answer the question.** 🎧
   What is implied by the professor when she says this? 🎧

   Ⓐ Most students are very involved in the lecture.
   Ⓑ Most students are eager to learn about Old English.
   Ⓒ Most students pay dearly when they answer incorrectly.
   Ⓓ Most students are not interested in the lecture.

3. Listen again, and fill in the blanks.

W1: Okay, everyone. Calm down. I know you are all really excited about being able to read a little bit of Old English. I congratulate you. Job well done, but we've _____ yet to go. Now it is time for us to take a look at the history of English. Who can tell me where English _____?

W2: That's easy! England, of course. Everyone knows that the language is named after the country!

W1: Uh, well, that's partly correct. English is a West Germanic language. It came from the Anglo-Frisian _____ to Britain by settlers from parts of what is now northwest Germany and the northern Netherlands. At first, Old English was a group of dialects _____ origins of the Anglo-Saxon kingdoms of England. The original Old English language was then influenced by _____. The first was by language speakers of the Scandinavian branch of the Germanic family. They _____ parts of Britain in the 8th and 9th centuries. The second was the Normans in the 11th century, who spoke a variety of French. These _____ English to become "mixed" to some degree. Now what kind of effect do you guys think this mixing had on English?

W2: Wouldn't that have made English pretty diverse, Professor?

W1: I see somebody is _____! Exactly! English became a very rich, elaborate _____. And later, English developed into a borrowing language of _____ with a huge vocabulary. So, what about modern English? Who can give us an idea of when it began?

M: I believe it was around the, um, 15th century, wasn't it?

W1: Yes, it was. Modern English is often dated from the _____, which took place mainly during the 15th century. English was also influenced by the spread of a _____ dialect in government and administration and by the standardizing effect of printing. By the time of William Shakespeare, around the, uh, middle to late 16th century, the language had become clearly recognizable as modern English.

4. Complete the following summary.

English is a West-Germanic language that _____ German and the Netherlands and was _____ England by settlers. Two _____ by the Scandinavians and Normans heavily influenced the language by _____ diverse and elaborate. Modern English began around the 15th century. It was affected by the _____ dialect of the government. By the time of Shakespeare, modern English was a clearly recognized language _____ its own.

later invasions	standardized	making it more
originated in	brought to	which stood on

Listen to part of a lecture, and answer the questions. 5-08

Ecology

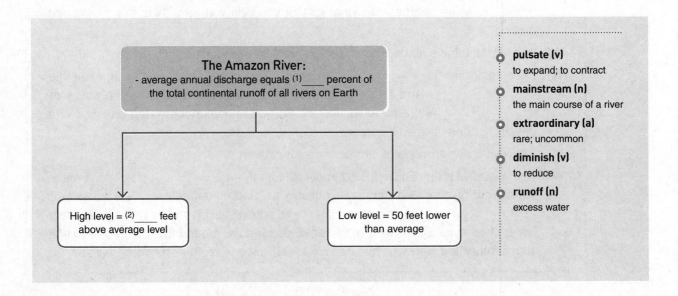

The Amazon River:
- average annual discharge equals (1)_____ percent of the total continental runoff of all rivers on Earth

High level = (2)_____ feet above average level

Low level = 50 feet lower than average

- **pulsate (v)**
  to expand; to contract
- **mainstream (n)**
  the main course of a river
- **extraordinary (a)**
  rare; uncommon
- **diminish (v)**
  to reduce
- **runoff (n)**
  excess water

1. **What is implied when the professor uses words such as "pulsate" and "surge"?**

   Ⓐ The professor is imparting basic information.
   Ⓑ The professor is emphasizing the power of the Amazon.
   Ⓒ The professor is bored with his own words.
   Ⓓ The professor is trying to downplay the size of the Amazon.

2. **Why does the professor make a point of relating the Mississippi River in the lecture?**

   Ⓐ To show his pride in the American river
   Ⓑ To show how the Mississippi cannot be matched
   Ⓒ To show how the Mississippi pales in comparison to the Amazon
   Ⓓ To show that the Amazon lacks the surge of the Mississippi

3. Listen again, and fill in the blanks.

The Amazon River _____, surging once a year. From November through May, the volume of the, uh, _____. For example, as stated in your text, on June 1, 1989, the level of the river at Manaus, 900 miles from the ocean, was 45 feet above low water, nearly reaching the 1953 all-time _____. Now, the Amazon's volume in that month far _____ of the next eight largest rivers on Earth, a pretty _____ if you think about it. It does this by the end of every May, even in years of normal flow. During the second half of the year, this, um, _____. All right, uh, yes, here it is in your text, page 372. In November of 1990, also around Manaus, _____ and sandbars were _____ for the first time in living memory. The river had fallen 50 feet to its lowest level on record this century. The only official studies of the main stream flow were done in 1963 and 1964 which, uh, were years _____ as, uh, having less than average rainfall by the U.S. Geological Survey. Measurements were made at Obidos, 600 miles inland, where the Amazon _____ a single channel, very narrow in comparison, a little more than a mile wide. Findings gave the average minimum discharge at 3 million cubic feet per second while the average maximum reached 8.5 million.

For comparison, our own Mississippi River at Vicksburg averages 620,000 cubic feet per second. It has been suggested that the Amazon's average _____ equals 20 percent of the total continental runoff of all rivers on Earth. Note this does not mean that the Amazon system holds one-fifth of the entire world's fresh water, as some other books have interpreted this data. In fact, all the Amazonia's waterways hold less than one ten-thousandth of the world's fresh water, most of which, by the way, is _____ in polar ice.

4. Complete the following summary.

The Amazon River experiences a _____ about once a year. This occurs between the months of November and May. Some areas _____ in the waterline by as much as 40 to 50 feet in the late '80s. During the other _____, the water recedes, exposing sandbars and _____ white sand. The average discharge of the river is between 3 and 8.5 million cubic _____. Finally, contrary to some published accounts, the Amazon holds less than one ten-thousandth of _____ fresh water.

beach-like	all the world's	large surge
reported increases	half of the year	feet per second

D Listen to part of a lecture, and answer the questions. ⊙ 5-09

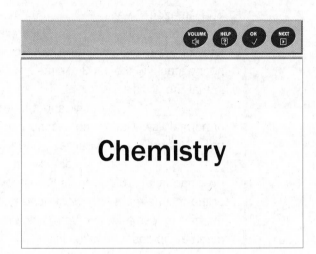

Chemistry

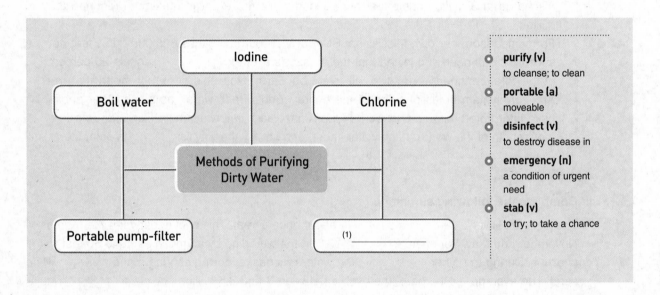

Iodine

Boil water

Chlorine

Methods of Purifying
Dirty Water

Portable pump-filter

(1)_____

- **purify (v)**
  to cleanse; to clean
- **portable (a)**
  moveable
- **disinfect (v)**
  to destroy disease in
- **emergency (n)**
  a condition of urgent
  need
- **stab (v)**
  to try; to take a chance

1. **What is implied about water purification during the lecture?**

   Ⓐ It is a simple task.
   Ⓑ It can be quite expensive.
   Ⓒ It takes a lot of time and effort.
   Ⓓ It isn't necessary to do all of the time.

2. **What does the professor imply is the most practical method of water purification?**

   Ⓐ Solar purification
   Ⓑ Boiling
   Ⓒ Chemicals
   Ⓓ Pump-filters

3. Listen again, and fill in the blanks.

M1: Could you close the door, please? Great. Thanks. Now today, class, we're going to discuss dirty water. That's right, dirty water, or more importantly, how _____ it yourselves so that you can drink it and not get sick. Sure, you can go out and buy _____ systems or _____, but there are other methods you can use if you don't have this stuff available. Who can name one?

W: Whenever my dad takes us all camping, he just boils it, and no one in my family has ever gotten sick.

M1: Sure. Boiling water on a portable stove or fire will _____. At higher elevations, though, the boiling point of water drops, so that several minutes of continuous boiling are required. Another option is just to be sure you _____ _____. Some of these, um, like the charcoal filter ones, don't remove the viruses. In this case, you have to _____ with a third method. Who can tell me what a third might be?

M2: How about electricity?

M1: Very funny. Not quite. No, actually, I was thinking of a _____. One is iodine, which kills many, but not all, of the most common, uh, pathogens in natural fresh water sources. Second, used only in _____, is chlorine-based bleach. Just add two drops of 5% bleach per quart of clear water, and _____, uh, covered, for about an hour. All right, now that is three so far. Anyone like to _____ at the last option?

W: Uh, sunshine?

M1: Bonus points for whoever said that in the back row. Yes, sunlight is another valid option. We call it solar purification. Water is placed in a _____, which is oxygenated by shaking. It is placed for six hours in full sun, which raises the temperature and gives an extended dose of _____, killing any microbes that may be present.

4. Complete the following summary.

Water purification is important when camping or doing other _____. If it isn't done, dirty or polluted water can be _____ beings. There are four _____ of purifying water in the outdoors: boiling, filtering, _____, and with the sun. Boiling is the easiest and most complete while _____ not kill all of the viruses. Iodine is a chemical for killing most pathogens in water, and sunlight, though _____, is another valid option.

filtering might	main methods	outdoor activities
time consuming	chemically	harmful to human

Integrated Listening & Speaking

A   Listen to the summary of the previous conversation and say the answers out loud by using the cue sentence words that are indicated in each answer. ⊙ 5-10

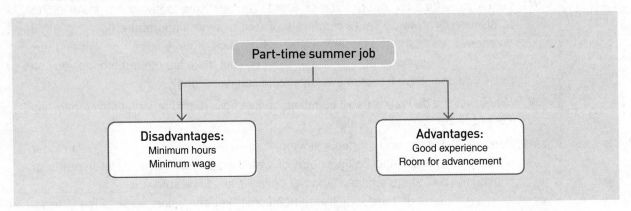

1. **What is the greatest advantage of the job?**

   (1) Experience is the _____.   (2) The _____.

2. **What are the students' responses to the professor's proposal?**

   (1) The students are _____.   (2) In response, the students _____.

3. **What is a minor disadvantage of the position?**

   (1) A minor disadvantage is _____.   (2) The students consider the _____.

B   Listen to the summary of the previous conversation and say the answers out loud by using the cue sentence words that are indicated in each answer. ⊙ 5-11

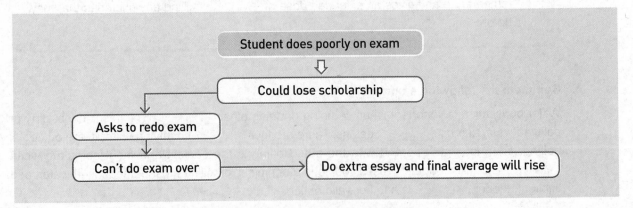

1. **Why is the student talking with the instructor?**

   (1) The student _____.   (2) The student _____.

2. **What is the instructor's reaction to the student's request?**

   (1) The instructor is very _____.   (2) The instructor's _____.

3. **What solution does the instructor offer?**

   (1) The instructor decides _____.   (2) The instructor has _____.

C Listen to the previous lecture and say the answers out loud by using the cue sentence words that are indicated in each answer. ⊙ **5-12**

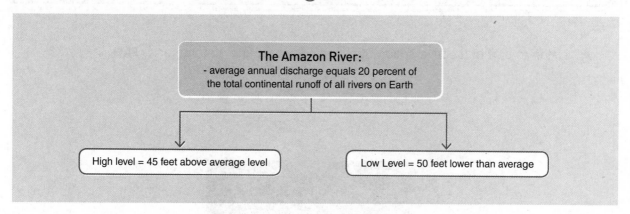

1. **What does this lecture teach us about the Amazon River?**

   (1) The Amazon is in _____.　　(2) Throughout the year, _____.

2. **What water level did the Amazon reach in 1989?**

   (1) The water level reached _____.　　(2) The water level rose _____.

3. **How does the Amazon compare to the Mississippi River.**

   (1) Compared to the Mississippi, _____.　　(2) The Amazon's average discharge is _____.

D Listen to the previous lecture and say the answers out loud by using the cue sentence words that are indicated in each answer. ⊙ **5-13**

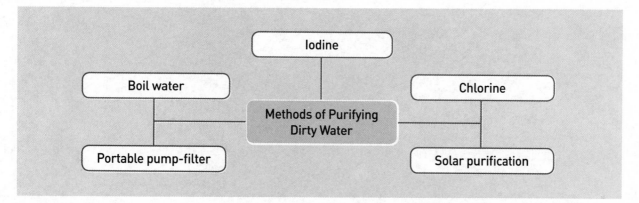

1. **What is the best method of water purification?**

   (1) The best _____.　　(2) Boiling is _____.

2. **What amount of time does solar purification take?**

   (1) Solar purification _____.　　(2) At six hours, _____.

3. **What is the focus of the lecture?**

   (1) The lecture focuses on _____.　　(2) In the lecture, _____.

Mini TOEFL iBT

VOLUME HELP OK NEXT

A Listen to part of a conversation between a student and a manager. 5-14

1. **What can be implied from this conversation?**

   (A) A student is complaining about her hours at work.

   (B) A student is trying to secure a job.

   (C) A student is upset with her manager at work.

   (D) A student doesn't have enough spare time to work.

2. **What can be inferred about the manager's feeling toward the student?**

   (A) The manager feels the student is promising.

   (B) The manager feels the student has a bad attitude.

   (C) The manager feels the student is lazy.

   (D) The manager feels that the student is highly intelligent.

3. **What does the student explain to the manager?**

   (A) She explains that she is too busy to work anymore.

   (B) She explains that being in a jazz band is more important than work.

   (C) She explains that she desperately needs a raise.

   (D) She explains her numerous qualifications.

4. **What are the main duties the manager talks about? Click on 2 answers.**

   (A) Handling money

   (B) Taking care of customers

   (C) Using a computerized register

   (D) Running many errands

5. **Listen again to part of the conversation. Then answer the question.**

   What is a concern the manager has about the student?

   (A) The manager thinks the student is over-qualified.

   (B) The manager believes the student might be too busy.

   (C) The manager believes the student doesn't have the right personality.

   (D) The manager thinks the student is arrogant.

B Listen to the part of a lecture in a biology class. ⊙ 5-15

Biology

1. **What is the professor's main focus in the lecture?**

   (A) How neurons communicate
   (B) The genetic make-up of neurons
   (C) Where neurons come from
   (D) Common problems with neurons

2. **How are neurons able to transmit information?**

   (A) Via target neurons
   (B) Via the brain
   (C) Via synapses
   (D) Via the blood stream

3. **What does the professor imply about neurons in children?**

   (A) Neurons do not increase in children.
   (B) Neurons develop slowly in children.
   (C) Neurons boost children's immune systems.
   (D) Neurons reduce in number as children grow.

4. **According to the lecture, what are neurons composed of?**
   Click on 3 answers.

   (A) Axons
   (B) Mitochondria
   (C) Cell bodies
   (D) Dendritic trees

5. **Listen again to part of the lecture. Then answer the question.**

   What does the professor mean when he says this?

   (A) The students should look at the picture of the neuron.
   (B) The students should understand his point better now.
   (C) The students should be confused by the picture.
   (D) The students don't understand what he's talking about.

6. **What are the two basic functions of synapses?**

   (A) They mutate and fertilize.
   (B) They expand and dominate.
   (C) They excite and inhibit.
   (D) They split and multiply.

⊙ Vocabulary Review

A Listen and choose the correct word that matches each definition. ⊙ 5-16

1. (A) farm   (B) film   (C) firm   (D) form
2. (A) relatively (B) relatives   (C) relived   (D) reliable
3. (A) penetrate   (B) conceptualize (C) create   (D) realize
4. (A) academy   (B) academic   (C) acronym   (D) acrobat
5. (A) accept   (B) inept   (C) adrift   (D) accepts
6. (A) expect   (B) accepting   (C) expecting   (D) expectation
7. (A) express   (B) excurse   (C) implore   (D) explore
8. (A) mechanical (B) naturalistic (C) creative   (D) artificial
9. (A) economics   (B) economy   (C) economically (D) economic
10. (A) emit   (B) intimidate   (C) imitate   (D) simulate
11. (A) excessive (B) extraordinary (C) exchangeable (D) explosive
12. (A) embrace   (B) embryo   (C) emergency   (D) embassy
13. (A) purge   (B) purify   (C) purchase   (D) purport
14. (A) exalt   (B) exact   (C) exceed   (D) exasperate
15. (A) fleeting   (B) flexible   (C) flash   (D) flattering

B Complete the sentences by filling in the blanks with the expressions in the box.

sweating buckets	zap	got it in you
take a stab	build up	ten bucks

1. Let your sister _____ at the poker game.
2. Jeff paid _____ for his sweater.
3. They need to _____ some savings before they can buy a car.
4. We were _____ while playing tennis yesterday.
5. I know you've _____ to do better in Spanish class.
6. I need to _____ this email to my boss.

This part provides lists of important vocabulary words in each unit. They are essential words for understanding any academic texts. Many of the words are listed with their derivative forms so that students can expand their vocabulary in an effective way. These lists can be used as homework assignments.

Vocabulary Wrap-up

Unit 1 • Listening for Main Ideas

● Step A

- [ ] acid
- [ ] barcode
- [ ] copperplate
- [ ] engraver
- [ ] heartburn
- [ ] ooze
- [ ] seismic

- [ ] amphibian
- [ ] beeswax
- [ ] detour
- [ ] etching
- [ ] intestine
- [ ] seep
- [ ] sphincter

- [ ] astronomy
- [ ] camouflage
- [ ] disaster
- [ ] gastric
- [ ] Mediterranean
- [ ] prudent
- [ ] esophagus

- [ ] ballistic
- [ ] circulation
- [ ] tectonic
- [ ] havoc
- [ ] nutrient
- [ ] reptile
- [ ] suffrage

● Step B

Noun	Verb	Adjective	Adverb
☐ revolution	☐ revolutionize	☐ revolutionary	☐ revolutionarily
☐ affiliation	☐ affiliate	☐ affiliated	
☐ theory	☐ theorize	☐ theoretical	☐ theoretically
☐ offense	☐ offend	☐ offensive	☐ offensively
☐ reservation	☐ reserve	☐ reserved	☐ reservedly
☐ extraction	☐ extract	☐ extractive	
☐ frustration	☐ frustrate	☐ frustrated	☐ frustratingly
☐ disconnection	☐ disconnect	☐ disconnected	☐ disconnectedly
☐ amendment	☐ amend	☐ amendable	
☐ irritation	☐ irritate	☐ irritable	☐ irritably
☐ eligibility		☐ eligible	☐ eligibly
☐ exposure	☐ expose	☐ exposed	
☐ recognition	☐ recognize	☐ recognizable	☐ recognizably
☐ removal	☐ remove	☐ removable	☐ removably
☐ association	☐ associate	☐ associative	

Unit 2 • Listening for Main Purpose

● Step A

☐ advent	☐ atmosphere	☐ carnivorous	☐ celestial
☐ clientele	☐ continent	☐ dispute	☐ enzyme
☐ exhaust	☐ flourish	☐ flytrap	☐ glacier
☐ obsolete	☐ pioneer	☐ pollution	☐ recyclable
☐ spew	☐ swampland	☐ tripod	☐ victim
☐ conversion	☐ landfill	☐ nitrogen	☐ planet
☐ polar	☐ premise	☐ registrar	☐ satin

● Step B

Noun	Verb	Adjective	Adverb
☐ precision		☐ precise	☐ precisely
☐ method		☐ methodical	☐ methodically
☐ exhaust	☐ exhaust	☐ exhausted	☐ exhaustedly
☐ flood	☐ flood	☐ flooded	
☐ pole		☐ polar	
☐ effect		☐ effective	☐ effectively
☐ economy	☐ economize	☐ economic	☐ economically
☐ theory	☐ theorize	☐ theoretical	☐ theoretically
☐ motor	☐ motorize	☐ motored	
☐ pace	☐ pace	☐ paced	
☐ advance	☐ advance	☐ advanced	
☐ fame		☐ famous	☐ famously
☐ organization	☐ organize	☐ organized	
☐ summary	☐ summarize	☐ summarized	
☐ information	☐ inform	☐ informed	
☐ availability		☐ available	☐ availably
☐ flexibility	☐ flex	☐ flexible	☐ flexibly
☐ preference	☐ prefer	☐ preferable	☐ preferably
☐ nerve		☐ nervous	☐ nervously
☐ shame	☐ shame	☐ shameful	☐ shamefully

Unit 3 • Listening for Major Details

● Step A

- ☐ allegiance
- ☐ ancestry
- ☐ aristocrat
- ☐ arsenal
- ☐ blockade
- ☐ confederate
- ☐ decorate
- ☐ dock
- ☐ federalism
- ☐ heritage
- ☐ influx
- ☐ invasion
- ☐ jargon
- ☐ monarch
- ☐ snowplow
- ☐ supreme
- ☐ ultimatum
- ☐ vassal
- ☐ vault
- ☐ withdraw
- ☐ zoning
- ☐ predominant
- ☐ immigrate
- ☐ integrate
- ☐ collapse
- ☐ distinct
- ☐ evolve
- ☐ hierarchy

● Step B

Noun	Verb	Adjective	Adverb
☐ distinction	☐ distinguish	☐ distinct	☐ distinctly
☐ shift	☐ shift	☐ shifted	
☐ colony	☐ colonize	☐ colonial	☐ colonially
	☐ predominate	☐ predominant	☐ predominantly
☐ uniqueness		☐ unique	☐ uniquely
☐ influx			
☐ evolution	☐ evolve	☐ evolving	
☐ chatter	☐ chat	☐ chatting	
☐ completion	☐ complete	☐ complete	☐ completely
☐ approver	☐ approve	☐ approving	☐ approvingly
☐ applicant	☐ apply	☐ applying	
	☐ solidify	☐ solid	☐ solidly
☐ balancer	☐ balance	☐ balanced	
☐ mob	☐ mob	☐ mobbish	
	☐ terrify	☐ terrible	☐ terribly
☐ scholar		☐ scholastic	☐ scholarly
☐ extension	☐ extend	☐ extending	☐ extendedly
☐ infusion	☐ infuse		
☐ domination	☐ dominate	☐ dominating	☐ dominatingly

Unit 4 • Understanding the Function of What Is Said

Step A

☐ accomplish	☐ aggression	☐ alert	☐ alumnus
☐ axis	☐ blitzkrieg	☐ chronological	☐ clockwise
☐ cluster	☐ confrontation	☐ coyote	☐ decoration
☐ designate	☐ dioxide	☐ elite	☐ emergency
☐ emit	☐ eruption	☐ famine	☐ genus
☐ grassland	☐ prey	☐ lava	☐ longitudinal
☐ marmot	☐ peninsula	☐ precipitation	☐ prelude

Step B

Noun	Verb	Adjective	Adverb
☐ perfecter	☐ perfect	☐ perfect	☐ perfectly
☐ manipulativeness	☐ manipulate	☐ manipulative	☐ manipulatively
		☐ clockwise	☐ clockwise
☐ lava		☐ lavalike	
☐ ozone		☐ ozonic	
☐ toxicity		☐ toxic	
☐ cultivation	☐ cultivate	☐ cultivatable	
☐ ascent	☐ ascend	☐ ascendable	
☐ descent	☐ descend	☐ descendable	
☐ transcript			
☐ unofficialization	☐ unofficialize	☐ unofficial	☐ unofficially
☐ inconvenience	☐ inconvenience	☐ inconvenient	☐ inconveniently
☐ grammaticalness		☐ grammatical	☐ grammatically
☐ evidence		☐ evidential	☐ evidentially
☐ chronology	☐ chronologize	☐ chronological	☐ chronologically
☐ confrontation	☐ confront	☐ confrontational	☐ confrontationally
☐ cluster	☐ cluster		

Unit 5 • Understanding the Speaker's Attitude

Step A

- [ ] accomplish
- [ ] achy
- [ ] aesthetic
- [ ] allotment
- [ ] anarcho-syndicalism
- [ ] angst
- [ ] antique
- [ ] apocalypse
- [ ] appendectomy
- [ ] archeological
- [ ] blast
- [ ] budget
- [ ] constable
- [ ] criticism
- [ ] dedication
- [ ] deliberate
- [ ] depict
- [ ] deputy
- [ ] drastic
- [ ] egotistical
- [ ] entrench
- [ ] existentialism
- [ ] expire
- [ ] formalism
- [ ] hemisphere
- [ ] hinge
- [ ] mannerism
- [ ] oscillation

Step B

Noun	Verb	Adjective	Adverb
[ ] note	[ ] note	[ ] notable	[ ] notably
[ ] probable		[ ] probable	[ ] probably
[ ] preference	[ ] prefer	[ ] preferential	[ ] preferentially
[ ] intellect	[ ] intellectualize	[ ] intellectual	[ ] intellectually
[ ] entrenchment	[ ] entrench	[ ] entrenched	
[ ] expiration	[ ] expire	[ ] expired	
[ ] contribution	[ ] contribute	[ ] contributed	
[ ] perseverance	[ ] persevere		
[ ] oscillator	[ ] oscillate	[ ] oscillated	[ ] oscillatory
[ ] couple	[ ] couple	[ ] coupled	
[ ] intersection	[ ] intersect	[ ] intersected	
[ ] proof	[ ] prove	[ ] proved	
[ ] enlargement	[ ] enlarge	[ ] enlarged	
[ ] bet	[ ] bet	[ ] betted	
[ ] complication	[ ] complicate	[ ] complicated	[ ] complicatedly
[ ] training	[ ] train	[ ] trained	
[ ] recovery	[ ] recover	[ ] recovered	
[ ] complaint	[ ] complain	[ ] complaining	[ ] complainingly
	[ ] scold	[ ] scolded	
[ ] reference	[ ] refer	[ ] referred	[ ] referentially

Unit 6 • Understanding Organization

Step A

- [ ] abiotic
- [ ] absorb
- [ ] affluent
- [ ] angiosperm
- [ ] anther
- [ ] argon
- [ ] blacksmith
- [ ] botany
- [ ] bust
- [ ] cerebral
- [ ] cognitive
- [ ] compulsory
- [ ] configuration
- [ ] criminology
- [ ] cynical
- [ ] deciduous
- [ ] doug
- [ ] entomology
- [ ] extermination
- [ ] flyby
- [ ] forensic
- [ ] fungus
- [ ] gamete
- [ ] gymnosperm
- [ ] habitable
- [ ] literacy
- [ ] microorganism
- [ ] optimally

Step B

Noun	Verb	Adjective	Adverb
declaration	declare	declarative	declaratively
complement	complement	complementary	complementarily
wanderer	wander	wandering	
reservation	reserve	reserved	reservedly
substitute	substitute	substituted	
slowness	slow	slow	slowly
affect	affect	affected	affectedly
thrower	throw	thrown	
digestion	digest	digested	digestively
absorption	absorb	absorbed	absorbedly
representative	represent	represented	
retrieval	retrieve	retrieved	
transfer	transfer	transferred	
help	help	helpful	helpfully
rub	rub	rubbed	
pat	pat	patted	
completion	complete	complete	completely
emphasis	emphasize	emphasized	
shift	shift	shifted	
rearrangement	rearrange	rearranged	

Unit **7** • Connecting Content

Step A

- ☐ afflict
- ☐ ape
- ☐ apparatus
- ☐ artistry
- ☐ astounding
- ☐ authenticity
- ☐ blubber
- ☐ broadband
- ☐ captivity
- ☐ contamination
- ☐ contentious
- ☐ contractual
- ☐ corrupt
- ☐ echolocation
- ☐ enduring
- ☐ genuine
- ☐ hibernation
- ☐ hoax
- ☐ insulate
- ☐ memorable
- ☐ micro-biology
- ☐ Paleolithic
- ☐ predatory
- ☐ pregnancy
- ☐ prototypical
- ☐ province
- ☐ pulse
- ☐ sensory

Step B

Noun	Verb	Adjective	Adverb
☐ corruption	☐ corrupt	☐ corrupted	
☐ communication	☐ communicate	☐ communicated	
☐ brutality	☐ brutalize	☐ brutal	☐ brutally
☐ selection	☐ select	☐ selected	
☐ depiction	☐ depict	☐ depictive	
☐ isolation	☐ isolate	☐ isolated	
☐ identicalness		☐ identical	☐ identically
☐ apparentness		☐ apparent	☐ apparently
☐ shape	☐ shape	☐ shaped	☐ shapely
☐ typicality		☐ typical	☐ typically
☐ maintainability	☐ maintain	☐ maintainable	
☐ enjoyment	☐ enjoy	☐ enjoyable	☐ enjoyably
☐ failure	☐ fail	☐ failed	☐ failing
☐ process	☐ process	☐ processed	
☐ perfect	☐ perfect	☐ perfect	☐ perfectly
☐ finance	☐ finance	☐ financeable	

Unit 8 • Making Inferences

Step A

☐ aggravate	☐ apparatus	☐ cancellation	☐ cerebellum
☐ dendrite	☐ desperate	☐ devotee	☐ dialect
☐ disguise	☐ disinfect	☐ elaborate	☐ endotherm
☐ enthusiasm	☐ errand	☐ excitatory	☐ extremist
☐ filter	☐ flunk	☐ frugal	☐ grassroots
☐ grizzle	☐ hallucination	☐ homeostasis	☐ hypothermia
☐ implore	☐ inhibitory	☐ innate	☐ intimidation

Step B

Noun	Verb	Adjective	Adverb
☐ acceptance	☐ accept	☐ accepting	
☐ respect	☐ respect	☐ respected	
☐ anxiousness		☐ anxious	☐ anxiously
☐ constant		☐ constant	☐ constantly
☐ satisfaction	☐ satisfy	☐ satisfiable	☐ satisfyingly
☐ extraordinariness		☐ extraordinary	☐ extraordinarily
☐ deliberateness	☐ deliberate	☐ deliberate	☐ deliberately
☐ harmfulness	☐ harm	☐ harmful	☐ harmfully
☐ aggravator	☐ aggravate	☐ aggravative	☐ aggravatingly
☐ imploration	☐ implore	☐ implorable	☐ imploringly
☐ tryingness	☐ try	☐ trying	☐ tryingly
☐ recentness		☐ recent	☐ recently
☐ mindfulness	☐ mind	☐ mindful	☐ mindfully
☐ report	☐ report	☐ reportable	☐ reportedly
☐ electricity		☐ electric	☐ electrically
☐ diminishment	☐ diminish	☐ diminishable	
☐ character	☐ characterize	☐ characterizable	

This section measures your ability to understand conversations and lectures in English. The listening section is divided into 2 separately timed parts. In each part you will listen to 1 conversation and 2 lectures. You will hear each conversation or lecture only one time. After each conversation and lecture, you will answer questions about it. The questions typically ask about the main idea and supporting details. Some questions ask about a speaker's purpose or attitude. Answer the questions based on what is stated or implied by the speakers.

You may take notes while you listen. You may use your notes to help you answer the questions. Your notes will not be scored. If you need to change the volume while you listen, click on the Volume icon at the top of the screen.

For some questions, you will see this icon: 🎧 This means that you will hear, but not see part of the question. Some of the questions have special directions. These directions appear in a gray box on the screen.

Most questions are worth one point. If a question is worth more than one point, it will have special directions that indicate how many points you can receive.

You must answer each question. After you answer, click on Next. Then click on OK to confirm your answer and go on to the next question. After you click on OK, you can not return to previous questions.

Actual Test

Conversation 1~5: Listen to part of a conversation between a student and a volleyball coach. 5-18

1. **Why does the student need to talk with the coach?**

   (A) To discuss an upcoming volleyball game

   (B) To inquire about volleyball tryouts

   (C) To talk about something unrelated to volleyball

   (D) To congratulate the coach on a great season

2. **Why does the coach suggest a combination lock?**

   (A) Because it is stronger than a key lock.

   (B) Because it would be more convenient.

   (C) Because he distrusts key locks.

   (D) Because combination locks are smaller.

3. **According to the coach, what are suicides?**

   (A) A secret energy drink

   (B) A sad repercussion of competition

   (C) A conditioning technique

   (D) An advanced play he is developing

4. **What is the coach's reaction toward the student's request to sign the petition?**

   (A) He is very receptive to it.

   (B) He is indifferent towards it.

   (C) He thinks it is petty.

   (D) He thinks it needs some work.

5. **What can be inferred about the student's impression of the coach?**

   (A) The coach is crass.

   (B) The coach is quite stubborn.

   (C) The coach is self-indulgent.

   (D) The coach goes out of his way for others.

Actual Test

Lecture 6~11: Listen to part of a lecture in a music history class.

Music History

6. **What is the lecture mainly about?**

   (A) The history of ragtime
   (B) The influence of ragtime on American music
   (C) The similarities between ragtime and classical music
   (D) The influence of ragtime on piano playing styles

7. **Why does the professor discuss sheet music?**

   (A) Because it became outdated due to ragtime.
   (B) Because it distinguished ragtime from jazz.
   (C) Because it limited the spread of ragtime.
   (D) Because it made ragtime difficult to record.

8. **What influence did the stride piano have?**

   (A) It made jazz easier to play.
   (B) It made jazz complex and distinctive.
   (C) It made jazz the most popular music of the 1920s.
   (D) It made jazz a clear successor to the Delta blues. *

9. **What does the professor imply about the probable future of ragtime?**

   (A) It will eventually die out.
   (B) It will never be as good as when it first started.
   (C) It will probably continue to influence new forms of music.
   (D) It will never live up to jazz.

10. **What did the revival of ragtime in the 1950s do for the genre?**

    (A) Many new ragtime songs were recorded.
    (B) It became the most popular genre of the age.
    (C) More ragtime concerts were held.
    (D) Many original ragtime artists were finally recognized.

11. **According to the lecture, what is a novelty piano? Check the correct boxes below:**

	Yes	No
It's an instrument similar to the blues piano.		
It's another term for a concert piano.		
It's another term for a player piano.		
It's a pianistic cousin of jazz.		
It's a Harlem version of the piano roll.		

Actual Test

Lecture 12~17: Listen to part of a lecture in a botany class. 5-20

12. What is the professor's lecture about?

- (A) Southeast Asia
- (B) The Venus flytrap plant
- (C) Tetra Stigma vines
- (D) Rafflesia plants

13. Why does the professor explain "passive carnivores"?

- (A) Because that's what a Venus flytrap is.
- (B) Because that's what a Rafflesia plant is.
- (C) Because that's what a Tetra Stigma vine is.
- (D) Because passive carnivores only live in Southeast Asia.

14. What are "pitchers"?

- (A) They are roots.
- (B) They are flowers.
- (C) They are leaves.
- (D) They are flies.

15. According to the lecture, what can be inferred about the relationship between flies and the Rafflesia?

Please check the correct box below:

	Yes	No
Rafflesia use flies as a food source.		
Rafflesia will use flies as a host on some occasions.		
Rafflesia sometimes feed Tetra Sigma vines flies on rare occasions.		
Flies pollinate Rafflesia.		
Flies attract other insects to Rafflesia so they can be eaten.		

16. What does the professor imply about Rafflesia arnoldii?

- (A) It's a very beautiful plant.
- (B) It's a very strange plant.
- (C) It's a plant that everyone should own.
- (D) It's a plant that can be found anywhere.

17. Why does the professor talk about the Tetra Stigma vine?

- (A) Because it's what Rafflesia lives on.
- (B) Because they are endangered.
- (C) Because they are Rafflesia's parasite.
- (D) Because they kill off Rafflesia's pitchers.

Actual Test

Conversation 18~22: Listen to part of a conversation between a student and a professor. 5-21

18. **What issue does the student have?**

   (A) The student doesn't care for her paper topic.

   (B) The student believes the topic of her paper is not all documented.

   (C) The student believes her paper topic is too complicated.

   (D) The student thinks her topic is too easy.

19. **What is the main idea of the student's original assignment?**

   (A) The habitat of the Alaskan Godwit.

   (B) The mating habits of the Alaskan Godwit.

   (C) The migration of the Alaskan Godwit.

   (D) The imminent extinction of the Alaskan Godwit.

20. **What aspect of the cuckoo does the professor defend?**

   (A) The cuckoo's intelligence

   (B) The cuckoo's appearance

   (C) The cuckoo's flight ability

   (D) The cuckoo's social skills

21. **Why does the student accept the Pink-footed Goose as an alternative topic?**

   (A) Because it is a beautiful bird.

   (B) Because the professor will lend her sources.

   (C) Because no one has written on it yet.

   (D) Because she has no other options.

22. **Why does the professor mention the cuckoo to the student?**

   (A) Because he feels it would be an easier topic to find information about.

   (B) Because he is an expert on the cuckoo.

   (C) Because it's an eccentric bird.

   (D) Because its migratory tendencies are not well documented.

Actual Test

Lecture 23~28: Listen to part of a lecture in a modern printing class. 5-22

23. What is the main topic of this lecture?

- (A) Gutenburg's printing press
- (B) Newspaper printing
- (C) 19th-century printing
- (D) 20th-century printing

24. Why does the professor explain alloy?

- (A) Because that's what "type metal" is.
- (B) To emphasize its importance to printing done in the 21st century
- (C) Because alloys were a new thing in the 19th century.
- (D) To emphasize its importance to the Gutenburg press

25. What was the result of the Linotype printing press?

- (A) It was less expensive than older models.
- (B) It required more people to operate.
- (C) It changed the publishing industry.
- (D) It was cleaner than older models.

26. What's a counterpunch?

- (A) A defensive tactic
- (B) A type of alloy
- (C) A punch used by boxers
- (D) A punch used to cut other punches

27. What's the attitude of the students?

- (A) They seem to know a great deal about the subject.
- (B) They don't seem to know much about the subject.
- (C) They seem intrigued by alloys.
- (D) They know more about printers than metals.

28. What does the professor imply about the Linotype printing press?

- (A) It was a process anyone could do with no training.
- (B) It's a much easier process than 21st-century printing methods.
- (C) It was a difficult task that required a craftsman throughout the process.
- (D) It was a much slower process than the Gutenburg printing process.

Actual Test

Lecture 29~34: 🎧 Listen to part of a lecture in a dramatics class. ⊙ 5-23

Dramatics

29. What is the professor mainly lecturing about?

- (A) The life of Robert De Niro
- (B) Method acting
- (C) Strasberg's influence on acting
- (D) How to become a professional actor

30. Why does the professor discuss Stanislavski?

- (A) Because Stanislavski ignored the art of method acting.
- (B) Because Stanislavski laid the foundation for the method acting movement.
- (C) Because Stanislavski personally brought method acting to Hollywood.
- (D) Because Stanislavski shunned method acting.

31. According to the professor, what is often confused?

- (A) The Method and the System
- (B) American Theater and Russian Theater
- (C) Robert De Niro and Al Pacino
- (D) Analytical and Introspective acting

32. Listen again to part of the lecture. Then answer the question.

What can be inferred when the student says this? 🎧

- (A) The student is demanding a direct answer.
- (B) The student is attempting to clarify an explanation.
- (C) The student is utterly confused.
- (D) The student is in need of more examples.

33. Why does the professor discuss Lee Strasberg?

- (A) Because he was an important Russian contemporary actor.
- (B) Because he rejected the acting methods of modern Europe.
- (C) Because he was an important influence on American theater and cinema.
- (D) Because he discovered method acting.

34. What can be inferred about the professor's opinion of method actors?

- (A) Their method is esoteric and hard to follow.
- (B) Their method should be respected because it is so old.
- (C) Their method is the most bizarre yet gets results.
- (D) Their method makes them better prepared than others.

How to
Master Skills for the
TOEFL iBT
Listening

Intermediate

Answer Book

Contents(Answer Book)

Unit 1 Listening for Main Ideas

Basic Drill

A   **1.** Ⓐ   **2.** Ⓒ   **3.** Ⓐ

🔘 **1-02**

W1: Wow, it's getting late. We've been studying in the library for a long time now.

W2: You're right. It's already dark outside. I'm kind of nervous about walking back to the dorm in the dark.

W1: Oh, well that's not a problem. We can call campus security to walk us back. Hey, they might even drive us.

W2: Really? I didn't know they did that.

W1: Yeah, it's a really great service. Hey, with the tuition we're paying, we should get walked back in the dark.

W2: Hey, I'm okay with paying tuition if it means safer campuses. This campus security thing is great!

🔘 **1-03**

W: All right, the first thing you need to do is register for your meal plan.

M: Where do I do that?

W: There's an office at the main dining hall on campus. Take your student identification card and a credit card. The meal plans are expensive!

M: But what if I really don't eat that much food?

W: That doesn't matter. All first-year students are required to get a plan for at least two meals a day. So it would be a really good idea if you ate at the dining hall for at least two meals a day. That way, you would actually get your money's worth.

M: So how much is this meal plan going to cost me?

W: I'm not sure because it changes from semester to semester. They'll have a pricing guide at the dining hall office.

🔘 **1-04**

M: Oh man, I'm running so late! I have to be at the Biology Building in five minutes!

W: Oh, well you had better hurry then. You can't take the usual path from here you know. You have to detour.

M: Detour? Why would I do that?

W: Don't you remember? They're building a new wing on the Chemistry Building. The path is going to be closed due to construction all semester. You have to go around the astronomy lab now to get to the Biology Building.

M: Oh that's right! I completely forgot. Okay, I really have to run then. I'll see you later!

B   **1.** Ⓒ   **2.** Ⓓ   **3.** Ⓑ

🔘 **1-05**

The earth has many natural disasters. Natural disasters are acts of nature that create havoc among the planet's creatures. One kind of natural disaster is a tsunami. A tsunami is a giant tidal wave that starts in the ocean. It causes major flooding where it hits. It can even sink entire islands so that they no longer can be seen from the surface of the water. One reason why a tsunami happens is underwater earthquakes. These quakes create a disturbance in the water and cause a large swell. This swell creates a wave, which moves until it hits land.

🔘 **1-06**

Women worldwide had to fight for the right to vote. Most governments thought that women couldn't make decisions about politics. In the 1800s, women started to fight against this. They became active in fighting for women's suffrage. Oh, suffrage means the right to vote. The first country to grant women the right to vote was New Zealand. This happened in 1892. Over the next hundred years, many more countries gave women voting rights. Many women around the world can now vote if they want to, but there are still countries that don't allow women to vote. Many battles in this fight have been won, but the fight for women's voting rights is not over.

🔘 **1-07**

The digestive system is vital in keeping humans and other animals alive. It lets animals take in food and pull out the nutrients. These nutrients are important to keeping an animal healthy. In humans, the digestive tract is made up of the mouth, the esophagus, the stomach, the small intestine, and the large intestine. Food is broken down in the mouth, esophagus, and stomach. Nutrients are taken out of the food in the small intestine. Food waste then goes through the large intestine. Here, more nutrients are pulled out or extracted. Finally, waste is passed out of the body through the colon. This is the bottom part of the large intestine. Without the digestive system, we wouldn't be alive.

Practice with Conversations

A   1. Ⓒ   2. Ⓑ

¹Toothpaste seeping out of tube

 1-08

W: So how are things going with your roommate?

M: Oh man, he's still really irritating me. I can't wait till the semester is over.

W: But Bob, the semester won't be over for two and a half months! You have to figure out how, you know, how to work this stuff out. Yeah, you have to talk to him.

M: Yeah, but I don't know what to say. I mean, I don't want to hurt his feelings or offend him or anything. But, seriously, if he doesn't get rid of those pizza boxes, I think I'm going to go ballistic.

W: See, this is why you have to talk to him. Because, you're obviously frustrated. I mean, I don't think it's unreasonable for you not to want empty food containers lying around the room. I mean, they could attract cockroaches. That's so gross!

M: And it's not just the pizza boxes, which, believe me, are bad enough! His socks are everywhere, his papers are all over my desk, and his tube of toothpaste is oozing and seeping all over our bathroom sink. He won't even put a cap on it! I really think it's unsanitary. I mean, I don't want to get sick.

W: Oh, man! That's really disgusting. You could definitely get sick from that. It's just so unhygienic. You just have to talk to him. Just be calm, and tell him that you don't appreciate his mess. Oh! You could even suggest that the two of you clean the room together once a week. If he has to clean up his own mess, maybe he won't make one!

M: Yeah, I suppose I could give that a shot. I really appreciate the suggestions. I mean, I guess I really do have to figure something out because we're not even halfway through the semester.

W: Hey, don't mention it. And if you need a pep talk or anything, you can always ask. I'm happy to be of assistance.

Bob is frustrated because his roommate is very messy. His roommate leaves food containers, socks, papers, and toothpaste lying around. Bob is concerned that because of the unhygienic room, he might get sick. The woman convinces Bob to talk to his roommate. She says it is important because Bob has to live with his roommate for another two and a half months. The woman suggests that Bob and his roommate clean the room together once a week. Bob appreciates the

woman's help.

B   1. Ⓐ   2. Ⓓ

¹needs a text book ²the library's copy

 1-09

M1: Hey, how's it going? Welcome back to school. Can I help you with anything?

M2: Yeah, actually, I hope so. I was looking for this book that I need for my, um, my research methods class. The professor really wants us to start reading this book now and going over material and stuff, and I can't seem to find it on the shelves.

M1: All right, well let me see if I can help you with that. What's the name of the book? Oh, and if you have the author, that would probably be really helpful, too.

M2: Okay, hold on. I have to find where I wrote it down. Okay, got it. The title of the book is *Methods of Educational Research*. And the author is, um, Wiersma.

M1: All right, let me enter that information into the computer to see if we have any in stock. Um, Wiersma, did you say? And *Methods of Educational Research*?

M2: Yeah, that was it.

M1: Wow, those disappeared quickly. We actually had a brand-new shipment come in yesterday – fifty textbooks – and they were gone by this morning.

M2: Oh, no! I knew I should have come by yesterday. I just got so carried away with school supply shopping. Are you expecting to get more in?

M1: Hmm… Yes, I think we're going to get another shipment in, probably in about a week. But it's going to be significantly smaller. I think just twenty books or so.

M2: Oh, man! I need to have two chapters read by next week already. I don't know what I'm going to do. What a horrible way to start out this semester!

M1: Well, I have a suggestion. You could put your name down to reserve one of the copies that'll be in, and in the meantime, maybe you could check the library to see if they have a copy on reserve. But if you're going to do that, you should probably do it quickly because I'm sure a lot more students are going to be in your position, you know.

M2: Yeah, I guess I'll try that. Um, okay, so where do I reserve a copy of the textbook?

M1: We can do that right here. But remember, you have to pick up the book within a week of delivery, or you'll lose your reservation, and it'll go to someone else.

M2: All right, thanks. Thanks for all your help.

A student is looking for a book at the campus bookstore. The shopkeeper informs him that the textbook is out of stock. He says a new shipment will arrive in a week. The student panics because his professor has already assigned several chapters of reading from the book. The shopkeeper makes a suggestion. He thinks the student should see if the book is on reserve at the library. That way, the student can do his reading without getting behind while he waits for the new shipment of textbooks.

C 1. (A) 2. (C)

[1] A barcode will be put on the student's ID card

🔘 1-10

W: All first-year students are required to do a one-on-one orientation with a librarian or a librarian's aid their first semester. So welcome!

M: Thank you.

W: Okay, so the first thing I'm going to do is walk you through how to borrow books from the library. Okay, so what you need to do first is make sure your identification card is registered at the front desk. The circulation desk officer will, um, scan your card, and then assign you a kind of, well, a barcode that will be swiped every time you borrow a book.

M: But why is that attached to my student ID card? I mean, couldn't I get a separate library card? That's how things were at my public library back home.

W: Well no, it's really important that your library card has a photograph of you on it for, um, for identification purposes. See, only students and professors and people affiliated with the university are allowed to borrow books from this library. So by attaching a barcode to your student ID, we're pretty much ensuring that you belong to this university. Plus, since your ID already has your picture on it, we don't, um, we don't have to worry about anyone else using your ID and taking out books.

M: Okay, I guess I can understand that. It's just a little weird to me to have one card for everything here. I mean, it already has my meal plan and a cash account on it, not to mention, it lets me back into my dorm.

W: Well, that's kind of a good thing. You don't end up carrying around a lot of cards.

M: Well, it's kind of bad, too. If I lose it, I can't do anything. I guess I have to be really careful.

W: I guess you do. It's not so hard. Don't worry.

M: Thanks. Okay, so the first thing I have to do before I can borrow books is, um, take my student ID to the circulation desk for a barcode?

W: That's right! Once you do that, you can start borrowing books!

A librarian is orienting a student to the book borrowing process. She tells him the first step is to get a barcode attached to his student identification card. She says that it is important that he has photo identification when borrowing books because only people affiliated with the university are allowed to borrow books. The student worries about having another account attached to his ID card because it already holds his money accounts, meal plan, and dorm entrance. He's afraid he will lose it. The librarian reassures him that he will be fine.

D 1. (A) 2. (A)

[1] a financial aid form

🔘 1-11

W: Hi, Professor. I was wondering if I could ask you for some advice.

M: Of course, that's what I do. What can I do for you?

W: Well, I was going over my financial situation, and I'm really aggravated about it because, well, I just don't think I'm going to be able to afford to stay at this university for more than a year. And I really would prefer not to transfer. I mean, I love it here.

M: Okay, well I'm sure we can figure something out. Um, have you filled out a financial aid form yet?

W: No, I don't think so.

M: All right, then that's your first task. That form will help to figure out your eligibility for loans and, um, need-based scholarships. Actually, I'm certain that you have to complete that form even if you're going for a merit-based scholarship.

W: Oh, wow. So where can I get it? And who do I turn it into? And what kind of information do they ask for?

M: Wow, that's a lot of questions. I'm pretty sure you can pick it up at the Financial Assistance Office. That is where you should return it as well. Oh! Actually, I think the Financial Assistance Office has set up an interface so that you can complete the form via the Internet.

W: Really? Wow, that's so convenient!

M: Yes, it really is. Um, just find the site for the university's Financial Assistance Office, and you can probably hyperlink to the form from there.

W: I think I'll do that right now. Wait, do you know what kind of information I'll need to fill out the form?

M: Um, I think it would be most prudent to fill out the form with a copy of last year's tax returns. That should have all the information you'll need.

W: Okay, great. I have a copy of that in my room.

M: Oh! And if you get the form in within the next couple of days, you might be eligible for some of the departmental scholarships we're awarding for next semester. We have both need- and merit-based scholarships available.

W: That's excellent! Thank you so much.

A student asks a professor for advice about receiving financial aid. Her professor tells her that in order to get a loan or a scholarship, she must fill out the financial aid form. The form can be found at the financial aid office or online. The professor urges her to fill out the form as soon as possible. He says this because there are departmental scholarships available for the following semester. The student is very grateful for her professor's help and advice.

Practice with Lectures

A   **1.** Ⓑ   **2.** Ⓑ
    ¹Carve image   ²Remove ground

🔊 **1-12**

M1: All right class, so now we've talked about Rembrandt and his life and a bit about his work. He was a really famous painter and engraver. The thing is though, that stuff isn't what made him most famous. Rembrandt pretty much revolutionized the art of etching. We talked a little bit about that technique before, remember? So, who can tell me what etching is?

W: Doesn't it involve burning an image onto a metal plate?

M1: That's right. Good job. The artist usually has a copper plate that he or she coats or covers with an acid-resistant substance. Um, this stuff is usually made of beeswax and resin, and this substance is called, um, bitumen. Altogether, it's called the etching ground. So what the artist does is cover the copper plate with the ground compound, all that stuff that I just mentioned, and he carves a design through it with a sharp tool. You have to carve pretty deep, actually, because you want to get through the ground to uncover the copper underneath. Then the artist exposes the plate to acid, and the parts that are uncovered by the ground get eaten away, and the metal is recessed into those areas, creating channels. So who knows what's done with the metal plates afterwards?

M2: They're used to make prints, right?

M1: Absolutely. Great job. Yes, after the ground compound is removed, ink is poured into the parts that have been eaten away. These channels hold ink really well actually. And then the plate is pressed onto moist paper, and you get a print. Rembrandt was a genius when it came to etchings. I think that after a while, etchings were all he did. Um, let's see, does anyone recognize this etching?

M2: I know that one. It's in a museum in Washington, D.C. Um, I think it's called "Woman and Arrow."

M1: Pretty close. It's called "The Woman with the Arrow." Rembrandt created this etching in, hmm, 1661, I think. Yes, it was 1661.

Etchings are created by covering a copper plate with a ground compound. Then, the artist cuts an image into the compound until the copper plate is exposed underneath. Next, the artist pours acid over the compound. The parts of the copper plate that are covered with the compound remain untouched. The other parts get eaten away by the acid. This creates channels. The artist removes the compound and pours ink into the channels. Finally, the plate is pressed onto moist paper. This creates a print.

B   **1.** Ⓑ   **2.** Ⓒ
    ¹the mouth and the stomach   ²Burning

🔊 **1-13**

After food is swallowed, the digestive process keeps going in the esophagus. The esophagus is basically a long tube. It pretty much goes straight up and down from your mouth to your stomach. At the top of the esophagus is the, um, the upper sphincter which is a ring-like muscle. This stays closed most of the time, for good reason. See, after you swallow, the upper sphincter opens up to let the food in. Then, it closes right away so that the food doesn't come back out.

Um, so once food is let into the esophagus, a process starts that's called, um, peristalsis, the wave-like movements of the muscles. During peristalsis, the muscles in the esophagus push the food down the tube. Picture a toothpaste tube. To get toothpaste out of the tube, you have to squeeze from one end to the other. That's what peristalsis is like, except that there's a wave-like motion from the top of the tube to the bottom. The food is pushed in front of the wave till it reaches the bottom of the esophagus. At the bottom of the, um, the esophagus, is the lower sphincter. When food gets to that point, the lower sphincter opens up to let food pass into the stomach. Then it closes up really fast so that the acids from the stomach can't get into the esophagus.

And speaking of acid getting into the esophagus, those acids are what causes the feeling called heartburn. Heartburn doesn't actually have anything to do with the heart. Actually, um, heartburn takes place in the esophagus. It's what happens when the lower sphincter gets weak. Gastric acids from the stomach enter the esophagus. They cause a burning feeling. See, these acids don't cause problems in the stomach because the stomach has, um, well it has a lining, kind of like armor, that keeps it from getting hurt. The esophagus doesn't have that kind of lining or armor, so gastric acids can really harm it.

After food leaves the mouth, digestion goes on in the esophagus. The esophagus is a long tube that connects the mouth and the stomach. Food enters the esophagus through the upper sphincter. Then, the food is pushed through the esophagus by a process called peristalsis. Peristalsis happens when the muscles squeeze food down the tube. Food leaves the esophagus through the lower sphincter. If the lower sphincter is weak, you can get heartburn.

C **1.** Ⓓ **2.** Ⓐ

[1]Plates meet each other at fault lines.

🔘 1-14

M1: The next chapter in our book discusses earthquakes. Um, well, I hope you've all read this chapter because I will be asking questions from the chapter for participation points today. Okay, to begin, the authors talk about the plate tectonic theory as a pretty widely accepted explanation for earthquakes. Who can tell me what this theory states? Yes, go on…

W: I think the authors said that the plate tectonic theory was that the earth's surface is made up of these large plates that are kind of disconnected. I think they move against each other.

M1: Very good. All right, so yes, the earth's surface is not one solid piece of land. Um, it's made up of these plates that move against each other. The worst earthquakes tend to happen where one plate is kind of pushed under another. These quakes start really deep in the ground. Other quakes, um, less severe quakes, happen where the plates slide against each other. Okay, so how many major earthquake zones are there?

M2: Three.

M1: And what are they?

M2: Um, one lies around the Pacific Ocean. I think another is called the, um, the trans-asiatic belt. I'm pretty sure that one goes across the Mediterranean countries and then across Asia. And the third, the third one is in the ocean, the mid-ocean ridges.

M1: Excellent. Okay, so does anyone have questions about plate tectonic theory?

W: Well, what about earthquakes that don't happen in these zones? I mean, aren't there ever earthquakes that, um, that don't occur around a seismic zone?

M1: Great question. Yes, I think that sometimes earthquakes do happen away from, um, seismic zones. These ones are tough to figure out though. So, quakes that don't occur along plate boundaries are called, um, intraplate earthquakes. I don't think that scientists have figured out the causes for those yet, but I think that they do agree that, um, there's a lot of, um, ground stress where these quakes happen.

One theory about why earthquakes happen is called the plate tectonic theory. The earth's surface is made up of plates that move against each other. The most severe quakes happen when one plate gets pushed underneath another one. Less severe quakes happen when plates rub against each other. Scientists don't really know what causes them. There are three major earthquake zones on the earth. But sometimes earthquakes happen away from the seismic zones due to ground stress.

D **1.** Ⓑ **2.** Ⓐ

[1]have the right to vote [2]give women the right to vote

🔘 1-15

A thing to note about the women's suffrage movement in this country is that women were fighting, um, I guess you could say it was a tough battle. Oh, by the way, suffrage means the right to vote. There had been a long history of women not having the right to vote. Even in the earliest democracies, in ancient Greece and Rome, women couldn't vote. And experts say that these times gave us the best thoughts and ideas of all time.

Anyway, let's just say that women had a lot of history to break down before they could vote. Right. Um, so women in Great Britain and the United States fought for the right to vote during the 1800s and 1900s. Women in Great Britain struggled in the same way American women did for this right. However, we're just going to look at American women and what they did. So the women's suffrage movement started in the U.S. around the same time as the anti-slavery movement. Um, that would have been during the, um, the mid-1800s. Right. So this is what happened. A group of really active women started pushing for anti-slavery laws. And while they were doing this, they found that women's issues in America also needed to be looked at.

So these women realized that something wasn't right about how women were treated. So this is what they did. They held a couple of, um, meetings in different parts of the country to draw women in those regions into the cause. Now, the problem was that there was no way of giving women the right to vote nationally. Now, states could give this right to women. But, that would only affect women in that state. Because of this, these women believed that it was vital to get an amendment, or change, to the Constitution to give women the right to vote. This would, um, give women the right to vote pretty much nationwide. So what they did was start a group called the National Woman's Suffrage Association. The purpose of the, um, the NWSA was to get an amendment to the Constitution.

There is a long history of a lack of voting rights for women. In the mid-1800s, American women started fighting for their right to vote. This started during the anti-slavery movement. While women were fighting for rights for others, they realized that they did not have many rights themselves. American women started meeting about what to do. They realized that the only way that all American women would get the right to vote would be to push for an amendment to the Constitution. So, they created the National Woman's Suffrage Association for that purpose.

Integrated Listening & Speaking

A

1. (1) Bob is frustrated because his roommate is messy.
   (2) Bob is frustrated because his roommate's stuff is all over the place.
2. (1) Bob's roommate leaves food containers, socks, papers, and toothpaste lying around.
   (2) The things lying around are food containers, socks, papers, and toothpaste.
3. (1) Ann tells Bob to talk to his roommate about the mess.
   (2) Ann thinks Bob should talk to his roommate.

🔊 1-16

Bob is very frustrated because his roommate is very messy. His roommate leaves food containers lying around the room, socks and papers all over everything,

and toothpaste seeping out of the tube and into the sink. Bob is concerned that because of the unhygienic room, he might get sick. Bob doesn't want to get sick because of a messy room. Bob asks Ann for advice about this situation. Ann convinces Bob to talk to his roommate. She says it is important because Bob has to live with his roommate for another two and a half months. Ann also suggests that Bob and his roommate clean the room together once a week. She thinks this will help because Bob's roommate will realize how messy the room is if he has to clean it. Bob appreciates Ann's help and thanks her for it.

B

1. (1) The student needs a textbook.
   (2) What the student needs is a textbook.
2. (1) The book the student needs is out of stock.
   (2) The campus bookstore doesn't have the book the student needs in stock.
3. (1) The shopkeeper suggests that the student reserve a copy and use the library's copy in the meantime.
   (2) The shopkeeper tells the student to use the library's copy until the new shipment arrives.

🔊 1-17

A student is looking for a book at the campus bookstore. The shopkeeper informs him that the textbook is out of stock. He says a new shipment will arrive in a week. The student panics because his professor has already assigned several chapters of reading from the book. The shopkeeper makes a suggestion. First, he suggests that the student reserve a copy of the book from the new shipment. That way, he can make sure to get a copy. Then, the shopkeeper thinks the student should see if the book is on reserve at the library. That way, the student can do his reading without getting behind while he waits for the new shipment of textbooks.

C

1. (1) The process explained is etching.
   (2) The lecture explains how to do an etching.
2. (1) The first step is to apply a ground compound to the plate.
   (2) First, you must put a ground compound on the plate.
3. (1) What happens last is the plate is pressed on moist paper.
   (2) The last step is when the artist presses the plate on moist paper.

Rembrandt was a famous artist in the 1600s. He did paintings and engravings, but he was most famous for his etchings. Etching is a technique that involves burning an image onto a metal plate. Usually, a copper plate is used. It can be done by applying a ground compound to a copperplate. The ground compound is made up of beeswax, resin, and bitumen. Then, the artist carves an image into the ground deep enough to reach the copper. The plate is exposed to acid, and the image gets burned into the plate. The artist then removes the ground compound and pours ink into the channels created by the acid. The plate is pressed onto moist paper. The image from the plate is transferred to the paper, creating a print.

D

1. (1) The esophagus connects the mouth and stomach.
   (2) The mouth and stomach are connected by the esophagus.
2. (1) Food enters through the upper sphincter.
   (2) The upper sphincter lets food into the esophagus.
3. (1) Heartburn feels like burning.
   (2) Heartburn causes a burning sensation.

The esophagus is an important part of the digestive system. It is a long tube that connects the mouth and stomach. After it leaves the mouth, food enters the esophagus through the upper sphincter. From there, a process called peristalsis pushes food down the tube. This process happens when muscles in the esophagus squeeze food down. When the food reaches the bottom of the esophagus, it goes to the stomach from the esophagus through the lower sphincter. A disease of the esophagus is called heartburn. Heartburn happens because the lower sphincter is weak. This lets acids from the stomach enter the esophagus and cause a burning feeling. The esophagus can't handle that because it does not have the special lining, or armor, that the stomach has. Stomach acids can destroy the esophagus because of this.

Mini TOEFL iBT

A 1. ⓓ 2. Ⓑ 3. ⓒ 4. ⓒ 5. ⓒ

W: Hi, Professor. I was wondering if I could ask you

something.

M: Of course. How may I be of assistance?

W: Well, I'm taking your developmental psychology class.

M: Right. I recognize you from the lectures. You sit in the first couple of rows usually, right?

W: Yes, that's me. Anyway, I'm taking this class with you, and I didn't do so well on the first exam. Well, I guess I did okay, but I'm not really satisfied with my grade. And I was wondering if you might be able to help me figure out how to bring it up for the next exam.

M: All right, well what did you get on the exam?

W: I got a B-. But I studied really hard, and I really need an A in this class for my graduate school application.

M: All right, well a B- isn't bad for the first exam. But since you're determined, let's figure out how you can get an A on the next two exams. That should bring you pretty close to an A for the class. And really, if you participate in class, I'll take that into account also. I mean, participation does count for, um, I think ten percent of your grade.

W: Okay, I'll try to participate more.

M: Great! That's an easy step to take. All right, so what did you do to study for this exam?

W: Well, um, I went over all of my lecture notes a few times and paid attention to, um, to definitions and theories. Oh! And I memorized Piaget's stages of development.

M: Well, that's a good start. And Piaget definitely came up on the exam a few times. What about the textbook? How did you review that material?

W: Well, um, I went over what I had highlighted when reading earlier this semester. And, um, I took notes on that stuff, and I, um, reviewed the notes a few times.

M: Well it sounds like you did everything right. Hm… Oh! What you should do for the next exam is talk to my teaching assistant for the class. I've given her old copies of exams from previous semesters, so you should try to, well, practice with those. And if you miss some of the stuff on those exams, well, then you know what you need to work on for the actual one.

W: Really? I can do that? I never knew that was an option!

M: You can certainly do that.

W: Great! And all the TA's information is on the syllabus, right?

M: Yes, it is. Email her before the next exam, but give yourself at least a week in case she doesn't get back to you right away.

W: Thanks, Professor. And I promise to participate more in class also.

M: Great! Student participation is my favorite part of my job. Good luck with everything!

 1. Ⓒ **2.** Ⓐ **3.** Ⓒ **4.** Ⓑ **5.** Ⓒ
6. Ⓑ

 1-21

All right, class. Today we're going to talk about reptiles. Now, as you probably remember, reptiles are cold-blooded animals that are hatched from eggs and have scales. Does this sound familiar to everyone? Okay, good. Now, I think the best thing to do would be to get into examples of reptiles. Let's see, um, raise your hand if you've ever heard of an animal called the horned toad. Okay, so many of you have heard of this creature. I see some questions in your eyes. You are probably wondering why we're going to talk about the horned toad since I just mentioned that we'll be discussing reptiles.

As you all know, a toad is an amphibian – an animal that starts out life living in water with gills and ends up living on land with lungs. So here is the issue with the horned toad – it's not actually a toad at all! The horned toad is actually a lizard! It's a reptile! The reason people confuse it for a toad is that it is kind of round. So from now on, if you hear of someone talking about a horned toad, let them know that it's actually a lizard.

Anyway, the horned lizard doesn't actually have horns. The things that look like horns are really just spiny scales. These scales act as protection for the lizard. If an animal is trying to eat the lizard, it will puff up, kind of like a balloon, and that will make the scales stick out. And when these spiny scales are sticking out, it's hard for other animals to swallow the lizard.

The horned lizard has other ways of protecting itself also. One of these ways is called camouflage. Does everyone remember what camouflage is? No? Okay, well camouflage is when an animal blends into its surroundings. The horned lizard does this really well. The horned lizard usually lives in deserts, and it is a, um, a brownish color. The lizard's color allows it to blend into the desert.

Some kinds of horned lizard have yet another way of protecting themselves. Now, this is kind of gross, but some of these lizards can shoot blood out of the corners of their eyes. This really confuses their predators. Also, this blood contains a substance that, um, that doesn't taste good. That makes animals that might have wanted to eat the lizard not want to eat it anymore.

Vocabulary Review

 A

 1-22

1. to cause dislike, anger, or insult (offend)
2. a series of actions leading to an end (process)
3. to change completely (revolutionize)
4. a delivery (shipment)
5. of a great degree, usually used in a negative context (severe)
6. not contributing to health (unhygienic)
7. general ideas about a body of fact, science, or art (theory)
8. a protective covering (armor)
9. to make certain (ensure)
10. a state or topic of disagreement (issue)
11. unhealthy because it's dirty (unsanitary)
12. having to do with the stomach (gastric)
13. a change or correction (amendment)
14. the wave-like movement of muscles in the esophagus that pushes food down the tube (peristalsis)
15. one who cuts figures, letters, or designs into wood or metal (engraver)

B

1. All right now, moving right along, the next topic to cover is the stomach.
2. Well, armor pretty much means protection.
3. A process is kind of like the way you get from the beginning to the end.
4. That lower sphincter stays closed for good reason.
5. So first of all, you cover the copper plate with a ground compound.
6. Now in just a minute, you'll see a filmstrip about earthquakes.

Unit 2　Listening for Main Purpose

Basic Drill

A **1.** Ⓐ **2.** Ⓒ **3.** Ⓓ
 1-24

M: Hey, so I think I might need a part-time job.
W: Really? Why?

M: I was just calculating my expenses for the semester, and if I want to have any fun, I'm going to need a little extra cash. I mean, I have enough for food and supplies and the basics. I just don't have enough to go out on the weekends.

W: So you're thinking like fifteen or twenty hours a week?

M: No, more like ten hours.

W: Oh, so you don't want to work a lot - just enough for a night out a week or so, right?

M: Yeah, that's basically it.

W: Oh, well, you should check the school paper's classifieds. They have listings for all kinds of part-time jobs around campus.

M: Thanks! I'll definitely check that out.

🔘 1-25

W: Hi, Professor, may I ask your advice?

M: Sure. What's the problem?

W: I've been working really hard in your class, but I'm having a little trouble understanding the material in the textbook.

M: Well the material is a little complicated. I've actually had quite a few students ask me for advice about this. So I think what you should do is take notes on the material while you're going over it. You know: key words, concepts, and such. And if that doesn't work, you could always go to the learning center. They'll help you with other tactics.

W: Oh okay. Thanks a lot. Oh, do you know how much they charge at the learning center?

M: Oh, those services are free of charge.

🔘 1-26

W: Hey, how're you going to study for this huge history exam?

M: Oh, man. I don't know, but I figure I'll be spending many long hours in the library.

W: The library? Really? I don't even know what the library's hours are anymore.

M: Wow, it really has been a while since you went last. The library's open twenty-four hours a day right now. At least till final exams are over. Then it'll go back to regular hours.

W: Oh, so studying at the library would be really convenient. I mean, I could be there all night if I needed to.

M: Yeah, you could. And the nice thing is that they've got all kinds of different couches and desks and tables. So, you could choose a variety of different places, depending on your mood.

W: Really? That sounds good. I get a little restless when I study, so different environments are good. And I'll bet it's really quiet, isn't it?

M: Yeah, it's really quiet. I've even napped there between chapters.

B 1. Ⓑ 2. Ⓑ 3. Ⓐ

🔘 1-27

Technology is useful to humans for many reasons. Unfortunately, it has also been used by humans to harm the environment. Pollution is one way in which the environment is harmed by people. For example, the factories that people build to produce goods emit smoke into the air. Many factories dump waste that they produce into rivers and the ocean. Additionally, cars, trains, and ships spew smoke into the air. Also, humans use computers a lot. New computers come out all the time and make old computers obsolete. Computers are not recyclable, so we have to throw them away. This fills up landfills.

🔘 1-28

The trickle-down effect in economics is a disputed theory. It states that big businesses should be allowed to do as they please because lower-level businesses will flourish from their successes. They should not be regulated or taxed by the government. Many economic theorists believe that this theory is only supported by right-wing economists. Others think that it's really not a valid theory at all. They don't believe that big businesses should be allowed to do whatever they want. Instead, they think that the government should regulate these businesses. They think that big businesses should be taxed so that the money will definitely be able to go to those who need it most.

🔘 1-29

The 1930s brought about a change in the film industry. This change greatly affected all in the industry, especially the actors. Before the 1930s, film was silent. It wasn't until the 1930s that the advent of "talkies" brought sound to cinema. Before the 1930s, actors like Charlie Chaplin were really popular. The films that Chaplin starred in are some of the most famous films from the silent film era. However, once sound was introduced into the film industry, Charlie Chaplin no longer got film roles. While he was a great actor in silent films, he was not good at doing speaking parts. His physical comedy did not translate well into sound. This sort of thing happened to many actors when the conversion from silent film to talkies took place.

Practice with Conversations

A   **1.** (A)   **2.** (C)

[1]Review class notes

🔘 1-30

M1: Wow, that final is going to cover a lot of material. We should probably start studying soon.

M2: Yeah, we need to figure out the best way to cover all this stuff in two weeks.

M1: Yeah, we definitely need a method. How many units do we have to cover?

M2: Um… okay. Let me check my syllabus. Okay, so according to the syllabus, we have to cover ten units worth of material from the textbook plus class notes.

M1: Well, the class notes are easy. We'll go over each of our notes and just fill in any blanks we might have.

M2: Yeah, that's a good plan. I didn't miss any classes this semester. Did you?

M1: I missed one a month and a half ago because I was sick. But I got the notes from someone the week after, so I have all the notes.

M2: Okay, so we've got class notes covered. Now we just have to get our units organized.

M1: Yeah, so that's going to be the time-consuming bit. Have you read all the units yet?

M2: Yeah, I have. You?

M1: Yeah. Okay, so I've got an idea. We'll each take half of the units to summarize. You know, we'll make an outline for each of them with key words, definitions, ideas, and such.

M2: Yeah, that sounds good. All right, so how's this? I'll do the first five units, and you take the second five units.

M1: Sounds good to me. And we should have the outlines done by next week so that we can have a week to go over the stuff.

M2: Yeah definitely. We'll do a couple of study sessions next week.

M1: Right, and hopefully, that'll be enough. Anyway, I'm going to start on these outlines. I'll see you later!

Two students are discussing the best method for studying for their final exam. According to the syllabus, they must go over ten units of material and all their class notes. Since they both have all the class notes, they will just look over them to fill in any holes they may have. They will also split the units they have to study in half. Each student will summarize and outline five units within one week's time. Then they will meet to go over the units and class notes together.

B   **1.** (A)   **2.** (C)

[1]Gain international perspective

🔘 1-31

W: Hi. Can I help you?

M: Hi, Professor. My name is John Smith. I was wondering if I could ask you something.

W: Of course, John. What can I do for you?

M: All right, well I know our final is in a week. And I know generally professors don't have to get the final grades in for two weeks afterwards. But the thing is, I've applied for a study abroad position that starts in four weeks, and I need to have all my grades in really early to be accepted to the program. So I was wondering if you'd be able to grade my exam early so I can complete the application process on time.

W: Hm… Okay, so when is the application deadline?

M: A week and a half from today. Three days after the final exam to be precise.

W: And which study abroad program is this?

M: I'm doing a Classics program in Rome. If I'm there for a semester, it'll take care of my Classics minor.

W: Wow, that sounds so exciting. So you're taking care of your minor first? And then you'll finish your major?

M: Yes. I'm already a little ahead on the Finance major, so I can afford to take a semester just focusing on the minor. Plus, it's a great way to travel and get a little international perspective.

W: I absolutely agree. I think all students should do a study abroad program. Anyway, back to your question. I'll make a note of your situation and copy that to my teaching assistant. And one of us will make sure to grade your exam first and get the grades to the registrar.

M: Thank you so much. I really appreciate it.

W: No problem. Glad to help. Good luck on the exam and in Rome!

M: Thanks!

A student asks his professor for a favor. The student is applying for a study abroad program in Classics in Rome. He needs his professor to turn in his grade early so that he may meet the application deadline. The professor is very pleased that her student is taking an opportunity to go abroad. The student is excited about learning new things and gaining a new perspective. The professor says she will make a note and inform her teaching assistant to get the student's grades to the registrar early.

C   **1.** (D)   **2.** (C)

[1]availability

M: Can I help you?

W: Yes, I heard that there are job openings here at the dining hall. Do you still have openings?

M: Yes, we do. Are you looking for a job?

W: Yes, I am.

M: Okay, well the way things work around here is that students who are eligible for work study usually have first dibs at the jobs. After that, we start hiring people who aren't eligible for work study. Are you eligible for work study?

W: Yes, I am. The Financial Aid Office actually sent me here. They said you might be hiring dining hall staff and that this would probably be the most flexible place to work around my classes.

M: Well, we definitely work around the students' class schedules around here. So, I'm going to give you an application to fill out. You just have to let me know what you want to do here in terms of whether you want to cook, serve, clean, work the register, or whatever. You rank the different positions in your order of preference. Oh, and you also need to let us know what your availability is. You know, what days and hours can you work? Then we'll match up your preferences and availability with what we need.

W: Oh, okay.

M: So if you want, you can just take a seat at one of the tables and fill out the application right away.

W: Ok great. Oh, how long after I turn in the application will I find out if I'm going to be hired?

M: Oh, you'll probably be hired if your availability matches what we need. You'll probably get a call in a week.

W: Oh okay, thanks! All right, I'm going to fill out the application. I'll turn it in as soon as I'm done.

A student is inquiring about open job positions at the dining hall. A cafeteria worker tells her that the dining hall is still hiring and asks if she is eligible for work study. The cafeteria worker says that work study students will be hired first. The student confirms that she is eligible. The cafeteria worker tells the student that she will need to fill out an application and indicate her position preferences and hours of availability. Then, the dining hall staff will match their need with the student's preferences and availability. The student will find out if she has a job in a week.

D   **1.** Ⓑ   **2.** False, True, True, False

¹participating in class   ²she participates

W: Hi, Professor. You wanted to see me?

M: Yes, I did. Well remember how a couple of months ago, you came to me and asked for my advice on getting your grade in my class up?

W: Yes, I do. And I want to thank you again for your advice.

M: Not a problem. You've done pretty well so far. Your exam scores have improved a lot. The only thing that hasn't really gotten better is your class participation. I'm kind of surprised about that. It's a really easy way to get an extra ten percent on your grade.

W: Oh, well I've tried, Professor. I just get really nervous saying stuff in front of the class.

M: Why is that?

W: I just really don't want to sound stupid in front of everyone.

M: Oh, no one's going to think you're stupid. You really do understand the material, you know. It shows from your test scores. You're doing really well in the class otherwise. Besides, we've got such a small class.

W: I know. I just can't seem to bring myself to raise my hand.

M: Well, this isn't usually my style, but if you'd like, I can call on you at first a couple of times. And then maybe after you answer a couple of questions, you'll be more comfortable raising your hand.

W: Well, I guess. I mean, we could try it.

M: Well, that's really all I ask. You see, if you participate, you might be able to bring your grade up to an A by the time the semester's over.

W: Oh, wow. I didn't know I was so close.

M: Well, you really are. It would be a shame if this was what was holding you back.

W: Ok, well, I'm really going to try. I promise.

A professor talks to his student about participating more in class. He tells the student that she is doing really well, and the student's grades have improved a lot. The only thing the student has not improved in is class participation. The student feels really nervous about speaking in front of the class. The professor suggests that he will call on the student first a couple of times. Then, when she is more comfortable talking in front of the class, she can volunteer answers on her own. The professor finally tells the student that if she participates more, she can probably get an A in the class.

Practice with Lectures

A   **1.** Ⓒ   **2.** Ⓓ

1the sun's rays and the atmosphere   2humans and their gadgets

🔊 1-34

Many people may not realize it, but the greenhouse effect and global warming are totally different things. The greenhouse effect is something that happens with all celestial bodies – planets, moons, and such – that have an atmosphere. Anyway, back to the greenhouse effect. The greenhouse effect is a process that happens when the sun's heat enters Earth's atmosphere. The sun's rays warm the earth, and the atmosphere keeps the heat in, just like a greenhouse. It's a very natural thing, and in most cases, the planet system knows how to balance itself out. Anyway, like I said, it's a pretty natural process.

Now all this gets messed up when humans, um, add stuff to Earth's atmosphere. That's when global warming, which is not a natural process, happens. See, what happens is that people create, um, things that create extra heat. For example, cars. We drive cars all the time. So we drive our cars, and our cars burn gas, and this exhaust is pretty hot. And the atmosphere keeps this heat around the planet. Plus, all of our machinery and our factories and stuff, they all produce heat. So all this stuff creates what scientists are calling global warming. Earth's surface and atmosphere just keep getting hotter.

Now global warming has many negative effects, but I think one of the biggest problems with global warming is the melting of polar ice caps and glaciers. See, our planet has huge chunks of ice at both of its poles. And when global warming happens, um, the overall temperature of the planet increases. And what this does is it makes polar ice melt. So when ice melts, it turns into water, which goes into our oceans. And that causes the level of water to rise. And this could also cause major flooding.

The greenhouse effect is a natural occurrence. All celestial bodies with atmospheres experience the greenhouse effect. The sun's rays warm the planet. The atmosphere keeps this heat around the planet. In contrast, global warming is a problem caused by man. The problem occurs when people start creating things that produce extra heat. Global warming causes the overall temperature of Earth to increase, which has negative effects. Most notably, global warming causes polar ice caps and glaciers to melt. This raises the water level of the oceans, which can cause flooding.

B 1. Ⓒ   2. False, True, True, False

1Trickle-down Effect   2Bookseller

🔊 1-35

M1: The next topic we have to discuss is the trickle-down effect. Now this is a theory that has been highly debated in economic circles. It's pretty complicated, but maybe we can figure it out together. Now, who can define the trickle-down effect? Yes?

W1: Okay, so I'm not sure about this, but I think the premise of the theory is that by large businesses doing well and making profits, everybody else does well, too. I mean, because the businesses spread their profits throughout the economy.

M1: Absolutely right. Now, it is still quite an abstract concept. So we're going to use an example that isn't quite the same, but it'll help us get an idea of the trickle-down effect. Okay. So let's say we have an author. This author writes a bestselling novel. Of course, the author will make a lot of money. But who else makes money? Any ideas?

M2: Um… the publishing company?

M1: Definitely. The publishing company will also make a lot of money because it will be printing many copies of the book. All right, who else will make money?

W2: The booksellers will definitely make money off of a best seller. They charge a mark-up, right?

M1: Right again. If a book is in high demand, and most bestsellers are, the booksellers can make a profit because of the mark-up price. They pay a certain amount of money to the publishing house for the books. Then, they charge the customer more. That way, they're making a profit. Let's see. Another industry that would stand to gain from an author writing a bestseller is the shipping industry. The books have to get from the publishing house to the bookstore. So, shipping companies would get business from that and profit. Anyway, are there any questions about this?

The trickle-down effect is a debated economic theory. It involves the profits of one business positively affecting connecting businesses and individuals in the economy. An example of how this theory works can be an author who writes a bestselling novel. The author will absolutely make money off of the book. Other companies who will profit from the book are the publishers, the booksellers, and the shippers.

C 1. Ⓒ   2. Ⓐ

1advance film   2special effects

So today, we're going to talk about how filmmaking was done before the 1930s. So before the 1930s, most filmmaking was done using what they called crank cameras. See, there were two types of cameras back then. There were motorized cameras and crank cameras. When using crank cameras, you had to crank the film forward by hand. Motorized cameras would forward the film automatically. But the motors on these cameras were so big and bulky that they were really hard to carry around. So instead, filmmakers used crank cameras.

Anyway, how these crank cameras worked was the cameraman would either hold the camera or have the camera on a tripod. Women didn't make films during this era, so we can correctly call the person holding the camera a cameraman. The cameraman would aim the camera lens at the scene he was trying to record. Then, he would crank the handle on the camera to advance the film. Now, this process could be pretty difficult. The cameraman had to crank the handle at a uniform pace so that the movie didn't seem rushed or delayed, which took lots of practice. But, once the cameraman had mastered this skill, he could alter the pace to make special effects. For example, the experienced cameraman could decrease the number of cranks for a scene. This would make the actions on film look rushed and kind of disconnected.

Also, for a good part of this time, films were shot on a single reel. This meant most films were pretty short – fifteen to twenty minutes, usually. Then, right before the First World War – which started in 1914, remember – filmmakers pioneered the double-reel process. This allowed for much longer films. This is also where the icon of the double-reel camera that we see everywhere comes from.

Filmmaking before the 1930s was very different from filmmaking today. During that time, there were two types of cameras – motorized cameras and crank cameras. Filmmakers generally used crank cameras because they were easier to carry. The cameraman would turn the handle on a crank camera to advance the film. This was difficult and took a lot of practice. When the cameraman had mastered this skill he could alter the pace to make special effects. Also, during most of this era, films were shot on a single reel. Then, just before 1914, the double-reel process was introduced. This is where the double-reel film icon comes from.

D   **1.** Ⓒ   **2.** Ⓐ

¹Took jazz around the world   ²Wrote and recorded many songs

W1: All right class, now that we know a little bit about jazz music, we're going to talk about some jazz musicians. Personally, I think there's no better place to start than with one of my favorites, Duke Ellington. He was born in North Carolina, but he didn't become famous till he moved to... does anyone know?

M: New York City! He played in Harlem, right?

W1: That's right! Duke Ellington got his first New York City gig at the Cotton Club in Harlem. Harlem was a hot spot for up-and-coming music and musicians back then. Anyway, that's where Duke Ellington started to be well-known. So yeah, after his first gig at the Cotton Club, Duke Ellington got a weekly radio show. And that spread his music everywhere. So then, a bunch of famous clientele started to go to the Cotton Club as well. This made the Cotton Club the most famous jazz club in Harlem. Anyway, the Duke made two major contributions to jazz. First of all, he brought jazz music to all corners of the world. His band traveled everywhere, to all continents. Secondly, he wrote and recorded hundreds of jazz hits. Can anyone name any famous Duke Ellington songs?

W2: Um... "Take the A Train."

W1: That's right! "Take the A Train" is probably one of his most famous songs. It's a song about the subway line you take in New York City to get up to Harlem and the Cotton Club. Some of the Duke's other famous songs are "Rockin' in Rhythm," "Satin Doll," "New Orleans," and "Crescendo in Blue."

Duke Ellington was a famous jazz musician from the early twentieth century. He was born in North Carolina in the late 1800s, which was where he started taking music lessons. He got his first big gig in New York City at the Cotton Club. This gig made him famous. It also made the Cotton Club the most famous jazz club in Harlem. The Duke and his band traveled all around the world, including Europe and Asia. One of his most famous songs is called "Take the A Train."

Integrated Listening & Speaking

1. (1) The purpose of this conversation is to decide the best way to study for a final exam.

    (2) Two students have this conversation so that they can figure out how to study for a final exam.

2. (1) The final exam will cover all of the class notes and ten units from the textbook.

    (2) The information on the final exam will come from all the class notes and ten units from the textbook.

3. (1) The students' outlines will include key words, ideas, and concepts from each unit.

    (2) The students will include in their outlines key words, ideas, and concepts from each unit.

🔘 **1-38**

Two students have a final exam in two weeks' time. They are discussing the best method for studying for their exam. According to the syllabus, they must go over ten units of material from their textbook and all their class notes. The students confirm that they both have all of the class notes. Since they both have all the class notes, they will just look over them to fill in the holes they may have. The students decide the best way to cover the material from the textbook is to divide the units between them. Each student will summarize and outline five units within one week's time. In their outlines, they will include key words, ideas, and concepts from each of the units. They decide on a one-week deadline to complete the outlines. After that, the students will have a study session. They will meet to go over the units and class notes together as a final step in their exam preparation.

B

1. (1) The purpose of this conversation is to find out if the dining hall will hire the student.

    (2) The student has this conversation because she wants to work at the dining hall.

2. (1) The student could work as a cook, a food server, or a cashier.

    (2) The jobs at the dining hall include cook, food server, and cashier.

3. (1) The student will find out if she has a job in a week.

    (2) The dining hall staff will contact the student in a week.

🔘 **1-39**

A student is inquiring about open job positions at the dining hall. A cafeteria worker tells her that the dining hall is still hiring and asks if she is eligible for work study. The cafeteria worker says that work study students will be hired first. The student confirms that she is eligible. The cafeteria worker tells the student

that she will need to fill out an application and indicate position preferences and hours of availability. In terms of position preference, the cafeteria worker tells the student that she can work as a cook, a food server, or as a cashier. Once the student completes the application, the dining hall staff will match their need with the student's preference and availability. The student will find out if she has a job in a week.

C

1. (1) The purpose of this lecture is to explain the difference between the greenhouse effect and global warming.

    (2) The topic of this lecture is how the greenhouse effect and global warming differ.

2. (1) The greenhouse effect is caused by the atmosphere keeping heat from the sun's rays close to Earth.

    (2) What causes the greenhouse effect is when the atmosphere keeps heat from the sun's rays close to Earth.

3. (1) A negative effect of global warming is it causes polar ice caps and glaciers to melt.

    (2) A bad thing that happens with global warming is that polar ice caps and glaciers start to melt.

🔘 **1-40**

The greenhouse effect is a natural occurrence. All celestial bodies with atmospheres experience the greenhouse effect. The sun's rays warm the planet. In turn, the atmosphere keeps this heat around the planet. In contrast, global warming is a problem caused by man. It is not a natural occurrence. More specifically, it is caused by the machines that people create, such as cars. Cars produce extra heat, and Earth's atmosphere holds this heat in. Because of this, global warming causes the overall temperature of the earth to increase, which has negative effects. Most notably, global warming causes polar ice caps and glaciers to melt. This raises the water level of the oceans, which can cause flooding.

D

1. (1) The purpose of the lecture is to explain what filmmaking was like before the 1930s.

    (2) The lecture is about what filmmaking was like before the 1930s.

2. (1) Filmmakers didn't use motorized cameras because they were big, bulky, and difficult to carry around.

    (2) Filmmakers preferred crank cameras because

they were lighter than motorized cameras.

3. (1) Cameramen created special effects by changing the pace of the crank.
   (2) Special effects were created by changing the pace of the crank.

🔘 1-41

Filmmaking before the 1930s was very different from filmmaking today. During that time, there were two types of cameras – motorized cameras and crank cameras. Filmmakers generally used crank cameras because they were easier to carry. Motorized cameras were big and bulky. Crank cameras were placed on a tripod, and the cameraman would turn the handle on the camera to advance the film. This was a difficult skill to master and took a lot of practice. When the cameraman had mastered this skill, he could alter the pace to make special effects. For example, he could crank slower to make the action in the film look disconnected. Also during most of this era, films were shot on a single reel. Then, just before 1914, the double-reel process was introduced. This is where the double-reel film icon comes from.

Mini TOEFL iBT

A   1. Ⓒ   2. Ⓐ   3. Ⓑ   4. Ⓑ   5. Ⓓ

🔘 1-42

M: So, where do I check these books out?

W: You'll have to go downstairs to the circulation desk. It's at the bottom of the stairs to the right.

M: Oh, okay. So how long can I keep the books?

W: Well our general lending time is 4 weeks. Most students find that that's sufficient.

M: What if I need them for more time though?

W: Well you can always renew your due date. And there are actually a couple of ways you can do that. You can bring the books back and renew them at the circulation desk. Or you can just extend them online. You just have to create an account on the library's website. And one of the options on that page is "Renew Library Materials."

M: Ok, that sounds easy enough.

W: Yeah, it really isn't that complicated at all. It's pretty easy to take care of actually if that's what you need.

M: Okay, great. Oh, hey, my roommate said there might be a time when I need to turn the books in earlier. Is that true?

W: Yes, it is. That doesn't happen very often, but every now and then someone will need the book you've

checked out. And if that happens, they can recall it, which means that they can request it. Now, they can't do that unless you've had the book for more than a week. But if you checked a book out over a week ago and someone else needs it, that person can recall it.

M: Okay, so what exactly does that mean?

W: Well, if one of the books you borrow gets recalled, you'll get an email. So make sure you check your email daily. And after that, you'll have twenty-four hours to return the book.

M: What happens if I can't bring it back in twenty-four hours?

W: You have to figure out a way to do that. Otherwise you get charged a really steep fee. It ends up being $10 a day.

M: Oh wow. That's a lot of money.

W: Yeah, it is.

M: Okay, what if I still need the book? Then what happens?

W: Well you have to bring it in, and the person who recalled it will pick it up. But after a week, you can recall it yourself.

M: Really?

W: Yeah. So it's not such a huge deal. Besides, it hardly ever happens. So go check out your books, and don't worry about it.

M: Thanks!

B   1. Ⓑ   2. Ⓒ   3. Ⓐ   4. Ⓐ Ⓑ
       5. Ⓑ   6. Ⓑ

🔘 2-01

M1: All right class, we're going to continue our botany unit with a discussion about the Venus Flytrap. Now, the Venus Flytrap is a carnivorous plant. It's kind of strange that a plant would use animals for food since this usually happens the other way around. But the flytrap does. Anyway, who can tell me what a Venus Flytrap eats?

M2: Flies!

M1: Of course. Flies. But flies aren't the only thing the flytraps eat. What else?

W1: Spiders?

M1: Very good. Basically, the Venus Flytrap will eat any insect or spider that gets caught in its leaves. The way they work is that they have these trigger "hairs" on the ends of their leaves. If something touches these hairs in rapid succession twice, the leaves will close on the bug, forming a trap. Now, why do you think the flytrap waits till something touches the hairs twice?

W2: Um, because it may not be a bug?

M1: Well, yes. Say it's raining. If the flytrap didn't wait for the second touch, it'll be closed through an entire rainstorm, and it wouldn't get any food. See, if the trap closes, it stays closed for a few hours. And if there's nothing in the trap, that's a lot of potential food that the flytrap has missed out on. Okay, so let's say a flytrap catches a spider. The leaves of the trap close, and end up sealing the spider in. The trap becomes something of a stomach. Then the flytrap will start to digest the spider by secreting enzymes into the trap. This process takes about ten days. That's a long time just to digest! Then, the trap will open up again and await its next victim. Now why do you think flytraps need to eat bugs?

M2: They need the food!

M1: Close, but not exactly. They need the nutrients that the bugs bring. See, flytraps are found in the swamplands of the Carolinas. The soil there isn't really rich in nutrients. So they need to find another way to get the kind of nutrients they need, particularly nitrogen and some minerals and vitamins. They get all their energy from the sun, but unlike other plants, they can't get nutrients from the soil because the soil doesn't have enough. So they have to eat bugs.

Vocabulary Review

A

 2-02

1. a three-legged stand (tripod)
2. a procedure or process (method)
3. based on general ideas rather than specific examples (abstract)
4. exact (precise)
5. having to do with something in space (celestial)
6. a claim or right (dibs)
7. beyond the boundaries of one's country (abroad)
8. a large body of moving ice (glacier)
9. a summary outline of a course (syllabus)
10. net gains minus expenses (profit)
11. a more favorable option (preference)
12. a term into which an academic year is divided (semester)
13. a body of people served by an establishment (clientele)
14. strong feeling of regret (shame)
15. qualified to participate or be chosen (eligible)

B

1. That isn't the way I usually do things, but I guess it would be okay this time.
2. It's kind of hard to explain an abstraction, but it's just like something based on an idea.
3. People think global warming and the greenhouse effect are the same thing. On the contrary, they're quite different.
4. Anyway, back to what we were discussing.
5. That was the way things were back a long time ago, but I digress. We were talking about how things are now.
6. So, even though global warming and the greenhouse effect employ similar processes, they're not exactly the same thing.

Unit 3 Listening for Major Details

Basic Drill

A 1. ⓒ 2. ⓒ 3. ⓓ

2-04

M: Excuse me. I need to see your school ID before you can enter.

W: Well, that's the problem. I lost my purse, and my ID was in it. What can I do?

M: That's not a problem. Just show me some other photo ID.

W: Umm, everything was in my purse - my driver's license, credit cards, everything.

M: I see, but I can't let you in. Do you have any other ID?

W: Yeah! I have a passport. It's in my room.

M: Uh, you know you can't get to your room without your ID?

W: Are you kidding? Come on!

M: Okay, I will follow you to your room. Then you can show me your passport.

2-05

W: Hello, Matt. Come here.

M: Yes?

W: I want to tell you that your paper on American federalism was excellent. I think you should try to get it published.

M: Oh my God, really?

W: Yes. You have some good points that haven't been discussed very much. If you want, I will send it to a friend who is the editor of "Politics Magazine." What do you think?

M: That's great.

W: Have you thought about graduate school? I really think you have a future in political science.

M: I have thought about it a bit.

W: Really consider it. You are a great writer, and you always produce good work.

M: Okay, thanks.

◉ 2-06

W: Hello, do you need anything?

M: Yes, I just need to tell you I am going to miss orientation. So when can I get the information I will miss?

W: You will miss orientation? Why?

M: I am going to take a trip to New York with a friend.

W: That's it? You need to come to orientation. You will get your class schedule, room assignment, fix any schedule problems, and learn about your professors. Trust me; it is very important.

M: Really? I didn't know that. I thought it wasn't a very big deal. Okay, I will cancel my trip. That will be disappointing.

W: That's a good decision. Make sure you are here before nine o'clock.

B 1. (D) 2. (C) 3. (D)

◉ 2-07

The Cuban Missile Crisis is recognized as the peak of the Cold War. At the time, the Soviet Union had a severe disadvantage in their nuclear arsenal compared to America. In an attempt to catch up with the U.S., Nikita Kruschev ordered nuclear missiles to be based in Cuba. President Kennedy feared having nuclear weapons based only 90 miles from American territory. Kennedy decided to use a naval blockade of Cuba as well as an ultimatum, but preparations for a full invasion were being made. To solve the crisis, Kruschev and Kennedy agreed publicly to have the missiles withdrawn in return for an American promise not to invade Cuba. In secret, Kennedy also agreed to withdraw American missiles from Turkey.

◉ 2-08

Perhaps the most famous building in America is the Empire State Building. The building represents the country's transition into the modern era, not only in its size, but its design as well. For example, its well-known shape was designed because of the New York City Zoning Law of 1916. This reduced the amount of shadows in the city. Also, the top of the 102-story building was originally intended to be a dock for airships. This idea was abandoned after a few failed tests, but the building retained the shape. Since the collapse of the World Trade Center, it is again the tallest building in New York, and some consider it to be the 8th Wonder of the World.

◉ 2-09

Sociologists often call America a melting pot. In a melting pot, all the parts melt and are mixed together to form something new. America is a country made by immigrants. The original settlers were from England, France and Germany. Later, large numbers of Irish, Italian, Chinese, and Latin immigrants made a new home in the USA. All of these people have added to the mixed American culture. For example, Chinese and Mexican foods are very popular. Also, some Americans have studied Spanish, and many people can understand a basic amount of the language. Many pubs have Irish themes, and many cities hold large parades for St. Patrick's Day.

Practice with Conversations

A 1. (D) 2. (B)

¹getting married ²waiting on two books

◉ 2-10

W1: Hi, Susan. You wanted to speak to me about something?

W2: Yes, I was wondering if I could talk to you about the term paper due in two weeks.

W1: Sure. What's up?

W2: My sister is getting married next weekend, and I'm the maid of honor, so this week is a little crazy. I was wondering if I could have an extension on the term paper.

W1: Well, how much do you have done already? With a paper this size, I would expect that you would have the majority of it taken care of by now.

W2: Well, I have taken care of most of it. The delay has been in two of my sources. I needed to request them from a library across the state, and it's just taken a really long time for them to get here. I requested the books almost a month ago. And they're really important to my paper. I just feel that it would be incomplete without those sources.

W1: So when do you expect the sources to arrive?

W2: Well, according to the library, they should be here tomorrow. But I won't get time to go through them until next week.

W1: Well, if you turn in your outline and your paper as it is tomorrow in class, I can grant you a one-week extension.

W2: Thanks so much! But there is a problem.

W1: Oh really? What is that?

W2: Well, tomorrow I must meet my sister about her wedding. I am going to leave at 6 AM, so I will miss all my classes tomorrow. What can I do?

W1: How about this… why don't you slip your paper and the outline under my office door before you leave? The building is unlocked at 6. Can you leave after that?

W2: Yeah, I can do that. Thanks.

Susan asks her professor for an extension on her term paper. Her sister is getting married, and she won't have time to finish the paper before the deadline. The professor wonders how much work the student has done so far. Susan tells her that the paper is mostly written, but she is waiting for two more books from the library to finish. The professor tells her to bring what she has and an outline for the paper to class, and she will get a one-week extension.

B 1. Ⓒ 2. Ⓐ

¹he will hang posters instead ²hang posters and wall hangings instead

🔘 2-11

M1: Hey, can I ask you a question?

M2: Sure. What's up?

M1: I was just wondering how old this dorm is.

M2: It's definitely really old. It was built the same year as the college.

M1: Well, I was wondering what the protocol is for painting my room. Right now it's this really gross, pale green color, and I just want to make it more livable.

M2: Well, I definitely understand your wanting to repaint your room. But you have to get all paint approved by the Housing Department. And you also have to repaint it back at the end of the year.

M1: Really? That's so much work. Why do you need to get paint approved?

M2: They just need to make sure you're using paint that is safe. You know, lead-free and stuff.

M1: Oh, well that makes sense. How long does that process usually take?

M2: Well depending on how busy they are, it can take up to a month.

M1: Really? That's such a long time for an eight-month stay.

M2: Yeah, it is. Most students just end up putting up wall hangings and posters. It saves a lot of time and effort. And there isn't nearly as much red-tape around that.

M1: Yeah, I can understand that. I might end up doing the same thing.

M2: Well it's a lot easier. It's definitely a much simpler process.

M1: Yeah, I guess I'll try that. Can I put in the paperwork with the Housing Department and then cancel later? Just in case the posters look okay. If they don't look good, then I have already started the process of the request.

M2: I don't see any problem with that. It's a good idea. Go for it.

M1: Okay, thanks for your help.

A student does not like the color of his dorm room. He wants to paint it a different color. His resident advisor says he must get the paint choice approved by the Housing Department. This process can take up to a month sometimes. According to the resident advisor, most students just put up posters and wall hangings instead. The student thinks that that might be easier to do.

C 1. Ⓒ 2. Ⓒ

¹Be polite ²Call back

🔘 2-12

M: Hey, can you help me?

W: Yeah, what do you need?

M: I am thinking about applying for some internships, but I really don't know how. Can you help me get the ball rolling?

W: Yeah, have you worked on your resume? You need a current resume.

M: Okay, what else?

W: With your resume, make a cover sheet. It's basically your way of personalizing your resume and telling someone why you are different and why they should choose you. Also, you should have a solid reference sheet.

M: What is that for?

W: You want people on there that can tell prospective employers you will be a good employee. Talk to your teachers, coaches, former employers, and counselors. Ask them ahead of time if you can use them on your reference sheet.

M: That sounds great. Anything else?

W: Oh, there is plenty. If they call for an interview and you miss the call, call back ASAP, no matter what. That shows you care, and you never know how long they will be waiting for you. At the interview, show up early, dress nicely, and be polite. You can never be too polite. Wait for them to sit, and call them sir or ma'am. All those things. At the end, thank them for their time.

M: Wow, this seems like a lot of work.

W: I know, but these things are important.

M: Will everyone else be doing this?

W: Well, the smart people.

M: How do you know all this?

W: I just came back from the Career Center, and they gave me this info. Oh my God, I almost forgot. Make follow-up calls.

M: When?

W: After you give them your resume, call them in a few days just to confirm they got it. Ask if they need anything else, and ask when you can come in and talk to them.

A student needs help applying for an internship. Another student gives him advice. He must make a current resume. With his resume, he should include a cover sheet to tell prospective employers why he would be a good employee. Also, he should have a reference sheet of people prospective employers can contact. At an interview, he should dress nicely and be very polite. It is also important to make follow-up calls after he gives his resume. This shows he is interested. He can also check to see if they need anything else.

D   **1.** Ⓐ   **2.** Ⓒ

¹talks too much ²do not talk enough

 2-13

W: Tim, come here.

M: Yes, ma'am?

W: I want to talk about your assignment.

M: Really? Did you like it?

W: No, the story was okay, and our class is a creative writing class, but there is a lot of room for improvement.

M: Oh… Okay. Well, what was wrong?

W: First of all, your story was not balanced at all. Your main character talks way too much. At times, I thought I was reading a play. Do you know why?

M: No.

W: I will tell you. Because in a play, the writer only writes what people say and only a tiny bit about their actions, and then the actors do the rest. Are you writing a play?

M: No, I wasn't, I just…

W: You just nothing. You are not writing a play. You need to describe things. Tell me what is going on. For example, your main character says "What a wonderful tree."

M: It was a…

W: Stop talking. I know it was a wonderful tree because he says so, but tell me why it was a wonderful tree. Describe it to me. Don't make me guess.

M: Was there anything else?

W: Yes, in fact there was. I don't know if your other characters talked. Just your main character. Let everyone else talk, and add a few more characters. This paper was terrible. Do you understand?

M: Yes ma'am, I understand. Less talking by the main character.

W: Oh my God, are you listening to me? More talking by other people. And more characters. Your favorite book is *The Lord of the Rings*, right? Do you know why some scholars like that book? Of course you don't. They like it because the author made so many characters. And each character is unique. Make more characters, make them come to life, make them talk, and have less talking by your main character. That's all.

The professor is telling her student why his creative writing assignment is not good. She tells him that the main character is talking way too much, almost like in a play. He needs to describe more. She very rudely tells him this. In addition, he must make his other characters talk more. They do not talk enough. She uses the example of *The Lord of the Rings* to tell him he needs more characters and, through their words, make them come to life.

Practice with Lectures

A   **1.** Ⓑ   **2.** Ⓓ

¹Abraham Lincoln ²Importance of freedom in the nation

2-14

M1: All right, guys. Since we've been talking about the Civil War for a while, it's about time for us to talk about another important thing that's related to it. We're going to shift gears a bit and talk about the Gettysburg Address. Who can tell me who gave the

Gettysburg Address?

W: That's easy! Everyone knows it was Abraham Lincoln!

M1: That's right! President Lincoln gave the Gettysburg Address. Now who can tell me when he gave this address?

M2: Didn't he make the speech after the Battle of Gettysburg? I think the week after the battle, right?

M1: No, not quite. I know it makes sense that he would give the Gettysburg Address after the Battle of Gettysburg, but actually, he gave it almost half a year after the Battle of Gettysburg was fought. Lincoln made the speech at the battleground at Gettysburg. That's why it's called the Gettysburg Address. Now there are a number of reasons why this speech is famous. Probably the most important reason is its content. Lincoln spoke about the importance of freedom in the nation. One thing that we have to note is that whenever he talked about the United States, he called it a "nation," not a "union." Can anyone tell me why this distinction is important?

M2: Well, probably because he wanted to make it a point not to exclude the Confederate States. By saying "nation," he was making a point that the Union states and the Confederate States were both part of the same country. That country was formed by the same people, and they're all basically the same people.

M1: Excellent! That's exactly right. By talking about everyone as a nation, he made sure to include everyone who was fighting the war. This helped motivate the North as well as welcome back the South after the war.

The Gettysburg Address was a famous speech given by President Abraham Lincoln. He gave this speech on the battleground at Gettysburg half a year after that battle was fought. The Gettysburg Address is famous mostly because of its content. In this address, Lincoln talked about the importance of freedom in the nation. The language he used was very important. This is because he did not exclude soldiers from either side of the war.

B 1. (A) 2. (B)

¹big, open, dull spaces ²splendid structures

🔘 2-15

W1: So we're going to move forward in our discussion on architecture and visit Turkey. Now, Turkey was once a part of the Ottoman Empire, so when we talk about Turkish architecture from a long time ago, we are generally referring to Ottoman architecture. So who can tell me what years the Ottoman Empire lasted from?

W2: I am not sure, but didn't it start about 500 BC and fall about 500 AD?

W1: No, you are thinking of the Roman Empire, which did play a huge role in the founding of the Ottoman Empire, but that is not correct. Anyone else?

M: It lasted a really long time, didn't it? From about 1300 AD till 1920 AD?

W1: Yes, that's exactly right. But the architecture of the Ottoman Empire flourished during the 14th and 15th centuries. So who can tell me some of the key characteristics of Ottoman architecture?

W2: Oh! They used a lot of domes, didn't they?

W1: Yes, they did. They actually made the dome a really popular architectural structure. Okay, anyone else?

M: Um… I think I read something about vaults.

W1: Great! Vaults are very much Ottoman architectural structures. Great job, guys! So in addition to domes and vaults, the Ottomans also used a lot of semi-domes and columns. Now, if you'll remember, the Greeks originally popularized the column. But it's such a functional structure that many groups of people have used it throughout history. So what the Ottomans did with these structures is that they used it to make mosques more beautiful. Before the Ottomans, mosques were usually these big, open, dull places. But the Ottomans designed mosques to be quite splendid. You can see examples of their mosques all around Turkey.

M: I heard that their houses had doors on the roof, is that correct?

W1: It is correct, but we will talk about that next week.

Turkish architecture usually means Ottoman architecture. The Ottoman Empire lasted from 1300 AD till 1920 AD, and its architecture flourished during the 14th and 15th centuries. The Ottomans popularized the use of domes, vaults, and semi-domes. What the Ottomans mostly used these structures for was to create beautiful mosques. Before the Ottomans, mosques were really plain and boring. Afterwards, they were very lovely.

C 1. (B) 2. (A)

¹America ²Latin countries

🔘 2-16

Hello, class. Last week we talked about the United States being a melting pot, where all the different immigrants mix together to create something new. Well, everything has exceptions, including our melting pot, right? Okay, inside the Mississippi River Valley, there is a large area that is part melting pot and part garden salad. In Louisiana, or more specifically, New Orleans, there have been a few major cultural influences that are different from the rest of the United States. Unlike the rest of the United States, which was colonized by England and Spain, New Orleans was predominantly a French settlement. It also was a unique slave culture.

While the rest of the U.S. was a melting pot, mixing all its parts to create something new, New Orleans became a garden salad. Right now you are asking yourself, "What does she mean by garden salad?" A garden salad has many parts that are combined to make a new flavor. Each piece retains its original identity, but combined they make something new, and hopefully better. This contrasts to the melting pot because in a melting pot, all pieces lose their identity to form something new.

So in New Orleans, we have a French beginning, with French culture, food, language and lifestyle. Added in over the centuries is a bit of a Spanish influence, when Spain controlled the territory for about 50 years after the French and Indian War. After that is the American/English influence after President Jefferson bought the territory from France. And lastly is an influx of Latino culture from Mexico and the Caribbean.

The result now is that New Orleans has a distinct culture apart from the United States. Because of their French ancestry, they have different jargon, such as they say "I'm making groceries," instead of our "I am grocery shopping." Again, this is because the French influence. In French, the direct translation is "to make groceries," not "to buy or go shopping."

Most of the United States is considered a melting pot because the different immigrants mix together. Inside the Mississippi River Valley, New Orleans is different from the rest of the USA. It is a garden salad. Its different pieces have retained their identities. New Orleans was heavily influenced from its French beginnings. Later, Spainish, American, African, and Latin immigrants all added to the culture of the city. One example of this difference is the jargon. The local jargon has a heavy French influence.

D　**1.** Ⓒ　**2.** Ⓐ

[1]to save money

Ⓞ **2-17**

We will keep talking about the idea of a language evolving. I talked about how war changes a language because one culture can dominate another and infuse aspects of its language into a new language. Today, I

will talk about another way a language can change. It is… can anyone guess? Technology.

My example will be, hmm, a cell phone. Cell phones have changed and are currently changing the way we communicate with each other. Only 50 years ago, phone conversations were considered private affairs. For example, if I was at your house, and your phone rang, I would leave the room so that you could have a private conversation. With cell phones, people have conversations everywhere, at restaurants, on dates, umm, even on public transportation you can see people chatting away.

Now people are talking about what was considered private in public. We will talk about work, people we hate, our relationships, and plans in front of complete strangers. The things we now talk about on the phone would have been considered extremely rude to say in public 50 years ago. Back then, you would be slapped by someone for talking about your boyfriend or girlfriend or a party you went to the night before.

Umm, what else? We are changing how we talk as well. We all get phone bills, so talking on the phone means you are using money. So, the faster you talk, the less money you use. This means we often start and end our phone conversations quickly. Before, we would take our time on the phone, ask someone how they are doing, chit chat for a bit, and then get to the point. We would slowly end the conversation, often saying bye two or three times. Now, we just say the point then maybe a goodbye, and the conversation is over. That would have been so rude only 20 years ago.

English is an evolving language. One way a language can evolve is through technology. Cell phones have changed how we speak. Cell phones allow us to speak in public places. This has changed what we consider private. Many things we discuss in public were once considered private and should not be spoken in public. Also, people talk quickly on cell phones to save money. This has shortened conversations. We often do not greet people the same as we did, and we end conversations without saying "bye."

Integrated Listening & Speaking

A

1. (1) The student cannot finish her paper after she gets the sources because she must attend her sister's wedding.

(2) The student will be attending her sister's wedding, so she will not be able to finish the term paper after she gets the sources.

2. (1) Susan must turn in her outline and the incomplete paper.

(2) The professor tells Susan to hand in her paper as is along with her outline.

3. (1) The student will not go to class tomorrow because she must meet her sister.

(2) Susan will go home to meet her sister, so she cannot attend class tomorrow.

2-18

Susan has a major paper due in two weeks. She asks her professor for an extension because she has been waiting to get two major sources from a library across the state. She feels these two sources are really important to her paper. To make it even worse, her sister is getting married, so even after she gets the sources, she will have no time to do the paper. The professor understands her situation and tells her to turn in her outline and paper tomorrow in class. Susan will be leaving to meet her sister tomorrow, so the professor tells her to leave the paper under her office door.

B

1. (1) The female student knows so much because she is returning from the Career Center.

(2) The female student just visited the Career Center, so now she knows a lot of information about getting an internship.

2. (1) The student should call after he drops off his resume to show he is really interested in the job.

(2) To show the student is sincerely interested in a position, he should make a phone call after he gives prospective employers his resume.

3. (1) A cover sheet allows the student to personalize his resume.

(2) In order to personalize his resume, the student should also submit a cover sheet.

2-19

A male student asks a female student for help with getting an internship. The female student has just returned from the Career Center, so she has lots of good advice. The first step is to update his resume. Along with his resume, he should personalize it with a cover sheet. Whoever is interviewing him will need references, so he should have a reference sheet. Next, he must be very polite. He should dress nicely and wait to be seated. Lastly, he should immediately return any phone calls and also call after he has dropped off his

resume. This will prove he is interested in the position.

C

1. (1) The biggest influence on Turkish architecture was the Ottoman Empire.

(2) The Ottoman Empire was a very big influence on the development of Turkish architecture.

2. (1) The peak of Ottoman architecture was the 14th and 15th centuries.

(2) The height of architecture in the Ottoman Empire started in the year 1300 and ended about 1500 AD.

3. (1) Some common characteristics in Turkish architecture are domes, semi-domes, vaults, and columns.

(2) Domes, semi-domes, vaults, and columns are very popular designs in Turkish architecture.

2-20

Turkish architecture is actually Ottoman architecture because the Ottoman Empire heavily influenced the style of the Turks. The Ottoman Empire lasted from 1300 to 1920 AD, but its architectural peak came in the 14th and 15th centuries. Some characteristics of Ottoman architecture are domes, semi-domes, vaults and columns. They used these designs to make mosques more beautiful. Before they added these designs, mosques were big, open, dull spaces. Even today, the mosques of Turkey still have Ottoman-style domes and columns. Another example of Ottoman influence on Turkish architecture is having a door on the roofs of houses.

D

1. (1) The city has its own culture, and the new pieces keep their old identity while adding to the city's culture.

(2) The city's culture is made of many pieces that retain their original identity but still add to the culture of the city.

2. (1) All of the pieces become part of American culture and lose their original culture.

(2) The pieces no longer have an original identity and become part of the culture of America.

3. (1) The people of New Orleans say "making groceries" because of their French heritage.

(2) Due to their French origins, people in New Orleans say things like "making groceries."

2-21

Parts of the Mississippi Valley, specifically the city of New Orleans, are different from the rest of the United

States. New Orleans is compared to a garden salad because all of the cultural influences have kept their old identity. Like in a garden salad, all the pieces keep their taste, but combined, they make a new flavor. The rest of the United States is compared to a melting pot. New pieces are added, and they lose their identity when they combine with the rest of the pot and create something new. For example, because of their French heritage, in New Orleans, the jargon is different. For example, they say "making groceries" instead of "going shopping."

Mini TOEFL iBT

A   **1.** Ⓑ   **2.** Ⓒ   **3.** Ⓒ   **4.** Ⓓ   **5.** Ⓑ

🔘 2-22

M: Hello, can I help you?

W: Yes, please. I just have a few questions.

M: Sure, I will see if I can get them answered.

W: Okay. First of all, I have a car on campus, and I just wanted to make sure I understood all the possible fees. I got the guidebook, and I downloaded it on my computer, but I am not sure if I understand everything completely.

M: Of course. Some of those rules are a bit strange to people outside of our state.

W: Yeah, first, it says I have to park on alternating sides of the road. What exactly does that mean?

M: Okay, here in Minnesota, it snows a lot. So the snowplows need to have open paths to plow. City law says you must park on alternating sides of the road. This means, on even dates, for example, today, is the 20th, so you must park on the even side of the road. One side of the road will have addresses like 910, 912, and 914 the other side will be 911, 913, and 915. So you must park on the even side. Does this make sense?

W: Yes, I understand. But then I must go move my car every day?

M: Yup, that's what it means.

W: Wow, that can get pretty annoying. When? Just during winter? When there is snow on the ground?

M: Nope, always. Even in the summer you must do this. Also, remember that if you park at 10 p.m. at night, on the 13th of the month, think about the next day. The next day would be the 14th, so you must be on the even side of the street. It can get a bit confusing. What is your next question?

W: Well, I just got my car, so I don't have a parking permit. How much time do I have until I need it?

M: Oh, you should buy it now. A semester pass costs thirty dollars, and a year-long pass costs fifty dollars.

W: I don't have enough money right now. What can I do?

M: You can park off campus. Or you can hope security doesn't notice you, or you can bring your car back home until you buy a pass.

W: I see. I think I'll have enough money in a few days, so I will take my chances until then. Thanks.

B   **1.** Ⓓ   **2.** Ⓐ   **3.** Yes/No/Yes/No/Yes
4. Ⓓ   **5.** Ⓒ   **6.** Ⓑ

🔘 2-23

Today we are going to start a big unit on government. Before the rise of the nation-state and absolute monarchies, Europe went through a period known as feudalism. Like our concept of democracy, feudalism had many forms and varied by location and time period. Let's see, feudalism originated by mixing Roman law with Germanic tradition. The Germanic warriors that lived about 3,000 years ago had a tradition of electing a supreme warrior as leader. After battles, he would collect all of the spoils and distribute them fairly among all the warriors. The term feudalism is defined by three principle terms. There are lords, vassals, and fiefs.

Okay, a lord, in feudalism, is a person that owns land. He temporarily gives this land to another person, called a vassal. The vassal enters this contract so he may gain the land. Land sizes varied, from the size of a small farm, to huge counties. The vassal gained the revenues generated by the land, usually in the form of farming products.

What did the lord get? At this time, there were no standing armies. There were no professional soldiers. The vassal swore allegiance to the lord. In times of trouble, the lord could call upon the vassal to fight for the lord. This guaranteed the security of the lord.

Other details were often included in feudal deals. For example, since the lord still owned the land and merely lent the land to the vassal, the lord still had to maintain the land and defend it. The vassal, many times, would be required to grind his wheat and bake his bread in the ovens and mills owned by the lord, who then could collect taxes.

Umm, oh yes, the vassals also acted as counselors to the lord. During times of crisis, the lords would often hold meetings, calling together all the vassals to help them decide major decisions, such as to go to war or not.

Ahh, lastly, feudalism had many levels. What I mean is, a king could be a lord, giving aristocrats large lands, who then became his vassals. Those aristocrats were lords themselves, dividing up their land to lesser vassals. The top of this hierarchy was the emperor, who was the lord to his vassal kings.

Feudalism declined when lords became strong enough to maintain a standing army and did not require the services of their vassals.

Vocabulary Review

A

 2-24

1. grand (splendid)
2. people that permanently move to a different country to make a new home (immigrants)
3. mostly (predominantly)
4. language used by a group of people that is different from the rest of the speakers of that language (jargon)
5. slowly changing, usually to become better (evolving)
6. the main reason or purpose (point)
7. a supplier of information (source)
8. a series of actions to an end (process)
9. a paper listing relevant information that is given when applying for a job (resume)
10. even; not relying on one thing (balanced)
11. a person whose job is to study a subject (scholar)
12. to talk about something that is not important (chatting)
13. an increase in a length of time (extension)
14. very small (tiny)
15. to control, or have the most influence (dominate)

B

1. The Harry Potter book series is named after its main character.
2. The characters in the movie were very great. The writer made them come to life.
3. I am working on my term paper. It is worth 30 percent of my grade.
4. Don't be rude at the interview, don't leave without saying "bye," wait to be seated, and dress nicely.
5. Getting married is what Jenny looks forward to every day. She needs to find a boyfriend soon.
6. John wants to decorate his dorm room with lots of movie posters when he goes to college.

Unit 4 Understanding the Function of What Is Said

Basic Drill

A   1. Ⓐ   2. Ⓒ   3. Ⓓ

 2-26

W: Hi, I registered last year to have the same roommate again this year, but I have a new roommate. What happened?

M: Well, let me see, what is your name and room number?

W: My name is Emily Davis. I live in Emerson 216.

M: Okay, I have your registration form here. Look here. You didn't fill it out completely.

W: Really? What is wrong with it?

M: You didn't put your roommate's last name on the form. It just has her first name. We didn't know who your roommate was.

W: Couldn't you just look up who I lived with last year?

M: Well, that is your job. But if your new roommate agrees and your old roommate wants to move in, you can do that. But they must change rooms by tomorrow.

W: Okay, I will go talk to my roommate now. Thank you!

2-27

M: Hello Professor Smith, can I talk to you?

W: Sure. What can I do for you?

M: I was wondering if I could get an extension on the report we will turn in tomorrow. I don't need much time, just maybe two more days.

W: I have never let students turn in work late. I said that on the first day of my class. You know that is my policy.

M: I remember, but I was hoping you would understand. I need the time because I work so much. My parents don't pay any of my tuition, and I didn't get many need-based scholarships.

W: I understand that must be difficult for you, but I already told you my policy.

M: Please! If I don't get this extension, I don't think I can stay in school. That is how important this is.

W: You do whatever you must, but I can't change my policy.

2-28

M1: Hi, John. I want to talk to you about your papers.

M2: Is something wrong with them?

M1: Yes, there is. I have noticed in all of your work that there are a few common problems.

M2: Please tell me so I can correct them or explain them.

M1: Of course! First, you have lots of grammar mistakes. These are not excusable. Double check these, use your grammar guidebook, and have it proofread. Grammar mistakes are terrible. Do you understand?

M2: Okay, I usually write my papers at night, so I am tired, I can fix that. What's the other problem?

M1: Your thesis is never clear. It is very important that your thesis be clear and simple. I didn't understand your thesis on your last paper until page two. Just say it, clean and simple, OK?

M2: I know. I have always had trouble with that. I will work harder on my thesis.

B   **1.** Ⓑ   **2.** Ⓑ   **3.** Ⓑ

🔘 2-29

Many people think that tomatoes are vegetables, but they really are not. Tomatoes are actually a fruit. The definition of a fruit is the sweet tasting part of a plant that contains the plant's seeds. Unlike a fruit, vegetables are plants that are eaten without seeds. Usually it is a root or leaf, like carrots or spinach. A tomato has seeds, and people eat the part of the plant around the seeds. Most people think tomatoes are vegetables because they are not sweet and they taste like vegetables.

🔘 2-30

Scientists divide the depths of the ocean into two different layers. The top layer is called the surface layer. Below the surface layer is the deep water. The surface layer's depth varies, but is usually a few hundred meters. The surface layer is the part of the ocean that is affected by the wind, rain, waves, tides, and other weather events. All of these factors constantly mix the surface layer and make it less dense than the deep waters. The layer that divides the deep waters and the surface layer is called the pycnocline. The gradual movement of the surface layer is called the current. The current does not affect the deep waters.

🔘 2-31

Global warming is a theory that Earth's average temperature is constantly rising due to an increase in human activities. Industry and fuel emissions from cars are emitting carbon dioxide and other gases into the atmosphere at a very high rate. These gases create holes in the atmosphere, therefore allowing more of the

sun's heat to pass through the atmosphere. The rise in temperature has several effects on the planet, like a rise in the sea level, changes in precipitation, and other extreme weather events, such as floods, heat waves, and tornados. The average temperature of the Earth has risen 1.1 degrees Fahrenheit since 1900 and is expected to increase another 11 degrees by the year 2100.

Practice with Conversations

A   **1.** Ⓐ   **2.** Ⓒ

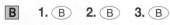
¹Pay the fee

🔘 2-32

M: Boston College Registrar's Office. What may I do for you?

W: Hello, I am currently a graduate student at Boston College. I am going to apply for an internship this summer, and I need some documents from the school.

M: Okay, what documents do you need?

W: I need three copies of my transcript, but a friend of mine said you can only get one copy at a time.

M: Your friend is wrong. You can get as many copies as you want, but after the first, you must pay a fee.

W: No problem, how much do they cost? And can you mail them to me?

M: For the cost, that depends. Do you want official transcripts or unofficial ones?

W: I need official ones.

M: Okay, each extra one will cost three dollars. You will need to come get them though. We only mail them to alumni. I am sorry if that causes any inconveniences. I really don't know why we have that policy. Is that okay?

W: Sure, I can come get them. What exactly must I do?

M: Come to the Registrar's Office, fill out a form, and pay the money, and we will have them ready by the next business day. How is that?

W: Sure, but one more thing. What time are you guys open?

M: Regular office hours, but we are closed during lunch from twelve to one.

W: Okay, I will swing by tomorrow. Thanks.

M: Sure, is there anything else I can do for you?

W: I almost forgot! The transcripts must be in a sealed official envelope with an official school stamp on the flap. Is that a problem?

M: No, we can do that. When you fill out the request

form, write that down just to make sure you get them exactly how you want them, okay?

W: Got it. Thanks.

M: Goodbye.

A graduate student at Boston College needs three copies of her transcripts. The worker at the Registrar's Office tells her that she must come to the office, fill out a form, pay a fee of six dollars, and she can get the transcripts the next day. The student wants the transcripts mailed to her, but the office will only mail them to alumni, not current students. The student also needs the transcripts sealed in an official envelope. To get that, she must write it on the request form.

B 1. Ⓓ 2. Ⓒ

[1]Not many primary sources [2]Did not discuss people

🔘 2-33

M: Hello Professor. May I talk to you? Are you busy?

W: Go ahead.

M: I was wondering if I could talk to you about my grade on the report we just got back.

W: Sure, is there a problem?

M: Well, you gave me a B, but I think I deserved a higher grade. I thought I was going to get an A on this.

W: Why don't you tell me why you think you deserve an A?

M: Sure, first, there were only two grammatical mistakes in the report, so you shouldn't have knocked me down for that. My thesis was very clear. My thesis was "England actually won the War of 1812." I supported it with a lot of evidence, I cited all my work, and I fulfilled your page requirements, so I really don't understand how you gave me a B.

W: Yes, I remember your paper, so why do you think I gave you a B then?

M: Honestly, that is why I am here. I really don't know.

W: Okay, well you tell me what was not good in that paper.

M: Okay, sometimes my writing is not clear, I know that is not one of my strong points. I didn't use very many primary sources. I know you wanted us to use that, but I couldn't find a lot, and I think that is not fair if you gave me a B because I didn't have enough primary sources.

W: No, that is not it. Your paper stated that England won the War of 1812, correct?

M: Yes.

W: And you pointed out all the military victories and political victories they had as well as the treaty that ended the war, right?

M: Yes.

W: Well, the assignment was to describe how a war affected the people of the countries fighting it. Did you talk about the people of Canada, America, or England?

M: No, I didn't.

W: Okay then, that is why you got a B. Understand?

M: Yes, okay, bye.

A student talks to a professor about his grade on a paper. He believes his paper was good, and he deserved an A on it. He tells the professor why his paper was good: he had few grammatical errors, a clear thesis, and lots of evidence, he cited his work, and he wrote the appropriate length. The professor asks him the details of his paper, which was about the War of 1812. The student did not do the assignment properly because he did not discuss the people affected by the war.

C 1. Ⓓ 2. Ⓒ

[1]a nurse or a teacher

🔘 2-34

W: Hello, Mr. Gray. I have an appointment with you now.

M: Sure, your name is Heather, right?

W: Yes, I want to change my major, but I was told I must get permission from you.

M: You are now studying history, right?

W: Yes, I want to change to a chemistry major. What do I need to do?

M: Well, first, tell me why you want to change.

W: When I was a freshman, I really liked history, so I decided to study it. In fact, I still like history a lot, and the professors are really good. I am sure I will keep taking history classes. But I have been thinking about my future a lot lately, and history doesn't seem like a good major for my future.

M: Keep going.

W: Well, a few of my friends were talking about how much money doctors can make, so I thought about it, for a long time actually, and I decided I want to go to medical school. History won't help me get into medical school, but chemistry can.

M: How long have you thought about this?

W: Hmm, about 6 weeks. Like I said, I have thought a while about it. My cousin is in medical school, and we talked about what it would take to get in and become a doctor.

M: Okay, that is good, but what will you do with your degree if you don't get into medical school?

W: I have thought about that too. There is big demand for nurses. I also am getting a minor in education, so I could be a teacher. Or I could be a temporary teacher until I get into medical school.

M: Have you taken any chemistry classes?

W: Yes, I have taken two. I got an A in General Chemistry and a B in Chemical Analysis. I actually have a note from the professor supporting me.

M: Sounds good. Let's get you changed.

A student made an appointment to talk to her counselor. She is currently a history major, but she wants to change to become a chemistry major. She needs permission to change her major. The counselor asks her some basic questions to make sure she is making the right decision. The counselor determines the student has thought about it long enough, the change will help her future, and the student has performed well. The counselor decides the change in majors is good for the student and grants her permission.

D 1. Ⓑ 2. Ⓓ

¹present the invasion ²Battle map

🔘 2-35

W: Hi John. Let's brainstorm for our project now.

M: We already decided our presentation will be on the German *blitzkrieg* of Poland in World War 2. I think we should split it up in halves, chronologically.

W: How about I do the prelude to the confrontation and you do the actual battles?

M: I think the battles will be difficult for everyone to follow, so let's have some kind of visual aid to help out.

W: Good idea. This time I don't want a bad grade. Got any ideas?

M: Yeah, we can have a battle map - a map of Poland, with the terrain and cities. Then we can have markers to designate the German and Polish forces. As one of us talks, the other moves the pieces on the map so people can see them moving throughout the country.

W: That's a great idea. I have another idea. We can have another sheet listing each major unit, the individual forces in that unit, and the commanders. That way we can refer to them by their unit names or their commander, and people will understand.

M: Oh, I like that. Then we could have one more map, too. As we move the units around, the map will become clustered, so we can have another map with the names of all the important places listed in big writing, so people will know where everything is.

W: This is going to be a great project. For the background information, I think we need to cover the political situation as well as the previous German aggression in Europe.

M: I don't know if we will have enough time. Is it that important?

W: Yeah, it is. Poland was the first actual military conflict of the war in Europe, so showing what had happened in the previous years will help people understand why certain events happened, like why Poland was unprepared.

Two students are brainstorming for a project. They decide to split the work in half. One student will present background information, and the other student will present the German invasion of Poland. They need three visual aids. The first visual aid will be a map of Poland with army units to move around the map. The second will be a list of all the units involved and their commanders. The last will be a map of Poland with the names of all the important locations written very clearly on it.

Practice with Lectures

A 1. Ⓒ 2. Ⓓ

¹Longitudinal axis ²Plane turns up or down

🔘 2-36

Hello class. Today we are going to talk about the controls of an airplane. Umm, but as you know, I like to talk a bit about the history of things. People generally credit the Wright brothers for having accomplished the first manned flight of an airplane. Their work is very astonishing when you consider they had to do all their own research and there was little precedence for them to look to. Even something as simple as controlling the airplane had to be imagined, tested, developed, and perfected.

Over the past 100 years, the technology of airplanes has changed, but the controls are still similar. Today, airplanes have three basic turns: turning up and down, turning left and right, and spinning. Airplanes turn by manipulating fins that are designed in their wings. When a pilot moves the fins in the air stream, they react with the air pressure to turn the aircraft.

You see, an airplane has three axes. A turn in the lateral axis can make the plane move up or down. A turn in the longitudinal axis can make the plane spin or roll. The third axis is the vertical axis. This turns the plane left or right.

Each axis has its own set of fins on the aircraft. To make a turn on the lateral or vertical axis, a pilot needs only to turn the fins in the direction of the desired turn. For example, if the pilot wants to turn left, he would turn the vertical axis left. The air stream that flows around the aircraft would change, and the aircraft would turn right.

In order to turn on the longitudinal axis, the pilot must do something a little different. For this axis, a turn is achieved by manipulating the fins in the same direction. To achieve a spin, the fins go in opposite directions. For example, to spin clockwise, the right fin would turn down, so the right side of the aircraft drops. The left fin would turn right, so that the left side of the aircraft would rise. With one side rising and one side dropping, the aircraft then would perform a spin or roll.

Airplanes have three axes. Each axis has its own set of fins built into the aircraft's wings. The fins turn and react with the air stream to enable the airplane to turn. Three basic turns are capable. The airplane can turn up or down on the lateral axis, left or right on the vertical axis, or it can spin on the longitudinal axis. For the first two types of turns, the fins turn in the direction of the desired turn. For a spin, the fins turn in opposite directions.

B　**1.** Ⓓ　**2.** Ⓓ

[1]Lava [2]Toxic gases destroy ozone

🔘 2-37

M1: We have studied the causes of volcanoes. Now I want to discuss the effects volcanoes have on the Earth. We can classify the effects into three different categories. Can anyone take a guess what they are?

W1: Well, I am sure one of them is lava or is related to lava.

M1: Yes, you are right. There are a few different kinds of lava flows. All of them can completely destroy the immediate environment, but later they are very beneficial to plant life. Lava, when it is not hot, is a great fertilizer for plants. They also emit lots of ash. We will get into that tomorrow. What other categories are there besides lava and similar emissions?

M2: What about other kinds of emissions, like gas? Volcanoes emit toxic gases, right?

M1: Yes, volcanoes emit many toxic and harmful gases, such as carbon dioxide and sulfur dioxide. Of course, not all the gases released are harmful, like water vapor, but others wreak havoc on our atmosphere. When sulfur dioxide reaches the atmosphere and reacts to change into sulfuric acid, it increases the Earth's albedo. What is the albedo?

W1: The albedo reflects the sun's heat. That reaction increases the Earth's albedo.

M1: Yes, why?

W1: Doesn't that mean volcanoes can actually reverse the effects of global warming and cool the Earth down?

M1: Very good! The eruptions of the past half century have actually increased the albedo enough to cool the surface of the Earth by half of a degree Fahrenheit. But, many of the gases emitted also destroy the ozone or can create acid rain. What other effects are there?

M2: In the movies, all the animals run away before a volcano.

M1: You almost got it. There are volcanic side effects. There are events that occur because of volcanoes, but are not emitted from volcanoes. Any guesses?

W2: Earthquakes. Earthquakes and volcanoes occur near faults and often accompany each other. Sometimes volcanoes cause small earthquakes.

M1: Yes, also, there are hot springs, geysers, fumaroles, and mud pots.

Volcanoes have three basic categories of effects on the Earth. First, volcanoes produce lava. Lava can destroy or severely damage anything that lies in its path. Later, lava works as a good fertilizer. Second, volcanoes emit several gases into the atmosphere. Some of the gases are beneficial. They can help to increase the albedo. Other gases can damage the ozone or create acid rain. Last, there are several other side effects, such as geysers and earthquakes.

C　**1.** Ⓒ　**2.** Ⓐ

[1]Central Asia and Russia　[2]Humans have little contact

🔘 2-38

Today, we are going to compare two different species that are the same genus. The two animals we will compare are the Olympic Marmot and the Bobak Marmot. First, they live a world apart. The Olympic Marmot lives in a small area in North America. It lives on the Olympic Peninsula in Washington state. Excluding Alaska, it is the northwesternmost part of the United States. Oh, yeah, and Hawaii is farther west. The Bobak Marmot's home is on the other side of the world, in the steppes of Russia and Central Asia. Even though they are both marmots, they prefer different areas to live. The Olympic lives in the alpine meadows near the Olympic Mountains. The Bobak is not like most marmots and lives in rolling grasslands and also has been known to live near cultivated fields.

Let's go on to defense calls. All species of marmots have calls and whistles to alert others of predators. The Olympic Marmot has much more developed calls though. Most research shows that the Bobak Marmot only has one call. This call communicates any and all forms of predators. Some studies have hinted that their call can change depending on the terrain. In flat areas, the call is slow. In rugged terrain, the calls tend to be faster.

Umm, okay the Olympic Marmot's calls are much more advanced. Their calls are categorized into ascending, descending, flat, and trills. The different calls are used to designate the type of predator, for example a bird of prey versus a bear. The trills are believed to be used for very dangerous situations.

Olympic Marmots' natural enemies are mainly the coyote and puma, but to a lesser extent birds of prey and bobcats. Bobak Marmots' natural enemies are similar animals, large cats and packs of hunting canines. This may sound strange, but Bobak Marmots have been a source of emergency food for many Russian people. In times of extreme hardship and famine, the Bobak Marmot has been used as food and clothing. Due to this, you can guess the Olympic Marmot is less shy around people.

Two different species of the Marmot genus are the Olympic Marmot and the Bobak Marmot. The Olympic Marmot lives near the Olympic Mountains in the Olympic Peninsula of Washington state. The Bobak Marmot lives in open grasslands in Central Asia and Russia. Both animals have calls to warn other marmots of a predator, but the Olympic Marmots' calls are more advanced and recognize different kinds of predators. The Bobak Marmot has been eaten by Russian people during famine, and it has also been used as a source of fur for clothes.

D **1.** (C) **2.** (A)

[1]Walter Camp [2]Many deaths

🔘 3-01

M1: Let's talk about what some people consider the most popular sport in America. Football was derived from soccer. Versions of soccer were played all over the world. The Chinese played a game called cuju over 2,200 years ago. Native Americans were playing a game like soccer before Europeans arrived in the Americas.

W: How much influence did the Native Americans have on football? Did settlers play with them?

M1: I am sure settlers and Native Americans played, but that had almost no influence on the development of football. Football became popular by elite college students playing the game around the 1820s. It was mainly an unorganized version of mob style soccer. Harvard played a game similar to rugby. In 1874, McGill University of Montreal played Harvard. Harvard adopted the Canadian version of football, which was much more similar to today's football. Harvard spread that style of football to other schools, who were playing a soccer-style game.

M2: You mean Canadians were playing American-style football before Americans?

M1: Not quite. They were playing a game similar to rugby, but they did influence the development of football. By 1883, a coach named Walter Camp made some major changes to the game, such as reducing the number of players from 15 to 11, adding the line of scrimmage, and adding a rule if the ball is not moved five yards after three downs, the other team would gain control of the ball. This rule was created to thwart Yale's strategy of controlling the ball without attempting to score.

W: Didn't Harvard and Yale hate each other?

M1: Football was very dangerous. Harvard invented the flying wedge, which almost killed 7 Yale players in one game. 18 players were killed in 1905. This led to more changes, such as the forward pass and adding a fourth down. After this, the game was pretty similar to our football today.

🔘 3-02

American Football is derived from European soccer. In the 1820s, American universities made the sport popular, but they played a game similar to soccer. Harvard played a game more like rugby. They then played a Canadian football team and adopted the Canadian style of football. Harvard passed on this style to the rest of the American universities. Walter Camp changed the game even further by adding downs and the line of scrimmage and reducing the number of players. The large number of deaths resulted in more changes, like the forward pass and a fourth down.

Integrated Listening & Speaking

A

1. (1) The student cannot get her transcripts mailed because the school only mails them to alumni.

(2) The student is not an alumnus, so she cannot get

her transcripts mailed.

2. (1) The student needs three transcripts for her application.

(2) The application requires the student to provide three transcripts.

3. (1) The student must go to the Registrar's Office, fill out a request form, and pay a fee.

(2) After the student goes to the Registrar's Office, fills out a form, and pays a fee, she can get her transcripts.

3-02

A Boston College graduate student will apply for a summer internship. She needs three copies of her transcript for her applications. She thinks it might not be possible to get three copies. The office worker tells her she can get as many copies as she wants, but she must pay three dollars for each extra copy. The student wants the transcripts mailed to her, but the Registrar's Office will only mail transcripts to alumni. The student wants to know how to get the transcripts, and the worker tells her she must come to the Registrar's Office, fill out a request form, and pay the fee. Then she can get the transcripts the next business day.

B

1. (1) The student talks to the counselor to get permission to change her major.

(2) The student has this conversation because she needs permission from the counselor to change her major.

2. (1) The job the student wants is doctor.

(2) The student wants to be a doctor.

3. (1) The student's current major is history.

(2) The student is currently a history major.

3-03

A student has an appointment with her counselor. The student currently is a history major, but she wants to change her major to chemistry. She needs to get permission from her counselor to change her major. The counselor asks her some questions about how making the change will help her and if it is a good idea. The counselor learns the student has thought about the decision for six weeks, has done well in her chemistry classes, and has a goal to become a doctor. She also has a plan in case she cannot get into medical school. The counselor decides it is a good decision. The counselor gives her permission to change her major.

C

1. (1) The Olympic Marmot lives in alpine meadows

near mountains.

(2) The Olympic Marmot's home is close to mountains in alpine meadows.

2. (1) The purpose of the marmot's calls is to warn other marmots of predators.

(2) The marmot will call to other marmots because a predator is near.

3. (1) The Bobak Marmot served people as an emergency source of food and clothes.

(2) People used the Bobak Marmot to eat and make clothes during times of emergencies.

3-04

A professor is discussing the differences of two animals. They are different species but the same genus. The first is the Olympic Marmot, which lives on the Olympic Peninsula in Washington state. The other is the Bobak Marmot. The Bobak lives in Central Asia and Russia. The Olympic Marmot lives in alpine meadows near mountains. The Bobak Marmot lives in rolling grasslands and near cultivated fields. Both animals have a call to alert other marmots of the presence of predators. The Bobak Marmot has one call for all predators. The Olympic Marmot has several calls to distinguish different types of predators. The Bobak Marmot has been used as a source of food and clothes by some people.

D

1. (1) The gas emissions from volcanoes increase the albedo.

(2) The albedo is increased by the gas emissions from volcanoes.

2. (1) Lava destroys the surrounding environment and then serves as a good fertilizer for plants when it cools.

(2) At first lava can destroy the surrounding environment, and then it helps plants by being a good fertilizer after it cools.

3. (1) Two of the gases emitted from a volcano are carbon dioxide and sulfur dioxide.

(2) During an eruption, volcanoes will emit gases such as carbon dioxide and sulfur dioxide.

3-05

Volcanoes have three different kinds of effects on the Earth. The first category is the lava and ash that are emitted from the volcano. Lava can cause lots of damage to the surrounding environment. Later, after it has cooled, lava is a good fertilizer for plants. The second category is the different gas emissions from the volcano. Many of the gases emitted are toxic or harmful to the ozone, like carbon dioxide and sulfur dioxide. Other gases help increase the albedo in the ozone, and that causes the Earth's temperature to cool. The third category is the side effects the volcano can have, such as earthquakes, geysers, and hot springs.

Mini TOEFL iBT

A 1. Ⓒ 2. Ⓒ 3. Ⓐ 4. Ⓓ 5. Ⓑ

◉ 3-06

W: Hi, Professor Clark. Remember I wanted to talk to you about my internship?

M: Yes, of course. Tell me about the internship you are looking at.

W: Okay, the internship is with Nike. I will be on their advertising team. Basically, what they want is to attract more kinds of buyers. For example, Nike is currently really popular with people age 29 and younger, but a lot of older people buy other brands. My job will be to talk to the people that do not buy Nike and find out what kind of advertisements would interest them. I think it will be really fun, and I can get paid for it, a little bit at least.

M: Money is good. I thought you were a communications major. Did you change?

W: No, I didn't.

M: I think you would have a better chance at getting an internship in your major. Like last summer, you did that internship with a magazine.

W: No, it was a newspaper. *The Chicago Tribune*.

M: Right, I am sorry. It was a newspaper. You know, I actually talked to the people that looked over your application, and one of the reasons you were accepted is because the internship directly applies to your major. I really think you should stick with a similar internship.

W: You think so? Hmm, because I really like the Nike one. I can travel and maybe get some free shoes or clothes.

M: Now I see. You are looking at that stuff. Honestly, don't do that. Shoes are nice, and clothes are nice, but the point of an internship is to learn, not to travel and get stuff. Look into some magazines or other newspapers. You have experience now as a journalist, and that is very valuable. You are ahead of most of the other applicants.

W: I see your point. Do you think I could do both? Then I could be happy traveling with Nike and gain all the knowledge and experience in journalism.

M: That's not a good idea. You must commit yourself.

I strongly urge you to do a similar internship like the one you did last year. If you are thinking about changing your major, then look into Nike, but if you are staying in communications, then go for a newspaper.

W: I guess you are right. Are you good at writing letters of recommendations?

M: Yes, I am. Don't worry.

B 1. Ⓓ 2. Ⓒ 3. Ⓐ 4. Ⓐ 5. Ⓐ
6. Yes/No/No/No/Yes

◉ 3-07

W: Let's talk about current American houses. Current American houses are very different from the housing styles of the past few hundred years. The biggest change in housing style comes from the location of the houses. 100 years ago, people lived in the country or the city. There has been a trend of people moving into suburbs. Why is this important?

M: Well, the suburbs are cheaper, and there are fewer people.

W: Yes, how are the suburbs cheaper? Do you mean buying a pizza at a lower price affects houses?

M: Of course not. Hmm, well, the cost of land is cheaper.

W: Yes! Exactly! Land costs a lot less in suburbs. Land is also more available there. That means houses can get bigger without needing to build more stories. There are two big things there. First, there are no more homes built above a store. Those second-story homes are only located in the cities. Next, houses can be built on larger areas of land for a cheaper price. This means more people can afford a large home. What technological developments have changed American homes since the turn of the century?

M: I am sure there are many. There have been many changes in the kitchen, hmm, what else?

W: Not really the kitchen, but you are close. Fireplaces have been replaced by heaters, meaning most homes don't have fireplaces, or they are just for decoration. Many American families now have more than one car, meaning they have multi-car garages. There have been social changes as well. The middle of the 20th century gave rise to the nuclear family. Also, as farming became less popular, households have shrunk. An average family has only two or three kids. Now bedrooms are bigger and more personal. Many families have fewer people in the house but bigger houses, so bedrooms often have only one or two people in them. This is a big contrast to the bedrooms on farmlands or in cities with several people in one room.

M: Why do all the houses in suburbs seem to be identical?

W: That is because they are built too quickly. There is a huge demand to move out of the cities, so houses are not individually designed and built. Developers build several houses at the same time using a similar style for each one. It is more efficient.

Vocabulary Review

A

🔊 3-08

1. a record of classes taken and grades (transcript)
2. changing or controlling (manipulating)
3. placed too closely together (clustered)
4. a previous experience (precedence)
5. a classification of land, such as forest, desert or mountain (terrain)
6. a first year student (freshman)
7. getting lower (descending)
8. a group of uncontrolled people that act emotionally (mob)
9. facts to support an idea or opinion (evidence)
10. an idea that has been made the best possible (perfect)
11. ordered by time, usually oldest to newest (chronologically)
12. an irritation or bother; something you don't want to do (annoyance)
13. a title given to students by a school after completing a program of study (degree)
14. poisonous (toxic)
15. a category of an animal that is more general than species (genus)

B

1. The bank near the river is open late. It doesn't have regular office hours.
2. John answered first, and then the children each answered in a clockwise order.
3. During the 1800s, there were many conflicts between American settlers and Native Americans.
4. The teacher wants me to use primary sources, but I can't find any diaries or journals.
5. The mail usually arrives in three business days.
6. I didn't understand the situation because I didn't have enough background information.

Unit 5 Understanding the Speaker's Attitude

Basic Drill

A 1. Ⓑ 2. Ⓓ 3. Ⓓ

🔊 3-10

M1: Hello, this is the Student Service Center. How may I help you today?

M2: Hi, I'm calling from my dorm room. I'm in Building B, room number 412. My door is broken. Could someone come up and fix it?

M1: Okay, no problem. You'll need to come down to the main office and fill out a repair request form.

M2: But I have finals coming up. I'm really busy. The hinge on the door is just missing a bolt. It would only take five minutes to fix. Couldn't you just send someone? I promise I'll fill out the request later.

M1: I'm afraid we can't give preferential treatment. You'll just have to come down and fill out the form before we can do anything.

🔊 3-11

M1: Hi, Mr. Jehosephat. May I speak to you for a second?

M2: Hi, David. How can I help you today?

M1: Yeah, I'm a little behind on my interview project.

M2: Aha, I see.

M1: Well, I know you are friends with the manager over at the Intel office in Pasadena.

M2: Oh yes, Bob Nilfordson. We play golf sometimes.

M1: Well, I was hoping you could call him and ask if he would get together with me for an hour tonight, so I can complete this interview project.

M2: David, you know I can't do that. It just wouldn't be fair to the other students.

M1: Okay, I understand. But I have to warn you that my project will probably be late.

🔊 3-12

M: Hi Jennifer. Can I speak to you for a moment?

W: Sure, Dr. Kline. What is it?

M: Let's take a look together at this report you handed in yesterday. I can't accept it from you.

W: Oh, but why? I worked so hard on it.

M: That may be the case, but you've forgotten two very important requirements. First of all, you didn't cite your sources.

W: Aha, I see. I can go back and do that easily.

M: Secondly, this paper is single spaced. I specifically told you I needed your reports to be double spaced. I need the extra space to write my comments between the lines.

W: Okay. I'll fix it right away and hand it back to you after lunch.

B 1. Ⓑ 2. Ⓒ 3. Ⓐ

🔵 3-13

Today, I want to tell you about Avram Noam Chomsky. He was born in Philadelphia in 1928. He most notably created the theory of generative grammar. This is considered to be one of the most significant contributions to the field of theoretical linguistics. But Chomsky is far better known for his political activism than his work in linguistics. He has strongly criticized the foreign policies of the United States and other governments. He describes himself as a libertarian socialist and a sympathizer of anarcho-syndicalism. Chomsky is a key intellectual figure in left wing politics of the United States. Between 1980 and 1992, Chomsky was the most cited source of any living scholar. He is the eighth- most cited scholar overall.

🔵 3-14

All right class, today I want to tell you about the architecture of Turkey. Most of its great works come from the Ottoman Empire. The Ottomans ruled Turkey and the surrounding areas for over six hundred years. Their architects achieved the greatest level in all of the Islamic lands. They mastered the technique of building vast inner spaces. These spaces were confined by seemingly weightless domes. Furthermore, they achieved perfect harmony between the inner and outer spaces, as well as between light and shadow. The plain mosque of the past was transformed by the Ottomans into a sanctuary of aesthetic and technical balance.

🔵 3-15

Okay, today I want to spend some time discussing the manager-employee relationship. There are various styles of management that a manager can employ to accomplish his goals. Let's consider two very different styles of management. An autocratic manager makes all of the decisions. The advantage of this style is that all of the decisions are consistent. A danger of this style is that employees may become overly dependent on the manager. The opposite of the autocratic style is the *laissez-faire* style. This kind of manager simply allows the employees to manage themselves. This can bring out the best in highly creative individuals. But in many cases, it is not deliberate and is the result of poor management.

Practice with Conversations

A 1. Ⓑ 2. Ⓓ

[1]posters and brochures

🔵 3-16

W: Hi, Dr. Caruso. May I have a moment of your time?

M: Hello, Mary. Sure, what's up?

W: Well, I'm working on my final project for my international business development class. I have to assemble a presentation as if it were a campaign to increase tourism for Guatemala. Since you're the Professor of Latin American Studies, I was hoping you might have some supplements that I could add to my presentation to spruce it up. You know, like some posters or brochures.

M: Hmm, let me think for a second. Well, I have an ancient Aztec spearhead and some examples of Stone Age pottery and weaving. Would those archeological antiques be of any use if I loaned them to you?

W: Uh, those sound interesting. But I was hoping for something more modern. I was thinking you might have some of those big laminated posters, some enlarged photographs, or maybe some information about the tourism industry.

M: Aha, I see. You're doing a booth to educate people about visiting Guatemala. Okay, I can help. But I don't have the materials here. Let me give you the telephone number for the Guatemalan Embassy downtown. I know the deputy ambassador there. I'm sure she would be happy to furnish you with some public relations materials. I know they have packets of posters and brochures that they hand out for free.

W: Thank you so much. That sounds like just what I need. I'll call them right away.

M: Sure, let me just check my rolodex here for Marta's phone number. I'll call her and put in a good word for you. She's always very helpful when I refer students. Let me tell you about one time. Last year, we took a study trip there, and two of my students lost their passports. There was a mix-up with immigration, and I called her. She got it all sorted out for us.

W: Wow, it's good to have connections I guess.

M: You bet it is!

Mary tells her professor that she is working on a final project for her international business development

289

class. She needs to make a campaign to increase tourism to Guatemala. She asks her professor if has any supplements she could use in the presentation. He offers her some archeological antiques, but those are not what she's looking for. Then he offers to connect her with the Guatemalan Embassy. He says that they will probably have some materials for her to use. She thanks him. Then he tells her a story about the time when his friend at the Guatemalan Embassy helped him recently.

B 1. Ⓑ 2. Ⓐ

¹Reconnection fee

🔘 3-17

W: Hi, Mr. Shanks. I'm Marcy Walker from room 322. I have a problem. My phone line is dead. I can't call my parents. I can't access the Internet. And I need to do research for my final project. This is the worst time on Earth that this could have possibly happened to me. What should I do? Can you help me get the phone turned back on?

M: Okay, Marcy, I know why your telephone line was shut off. It's because you didn't pay your bill for the last two months. It's not up to me whether your phone gets shut off or not. It's up to the phone company. They'll let you pay your bill a month late. But if you are two months late, they shut your phone off.

W: Yeah, it's a real pain in the neck. I didn't pay my bill on time because I spent the money reserved for the phone bill in my budget on shopping and drinking.

M: That was not very smart. Now you are going to have to pay your bill as well as a late fee of 2%. Then you'll have to fill out a reconnection form and wait for the service technician to schedule an appointment to reconnect your line. Then you'll have to wait for him to show up here at the main desk. Then, after it's reconnected, on your next bill, you're going to have to pay a $50 reconnection fee. All this trouble is because you were late paying your bill. What does this complication teach you?

W: I guess I'm going to have to get a part-time job to afford all of this.

M: Well, I'm looking for someone to work at the front desk at night and on weekends. I can give you twenty hours a week at minimum wage.

W: Oh, Mr. Shanks! You're a lifesaver. Thank you so much.

M: Sure. You can start training tomorrow at 5 p.m.

Marcy Walker tells her dorm manager that her telephone line has been shut off. She is upset because she can't access the Internet or call her parents. He tells her that the phone was shut off because she didn't pay her bill for two months. Then he tells her she will have to pay a late fee and a reconnection fee. He scolds her for not paying her bill. She admits that she didn't pay her bill because she spent her money on other things. Then the dorm manager offers her a part-time job working at the front desk. He tells her she can work 20 hours per week for minimum wage. She is happy and agrees.

C 1. Ⓒ 2. Ⓓ

¹comparisons and contrasts ²discusses the differences

🔘 3-18

M1: Dr. Simmons, hi, how are you doing? I haven't seen you since last year!

M2: Hey there, Fred. Long time no see. I'm feeling great. I had an appendectomy last summer. I was in the hospital for two weeks. That was tough. But I'm fully recovered now and feeling great. My body is one hundred percent shipshape! So how are you? I hear you're a student teacher these days.

M1: That's right. I'm really enjoying being on your side of the classroom. I'm teaching the Freshmen Introduction to Modern Literature Course.

M2: That's what I heard. As a matter of fact, that's why I called and asked you to meet me here today. The university has assigned me to observe your class next week on Tuesday, and I wanted to tell you in person.

M1: Oh really? Did I do something wrong? Was there a complaint?

M2: No, no, nothing of the sort. It's just a routine yearly evaluation that the university does on all new student teachers.

M1: Hmm, okay. I'm just surprised because I would think they would have told me about it earlier.

M2: Well, you know, the university administration likes to use the element of surprise sometimes. They want me to observe your normal teaching style. Speaking of which, what are you teaching this semester?

M1: I'll email you my syllabus and lesson plans before you come in. But in brief, I'm doing a compare and contrast unit, where we read a novel and then watch the Hollywood adaptation and discuss the difference.

M2: That sounds really interesting. Which books and movies are you doing?

M1: First we're reading and watching William Golding's *Lord of the Flies*. Then we're going to do Shakespeare's *Hamlet*, with the Kenneth Brannaugh film adaptation. Then, if we have enough time, we'll take a look at Joseph Conrad's *Heart of Darkness* with Francis Ford Coppala's *Apocalypse Now* for the film portion.

M2: Wow! That's a heavy syllabus.

M1: Yeah, do you think it's overambitious?

M2: Maybe a little.

Dr. Simmons and Fred meet. Dr. Simmons tells Fred that he was in the hospital for an appendectomy. He says his body is fully recovered now. Fred says he enjoys being a student teacher. Dr. Simmons tells Fred that the university administration is sending him to observe Fred's class. Dr. Simmons asks Fred about what he's teaching. Fred tells Dr. Simmons about a unit he's teaching that compares and contrasts novels and their Hollywood adaptations. Fred asks Dr. Simmons if he thinks this syllabus is overambitious. Dr. Simmons says it is a little overambitious.

D   **1.** Ⓒ   **2.** Ⓑ

¹old bathroom

  3-19

M : Hey, Sheila. What's up sister?

W: Oh, Ryan, I'm mad at you. Why didn't you call me yesterday like you said you would?

M: Oh, sorry for not calling. I forgot. I was busy getting chewed out by the resident manager of my dorm.

W: Really, what did you do wrong?

M: Nothing really. Reilly, my roommate, and I were just listening to the new Slayer album. We didn't even have the stereo at full blast. But the walls in that old building are so thin. The pre-med students next door were trying to study. They called and complained to the resident manager. Are the walls that thin in your building?

W: Oh yeah, totally. But our resident manager never scolds us. That's because we live next door to her, and we hear her television turned up loud all the time. We have blackmail material on her. Ha ha.

M: That's cool. I wish my resident manager would loosen up. He said if we get another noise complaint, he's going to refer us to Student Housing Services, and they're going to put us on probation.

W: That's bad. You should get out of the dorms and move into an apartment near campus anyways. I hate living in the dorms. The bathrooms are so old. They look and smell like my grandmother's house.

M: Yeah, the plumbing does seem sort of ancient. Plus I think there may be a family of rats living in the ceiling and walls. I can hear them scratching around at night.

W: That's disgusting. Remind me not to visit your dorm. So what about the apartment? Have you thought about it?

M: Yeah, I asked my dad if he would help me get out of the dorms. But he said I had to spend at least one year there before he would consider helping me get an apartment.

Sheila and Ryan meet. Sheila is mad at Ryan for not calling her. He says he didn't call her because he was busy being chewed out by the resident manager of his dorm. His resident manager was angry because he played music too loudly. Some students next door called and complained. Sheila says her resident manager never scolds her. Sheila tells Ryan he should leave the dorms and move into an apartment. She hates living in the dorm. She thinks they are old and dirty. Ryan says he thinks there are rats living in the ceiling and walls of his dorm. But his father will not help him get an apartment.

Practice with Lectures

A   **1.** Ⓐ   **2.** Ⓑ

¹300 ²3,500,000

 3-20

W1: Good afternoon, class. Today we are going to discuss the construction of one of the world's most famous tourist attractions. It's located in the middle of Paris, France.

W2: You're talking about the Eiffel Tower, designed by Gustave Eiffel and built between 1887 and 1889.

W1: That's absolutely correct. The Eiffel Tower today remains the tallest structure in Paris, standing 300 meters high. The iron structure of the tower weighs a total of 7,300 tons. It took 300 workers to join together 18,038 pieces of puddle iron with three and a half million rivets to erect the tower.

M: That doesn't sound like such a big deal.

W1: In a way, you're right. By today's standards, building that kind of structure would be quite easy. But for the time, it was the tallest structure in the world. It held the record for over 40 years. The tower was erected to be the entrance arch for the 1898 World's Fair in Paris. Did you know that only one worker died during construction? He was killed when he fell down the elevator shaft.

W2: Well, as famous as it is, I still think it's ugly. It looks like the skeleton of a building.

W1: You wouldn't be the only one who has thought the tower was an eyesore. Many members of the French public did not approve of the tower. One famous novelist even ate his lunch at a restaurant near the tower because he felt it was the only place he could eat without having to see it.

W2: Ha ha!

W1: And furthermore, the city government of Paris had an agreement with Gustave Eiffel that after twenty years, rights to the tower would be theirs at which time they would tear it down. But since it proved to be a valuable antenna used for radio communications, the city allowed Eiffel's permit to expire. By that time, the tower was so firmly entrenched in French history that they could not tear it down.

The Eiffel Tower was designed by Gustave Eiffel. It is still the tallest structure in Paris. The iron structure of the tower weighs 7,300 tons. It took 300 workers to join 18,038 pieces of puddle iron and three and a half million rivets to erect the tower. It held the record for tallest building in the world for over 40 years. The Eiffel Tower was the entrance arch for the 1898 World's Fair. Only one worker died during its construction. By the time the tower's permit expired, it was so firmly entrenched in French history that the government could not tear it down.

B   **1.** Ⓓ   **2.** Ⓐ

¹Media ²Message

 3-21

Good afternoon, everybody. Do you remember a movie called *Lord of the Rings* (*LOTR*)? I'll bet you either saw it or heard about it. The reason you know about it is because it had a successful advertising campaign around the world! To create a successful advertising campaign, you need the four Ms. Those Ms stand for Marketing, Media, Money, and Message. Let's take a look at how the four Ms added up to the huge success of *LOTR*.

First of all, the advertisers of *LOTR* had great marketing strategies. That means that aside from the actual movie, the film studio hired marketing companies to come up with many other products with the *LOTR* brand logo on them. That includes *LOTR* toys for kids, t-shirts, drinking glasses, posters, OST, and many other products. The act of putting the brand name, in this case, *LOTR*, in

front of people's eyes in as many places as possible is called good marketing!

Secondly, the *LOTR* advertising campaign saturated every form of media possible. That means that there were commercials for *LOTR* on television commercials, movie previews in theaters, on the radio, and on the Internet. There were even *LOTR* billboards posted on the highways in major American cities! Anyplace you looked, there was *LOTR*.

Thirdly, the producers of *LOTR* had the money to invest heavily in the various campaigns that were necessary to promote their product. In this case, the more you invest, the higher profits you reap. If the studio couldn't afford to spend as much on advertising as they did, the movie wouldn't have been so successful. Money is an important ingredient for a successful advertising campaign. Always!

Finally *LOTR* contained great messages. The messages in the movie were about friendship, perseverance, and the triumph of good over evil. People loved the movie and the products surrounding it because they loved the messages it portrayed. You can have the best advertising campaign on Earth, but if your product's message is bad, no one will buy it!

The professor uses the movie *Lord of the Rings* as an example of a successful advertising campaign. He says that the advertisers of *LOTR* were successful because they used the four Ms. The first M is for marketing. *LOTR* employed various marketing strategies, such as selling t-shirts, posters, toys, and drinking glasses. The second M is for media. The advertisers of *LOTR* saturated as many forms of media as possible. The third M is for money. The producers of *LOTR* had enough money to invest heavily in their project. The fourth M is for message. *LOTR* had a positive message that people liked. All of these Ms added up to success for *LOTR*.

C   **1.** Ⓑ   **2.** Ⓑ

¹El Nino: ²South America

3-22

Okay, class, today I'm going to provide you with overviews of the El Nino and La Nina weather phenomenon. These patterns are not easy to understand, so pay close attention.

The El Nino Southern Oscillation (ENSO) is a global coupled ocean-atmosphere phenomenon. Pacific Ocean signatures such as El Nino and La Nina are major temperature fluctuations in surface waters of the Tropical Eastern Ocean. El Nino signifies a rise of 0.5. Celsius or more and La Nina a drop of the same that is sustained for a period longer than five months.

Many of the countries most affected by ENSO events are developing nations on the continents of South America and Africa. Their economies are largely dependent on agricultural and fishing sectors as a major source of food supply, employment, and foreign exchange. New capabilities for predicting these events can have a great socio-economic impact.

These episodes usually occur irregularly every 2-7 years. They usually last one or two years. The effects of El Nino are very wide ranging. Many places experience weather that is the reverse from their normal climate. Some areas even experience terrible flooding due to excess rainfall or forest fires because of heavy drought. Aside from the drastic weather changes around the southern hemisphere, the fishing and manure industries in South America are heavily affected.

In the normal Pacific pattern, equatorial winds gather. Then warm water pools towards the west. Cold water upswells along the South American coast. Since fish follow the cool nutrient-rich water, this brings them up the coast where they support the local fishing industry. When El Nino takes effect, the warm water flows toward the South American coast. The absence of cold upswelling increases warming and sends the fish population out to sea instead of along the coast. These conditions are severely damaging to local fishing industries.

The causes of El Nino and La Nina temperature changes are still undiscovered. But many scientists are dedicating their careers to better understanding this global weather phenomenon.

El Nino and La Nina signify a temperature change of 0.5° Celsius higher or lower than normal for more than five months. Countries on the continents of South America and Africa are the most affected by El Nino. These episodes occur irregularly every 2-7 years. They reverse normal climates. An example of El Nino in action is when the warm water flows towards the South American coast. The absence of cold water upswelling sends the fish population out to sea. This is due to the fact that fish follow the cool nutrient-rich water. The causes of El Nino are still not fully understood by scientists.

D **1.** Ⓐ **2.** Ⓒ

₁A glass is half full

3-23

M1: Welcome, class. I'd like to start this class off with a question. Who here can tell me which great philosopher said, "I think, therefore I am"?

W: Ooh, I've heard that before. Was it… Jean Paul Sartre?

M1: That's a good guess, but no. This philosopher lived almost three hundred years before Jean Paul Sartre. His name is Rene Descartes. He is considered the founder of modern philosophy.

M2: Was he an existentialist?

M1: No, he wasn't. Descartes was a natural philosopher. He was also a mathematician. His love for math and philosophy intersected. He felt math could be used to prove truth about the universe. But it's interesting that you brought up the existentialists. That's an important group from modern western philosophy. Let's talk about an early existentialist named Soren Kierkegaard.

M2: Why?

M1: Soren Kierkegaard was a Danish philosopher who lived in the 1800s. He made a very important statement on truth. He said, "All truth is subjective."

W: Does that mean that up is down, black is white, and two plus two equals five?

M1: No, his viewpoint was not that drastic. Kierkegaard just thought that each person experienced a different version of the truth based on the perspective from where they were standing. For example, two men are looking at a glass of water. One man says the glass of water is half empty. The other man says the glass is half full. Their opinions seem to be conflicting. Are they? No, they are both right. Each man possesses his own truth. Neither one is more right or more wrong. Their truths are simply subjective. This was a precursor to the existentialist view that each person is alone in their relationship with the rest of the universe. This viewpoint, called the doctrine of Solipsism, has gotten a lot of criticism from other branches of philosophy. It's accused of being selfish and egotistical.

M2: But it makes sense to me!

M1: Sure, existentialism and teen angst have always gone hand in hand.

The professor begins the lecture with the quote, "I think, therefore I am." It is from Rene Descartes. Descartes was a natural philosopher. He was also a mathematician who believed math could be used to prove truth about the universe. Soren Kierkegaard was an early existentialist. He said, "All truth is subjective." The professor and students then discuss the meaning of truth to individual people. Kierkegaard's statement on truth led to the doctrine of Solipsism, that all individuals are alone with the rest of the universe. Solipsism has suffered much criticism from other branches of philosophy for being selfish and egotistical.

Integrated Listening & Speaking

A

1. (1) She is working on her final project.
   (2) Mary has to complete her final project.
2. (1) No, those are not what she's looking for.
   (2) No, the antiques are not what Mary wanted.
3. (1) The professor says they will have the proper materials for her project.
   (2) He says they will probably have the right materials for her to use.

🔊 3-24

Mary is working on a final project for her international business development class. She's making a campaign to increase tourism to Guatemala. She hopes her professor has some supplements she can use in her project. He has some archeological antiques he offers her. But those are not what she's looking for. He offers to call his friend at the Guatemalan Embassy. He thinks they will probably have some materials for her to use. She thanks him. There was a time when his friend at the Guatemalan Embassy helped him recently. He tells Mary the story.

B

1. (1) The line to her dorm has been shut off.
   (2) She tells him that her telephone line is not working.
2. (1) He tells her it's because she didn't pay her bill for two months.
   (2) He says the problem is that her bill has gone unpaid for two months.
3. (1) He offers her a parttime job working at the front desk.
   (2) He says she can have a job as a front desk worker.

🔊 3-25

Marcy Walker's telephone line has been shut off. She can't access the Internet or call her parents, which upsets her. The manager knows that her phone was shut off because she didn't pay her bill for two months. He explains that she will have to pay a late fee and a reconnection fee. He scolds her. She should have paid her bill. She admits that she spent the money for her

phone bill on other things. The dorm manager offers Mary a part time job. She'll be working at the front desk. He offers her 20 hours per week for minimum wage. She thanks him. She will begin training tomorrow.

C

1. (1) An example of a successful advertising campaign is *The Lord of the Rings*.
   (2) *The Lord of the Rings* is a successful advertising campaign example.
2. (1) They saturated as many forms of media as possible.
   (2) As many forms of media were saturated as possible.
3. (1) It had a positive message that people liked.
   (2) The message, which was positive, was liked by people.

🔊 3-26

An example of a successful advertising campaign is the one from *The Lord of the Rings*. The advertisers of *LOTR* were successful because they used the four Ms. Marketing is the first M. *LOTR* employed various marketing strategies, such as selling t-shirts, posters, toys, and drinking glasses. Media is the second M. The advertisers of *LOTR* saturated as many forms of media as possible. Money is the third M. The producers of *LOTR* had enough money to invest heavily in their project. Message is the fourth M. *LOTR* had a positive message that people liked. All of these Ms added up to success for *LOTR*.

D

1. (1) The professor began the lecture by saying, "I think, therefore I am."
   (2) "I think, therefore I am." is the famous statement which the professor began his lecture with.
2. (1) He believed that math could be used to prove truth about the universe.
   (2) The truth about the universe could be proved with math.
3. (1) "All truth is subjective."
   (2) "Every truth on the Earth is subjective."

🔊 3-27

The quote, "I think, therefore I am." is from Rene Descartes. He was a natural philosopher. Descartes was also a mathematician. He believed math could be used to prove truth about the universe. Kierkegaard was an early existentialist. He made the statement, "All truth is subjective." The meaning of truth to individual people is discussed. Soren Kierkegaard's important statement on truth led to the doctrine of Solipsism. This is the view that all individuals are alone with the rest of the universe. Other branches of philosophy have criticized Solipsism for being selfish and egotistical.

Mini TOEFL iBT

A   1. Ⓓ   2. Ⓐ   3. Ⓒ   4. Ⓓ   5. Ⓑ

🔊 3-28

W: Hi, there. Are you the janitor in this building?

M: Oh, hello. Yes, I am.

W: Okay, my name is Rachel Morse. I live on the third floor. I just wanted to tell you that the hand dryer in the shared bathroom on that floor is broken.

M: Oh yes, I seem to remember hearing about that. You know, with the construction in the basement and all of the new students arriving next week, I'm busier now than ever. I'm going to try to get up there and fix that dryer as soon as possible.

W: Well, I think you should know that it's been broken for more than a month now. You aren't doing your job well! You should have already done something about it by now.

M: Now just wait a minute. I'm really busy these days. I have to paint rooms and repair holes in walls and floors and scrape gum from garbage cans. All of these messes are made by you students. I don't need a freshman like you telling me how to do my job! You've probably never done any hard work in your life.

W: Yeah, I'm telling you that I don't like to wash my hands and then not be able to dry them. Cold wet hands get sore and achy in the winter. And they smear ink on my paper when I'm writing, and they get my clothes wet. It's unacceptable, and I want you to do something about it, or I'm going to complain to the administration!

M: I've never been spoken to by a student like this before. You're not my boss. You are a child, and this school is your playpen! I suggest you start bringing a clean towel to the bathroom with you to dry your hands.

W: Look, I'm sorry for being so disrespectful. I wasn't looking to start a fight. I just think it would be nice if you could find a few spare minutes to get that hand dryer working.

M: Hmm. Okay. I didn't want to fight with you either. The motor in the hand dryer is probably burned out. I'm going to put in a parts request at the school's supply office. It'll take a week for the new motor to come. I

promise I'll try my best to get it installed by the week after next. I hope that's good enough for you.

W: Yes, it is. Thank you. Have a nice day.

B   1. Ⓑ   2. Ⓓ   3. Ⓐ   4. Ⓐ Ⓑ Ⓓ
  5. Ⓒ   6. Ⓓ

🔊 3-29

Good morning, class. Let's begin with the realists. Realist painting arose in the late 1500s when Carvaggio went against the prevailing European style of Mannerism, which flaunted figures in graceful but unlikely poses. Carvaggio painted normal people, in real tones of flesh and blood, awkward and ugly, as they truly are in real life.

Rembrandt was a Dutch master of realist painting. He totally renounced the ideal. He embraced the life around him in his work.

Now, Edgar Degas was both a realist and an impressionist. Looking at his work creates a perfectly natural bridge between one school of painting to the other. Degas was one of the founding painters in the impressionistic movement. This movement began as a loose association of painters in Paris. The name of the movement comes from Claude Monet's painting *Impression, Sunrise*. The characteristics of this movement are visible brushstrokes, light colors, open composition, emphasis on the changing qualities of light, ordinary subject matter, and unusual visual angles. The influence of this movement spread to music and literature.

Interestingly, it was a group of French realist landscape painters called the Barbizon school who directly led to the impressionists. The realist nature scenes of John Constable influenced a younger generation of painters to abandon formalism and draw their inspiration directly from nature. One of these painters, Jean Francois Millet, extended the idea from landscapes to figures. He depicted peasant figures, peasant life, and their work in the fields. In his painting *The Gleaners*, Millet portrays three peasant women working hard at the harvest. The painting depicts no drama and no story, simply three women working hard.

Now, class, I want to share with you my favorite impressionistic painting. This is Georges Seurat's *Sunday Afternoon on the Island of La Grande Jatte*. This incredible painting simply depicts all different people from different classes of society enjoying a sunny afternoon in the park. If you look closely, you'll see that all of the color is applied in points, or unmixed dots, instead of brushstrokes. It allows the eye of the viewer to blend the colors optically instead of having them blended on the canvas. It took Seurat two years to complete. It now hangs in the Art Institute of Chicago.

Vocabulary Review

A

 3-30

1. memorable and worthy of recognition (notably)
2. ruling absolutely (autocratic)
3. a safe place (sanctuary)
4. the metal bracket that holds a door in place and allows it to swing (hinge)
5. to list or make mention of something (cite)
6. likely (probably)
7. metal bolts used to hold metal together (rivets)
8. an organized effort to achieve a goal (campaign)
9. to maintain over a period of time (sustain)
10. an enriching additive (supplement)
11. an officially appointed assistant to one holding an official office (deputy)
12. one's allotment of money for a period of time (budget)
13. surgery to remove an appendix from a human (appendectomy)
14. trying to accomplish more than one is capable of (overambitious)
15. to reprimand someone verbally (scold)

B

1. Yeah, it's a real pain in the neck.
2. This can bring out the best in highly creative individuals.
3. They mastered the technique of building vast inner spaces.
4. I'm afraid we can't give preferential treatment.
5. I need the extra space to write my comments between the lines.
6. I'm a little behind on my interview project.

Unit 6 Understanding Organization

Basic Drill

A   1. ⓒ   2. ⓒ   3. ⓒ

3-32

W: Hi, Professor Higgins. I was hoping I could ask you some questions about declaring a double major.
M: Oh, hi, Mary. Sure, I can spare a few minutes. I've had a lot of students do double majors in my department and others before. What subjects were you thinking about declaring?
W: I was thinking that I'd like to do a double major in criminology, in your department, and sculpture.
M: Hmm, criminology and sculpture. That's a social science and a fine art. That could be a problem. You see, the best double majors are two subjects that complement each other. For example, majors in criminology and forensic science go together well if you want to become a forensic detective.

3-33

M: Hi, I'm wondering if you can help me find Plato's *Dialogues*. I have to do a report on *Republic: Book X.*
W: Okay, let me check. Hmm, all of our copies seem to be out.
M: Oh no. They must have been checked out by the other students in my class. This report is due in two days.
W: Yes, you should have reserved a copy if you knew you'd need it.
M: Reserve a copy? I didn't know I could do that. How?
W: Do you see that desk over there by the water fountain?
M: Sure.
W: That's the Reservations Desk. The clerk there will reserve any book you ask her too. All you have to do is fill out a reservation card. Then, when the book comes in, they'll save it and call you.
M: Wow, wish I'd known that!

3-34

M1: Hi, do you work here?
M2: I sure do. How can I help you?
M1: I heard you might be hiring cashiers.
M2: We've actually just hired two new cashiers. That position is filled. But I'm sure there're jobs for kitchen workers. We always need more of those.
M1: Oh yeah? What does that entail?
M2: Washing dishes, cleaning up before and after lunch, that sort of thing.
M1: Hmm, that doesn't sound like my cup of tea. I think I'm going to have to keep looking around.
M2: Sure, I don't blame you. Another place you might look is the bulletin board at the Student Job Center. I heard you can always find different jobs there.
M1: Thanks, I'll try there.

B 1. Ⓓ 2. Ⓐ 3. Ⓑ

🔘 3-35

Okay, class, today I want to talk about my favorite heavenly body, the comet. It is a small body that orbits the solar system. It also exhibits a coma, or atmosphere, and a tail. These are primarily due to the effects of solar radiation upon the comet's nucleus. The nucleus is a minor body composed of rock, dust, and ice. Due to their origins in the outer solar system and the fact that they are heavily affected by close approaches to the major planets, comets' orbits are constantly changing. Some comets are destroyed when they near the sun while others are thrown out of the solar system forever.

🔘 3-36

Good morning, class. Today we are going to talk about something everybody likes on their pizza but not growing between their toes: a fungus. Fungi are eukaryotic organisms that digest food externally. Then they absorb the nutrient molecules into their cells.

Along with bacteria, fungi are the primary decomposers of dead organic matter in most terrestrial ecosystems. Many fungi have important symbiotic relationships with many other organisms. Mycorrhizal symbiosis between plants and fungi is particularly important. Over 90% of all plant species engage in some sort of mycorrhizal relationship with fungi and are dependent on that relationship for survival. As I mentioned at the beginning of the lecture, fungi are also used extensively by humans.

🔘 3-37

Greetings to you all. I hope you listen carefully today because I want everyone to remember what I tell you. Although traditional studies of memory began in the realm of philosophy, the late nineteenth and early twentieth century put memory with the paradigms of cognitive psychology. In recent decades it has become one of the principal pillars of a new branch of science that represents a marriage between cognitive psychology and neuroscience called cognitive neuroscience. There are several ways of classifying memories, based on duration, nature, and retrieval of information. From an information processing perspective, there are three main stages in the retrieval of memory. These are encoding, storage, and recall.

Practice with Conversations

A 1. Ⓓ 2. Ⓒ

[1]Tuesday morning calculus class is too advanced
[2]Chemistry 101 is a prerequisite class; cannot drop

🔘 3-38

M: Hi, who should I talk to about changing my class timetable for this semester?

W: You can talk to me about it. I'm the registrar's assistant.

M: All right, great. You're just the person I need to talk to. Okay, so, I want to join the recreational hockey league. So I'm going to have to shift my calculus class to Tuesday mornings, my Intro to Modern Literature course to the night class, and maybe drop Chemistry 101.

W: Hmm, that sounds like a lot of rearranging. Are you sure you want to do that just to join the hockey league?

M: Oh, totally, for sure. Hockey versus Chemistry 101… Which one would you choose?

W: Do you want to graduate with a useful degree in four years?

M: Yeah, but that's not for years. I need to get some exercise this winter. That seems more important right now.

W: Okay, I'm looking at your schedule here, and I'm seeing some problems. First of all, the night class for Intro to Modern Literature is all full. There's no way you can get in there.

M: Oh, that stinks.

W: Well, that's just too bad. Secondly, you can transfer to the Tuesday morning calculus. But I have to warn you, it's an accelerated class. That means that they move through the book a lot faster than the low level class you're currently in. Are you prepared to keep up with the increased course speed? Is calculus one of your strong suits?

M: Well no, but maybe I could…

W: Finally, about dropping Chemistry 101. Your major is Microbiology. You have to have Chemistry 101 as a prerequisite to take most of the other classes in your major. If you drop it this semester, it'll hold you up from taking any other courses in your major next semester. You could set your entire education back a year just to play recreational hockey. Do you really want to do that?

M: Hmm, I guess I'd better not. Thanks anyway.

W: No problem. Have a nice day!

A student wants to change his schedule so he can join a recreational hockey league. He wants to shift his classes to different times. He also wants to drop his Chemistry 101 class. The assistant tells him that the classes he wants to change into are either full or too advanced for him. She also tells him that he might not be able to graduate in four years if he drops Chemistry 101. The student changes his mind and decides not to play hockey.

B 1. Ⓑ 2. Ⓐ

¹get them online anytime

🔘 3-39

W1: Good morning, Mrs. Lassiter.

W2: Hi, Sally. You were absent yesterday. I hope you're feeling okay.

W1: Oh, uh, yeah, I'm feeling better now. I was uh, oh, at home, sick in bed all weekend. Actually, that's why I was coming to speak with you.

W2: Sick in bed? Oh, that's terrible. I was worried your absence had something to do with the big football game on Sunday and all the partying that was going on Sunday evening.

W1: Oh, Mrs. Lassiter, no way, not me. I'm not into any of that, football or partying.

W2: Hmm, okay. So how can I help you today?

W1: Well, I know you handed out the review sheets for the final exam yesterday, and I was hoping to get them.

W2: Oh yeah, those review sheets. You know, I hate to tell you this, but I'm all out. I ended up giving away my master copies by accident. You'll have to get them from one of your classmates.

W1: Oh, Mrs. Lassiter, I'm begging you. The class is graded on a curve. None of my classmates want to help me. I might get a higher score than them. No one will loan me the sheets!

W2: My, you do seem to be in a predicament. Sally, I have to confess something. I was watching the game on television on Sunday, and I saw you in the crowd. You were on campus television! You didn't look very sick to me.

W1: Okay, you busted me. I was at the game. I missed class because I partied too much. You caught me in a lie. But now will you help me?

W2: I'll tell you again what I told you at the beginning of the semester. You can access any of the handout sheets for this class from my website under the link that says "handouts". What do you think about that?

W1: Oh yeah. Now I remember. Okay, thanks.

Sally was absent from class. She tells the professor she was sick all weekend. She asks for some important review sheets for an upcoming exam. The professor tells her she's all out. She recommends Sally ask her classmates. Sally is upset because her classmates won't help her. The professor tells Sally that she saw her on television at the football game. Sally confesses she wasn't really sick. The professor tells her that she can get the handouts from her website online.

C 1. Ⓒ 2. Ⓒ

¹they write angry letters ²protested successfully last year

🔘 3-40

M1: Hey, Benny. Let's go over to the recreation room and shoot some pool or play some video games.

M2: Oh, Doug, haven't you heard? The recreation room is closed.

M1: No way! Why? I love that place! I usually go there every day!

M2: Well, you won't be going there anymore. It's been shut down and gutted. They're turning it into a Student Employment Center. It's going to be a place for company recruiters to set up booths and for career counselors to hold resume building sessions.

M1: Yuck, career counseling, company recruiters. That sounds like no fun! This is a total outrage. I'm going to do something about it. Do you want to help me?

M2: What are you going to do about it? They've already closed the place. It's too late!

M1: It's never too late. We can chain ourselves to the front door so the construction workers can't go inside and tear it apart. We'll stage a protest and get all of our friends to come.

M2: I don't think any of my friends would come. They're all interested in going to the career center to set up jobs for after they graduate. Maybe we should write the president of the university some angry letters.

M1: I like that idea, but I don't think it would get anywhere. People write him angry letters all the time, and I don't think he even reads them. He has employees who screen his mail and toss out the angry letters.

M2: I'm not so sure about that. Last year, the school administration tried to take away the benches and ash trays in Langley Park. You know, the place where everybody likes to gather and talk.

M1: Yeah, I know about it, but I've never been there.

M2: Yeah, well, they tried to take it away. All of the students who went there regularly were so upset. They held a protest. In the end, the administration didn't remove the benches.

M1: Sure, but I'll bet one of the protester's fathers works at the school.

M2: Hey, don't be so cynical.

Two friends meet and chat. Doug wants to go to the recreation room on campus to play some games. Benny tells Doug that the recreation room has been closed. It is being changed into a Student Employment Center. Doug is upset. He wants to stage a protest. Benny doesn't think the protest would be effective. He wants to write angry letters to the president of the university. Doug likes the idea, but doesn't think it would work. Benny tells Doug about a time when a student protest stopped the administration from removing some benches that students liked.

D　**1.** Ⓑ　**2.** Ⓓ
　　[1]Hungary [2]Budapest

🔘 4-01

M1: Hi, Mr. Jones. May I speak with you for a few moments?

M2: Okay, Mark, how can I be of service to you today?

M1: I heard you were in charge of the student exchange program for the international studies department.

M2: That's right, Mark. I am. Are you interested in studying abroad?

M1: Well, I'd never thought about it before. But I've been reading my course book and they recommend spending a semester abroad for students like me majoring in international law, like me.

M2: That's absolutely correct. For students in your major, it's recommended that you spend six months to a year abroad. It prepares you for the type of work you'll be doing, and it helps you determine your country or region of focus. So where do you think you'd like to study?

M1: Well, I've been thinking about a few places. I've always wanted to go to the Sudan.

M2: The Sudan! Aren't they in the middle of a civil war? Do you really want to go there?

M1: Well, I've been reading about it, and I think I could help save some lives or something.

M2: Hmm, do you really think you can stop genocide single-handedly? I don't think that's a very realistic place for you to get much studying done. Do you have a second or third choice?

M1: Yeah, you're probably right. My parents are Hungarian. So I speak Hungarian fluently. It would be easy for me to study in Budapest since I speak the language.

M2: Now that is a much more realistic idea, Mark. I actually know of a good law school located in Budapest. We have some of their students studying

here now. Maybe I could introduce you to them, and you could make some connections.

M1: That would be great. I'd love to make some friends that I could call if I went there. It would be nice to know some people right away.

Mark is interested in studying abroad. He talks to Mr. Jones, who is in charge of the student exchange program. Mr. Jones asks Mark where he would like to study. Mark says he would like to study in the Sudan. Mr. Jones says it is an unrealistic idea because the country is in civil war. Mark says his second choice is Budapest because he speaks Hungarian fluently. Mr. Jones thinks it's a good idea. He offers to introduce Mark to some Hungarian exchange students at the school.

Practice with Lectures

A　**1.** Ⓒ　**2.** Ⓒ
　　[1]ovule [2]Abiotic

🔘 4-02

Okay, class, today I want to tell you about the process of pollination. Pollination is an important step in the reproduction of seed plants. This is the name for the transfer of pollen grains to the plant carpel. The carpel is the structure that contains the ovule. The pollen grains are the male gamete, and the ovule is the female gamete. The receptive part of the carpel is called a stigma in the flowers of angiosperms and a micropyle in gymnosperms.

The study of pollination brings together many disciplines, such as botany, horticulture, entomology, and ecology. Pollination is important in horticulture because most plant fruits will not develop if the ovules are not fertilized. The pollination process as interaction between flower and vector was first addressed in the 18th century by Christian Konrad Sprengel.

The process of pollination requires pollinators as agents that carry or move the pollen grains from the anther to the receptive part of the carpel. The various flower traits that attract different pollinators are known as pollinator syndromes.

One method of pollination common with plants is entomophily, which is pollination by insects. Bees, wasps, butterflies, and flies are just a few of the insects that usually take part in this process. Another method is called zoophily. This denotes pollination by vertebrates, such as birds or bats. The hummingbird and the honeyeater are helpful with this process.

Yet another method of pollination is anemophily, which is by the wind. This is common with many types of grasses and deciduous trees. In the case of aquatic plants, pollination by water is called hydrophily. All of these pollination processes are covered by two categories, biotic and abiotic pollination. Biotic covers pollination by organisms, including entomophily and zoophily. This includes 80% of all pollination. Abiotic pollination covers all types not carried out by other organisms, including anemophily and hydrophily. Of the 20% this covers, 98% is by wind and just 2% by water.

Pollination is important for the reproduction of seed plants. Many plants will not develop if their ovules are not fertilized. The process of pollination requires pollinators to act as agents and carry pollen grains from the anther to the carpel. Pollination can either be carried out by biotic or abiotic means. Biotic refers to pollination by other living organisms. This often includes hummingbirds, bees, and bats. Abiotic refers to pollination by natural means, such as wind or water. Most pollination is biotic.

B   **1.** Ⓓ   **2.** Ⓐ
¹rubbing belly

🔘 4-03

M1: All right class, let's get started. I'd like to begin today's class with a simple activity. With your left hand I want you to pat yourself on the head. With your right hand I want you to rub your belly with a circular motion. Can you do it?

M2: Hey, this is really difficult! I can't do it!

W: I've got it! It just takes a lot of attention. Check this out!

M1: Okay, everyone can stop now. I asked you to do this because I wanted you to notice how difficult it is for your brain and nervous system to coordinate two different actions at the same time. This is called splitting your attention. Attention is the cognitive process of selectively concentrating on one thing while ignoring other things. One example is listening carefully to what someone is saying while ignoring other conversations in the room. This is called the cocktail party effect. Attention can also be split, such as when a person drives a car and talks on a cell phone. Sometimes our attention shifts to matters unrelated to the external environment. This is referred to as mind wandering or "spontaneous thought."

W: But I was able to pat my head and rub my belly at the same time. What does that mean about me?

M1: Well, that means that you are capable of splitting your attention. That reminds me of the most famous definition of attention by one of the first major psychologists, William James. He said, "Everyone knows what attention is. It is the taking possession by the mind in clear and vivid form, of one out of what seem to be several simultaneously possible objects or trains of thought. It implies withdrawal from some things in order to deal effectively with others."

W: Hmm, that sounds interesting. But how is the action of rubbing my belly and patting my head linked to focusing my mind?

M1: Good question. It is linked because your cerebral cortex controls your fine motor skills, which is what those motions require.

Coordinating the brain and nervous system to do two different actions at the same time is called splitting attention. Attention is the cognitive process of selectively concentrating on one thing while ignoring other things. William James was one of the first major psychologists. He defined attention as "the taking possession by the mind, in clear and vivid form, of one out of what seem to be several simultaneous possible objects or trains of thought." The attention of one's mind is linked to the cerebral cortex, which controls fine motor skills.

C   **1.** Ⓑ   **2.** Ⓒ
¹Public school system ²16 years

🔘 4-04

Okay, everyone, today I'm going to tell you about the development of the American educational system. The first American schools opened during the Colonial Era. As the colonies began to develop, many began to institute mandatory education schemes. In 1642, the Massachusetts Bay Colony made "proper" education compulsory. Similar statutes were accepted in other colonies in the 1640s and 1650s. Virtually all of the schools that opened as a result of this were private. Most of the universities which appeared between 1640 and 1750 form the contemporary Ivy League, including Harvard, Yale, Columbia, Brown, the University of Pennsylvania, and several others. After the revolution, an even heavier emphasis was put on education. This made the United States have one of the highest literacy rates of the time.

The school systems remained largely private and unorganized until the 1840s. Education reformers such as Horace Mann of Massachusetts began calling for public education systems for all. He helped to create a statewide system of "common schools," which referred to the belief that everyone was entitled to the same content in education. These early efforts focused primarily on elementary education.

The common-school movement began to catch on. By 1900, 31 states required 8-to-14-year-olds to attend school. In 1918, every state required students to complete elementary school. Lessons consisted of students reading aloud from their texts, such as the *McGuffery Readers*, and emphasis was placed on rote memorization. Teachers often used physical punishments, such as hitting students on the knuckles with birch switches for incorrect answers.

Secondary education progressed much more slowly, remaining the province of the affluent and domain of private tutors. In 1870, only 2% of 14-to-17-year-olds graduated from high school. The introduction of strict child labor laws and growing acceptance of higher education in general in the early 20th century caused the number of high school graduates to skyrocket. Most states passed laws which increased the age for compulsory school attendance to 16.

The first American schools opened during the Colonial Era. After the revolution, a heavier emphasis was placed on education. School systems remained private until the 1840s. Then educational reformers began calling for public education systems. They believed everyone was entitled to the same content in education. By 1900, 31 states required 8-to-14-year olds to attend school. Secondary education progressed more slowly. In the early 20th century, strict child labor laws and growing acceptance of higher education caused the number of high school graduates to skyrocket.

D 1. (B) 2. (A)

¹Nitrogen ²Argon

4-05

W1: Okay everyone, today we are going to talk about the fourth planet from the sun. It's named after Mars, the Roman god of war. Until the first flyby of Mars by Mariner 4 in 1965, it was thought that there were channels of liquid water on the planet's surface. People called these the Martian canals. Observations later showed that these channels do not exist. Still, of all the planets in our solar system after Earth, Mars is the most likely to harbor liquid water and possibly life.

M: What about time on Mars? I heard it takes longer to travel around the sun than the Earth.

W1: Very good. That's right. Mars has a similar axial tilt to Earth, so it has similar seasonal periods. But it's further from the sun and takes longer to orbit. So a Martian year is 687 Earth days long. Interestingly enough, the solar day on Mars is almost the same as Earth, being approximately 24 hours, 39 minutes, and 35 seconds.

W2: What about its atmosphere? Is it possible for humans to breathe on Mars?

W1: Well, Mars has an atmosphere. But since it contains only traces of oxygen, you wouldn't want to breathe it. The Martian atmosphere is 95% carbon dioxide, 3% nitrogen and 1.6% argon. During the winter months, the atmosphere gets so cold that it condenses into thick slabs of dry ice.

M: But earlier, you said that it's possible for life to exist there. What kind of life could live in that kind of atmosphere?

W1: That's an interesting question. Some evidence suggests that the planet was once significantly more habitable than it is today. But whether living organisms ever existed there is still an open question. The Viking probe of the mid-1970s carried experiments designed to detect microorganisms in Martian soil and had some positive results. But these were later disputed by many scientists.

Mars is the 4th planet from the sun. Canals on the planet's surface that were once believed to exist do not. But Mars is still the most likely place in the solar system, besides Earth, to harbor liquid water and possibly life. Mars has seasonal periods similar to Earth's. But its year is almost twice as long. The Martian atmosphere contains only traces of oxygen. During the winter months, the atmosphere gets so cold that it condenses into dry ice. Whether living organisms exist on Mars is still an open question.

Integrated Listening & Speaking

A

1. (1) Doug suggests they go to the campus recreation room.
   (2) Doug makes the suggestion to go to the campus recreation room.

2. (1) Benny tells Doug some bad news about the recreation room being closed.
   (2) Benny tells Doug some bad news that the recreation room has been closed.

3. (1) Benny makes the suggestion that they write some

angry letters to the president of the university.
  (2) Benny suggests that they write angry letters to the university president.

◉ 4-06

Doug suggests that he and Benny go to the campus recreation room and play some pool or video games. But Benny tells Doug the bad news that the recreation room has been closed. He tells him it has been changed into a Student Employment Center. Doug is really upset at this news. He wants to stage a protest, but Benny doesn't think it would be effective. He doesn't think any of their friends would support them. He suggests they write angry letters to the university president. Doug doesn't think this idea would work. But Benny tells him about a time when a student's protest changed the administration's decision to remove some benches.

B

1. (1) His major requires it in international law.
   (2) It is required by his major in international law.
2. (1) Mr. Jones is in charge of the student exchange program.
   (2) Mr. Jones runs the student exchange program.
3. (1) His parents taught him to speak fluent Hungarian.
   (2) He was taught fluent Hungarian by his parents.

◉ 4-07

Mark is interested in studying abroad since it is required by his major in international law. Mr. Jones is in charge of the student exchange program. He tells Mark that studying abroad will help him decide the area of focus for his major and asks where his first choice to study is. Mark wants to study in the Sudan, but Mr. Jones thinks it's a bad idea because the country is in a civil war. He asks Mark his second choice, and Mark answers Budapest. He wants to study there because his parents taught him to speak fluent Hungarian. Mr. Jones offers to introduce Mark to Hungarian exchange students so he can make some connections.

C

1. (1) He asks them to pat their heads with one hand and rub their bellies with their other.
   (2) He tells them about patting their heads with one hand and rubbing their bellies with the other.
2. (1) He says it's a cognitively selective process of concentrating and ignoring things.
   (2) He explains that it is the cognitive process of selectively concentrating on one thing while ignoring other things.
3. (1) It's linked by the cerebral cortex and fine motor

skills.
  (2) It's linked to the cerebral cortex, which controls fine motor skills.

◉ 4-08

The professor asks his students to split their attention by patting their heads with one hand and rubbing their bellies with their other. This is an example of the difficulty of splitting one's attention. He explains that attention is the cognitive process of selectively concentrating on one thing while ignoring other things. The professor tells them about William James, who was one of the first major psychologists. James's definition of attention defines it as the mind taking possession of several simultaneous objects or trains of thought. The student wants to know how attention is linked to physical actions. Then the professor explains that a person's attention is linked to the cerebral cortex which controls fine motor skills.

D

1. (1) He begins by explaining that the first American schools opened during the Colonial Era.
   (2) He begins with an explanation of the first American schools and their opening during the Colonial Era.
2. (1) A heavier emphasis was put on education by the U.S. after the revolution.
   (2) The U.S. put a heavier emphasis on education after the revolution.
3. (1) Many of the teaching methods were by rote memorization and punishment for incorrect answers.
   (2) Many teaching methods were rote memorization that included punishment for incorrect answers.

◉ 4-09

The professor begins the lecture by explaining that the first American schools opened during the Colonial Era. The Massachusetts Bay Colony was the first to make education compulsory. After the revolution, the U.S. put a heavier emphasis on education, which gave them one of the highest literacy rates. Then he says that the education reformers began calling for public school systems in the 1840s. Horace Mann was a reformer who believed everyone was entitled to the same educational content. But many of the teaching methods were by rote memorization and punishment for incorrect answers. Secondary education did not become common until the 20th century, when the number of high school graduates skyrocketed.

Mini TOEFL iBT

A 1. Ⓒ 2. Ⓓ 3. Ⓑ 4. ⒶⒸⒹ
　　5. Ⓐ

🔘 4-10

M1: Hello there. Do you work here?

M2: I sure do. But I'm a little busy right now. Could you just hang on a second?

M1: Look, I don't want to bother you. I'm just wondering what I have to do to use one of these computers. I'm kind of in a rush, and I need to check my email.

M2: Just a second. I'm about to level up on this game.

M1: Hey, buddy, I'm sorry to interrupt your game, but you'll just have to hit the pause button.

M2: Oh, I missed it! Thanks to you I missed getting a new level! Why should I help you now?

M1: Perhaps because you work here, this is a student facility, and I'm a student, and I want to use a computer now!

M2: Okay, hold your horses. If you want to use a computer, first you have to fill out a student usage form for us to file.

M1: Look, I'm running late for class, and I need to check my email for a study sheet I need for a quiz we're having in class today. Can you just help me out and let me check my email really quick?

M2: Sorry buddy, no one can touch these computers without filing a student usage card. Students are only allowed 100 hours of campus computer time per month, and we have to have a card on file for you to keep track of the time you spend. You obviously don't use the student computer lab very often.

M1: No, I usually just use my own. But my dorm is too far to run back to. Okay, it's an emergency. Where's the card? I'll fill it out.

M2: Uh, let me look. I'm not sure where I put them.

M1: Gosh, this is a real pain in the neck.

M2: Okay, here it is. Just fill out your name, address, telephone number, student number, and date of birth here.

M1: Here you go. All finished. Now can I use a computer?

M2: Sure, just show me your student ID, and you're set to go.

M1: I thought I had my ID card in here. Oh, I seem to have forgotten my wallet today. I... I don't have my ID card with me.

M2: I'm sorry. I can't let you use the computer without a student ID card.

M1: This is too frustrating. I give up!

B 1. Ⓒ 2. ⒷⒸ 3. Ⓑ 4. Ⓑ
　　5. Ⓐ 6. Ⓑ

🔘 4-11

M1: All right people, today we're going to be talking about something almost everybody here has used at one time or another: the bicycle! Who here rides a bike to class?

W: I just got a recumbent bicycle, but I didn't ride it to class today.

M1: Funny that you would mention a recumbent bike, because if you ask the International Union of Cycling, they don't consider that to be a true bicycle.

W: They sound like bike snobs!

M1: That may be the case, but they define the bicycle as a pedal-driven, human-powered vehicle with two wheels attached to the frame, one behind the other, with the seat positioned more or less above the pedals. Anyhow, I'm wondering if anybody can tell me why this child's toy is a significant invention in human history.

M2: Well, maybe because it's popular in places where people don't have cars.

M1: Great! That was just the answer I was looking for. Bicycles were first introduced in 19th century Europe, and now number over 1 billion worldwide. They provide the principal means of transportation in many regions. They are also a popular form of recreation and have been adapted for use in many other fields of human activity, including children's toys, adult fitness, military and local police applications, courier services, and cycle sports.

M2: Wow, I never thought about bikes so seriously.

M1: Well, let's first consider how the shape and configuration of the bicycle's frame, wheels, pedals, saddle, and handlebars have changed. Since the first chain driven model was developed around 1885, many important details have since been improved. On a modern bicycle, power is transmitted from the rider's legs to the rear wheel via the pedals, the crankset, chain, and rear hub. A cyclist's legs produce power optimally within a narrow pedaling speed range.

Now, let's go back to the earliest origins of the bicycle so we can see how much they've changed since then. The earliest known forbearers of the bicycle were known as velocipedes. One of these was known as the dandy-horse. It was used in France in the 1790s. Historians believe that it was merely a seat with two wheels and no steering or pedal mechanisms.

In 1839, a Scottish blacksmith named Kirkpatrick MacMillan added a mechanical crank to the rear wheel of a pushbike, creating the first true bicycle. It was copied and improved upon by other Scottish builders.

Vocabulary Review

A

🔘 4-12

1. to announce officially (declare)
2. required for submittal at a given time (due)
3. to hear incorrectly (misheard)
4. a regular pattern of circulation (orbit)
5. of or pertaining to a mutually beneficial relationship (symbiosis)
6. a place or area (realm)
7. specialized areas of subject matter and activity (disciplines)
8. the act of withholding one's attention (ignoring)
9. not public (private)
10. to be sped up, made faster, or more advanced (accelerated)
11. to change in any manner (shift)
12. to tell the truth after having deceived (confess)
13. the deliberate extermination of a people or nation (genocide)
14. to roam without an intended destination (wandering)
15. required by law (mandatory)

B

1. I'm so busy that I won't be able to spare a moment all day.
2. It's too bad that all of the copies of that new movie are checked out.
3. I'll take a cheeseburger, fries, a large coke, a salad, two cookies, a milkshake, three ice cream cones, and a cup of coffee.
4. Let's go to my bank's new branch. It's not busy at lunchtime.
5. It was an important step in the development of medical science.
6. The parents are calling for the principal to be fired.

Unit 7 Connecting Content

Basic Drill

A   1. Ⓐ   2. Ⓐ   3. Ⓒ

🔘 4-14

M: Well, ma'am, here's that essay assignment that's due tomorrow.
W: Hmm, hold on a minute there. Let me take a quick look at what you wrote.
M: I'm pretty sure I included all the details.
W: Hmm, actually, I don't think so.
M: Really?
W: Well, look at this. You have not explained the outcomes in any sort of detail at all.
M: What would you suggest I do?
W: Let's see, by the looks of this, rewrite your introduction section so that you can make the cause and effect transition later in the essay. Also, you need to give me more supporting evidence on the causes, so that you can easily describe the effects.

🔘 4-15

W1: Next. Hi there. That will be one meal ticket, please.
W2: Okay. Um, let's see, ah, just a second. I'm sorry. I think I've misplaced or lost my meal ticket.
W1: No problem. Maybe I can help you out. Do you have your student card with you?
W2: Just a second, I think I saw it in here. Um, yes, I have it.
W1: Okay. Um, go to the Student Information Desk just outside the cafeteria, and tell them you need one meal ticket credit. They'll take your name and student number and, um, issue you a meal ticket credit. You will have seven days to pay it back in cash at the same desk.
W2: That's great! Thanks!

🔘 4-16

M1: Sir, may I have a word with you?
M2: Sure.
M1: Well, I can't decide which grad school I should go to.
M2: Have you considered any overseas graduate programs?
M1: Ah, well, not really. Are there any advantages to studying overseas?
M2: Sure. I mean, not only would it give you a lot more choices of places where you can study, but, um,

also it would broaden your chances at getting some practical experience in your major.

M1: Well, ah, I never thought of that.

M2: You know, you really should think about it. Graduate students who study outside of their home countries are much more serious with their grad school research.

B　1. Ⓑ　2. Ⓓ　3. Ⓐ

🔘 4-17

When Europeans first discovered the Magdalenian paintings of the Altamira Cave, Spain, in 1879, they were considered to be hoaxes by academics and ignored. Recent reappraisals and increasing numbers of discoveries, however, have illustrated their authenticity and have indicated high levels of artistry of Upper Palaeolithic humans who used only basic tools. The age of the paintings in many sites remains a contentious issue, since methods like radiocarbon dating can lead to faulty data by contaminated samples of older or newer material, and caves and rocky overhangs are typically littered with debris from many time periods.

🔘 4-18

Until a few decades ago, humans were thought to be quite different from other apes, so much so that many people still don't think of the term "apes" to include humans at all. However, it is not considered accurate by many biologists to think of apes in a biological sense without considering humans to be included. The terms "non-human apes" or "non-human great apes" is used with increasing frequency to show the relationship of humans to the other apes while still talking only about the non-human species.

🔘 4-19

Dolphins are often regarded as one of the most intelligent animal species on earth, but it is difficult to say just how intelligent they are because of the complicated differences in sensory apparatus and response modes. They are social animals, living in pods of up to a dozen animals. In places with a high concentration of food, many pods can join temporarily, forming what is known as a super pod, and these groups may exceed 1,000 dolphins. These individuals communicate using a variety of clicks, whistles, and other vocalizations. Dolphins use these types of echolocation by emitting calls out to the environment. They listen to the echoes that return from various objects in the environment and then use these echoes to locate, range, and identify objects.

Practice with Conversations

A　1. Ⓓ　2. Ⓐ

¹change dates

🔘 4-20

W: Ah, yes, can I help you?

M: Well, yes you can. I need a favor from you.

W: What is it?

M: Well, I just got a phone call a few minutes ago informing me I was one of two people selected for a job interview.

W: Well, that's great news. When is the interview?

M: Ah, that's the problem. The interview is tomorrow afternoon at three o'clock.

W: Hey, wait a minute. You have a class presentation at that time tomorrow.

M: That's right. I was wondering if it would be possible to have my group's presentation time changed to the following day. I don't want to be absent, but I have to go to the interview.

W: Hmm, that could be a problem. Well, let's take a look at the presentation schedule. Maybe I can help.

M: Well, this is very important to me because I really need the money to finance my studies.

W: I understand. Now, let's see. Group A, hmm, they are scheduled to make their presentation two days from now. Here's what I can do. I'll call Group A's leader and see if your groups can switch presentation dates.

M: Oh, that would be great!

W: Well, this is on condition that Group A can make the change.

M: I understand.

W: Yes, hello. I need to ask a very big favor from your group. Would it be possible to change your presentation time to tomorrow afternoon at three o'clock? Really? Well, that's great! See you tomorrow at three o'clock then. Well, Group A can go tomorrow, so your group goes the following day.

M: Oh, thank you so much.

W: Just make sure you contact your group members and let them know about the change. That will be your job.

M: No problem. I'll get on it right now. Thanks again.

A student has suddenly been called for a job interview. The problem is he has a group class presentation at the same time as the interview. The student asks his professor if he can change the presentation time so that he can attend the job interview. The professor is willing to change the date on the condition that she can find another group who is willing to change their presentation date. The professor calls another group she thinks is willing to change dates. After communicating the problem, the other group is willing to change dates, and the student is thankful.

B   **1.** Ⓓ   **2.** Ⓓ

¹male student's notebook

🔊 4-21

W: All right. Are you ready to do this?

M: Yeah, let's study for that history test right now because I have another study group in about two hours.

W: Great. Let me get my notebook out, and we'll be ready to go. Let's see, um, chemistry, biology, um, oh no. Where is my history notebook?

M: Don't ask me. I have no idea.

W: You've got to be kidding. I had it at last night's lecture. I thought I brought it home. Which means it should be in my briefcase right now.

M: Hmm, maybe it's at home then.

W: No way. I don't leave any books lying around at home. My roommates tend to pick up things that are not theirs. Ah gee, I'm sure that book is lost. What am I going to do now?

M: Well, I have an idea. Why don't you photocopy my notes? Then we can study and make some last-minute notes on the photocopies.

W: Really? I can't thank you enough. You are a lifesaver. I just can't believe I lost my book.

M: No problem. There's a photocopier at the main entrance.

W: Great! Say, before I do that, I have a question about how you go about studying for an exam like this one.

M: Hmm, well, I got to tell you that I really look at the textbook very closely. You didn't lose your textbook, did you?

W: No, ah, I've got it in my briefcase right here.

M: Well, did you highlight the important sections during your readings?

W: Sure, who doesn't?

M: You'd be surprised. Anyways, read the highlighted sections carefully, and along with our study session now, we should both be in great shape to do well on the exam.

W: You're a lifesaver.

Two students are going to study for a test. One of the students has lost her notebook. She is worried that she will not be able to study for the test. The male student offers a solution. First, the female student should

photocopy his notebook. Then they should study together, making notations as they go along. Finally, the male student suggests that she also study the highlighted sections in her textbook. The female student is grateful for all of his suggestions.

C   **1.** Ⓓ   **2.** Ⓓ

¹lost on campus

🔊 4-22

W: Gee, I'm so lost. Oh, excuse me, I'm looking for the main micro-biology lab. Ah, you wouldn't happen to know where it is, would you?

M: Hmm, let me see. Well first of all, you are in the wrong building. This is the, ah, chemistry building.

W: Well that figures. This is my first week on campus, and I haven't a clue where anything is. To top it off, I'm late for yet another class. So, where exactly should I be going?

M: Well, hmm, let's see, I'm trying to figure out the easiest way to get you from here to the university hospital.

W: The university hospital?

M: That's right. That's where the main micro-biology lab is located. Hey, don't ask me why. I just work here. Anyways, ah, let's get you over there. First, do you know where the university hospital is?

W: I think so. Isn't it located on the corner of Alumni Drive and Ambassador Street?

M: That's right. So, from here you go, umm, yes, go out the main entrance of this building, and turn left. Follow the main pedestrian thoroughfare until you get to Ambassador Street. Got that so far?

W: Yeah, no problem. What do I do next?

M: Well, when you get to Ambassador Street, turn right, and walk about 200 meters until you get to the hospital. But, ah, don't use the main entrance. You will see a driveway that all the emergency vehicles use, and this leads to the Emergency Room entrance. Following me so far?

W: Got it. What's next?

M: Once inside, take the stairway down to the basement. Just follow the room directions on the floor map at the basement entrance. That's it!

W: How long a walk is it from here?

M: Oh, maybe, um, six minutes at the most.

W: I can't thank you enough. If I run, I should be able to make that class on time.

A female student who is new to the university is looking for a classroom but is hopelessly lost. She asks a university worker for directions. The worker explains she is in the wrong building and has about a six-minute walk to the building she needs to get to. So the worker gives the student walking directions to the correct building. The worker is careful to make sure the student understands the directions he is giving her. The student is very thankful for the directions as well as knowing where her next class is.

D   1. Ⓒ   2. Ⓑ

¹books

🔘 4-23

W: Hi, how are you today? I don't know if you remember me, but I was here a few days ago, um, trying to get my student ID card renewed.

M: Ah, right, I remember you. I had to get some information from the Registrar's Office regarding your current registration status.

W: That's right. Did you find out what the problem was?

M: Ah, as a matter of fact, I did.

W: Well, what was the problem? I've, um, been having a very hard time the past few days trying to use some of the university's services. Not only that, but I'm ineligible for discounts on books and supplies because I don't have a student card.

M: Yes, and well, I'm sorry for any inconvenience this has caused you. But, don't worry. I've got you set up with a valid student ID card.

W: So tell me. What happened?

M: Oh right. Well apparently, one of the office workers at the Registrar's Office failed to process your *Change of Major Request Form*. Because of that error, you were not officially registered as a student. You were actually listed as "withdrawn" from the school.

W: What? Are you serious?

M: Oh, don't worry, everything has been straightened out. The error has been corrected. Your *Change of Major Request Form* was processed and approved along with your tuition payment which has also been processed. That being done, we then were able to issue you a new student ID card. So, here it is.

W: Perfect! Am I ever glad that has been taken care of. Now I can buy my textbooks, get my meal plan taken care of, and ah, oh yeah, get my parking permit.

M: Oh, once again, I'm sorry for any problems this may have caused you.

A student needs to get her student ID card renewed. Unfortunately, there was a delay, so she had to wait. This caused her many problems, including not being able to buy discounted textbooks and supplies as well as not being able to use the university's student services. She is told her *Change of Major Form* was initially not processed, which led to her being denied a student ID card. Upon her next visit, she is told the problem has been corrected. She is issued a new student ID card and is now entitled to all of the benefits of having a valid ID card.

Practice with Lectures

A   1. Ⓓ   2. Yes/No/No/No/Yes

¹tools in the wild

🔘 4-24

M1: Well, let's start off this class by talking about the similarities of the cognitive skills between apes and humans. As you all know, humans and apes share many similarities, including the ability to use tools properly and imitate others.

W: Sir, can you explain how apes learn such skills?

M1: Well, ah, various studies have shown that baby chimps learned from experience while baby humans just imitated what they were shown. This gave scientists some key information in understanding the cultural aspects of ape life and the evolutionary similarities between humans and apes.

M2: Professor, can you give us any specific examples showing how, um, humans and apes are so similar?

M1: Sure. Let's take the gorilla. With, um, with 92-98% of its DNA being identical to that of a human, it is the next closest living relative to humans after the chimpanzee. A few individuals in captivity, such as, ah, Koko, have even been taught a subset of sign language.

W: Well, professor, isn't Koko an isolated case? I mean, I haven't heard of any other situations where gorillas have shown any kind of cognitive process.

M1: Actually, there's much more evidence available to support this fact. For example, a team of scientists observed gorillas using tools in the wild. A female gorilla, um, was recorded using a stick to gauge the depth of water while crossing a swamp. A second female was seen using a tree stump as a bridge and also as a support while fishing in the swamp. While this was the first such observation for a gorilla, um, for over forty years chimpanzees had been seen using tools in the wild, fishing for termites.

M2: Are you serious? You can count those examples on one hand. Surely, more observations are needed to infer that apes and humans have similar cognitive skills.

M1: Well that's true, and I agree, there have not been enough observations to make any valid conclusions, and that's why several field studies are currently underway. But, let's not forget about the studies we have discussed here. We should also be realistic, um, with the numbers of studies available since it's not easy to study apes in the wild.

Not long ago, humans were thought to be distinctly set apart from apes. Recent research has shown that this is not the case. For example, the DNA content of apes and humans is very similar, as well as the fact that some studies of apes in the wild have shown conclusive evidence of apes being capable of learning. We now know that certain species of apes are able to use tools. What is not known is the extent of apes' learning capabilities as well as the limit to what they can actually learn. Further studies are needed to answer these questions although this could be quite difficult to do.

B   **1.** Ⓐ   **2.** Ⓒ

¹louder

🔘 4-25

All right, are we ready to begin? Good. Last class we left off with, um, an introduction concerning the dolphin's ability to communicate with one another. As you know, dolphins are often regarded as one of the most intelligent animal species on Earth, but it is hard to say just how intelligent dolphins are. This is because of, um, this mammal's ability to communicate by using a variety of clicks, whistles, and other vocalizations. Now let's talk about the different ways dolphins communicate.

Okay, the first of these communication methods includes a form of echolocation, where dolphins locate an object by producing sounds and then listen for the echo. It works like this: um, broadband clicking sounds are emitted in a focused beam towards the front of a target. As the object of interest is approached, the echo grows, um, louder; and the dolphins adjust by decreasing the intensity of the inter-click interval and their emitted sounds. Anyway, we also know dolphins use different rates of click production in a, um, click train, which gives rise to the familiar barks, squeals and growls of the dolphin. A click train with a repetition rate over, um, let's see, yes, of 600 per second is called a burst pulse. Because of this process, it has been accepted by researchers that dolphins are able to form an "echoic image" of their targets. I guess you could say it's a lot like a submarine's sonar system.

Now let's see. Dolphins also communicate with body

movements and vocal bursts. These vocal bursts are produced using six air sacs near their blow-hole, since dolphins lack vocal cords. What these vocal bursts represent is not really understood. Yet, each animal does have a characteristic, frequency-modulated, narrow-band signature whistle, which is uniquely identifying. In this mode of communication, um, dolphins do use about 30 distinguishable sounds. However, many researchers scoff at the idea that this is a form of dolphin language.

Dolphins are considered one of the most intelligent animal species on Earth. This is because of their ability to communicate by using a variety of clicks, whistles, and other vocalizations. For example, the most effective method of communication they use is a form of echolocation, where they emit a series of clicking sounds to locate a target. This is done much like a submarine's sonar system. They also use whistles, which are unique for each individual. The use of body movements and vocal bursts is still not fully understood.

C   **1.** Ⓒ   **2.** No/Yes/Yes/Yes/No

¹The Big Sleep

🔘 4-26

Ah, now for today's lecture, we will explore some of the greatest American detective novels written by three of the best novelists of the twentieth century. My personal favorite is, well, *The Maltese Falcon*, written by the American author Samuel Dashiell Hammett. His most famous character, of course, was Sam Spade, a man who saw the, um, wretched and corrupt side of life but still retained his, um, tarnished idealism. Even though Spade was a tough guy, he was also a sentimentalist at heart, which makes him one of the most enduring detective characters ever created.

Well, next, um, we have American author Raymond Chandler, who based his main character, detective Philip Marlowe, initially on Hammett's Sam Spade. Marlowe first appeared in the novel *The Big Sleep*, published in, let's see, ah yes, 1939. Underneath the wisecracking tough guy public image, Marlowe was quietly philosophical and enjoyed chess and poetry. While he was not afraid to risk physical harm, he, hmm, never became violent merely to settle scores. Chandler's treatment of the detective novel, um, exhibited a continuing effort to develop the art form. His first full length book, *The Big Sleep*, was published when Chandler was, um, 51 years old while his last, *Playback*, when he was 70. Incidentally, all seven of his novels were produced in the last two decades of his life. I can say that all of these novels maintain the integrity of Philip Marlowe's character, but each novel has unique qualities of narrative tone, depth, and focus that set it apart from the others.

Finally, and I just love reading this guy's work. Author Mickey Spillane who created the fictional detective Mike Hammer in the book, *I, the Jury*. Hammer is in many ways the prototypical "tough guy detective" since he is brutally violent, and fueled by a, um, genuine rage that never afflicts Chandler or Hammett's heroes. While other detective heroes kind of bend the law, Hammer holds it in total contempt, seeing it as nothing more than a means to an end. And, well, this is contrary to Chandler's and Hammett's characters.

Some of the greatest American detective novels written were created by three authors: Samuel Dashiell Hammett, Raymond Chandler, and Mickey Spillane. Each of these authors created at least one memorable detective character that has endeared readers for over fifty years. Characters like Sam Spade, Mike Hammer, and Philip Marlowe had many similar attributes, yet each character has at least one major characteristic which sets them apart from all others. All three of these detective characters were characterized as tough guys, which probably makes them so memorable.

D   **1.** Ⓒ   **2.** No/No/Yes/No/No
¹South Africa ²Asia

🔘 **4-27**

M1: All right, here we go. We will begin this class with a discussion on cave paintings. As we have discussed previously, cave paintings were an important communication tool used by our ancestors for thousands of years. Cave paintings were relatively unknown until Europeans first encountered the Magdalenian paintings of the Altamira Cave, in Spain, um, in 1879.

W: Professor, could you tell us which cave has the oldest drawings?

M1: The place with the oldest cave art is that of the Chauvet Cave in southern France. It has been measured through radiocarbon dating back to 32,000 years. The cave was named after Jean-Marie Chauvet, who discovered it on December 18, 1994.

M2: Ah, sir, what's so special about the Chauvet Cave anyways?

M1: Well, the Chauvet Cave is uncharacteristically large, and the quality and, hmm, quantity of paintings found in it, makes it, well, unsurpassed compared

to other caves that have been found with similar paintings. The walls of the Chauvet Cave are covered with predatory animals like lions, panthers, bears, owls, rhinos, and hyenas. Um, as is typical of most cave art, there are no paintings of complete human figures. Researchers have found that the cave had been untouched for 20,000-30,000 years.

W: Ah, Professor, are there any other caves that have been discovered with similar paintings in other parts of the world?

M1: Oh, sure. For example, in South Africa, there are caves where the paintings are thought to have been done by the San people who settled in the area some, let's see, 8,000 years ago. The paintings depict animals and humans and are thought to represent religious beliefs.

M2: Are there any other examples?

M1: There are also rock paintings in caves in Malaysia and Indonesia. In Thailand, in the nineteenth century, there were some caves found along the Thai-Burmese border as well as other caves overlooking the Mekong River in Nakhon Sawan Province, which all contain galleries of rock paintings thought to be about 6,000 years old.

Cave paintings were an important communication tool used by our ancestors for thousands of years. Cave paintings were unknown to modern man until Europeans first encountered them in 1879. The best example is the Chauvet Cave, which is uncharacteristically large and has the best quality and quantity of cave art discovered so far. For example, the walls of the Chauvet Cave are covered with predatory animals such as lions, panthers, bears, owls, rhinos, and hyenas. As is typical of most cave art, there are no paintings of complete human figures.

Integrated Listening & Speaking

A

1. (1) The student's problem is that he has suddenly been called for a job interview.
   (2) Being suddenly called for a job interview has caused a problem for the student.

2. (1) The professor is willing to ask another group to change their presentation date.
   (2) To change the date of the presentation, the professor is willing to call another group.

3. (1) The other group is willing to change dates because they are ready.

(2) Because they are ready, the other group is willing to change dates.

4-28

A student has suddenly been called for a job interview. The problem is he has a group class presentation at the same time as the interview. The student asks his professor if he can change the presentation time so that he can attend the job interview. The professor is willing to change the date on the condition that he can find another group who is willing to change their presentation date. The professor calls another group she thinks is willing to change dates. After communicating the problem, the professor finds out that other group is willing to change dates because they are ready to go.

B

1. (1) The students need to study for a test.
   (2) The students are going to study for a test .
2. (1) The female student lost her notebook.
   (2) The female student can't find her notebook.
3. (1) The male student suggests that the female student photocopy his notebook and make study notes.
   (2) The male student tells the female student to photocopy his notebook and make study notes.

4-29

Two students are going to study for a test. One of the students has lost her notebook. She is worried that she will not be able to study for the test. The male student offers a solution. First, the female student should photocopy his notebook. Then they should study together, making notations as they go along. Finally, the male student suggests that she also study the highlighted sections in her textbook. The female student is grateful for all of his suggestions.

C

1. (1) The most effective method of communication for dolphins is echolocation.
   (2) An effective method of communication used by dolphins is echolocation.
2. (1) Dolphins can form an echo image of their targets.
   (2) Dolphins are able to create an echo image of their targets.
3. (1) The dolphin's intelligence can be accounted for in its vocalizations, such as whistles.
   (2) In a display of high intelligence, dolphins use vocalizations, such as whistles.

4-30

As you know, dolphins are considered one of the most intelligent animal species on Earth. This is because of their ability to communicate by using a variety of clicks, whistles, and other vocalizations. The most effective method they use is a form of echolocation. It's a lot like a submarine's sonar system. It works like this: first, broadband clicking sounds are emitted in a focused beam towards the front of the animal. Then, as the object is approached, the echo grows louder. The dolphins adjust by decreasing their emitted sounds and the intensity of the inter-click intervals. It has now been accepted that dolphins are able to form an "echo image" of their targets.

D

1. (1) Each author created at least one memorable character.
   (2) At least one memorable character was created by each author.
2. (1) Each detective's tough guy image was similar.
   (2) Similarly, each detective had a tough guy image.
3. (1) There are three authors mentioned in the passage.
   (2) In the passage, three authors are mentioned.

4-31

As I've mentioned before, some of the greatest American detective novels written were created by three authors: Samuel Dashiell Hammett, Raymond Chandler, and Mickey Spillane. Each of these authors created at least one memorable detective character that has endeared readers for over fifty years. Characters like Sam Spade, Mike Hammer, and Philip Marlowe had many similar attributes, yet each character has at least one major characteristic which sets them apart from all others. All three of these detective characters were characterized as tough guys, which probably makes them so memorable.

Mini TOEFL iBT

A 1. Ⓑ 2. Ⓐ 3. Ⓐ 4. Ⓐ Ⓓ 5. Ⓒ

4-32

M2: Good morning, sir. Thanks for seeing me on such short notice.

M1: No problem. How can I help you?

M2: Well, I'm here to see you about how I go about becoming a teaching assistant in the department next semester.

M1: Oh, good. We can always use some bright grad

students to take care of all those lengthy required course assignments that most professors just don't have the time to deal with.

M2: Well, I understand, and that's why I'm here. I think I'm a very capable student and feel I would do well as a teaching assistant. Do you have any advice on how I might make myself look like a reasonable candidate for the department's selection committee?

M1: Sure, no problem. Okay. Let's see, you first need to post your name on the department's teaching assistant candidate list. But before you do that, let's take a look at your up-to-date transcripts. Do you have a copy with you?

M2: Yes, sir, right here. Take a look.

M1: Hmm, all right, high grade average across the board, very good. Next, you have to submit a summarized paragraph of your current graduate studies research. You wouldn't have that with you, would you?

M2: Yes, sir. Ah, let's see, here it is. I…

M1: Great! Now let's take a look at that. Hmm, okay. Let me give you the rundown. As you know, a teaching assistantship is a contractual agreement between the university and student for a specified number of teaching hours. A teaching assistantship provides, um, teaching support to undergraduate courses and is a good way to make extra money for a considerable number of graduate students. I'm sure you already know this.

M2: Yes, sir.

M1: Good. Moving on then, a TA serves under the supervision of a course supervisor in one or more of the following capacities: as a marker, laboratory demonstrator, tutorial leader, or other supporting roles in the delivery or preparation of degree-credit courses.

M2: Understood.

M1: Okay, well, to wrap this up, a TA has a duty to acquire and maintain general knowledge of the content of the course as well as a thorough understanding of the components of the course for which she/he is directly responsible. Do you have any questions?

M2: No, sir. It sounds fairly simple. I think I will sign up right now. Thanks for your help.

Well, if you're ready, let's get started. Today's lecture will focus on the polar bear's ability to survive in the Arctic. As you know, polar bears are at the top of the food chain in the Arctic, so they are well-adapted to their habitat with their, um, thick blubber and fur, which insulates them against the cold.

For example, a polar bear's coat is about, um, 1 to 2 inches thick, and their white-colored fur also camouflages them from their prey. Um, camouflage means it makes it invisible. Anyways, moving along, their fur has a dense, wooly, insulating layer of under-hair which is covered by a relatively thin layer of guard hairs, which are about 6 inches long.

Now, these guard hairs are very stiff, shiny, and erect, and they stop the undercoat from matting when wet. This is good for the bear because water can then be easily shaken off before it can freeze. This excellent insulation keeps a polar bear warm even when air temperatures drop to, let's see, ah yes, -34. F. These stiff hairs grow on the soles of its paws, and these hairs insulate and provide traction on ice.

Amazingly, and I'm sure you all know this, polar bears are so well insulated they tend to overheat, so they move slowly and rest often to avoid this. Their thick undercoat does however, ah, insulate the bears to the point where they can overheat at temperatures above 50. F. Any excess heat is released at their muzzle, nose, ears, footpads, inner thighs, and shoulders. As we all know, polar bears also swim, and they do this to cool down on warm days or after physical activity.

Now this point is crucial. Contrary to popular belief, polar bears don't enter deep hibernation but enter a state of carnivore lethargy, um, which is another way of saying they can still hunt while they are almost asleep. Ah, only pregnant female polar bears hibernate. Hibernating females sleep soundly, but they're easily and quickly aroused. Incredibly, unlike most other hibernators, female polar bears give birth while hibernating. A high body temperature is needed to meet the demands of pregnancy, birth, and nursing. Finally, during the nursing period, the mother bears will not emerge from their caves while the cubs are very young. In this situation, the mother will not have eaten for an astounding nine months, and it relies on stored body fat for both her own nutrition and that of the cubs. Okay, are there any questions?

B 1. Ⓓ 2. Ⓓ 3. Ⓒ 4. ⒷⒸⒹ
5. Ⓑ 6. Ⓐ

Vocabulary Review

A

🔊 **4-34**

1. genuine or true (really)
2. similar or alike in every way (identical)
3. a slight, sharp sound (click)
4. the condition necessary for action (shape)
5. to continue; to preserve (maintain)
6. to meet or find something unexpected (encounter)
7. something done out of goodwill (favor)
8. to be given consent; to agree to (approve)
9. to raise money to use for something (finance)
10. not correct (wrong)
11. a lecture that is given to an audience (presentation)
12. a period of time where people are assembled (session)
13. the act of adding a person's name to a list (registration)
14. something that is considered true (belief)
15. related to people who walk (pedestrian)

B

1. You can count those examples on one hand.
2. I guess you could say it's a lot like a submarine's sonar system.
3. His most famous character, of course, was Sam Spade.
4. Hey, wait a minute! You have a class presentation tomorrow.
5. Ah, as a matter of fact, I did.
6. Am I ever glad that has been taken care of.

Unit 8 Making Inferences

Basic Drill

A 1. Ⓐ 2. Ⓓ 3. Ⓓ

🔊 **4-36**

W: Professor! I wanted to thank you for writing that wonderful reference letter for my scholarship application. I just found out this morning that I won the scholarship!

M: That's wonderful, Angela. There was no doubt in my mind that you wouldn't. You deserve it!

W: Oh, you're so kind. By the way, may I ask what exactly you wrote about me?

M: Well, I basically said that you are a joy to have in my seminar. You are insightful and quite intelligent. I also mentioned that you are one of the best writers that I have ever seen come through our department in many many years.

W: Wow, I just don't know how to thank you!

🔊 **4-37**

M: Excuse me, but I received this letter that I haven't paid my tuition and that all of my classes would be cancelled if it isn't paid by tomorrow. Can I get any kind of extension?

W: I think I can arrange that. May I ask why you haven't been able to pay yet?

M: Well, I'm waiting for my financial aid check to get here.

W: Oh, financial aid. Why didn't you just tell me that in the first place? In your situation, we can defer your tuition payment indefinitely.

M: Really! That's a relief to hear!

🔊 **4-38**

M: I'm sorry I haven't been more active in your class, Professor.

W: Is everything okay? Last semester you were much more talkative. You know that class participation is a major part of your final grade. You must contribute more to the discussions!

M: I know. I know. I just feel really intimidated with all of the upperclassmen in the class. Their views are so profound.

W: Oh, don't worry about that. They just have a little bit more experience than you, that's all. Last semester, you always had something intelligent to say, so I know you've got it in you. You just need to build up your confidence some.

M: All right, Professor. I'll try my best.

B 1. Ⓒ 2. Ⓓ 3. Ⓒ

🔊 **4-39**

In animals, the brain is the control center of the central nervous system. In most animals, the brain is located in the head, protected by the skull and close to the primary sensory apparatus of vision, hearing, taste, and olfaction. In humans, it is an organ of thought. While all vertebrates have a brain, invertebrates have either a centralized brain or collections of individual ganglia. Brains can be extremely complex. The human brain also has a massive number of synaptic connections, allowing for a great deal of parallel processing. For example, the human brain contains more than 100 billion neurons, each linked to as many as 10,000 others.

○ 4-40

Linguistic theories hold that children learn through their natural ability to organize the laws of language but cannot fully utilize this talent without the presence of other humans. This does not mean, however, that the child requires formal teaching of any sort. Nativist theorist Noam Chomsky claims that children are born with a language acquisition device in their brains. They are born with the major principles of language in place but with many parameters to set, such as whether sentences in the languages they are to acquire must have explicit subjects. According to Chomsky, when the young child is exposed to a language, the language acquisition device makes it possible for them to set the parameters and deduce the grammatical principles,because the principles are innate.

○ 5-01

The environmental movement is a diverse scientific, social, and political movement. In general terms, environmentalists advocate the sustainable management of resources and stewardship of the natural environment through changes in public policy and individual behavior. In its recognition of humanity as a participant in, not enemy of, ecosystems, the movement is centered around ecology, health, and human rights. The environmental movement is represented by a range of organizations, from the large to the grass roots. Due to its large membership, varying and strong beliefs, and occasionally speculative nature, the environmental movement is not always united in its goals. At its broadest, the movement includes private citizens, professionals, religious devotees, politicians, and extremists.

Practice with Conversations

A **1.** Ⓐ **2.** Ⓑ
¹GPA

○ 5-02

W: Hey, Adam. Did you get your report card in the mail yesterday?

M: Sure did, and get this. I flunked P.E.! Can you believe that? Mr. Andrews gave me an F! I can't understand why he would do this to me. I mean it is only P.E. after all! It should be an automatic A!

W: You too, huh! I thought my eyes were playing tricks on me when I first looked over my report card. English, A. Biology, A minus. Statistics, A. French, B plus. P.E., F. Woah! Hang on a second! Go back. P.E., F! How did that get in there? Am I hallucinating?

M: Wow! Wait a minute, Gloria. You got an A minus in Biology? How'd you pull that one off?

W: My friend is brilliant at science, so she helped me out a little bit.

M: A little bit! What'd she do? Disguise herself as you and take the tests for you!

W: No, she just gave me some pointers on how to study better. Anyways, what are we going to do about this P.E. grade? It's killing my G.P.A.! Speaking of killing, my parents are going to kill me once they find out I failed the easiest course out there!

M: Yeah, mine too! Let's think about it. We both dressed out every day, right?

W: Right. And we both participated in the activities each day, right?

M: Yeah, and I can't think of anything we might have done to irritate Mr. Andrews, can you?

W: No, he always seemed to like us, didn't he? I haven't got a clue! There must be some mistake here. Some typo or something. I guess the best thing to do is just go over to the gym and ask him about it. What do you think?

M: Yeah, and while we are over there we can ask him when we can retake the final exam that we missed ...

W: Final exam? Final exam! What final! You told me there was no final! What are you talking about!

M: Yeah, when you were absent a couple of weeks ago, Mr. Andrews told us there had been a change of plans and that we would have a final exam which would count for 50% of our grade. But, it completely slipped my mind until just now.

W: Adam!

Gloria and Adam are talking about their P.E. grades. They both flunked the class, and they don't understand why. They participated in every class and believe the professor liked them a lot. When they decide to go and talk to the professor, the truth comes out. Gloria realizes that Adam forgot to tell her about the final test they were supposed to take. Because Adam forgot, they missed the test and failed the class. Once she finds this out, Gloria becomes really aggravated with Adam for his mistake.

B **1.** Ⓒ **2.** Ⓐ
¹Minimum wage ²Good experience

W1: Okay, I've got an important job announcement to tell you about. Jeppsen Publishing is looking to hire two students as editorial assistants during the summer vacation. You both are my brightest students this year, so I thought I'd give you the first shot at it. This is an excellent opportunity for you to get a head start on your future since you are both thinking about publishing as a career.

M: Uh, how much are they paying?

W1: Well, it is only minimum wage. But think about it guys. The money really isn't the issue here. What is important is the valuable experience you'll gain from working in a real job setting.

M: Yeah, I know. I expected the minimum seeing how we are just students and all, and we don't have really any professional experience. It does sound like a great job though. Jeppsen is like one of the largest firms in the country. Many people would work for them for free just to get their foot in the door.

W1: You are exactly right. This is an excellent way for you to make valuable contacts within the company at a relatively young age. You never know, if they like you and, uh, you do well, who knows, they might offer you a full-time job that pays much more once you graduate from school!

W2: Oooh. It sounds really exciting! I've always wanted to work for them. Can you give us some more detailed information about the job? How many hours a week would we work, and what kind of duties would we have?

W1: I believe they want you to work a maximum of 25 hours a week. You'd basically be running errands for your supervisor, typing up memos, and taking notes during meetings. They said you would also have a chance to observe the senior editors when they are editing manuscripts. Who knows? You might even get a chance to meet some famous authors!

W2: Well, this all just sounds too good to pass up! I've already made my decision. I'm in!

M: Me too! Who knows! Maybe one of us will end up being the CEO one day!

A professor is telling two students about a summer job opportunity they have been chosen for. The professor explains how much they will make and what the duties of the job will be. Most importantly, the professor emphasizes how valuable the experience will be for the student's futures. The students are very excited about the chance and realize what an excellent opportunity it is for them. Both students decide to accept the jobs with great enthusiasm.

C **1.** Ⓑ **2.** Ⓒ

¹extra essay

M1: Excuse me, Mr. Adams? Do you have a minute?

M2: Sure. What's on your mind?

M1: It's about the test we had last week. I didn't do very well, and I was hoping I could take it again.

M2: A re-test, huh. You know, I don't usually allow students to take tests over unless they have a very, very good reason. Explain to me why I should make an exception in your case.

M1: Well, um, I'm afraid that if I get lower than a C on it, I could lose my scholarship. My academic scholarship states that I must maintain an A-average in all of my classes, and in your education class, my grade is slipping a bit.

M2: Hmm, let's see. Uh, yes, it looks like you got a C+ on the test last week, which has brought your overall average down to a B right now. Why do you think your grade has been slipping in my class? Is the workload too much?

M1: Honestly, sir, I haven't really had the time to study because of my part-time job. I've been working the night shift as a security guard to earn some extra money, but it has really been disrupting my academics, so I quit yesterday.

M2: Well, I respect your decision. I know how hard it can be supporting yourself and going to school full-time, too. I'm not going to allow you to retake the test, but I am going to assign you an extra credit essay. Once you complete the essay, I'll bump your score up on the test to a B+. This way, uh, you'll be able to get an A- or possibly even an A in the class, depending on how you do on the final. How does that sound to you?

M1: That sounds great! Thank you, sir, for being so understanding and giving me the opportunity to make up the extra points. I won't let you down!

A student is discussing a test he took in the professor's class the previous week. The student is not satisfied with his performance and is afraid he will lose his scholarship. He asks the professor if he can take it again. The professor asks the student why he believes he did so poorly. The student explains that he was too busy with a part-time job that he recently quit. Because of his honesty, the professor decides not to allow him to retake the exam but to do some extra credit work instead.

D   1. Ⓑ   2. Ⓒ

¹override code

🔘 5-05

W: Hello, excuse me! You haven't already closed up, have you? I need to check my mailbox real quick.

M: I'm sorry, miss, but yes, I've, uh, already closed up for the evening. Can't you just come back Monday morning?

W: I could, but I'm expecting a really special package from my father today. You see, it is my birthday, and he's sent me a new digital camera, and I was hoping I could use it this weekend when I go to the beach with my friends.

M: A new digital camera, huh. Well, uh, you see, the thing is the lock is on a timer, and it automatically opens and locks itself every morning and evening. It's a new type of security system they are trying out. If I had a key, I'd be glad to open back up so you could get your present.

W: Oh, no! You mean there's no other way for me to get in? I'm going to have to wait until Monday? What am I going to do? You've just got to help me out! I'm desperate!

M: Well, there is one other way now that I think about it. I remember my manager mentioning something about an override code in case of an emergency. It's a code I can punch in that will unlock the door. The problem is that I really hate calling my boss up and bothering him.

W: Oh, please! I'll do anything! Couldn't I give you a tip or something for all your trouble? How about ten bucks! Would that make calling your boss up a little bit easier to do? I've just got to open up that mailbox!

M: Oh, no, no, no. I can't accept your money. Keep it! You need it for your beach trip this weekend! You know what? Don't worry about it. I'm going to call my boss up right now. We'll have that camera of yours in a matter of seconds!

W: Oh, thank you so much! You are so kind!

An anxious student is speaking to a mailbox manager who has just locked up the office for the weekend. The student is expecting a birthday gift and hopes the manager will allow her to check her mail. Unfortunately, the door locks on an electric timer and will not open up until Monday morning. The student wants to use her gift over the weekend and implores the manager to help

her. The manager finds an alternative way to get inside. The student is very grateful.

Practice with Lectures

A   1. Ⓒ   2. Ⓑ

¹sweat, shiver, pant ²control body temperature

🔘 5-06

Warm-blooded animals maintain thermal homeostasis. What I mean is they keep their body core temperature at a nearly constant level regardless of the temperature of the surrounding environment: the outside climate. Okay. Now what we call this is endothermy.

Endothermy is the ability of some creatures to control their body temperatures through internal means such as shivering, fat burning, panting, and sweating. You all know what I'm talking about, right? When you shiver because it's so cold in the winter or when you are sweating buckets in the summer, all your body is trying to do is maintain that constant temperature of 98.6 degrees inside.

Now, um, there are some advantages and disadvantages to all of this. The advantages are increased enzyme activity and a constant body temperature, which allows warm-blooded animals to be active in cold temperatures. A big disadvantage is the, uh, need to maintain thermoregulation or, in other words, heat production, even during inactivity, otherwise the organism will die. That's right. It could mean life or death.

Heat regulation is one of the most important defense mechanisms in a warm-blooded organism. Is everyone following me? Sure? Great, so uh, for example, in the winter, there may not be enough food to enable an endotherm, for example, a hungry grizzly bear, to keep its metabolic rate stable all day. Um, so some animals, like our friend the grizzly, go into a controlled state of hypothermia called hibernation, or torpor. This deliberately lowers the body temperature to conserve energy. Everyone still with me? Good. Now, in hot weather, like when you were at the beach last weekend soaking up all those dangerous ultraviolet rays to make yourself look tan and pretty, endotherms expend considerable energy to avoid overheating. They may pant, sweat, lick, or seek shelter or water.

Warm-blooded animals are able to keep their body temperatures at a constant level. They use means such as shivering and sweating to do this. Another term for this temperature control is endothermy. Endotherms spend a great amount of energy to maintain body temperature, and if they don't, they could perish. Advantages of this regulation are increased enzyme activity and increased activity in cold weather situations.

B 1. Ⓐ 2. Ⓓ
[1]Normans [2]15th century

🔘 5-07

W1: Okay, everyone. Calm down. I know you are all really excited about being able to read a little bit of Old English. I congratulate you. Job well done, but we've got a ways yet to go. Now it is time for us to take a look at the history of English. Who can tell me where English originated?

W2: That's easy! England, of course. Everyone knows that the language is named after the country!

W1: Uh, well, that's partly correct. English is a West Germanic language. It came from the Anglo-Frisian dialects brought to Britain by settlers from parts of what is now northwest Germany and the northern Netherlands. At first, Old English was a group of dialects reflecting the different origins of the Anglo-Saxon kingdoms of England. The original Old English language was then influenced by two waves of invasion. The first was by language speakers of the Scandinavian branch of the Germanic family. They conquered and colonized parts of Britain in the 8th and 9th centuries. The second was the Normans in the 11th century, who spoke a variety of French. These two invasions caused English to become "mixed" to some degree. Now what kind of effect do you guys think this mixing had on English?

W2: Wouldn't that have made English pretty diverse, Professor?

W1: I see somebody is paying attention! Exactly! English became a very rich, elaborate layer of words. And later, English developed into a borrowing language of great flexibility with a huge vocabulary. So, what about modern English? Who can give us an idea of when it began?

M: I believe it was around the, um, 15th century, wasn't it?

W1: Yes, it was. Modern English is often dated from the Great Vowel Shift, which took place mainly during the 15th century. English was also influenced by the spread of a standardized London-based dialect in government and administration and by the standardizing effect of printing. By the time of William Shakespeare, around the, uh, middle to late 16th century, the language had become clearly recognizable as modern English.

English is a West-Germanic language that originated in German and the Netherlands and was brought to England by settlers. Two later invasions by the Scandinavians and Normans heavily influenced the language by making it more diverse and elaborate. Modern English began around the 15th century. It was affected by the standardized dialect of the government. By the time of Shakespeare, modern English was a clearly recognized language which stood on its own.

C 1. Ⓑ 2. Ⓒ
[1]20 [2]45

🔘 5-08

The Amazon River pulsates, surging once a year. From November through May, the volume of the, uh, mainstream swells. For example, as stated in your text, on June 1, 1989, the level of the river at Manaus, 900 miles from the ocean, was 45 feet above low water, nearly reaching the 1953 all-time high-water mark on the flood gauge. Now, the Amazon's volume in that month far exceeded the combined flow of the next eight largest rivers on Earth, a pretty extraordinary stat if you think about it. It does this by the end of every May, even in years of normal flow. During the second half of the year, this, um, regular flow diminishes. All right, uh, yes, here it is in your text, page 372. In November of 1990, also around Manaus, stretches of white beaches and sandbars were exposed to the sun for the first time in living memory. The river had fallen 50 feet to its lowest level on record this century. The only official studies of the main stream flow were done in 1963 and 1964 which, uh, were years estimated as, uh, having less than average rainfall by the U.S. Geological Survey. Measurements were made at Obidos, 600 miles inland, where the Amazon squeezes through a single channel, very narrow in comparison, a little more than a mile wide. Findings gave the average minimum discharge at 3 million cubic feet per second while the average maximum reached 8.5 million.

For comparison, our own Mississippi River at Vicksburg averages 620,000 cubic feet per second. It has been suggested that the Amazon's average annual discharge equals 20 percent of the total continental runoff of all rivers on Earth. Note this does not mean that the Amazon system holds one-fifth of the entire world's freshwater, as some other books have interpreted this data. In fact, all the Amazonia's waterways hold less than one ten-thousandth of the world's fresh water, most of which, by the way, is locked up in polar ice.

The Amazon River experiences a large surge about once a year . This occurs between the months of November and May. Some areas reported increases in the waterline by as much as 40 to 50 feet in the late '80s. During the other half of the year, the water recedes, exposing sandbars and beach-like white sand. The average discharge of the river is between 3 and 8.5 million cubic feet per second. Finally, contrary to some published accounts, the Amazon holds less than one ten-thousandth of all the world's fresh water.

D   **1.** Ⓐ   **2.** Ⓑ

[1]Solar purification

⊙ 5-09

M1: Could you close the door, please? Great. Thanks. Now today, class, we're going to discuss dirty water. That's right, dirty water, or more importantly, how to purify it yourselves so that you can drink it and not get sick. Sure, you can go out and buy portable drinking water systems or expensive designer mineral water, but there are other methods you can use if you don't have this stuff available. Who can name one?

W: Whenever my dad takes us all camping, he just boils it, and no one in my family has ever gotten sick.

M1: Sure. Boiling water on a portable stove or fire will kill most bacteria and viruses. At higher elevations, though, the boiling point of water drops, so that several minutes of continuous boiling are required. Another option is just to be sure you carry a portable pump filter. Some of these, um, like the charcoal filter ones, don't remove the viruses. In this case, you have to disinfect the water with a third method. Who can tell me what a third might be?

M2: How about electricity?

M1: Very funny. Not quite. No, actually, I was thinking of a couple of chemicals. One is iodine, which kills many, but not all, of the most common, uh, pathogens in natural fresh water sources. Second, used only in emergency situations, is chlorine-based bleach. Just add two drops of 5% bleach per quart of clear water, and let it stand, uh, covered, for about an hour. All right, now that is three so far. Anyone like to take a stab at the last option?

W: Uh, sunshine?

M1: Bonus points for whoever said that in the back row. Yes, sunlight is another valid option. We call it solar purification. Water is placed in a transparent plastic bottle, which is oxygenated by shaking. It is placed for six hours in full sun, which raises the temperature and gives an extended dose of solar radiation, killing any microbes that may be present.

Water purification is important when camping or doing other outdoor activities. If it isn't done, dirty or polluted water can be harmful to human beings. There are four main methods of purifying water in the outdoors: boiling, filtering, chemically, and with the sun. Boiling is the easiest and most complete while filtering might not kill all of the viruses. Iodine is a chemical for killing most pathogens in water, and sunlight, though time consuming, is another valid option.

Integrated Listening & Speaking

A

1. (1) Experience is the greatest advantage of the job.
   (2) The greatest advantage of the job is experience.

2. (1) The students are eager and react with enthusiasm.
   (2) In response, the students react eagerly and with enthusiasm.

3. (1) A minor disadvantage is that the pay is quite low.
   (2) The students consider the low pay to be a minor disadvantage of the job.

⊙ 5-10

A professor is explaining to two of her students about a job opening. It is a summer job at a publishing company. The professor goes on to explain that the students would make minimum wage and work about 25 hours a week. The students seem quite interested. Emphasizing the importance of experience, the professor shows how the job could be an excellent stepping stone for their future careers. She talks about how they would make great connections with those in the company. Ultimately, both students readily accept the job with great enthusiasm and look forward to their new positions.

B

1. (1) The student needs to redo an exam.
   (2) The student hopes to redo an exam.

2. (1) The instructor is very understanding and helpful.
   (2) The instructor's reply is helpful and understanding.

3. (1) The instructor decides to give the student extra credit work.
   (2) The instructor has the student do extra credit

work to bring up his average.

5-11

The student is having a conversation with his instructor. The student is concerned about a test he took the previous week. He hopes the instructor will allow him to take it again. If the instructor doesn't allow a makeup test, the student is afraid he will be in jeopardy of losing his scholarship. The instructor inquires the reason the student hasn't been doing so well in the class, and the student claims it has been due to a part-time job that has kept him really busy. In a very understanding manner, the instructor decides not to allow a makeup test but to allow the student to do an extra credit essay in order to improve his overall grade. The student is elated and thanks the professor enthusiastically.

C

1. (1) The Amazon is in constant change throughout the year.
   (2) Throughout the year, the Amazon is in constant change.
2. (1) The water level reached 45 feet above the low level line.
   (2) The water level rose to 45 feet above the low level line.
3. (1) Compared to the Mississippi, the Amazon's average discharge is over 10 times greater.
   (2) The Amazon's average discharge is over 10 times greater than the Mississippi's.

5-12

The Amazon River is a river in great flux most of the year. It experiences a great increase in water level each year, typically between the months of November and May. In June, 1989, the water level rose to 45 feet above the low level line, which nearly made it a record reading. That same month the volume of the Amazon was greater than the combined flow of the next 8 largest rivers in the world. The only official studies of the river capacity were done in the mid 1960s. In comparison to the Mississippi River in the U.S., the Amazon is a monster even during low rainfall seasons. The average discharge of the Amazon can reach 7 to 8 million cubic feet per second while the Mississippi averages 600,000.

D

1. (1) The best method of water purification is boiling.
   (2) Boiling is the best method of water purification.
2. (1) Solar purification takes about six hours.
   (2) At six hours, solar purification takes a long time.
3. (1) The lecture focuses on methods of water purification
   (2) In the lecture, methods of water purification are focused on.

5-13

Purifying water is very important for individuals who spend time camping and doing other outdoor activities. If people don't purify water from lakes, rivers, and other sources, they could become ill and possibly even die. Boiling water is one of the easiest and best methods of cleaning water. Another method is a water filter, though it does not always kill all the bad organisms in the water. A third method is using chemicals such as iodine or chlorine. Chlorine should only be used in emergency situations. Finally, people can use sunlight to sanitize their drinking water. Yet, solar purification takes a great amount of time, usually about six hours.

Mini TOEFL iBT

A 1. Ⓑ 2. Ⓐ 3. Ⓓ 4. ⒶⒸ 5. Ⓑ

5-14

W: Good afternoon. I'm looking for a part-time job and was wondering if you had any openings at the moment.

M: Well, actually, we do have a couple of openings. Because it is the beginning of the semester, we're really swamped right now and are actually understaffed. When would you be available?

W: I'd really prefer to work during lunch if that's possible. I have a really heavy load of classes this term, so my mornings are completely booked. I'm also in a jazz band, and we usually have our practice sessions in the evening, so that wouldn't really be a good time for me either. Would a lunch schedule be possible?

M: Let's see. Um, we have a cashier's position available. Hold on a second so I can check the schedule real quick. Uh, here it is, yes, the hours would be Monday through Friday from 11 a.m. to 2 p.m. Now, do you have any experience with using a computerized register and handling money? If you don't, don't worry about it. We would train you, and it is really very easy to pick up.

W: Sure! I worked at a bookstore for a few months last summer and used one of those kinds of registers. It was a really busy store right next to campus. I got really good at handling all the money and making change. It was a little stressful at first, but I think I, uh, adapted pretty well! By the end of the first month, they were actually asking me to train new employees!

M: Good! And the hours? Would that be a workable schedule with you? You sound like a very busy person! I don't want you to get in over your head!

W: The hours are perfect for me. My morning classes finish by ten, and I've only got one afternoon seminar each day, and that doesn't start until three. Um, I wanted to ask you about weekends. Would that be a possibility too? I could really use the extra money.

M: Of course! That wouldn't be a problem, and it would basically be up to you. Look, I think you would be an excellent addition to our staff. You have good experience and a great personality. I'll start you off at eight dollars an hour. Why don't you just come in next Monday at 10:30 so we can get you going!

W: Great! You just made my day! I'll see you on Monday!

B 1. Ⓐ 2. Ⓒ 3. Ⓓ 4. ⒶⒸⒹ
5. Ⓑ 6. Ⓒ

 5-15

Good morning, all. Everyone please grab a seat so we can get started. Thanks. Now, today's topic is neurons, a major class of cells in the nervous system. And the main role of these neurons is to process and transmit information. In vertebrates, um, you all remember what a vertebrate is, right? Good. Now, in vertebrates, neurons are found in the brain, the spinal cord, and in the nerves and ganglia of the peripheral nervous system. In the most basic of terms, the neuron is composed of a cell body, a dendritic tree, and an axon. In the classical view of the neuron, the cell body and dendritic tree receive inputs from other neurons, and the axon transmits output signals.

Everyone following me? Excellent. So, the way neurons are able to do this is that they have the ability to generate electrical impulses. They zap specific information through connectors to other neurons in what we scientists like to call a synaptic transmission. That's right! Neurons communicate with each other via synapses, where the axon of one cell touches the dendrite of another. Synapses can be excitatory or inhibitory. That is, they produce or stop signals, and will either increase or decrease activity in the target neuron. With me? Great. Now, some neurons in your cerebellum, that large part of your brain which controls many your movements, can have over 1000 dendrite branches which connect with thousands of other cells. And, um, on the other hand, certain neurons might have only one or two dendrites, each of which receives thousands of synapses. Getting the picture now?

Further, the human brain has a huge number of neurons and an even huger number of synapses. Now listen closely to this. Each of 100 billion neurons has on average 7,000 synaptic connections to other neurons. Most authorities estimate that the brain of a three-year-old child has about 1,000 trillion synapses. Of course, uh, this number declines with age and stabilizes when you are older, say in your early twenties, when the number of synapses ranges from 100 to 500 trillion synapses in most adults.

Vocabulary Review

A
 5-16

1. strong or solid (firm)
2. a comparison or in relation (relatively)
3. to understand or be aware (realize)
4. pertaining to school or scholastics (academic)
5. to receive or get (accept)
6. to anticipate (expect)
7. to make urgent (implore)
8. imitating nature (naturalistic)
9. thrifty or frugal (economically)
10. to fill with fear (intimidate)
11. rare; uncommon (extraordinary)
12. a condition of urgent need (emergency)
13. to cleanse; to clean (purify)
14. to surpass (exceed)
15. adaptable; elastic (flexible)

B

1. Let your sister take a stab at the poker game.
2. Jeff paid ten bucks for his sweater.
3. They need to build up some savings before they can buy a car.
4. We were sweating buckets while playing tennis yesterday.
5. I know you've got it in you to do better in Spanish class.
6. I need to zap this email to my boss.

Actual Test

Conversation 1~5

1. Ⓒ **2.** Ⓑ **3.** Ⓒ **4.** Ⓐ **5.** Ⓓ

🔊 5-18

W: Oh, hey, Coach. Got a minute?

M: Sure, but try to make it quick. I'm late for practice.

W: Say, the volleyball team has been going great since you took over. Great job! Anyways, I just wanted to tell you that we've been petitioning the school for a couple of weeks now to start a new ping-pong club, and I was wondering if you would join and support us. What do you think?

M: Ping-pong, huh. Great sport. That's good that you guys have started to do this. Our school can always use new clubs like this. I must say too that back in my day I was a pretty darn good ping-pong player. It's just that I don't believe I really, uh, have the time to coach you guys, that's all. I'm sorry.

W: Oh, no, no, Coach. We're not asking you to coach us! We don't need a coach. It's more of a social club than anything - just a bunch of students who like to get together and have fun. We won't be in any competitions or anything like that!

M: Ah, I see.

W: Yeah, well, anyways, all I need from you is your signature on our petition list. The school requires us to get one hundred signatures before they will consider the new club. We've got ninety-nine so far, and we just need one more!

M: Oh, I got it. Sure. I'd be proud to be the final signature on your petition. There you go!

W: Thanks, Coach. We really appreciate it. Listen, there's one other thing I wanted to talk to you about if you have time.

M: Sure.

W: Well, we're going to need a place to store all our equipment. You know all our balls and paddles, nets, and stuff like that. And I was, uh, wondering if you had any ideas on where we could do that. Do you guys have any extra storage space in the locker room?

M: Well, let's see. When would you need to start using a locker? Actually, how many lockers do you think you would, uh, need?

W: Oh, just one, and we'd probably start using it at the beginning of next month.

M: You know what? Our season is over next week, so

we won't be using most of the lockers until next year. We'll have plenty of space for you guys. Why don't you get with me at the beginning of next month, and we'll set you up? The only thing you'll need is your own lock.

W: A lock, huh. Any special kind? Should I get a key lock or a combination lock, Coach?

M: Well, uh, let's see. How many students do you think will be in this ping-pong club of yours?

W: Ummm, I'm not sure exactly. A lot of students have shown interest, so I would imagine fifteen or so at least. Why?

M: Well, if you're going to have that many, I would suggest a combination lock. That way you can just give everyone the combination, and you wouldn't have to go out and get X number of keys made. It would just be a bit easier, that's all.

W: That's a great idea, Coach! Wow, why didn't I think of that? I don't know what we'd do without you!

M: Ah, don't mention it. That's what I'm here for. Now, um, if there isn't anything else, I'm sure my players are wondering where the heck I'm at. Practice was supposed to start five minutes ago. You know what I have my players do if they are even one minute late to a practice?

W: No, Coach, what's that?

M: Suicides. You know what one of those is?

W: No, Coach. What's a suicide? It sounds pretty tough.

M: Well, it is. It's uh, basically a continuous series of wind sprints. You start from the baseline in the gym, that's the one under the basket. So, you start there, run out and touch the foul-line and then run back then touch the baseline again. But you don't stop there. Oh, no. You keep going, but this time you run out and touch the half-court line and then run back again to touch the baseline.

W: Wow, Coach that sounds so hard. Your players must be in tip-top shape, huh?

M: You've got that right. Conditioning is the key to championships. That's what I always say, conditioning. Without it, you've got... Woah! Look at the time! I've got to stop rambling and get to practice! We'll talk later!

W: Okay, Coach! See you later, and thanks again!

Lecture 6~11

6. Ⓓ **7.** Ⓑ **8.** Ⓑ **9.** Ⓒ **10.** Ⓐ

11. No/No/No/Yes/No

🔊 5-19

Okay. Let's carry on with some more American music history, shall we? For this lecture, I will discuss the effect that ragtime music had on the way the piano was played after, um, ragtime's inception. From a historic point of view, um, ragtime is an American musical genre enjoying its peak popularity, from, um, 1899 to 1918. Ragtime was the first truly American musical genre, preceding jazz. It originated in African American musical communities, descended from the jigs and marches played by all-black bands common in all Northern cities with black populations. Questions? Oh, no problem.

Well, ragtime began as dance music years before being published as popular sheet music for piano. Scott Joplin, the composer/pianist who was known as the, ah, "King of Ragtime" called the effect "weird and intoxicating." By 1897, several important early rags were published, and in 1899 Scott Joplin's *Maple Leaf Rag* was published. Now, some authorities consider ragtime to be a form of classical music. Additionally, the name swing later came to be applied to an early genre of jazz that developed from ragtime. So we can see early on that ragtime had a great influence on music in general at that time.

Okay. Now, let's get to its influence on the piano. To start, the heyday of ragtime was before the widespread availability of sound recording. Like classical music, and unlike jazz, classical ragtime was a written tradition, being distributed in sheet music rather than through recordings or by imitation of live performances. Ragtime music was also distributed via piano rolls for player pianos.

Let's talk about this piano roll. By definition, um, a piano roll is the medium used to operate the player piano, band/fairground organs, calliopes, and hand-cranked organs and pipe organs. Basically, a piano roll is a roll of paper with holes punched in it. The position and length of the perforations determined the note played on the piano. Well, the piano roll moves over a device known as the 'tracker bar,' which had 88 holes, um, or one for each piano key. When a perforation passed over the hole, the note sounds. Believe it or not, piano rolls have been in continuous mass production since around 1897. So, even though a piano roll was used to make a piano play without an actual person playing, we must remember that pianists actually created the music for the piano rolls. Confused? I hope not. Let's move on then.

Another change was called the novelty piano, which can be considered a pianistic cousin of jazz, and this appeared around the same time as the piano roll. Its originators were mostly piano roll artists from the Chicago area. Actually, the novelty piano was developed as a vehicle to showcase the talents of these professionals and was more often sold in the form of recordings and piano rolls than as sheet music.

Anyways, novelty piano slowly fell out of favor to, or was absorbed into, the new orchestral styles as the piano moved off center stage and took a support role. By, um, 1920, though, two new technologies had appeared which allowed the general public to hear music as performed by skilled musicians: the "hand-played" piano roll and the phonograph record.

Now, the most important new form of actually playing the piano in a live performance was called, ah, stride piano, used primarily in jazz. The distinctive technique originated in, um, Harlem, in or about 1919. It was partially influenced by ragtime, which features improvisation, blue notes, and swing rhythms. The over simplistic name "stride" comes from the "striding" left-hand movement. See how I'm doing it? As well, pedal technique further varied the left-hand sound. Quite frankly, stride piano is one of the most difficult styles of jazz piano playing because it takes years to master and is often confused with other jazz piano where the left hand alternates. Like this!

Okay, on a final note, a significant ragtime revival occurred in the 1950s. Ragtime styles of the past were made available on records, and new rags were composed, published, and recorded. A number of popular recordings featured, um, "prepared pianos," simulating the sound of a piano in an old honkey tonk. So, as you can see, we still have portions of piano ragtime music incorporated into the music we hear today.

Lecture 12~17

12. Ⓓ **13.** Ⓑ **14.** Ⓒ **15.** Yes/No/No/Yes/No
16. Ⓑ **17.** Ⓐ
🎧 5-20

Hi, everyone. Okay. Today, I will lecture on some pretty strange plants. As a matter of fact, the plants we will discuss are from the family Rafflesia, a parasitic plant. So, without further delay, I will begin. The Rafflesia is a genus of parasitic flowering plants. It contains, um... 15-19 species, all found in southeastern Asia, let's see, on the Malay Peninsula, Borneo, Sumatra, West Malaysia, and the Philippines. The flowers have no leaves and hardly any stem, just a huge, speckled, five-petal flower with a diameter of up to 106 cm, and it weighs up to 10 kg. Even the smallest species, um, R. manillana, has 15-inch-diameter flowers. The flowers smell like rotting meat, so we get certain local names for these plants which translate to, um, "corpse flower" or "meat flower." The vile smell that the flower gives off can sometimes attract flies, which these plants use as a food source. Additionally, it is parasitic on vines in the genus Vitaceae, spreading its roots inside the vine.

Now, let's talk about specific varieties of Rafflesia. I'll begin with the Nepenthes rafflesiana, a species of pitcher plant named after Stamford Raffles, the founder of Singapore. This plant has a very wide distribution covering, um, Borneo, Sumatra, Peninsular Malaysia, and Singapore. N. rafflesiana is extremely variable with numerous forms and varieties. For example, in Borneo alone, there are at least four distinct varieties. The most impressive form, known as N. rafflesiana gigantea, produces enormous pitchers. These pitchers, or heavily modified leaves, are used to capture and kill insect prey for nutrients.

Well, like it or not, all Nepenthes are, um, passive carnivores. They are classified passive because they have no moving parts, unlike their distant cousins the Venus flytrap, an active carnivore. Okay... So the N. rafflesiana kills by luring its prey into its, ah, pitchers, whose peristomes secrete sweet-tasting nectar. Once the insect is inside, it quickly finds the walls of the pitcher too slippery to scale and, as you may expect, drowns. Digestive enzymes released by the plant into the liquid break down the prey and, um, release soluble nutrients, which are absorbed by the plant through the walls of the pitcher. The carnivorous nature of Nepenthes is supposedly a consequence of, um, living in nutrient-poor soils since the main method of nutrient absorption in most plants, the root, is insufficient in these soils, so the plants have evolved other ways to gain nutrients. Let's see, yes, finally, N. rafflesiana enjoys hot, humid conditions most of the time, as found in tropical jungle lowlands.

Okay, so far so good. The next plant I will discuss is the, um... where are my notes, ah, here we go, Rafflesia arnoldii, another member of the genus Rafflesia. Not only is it the world's largest flower, but it is also one of the most bizarre and improbable organisms on the planet. There are some plants with larger flowering organs, for example, the Titan Arum and Talipot, but these are technically clusters of many flowers. Rafflesia arnoldii is the largest, and you can take this to the bank, because its flower attains a diameter of nearly three feet and can weigh up to, get this, 24 pounds!

It lives as a parasite on the Tetra Stigma vine, as its host, which grows only in undisturbed rainforests. While many parasites appear like normal plants, um, Rafflesia lacks any observable leaves, roots, or even stems, and this is what makes it so strange. A lot like fungi, Rafflesia individuals grow as thread-like strands of tissue completely embedded within and in intimate contact with surrounding host cells from which, um, nutrients and water are obtained. The only part of Rafflesia that is identifiable as distinctly plant-like are the, ah, flowers, although even these are bizarre because they attain a massive size and are usually reddish-brown and stink of rotting flesh. The flower is pollinated by, uh, oh my goodness, flies... which are attracted by its scent. Rafflesia arnoldii is very rare and fairly hard to locate. It is especially difficult to see in flower because the buds take many months to develop, and the flower lasts for just a few days.

Conversation 18 ~ 22

18. Ⓑ **19.** Ⓒ **20.** Ⓐ **21.** Ⓑ **22.** Ⓐ

🔊 5-21

W: Uh, excuse me, Professor. I wanted to talk to you about the paper due next Friday. I'm having some trouble finding enough information on the seasonal migration of the Alaskan Bar-tailed Godwits.

M: Ah, the Godwit, a fascinating species, yet a bit obscure I believe. There haven't been many studies on that particular bird though I do love the long brown bill. Did you know the Bar-tailed Godwit is the holder of the longest nonstop flight known for any bird, 6,835 miles from Alaska to New Zealand? Isn't that fascinating?

W: Of course, Professor. I was able to find that fact. Actually, it is stated in most of the resources I looked at. Unfortunately, it was about the only fact I was able to find on the Bar-tailed Godwit.

M: I see. Well, I thought it would be a little difficult researching the Godwit, but not that hard.

W: Well, yes it is, which is why I'm so concerned. The minimum length of the paper is, as you, uh, know, eight pages typed. I don't think I'll be able to find enough information for that length of a paper. I mean, I could probably stretch it to half that right now, but that would be pushing it.

M: Yes, I see your dilemma. Please understand that I did not intentionally want to put you in any distress. Please remind me when this paper is due.

W: It is due next Friday, sir.

M: Next Friday, hmm, I see. That gives you roughly one week to complete it, correct?

W: That's correct, sir. I'm really starting to panic because I have a number of other papers due next week, and then with finals the week after that, I'm worrying if I'm going to be able to put my best effort into this paper. And now I can't seem to find any info on the bird.

M: Well, I have an idea. Would you feel comfortable changing your topic this late in the game? I could assign you a more research friendly topic, and you could get to work on that. What do you, uh, think?

W: That might be a good idea as long as it isn't as obscure as the migrational habits of the Alaskan Godwit, Professor. What do you think would be a good topic?

M: Now, let's see. How about the cuckoos, which are genuine long distance migratory birds in the tropics? There's been tons written on them, of course, and I doubt you'll have any trouble finding enough stuff on them.

W: The cuckoo, huh? I'll be the laughing stock of our seminar. Can't you assign a bird with a better intellectual reputation than the cuckoo?

M: I do beg to differ. The cuckoo is a bird of impeccable intelligence. How most laymen think of the cuckoo as a silly, stupid bird is a misnomer!

W: Please, Professor! Can't you give me something different?

M: Oh, all right. Let's see here. Um, no, well, uh, how about the Pink-footed Goose? If I recall correctly, they migrate each year from Iceland to England. One of my colleagues has written four books on them, which I can let you borrow.

W: The Pink-footed Goose sounds perfect, Professor! And that would be wonderful if I could borrow those texts from you. I promise that I'll take excellent care of them and will return them just as they were.

M: I have the utmost trust in you.

W: Thank you, thank you, Professor. You've been very accommodating and patient with me, and I appreciate that. Most professors wouldn't have gone out of their way just for one student like you have. Thanks!

M: Oh, don't mention it. I know you guys are under a lot of pressure these days with all the new academic requirements, and it is the least I can do to help you out once in a while when I can. Now, why don't you get out of here and start to work on that paper? I'm really looking forward to, uh, reading about the Pink-footed Goose.

W: Okay, Professor. I will, and I won't let you down! Thanks again! Bye!

Lecture 23~28

23. Ⓒ **24.** Ⓐ **25.** Ⓒ **26.** Ⓓ **27.** Ⓑ
28. Ⓒ

🔘 5-22

W1: Good evening. Everyone ready? Okay. Tonight we will discuss some of the details of the modern printing process. I will begin with the changes in the printing process introduced in the 19th century. First of all, does anyone know the first step a 19th-century printer had to do in order to print something?

W2: I haven't a clue.

W1: Well, make sure you take good notes then. Okay, the first step in the 19th-century printing process was to create the typeset. Let me explain. By the 19th century, printers began using what we now call the hot metal typeset. Hot metal typesetting is a method, um, of creating a relief printing surface by injecting a molten metal alloy into a matrix.

M: Ma'am, I don't want to sound uninformed, but, ah, what's an alloy?

W1: You're kidding? Hmm. An alloy is simply a mixture of metals to create a new metal. Anyways, this alloy was typically an alloy of lead, tin, and a small amount of antimony. The resulting lines of type could range in size from 6 pt. to 24 pt. It was pioneered by the companies Monotype and Linotype in the late 19th century, and their typesetting machines dominated the industry for the next century.

W2: You mean they were using this in the 20th century?

W1: Oh sure. Remember, computers weren't commonplace in the printing industry until the 1980s. Anyways, moving along, the Linotype machine uses a 90-character keyboard to create an entire line of metal type at once. This allows much faster printing than with the Gutenburg-style system, um, in which operators placed down one letter at a time. The machine revolutionized newspaper publishing, making it possible for a relatively small number of operators to set type for many pages on a daily basis.

M: You mean this was the first new printing process since Gutenburg?

W1: Correct. Let me explain how it works. This new

process was produced by Ottmar Mergenthaler in 1886. His Linotype machine was 2.1 meters tall. First of all, a typesetter would put the letter molds to be used to form a line on a page. Once an entire line of molds was assembled, the machine poured molten type metal, which is an alloy of lead, tin, and antimony, into the stacked-up molds. This produced a complete line of type in reverse, so it would read properly when used to transfer ink onto paper. The lines of type were then assembled by hand into a page. Are we good so far?

M: You mean this was all done by hand?

W1: Naturally. But the most difficult process was punch cutting.

M: Well, what's that?

W1: Well, the cutting of letter punches was a highly-skilled craft requiring much patience and practice. The punch-cutter began by, um, transferring the outline of a letter design to one end of a metal bar. Do you understand?

M: Yeah, it sounds pretty basic.

W1: Good. Okay. Next, the outer shape of the letter punch could be cut directly, but the internal curves of a small punch were particularly difficult, as it was necessary to cut deep enough and straight into the metal. This was almost never done with cutting tools, so they used what is called a counterpunch, which is a type of punch used in the cutting of other punches.

W2: You mean they used a counterpunch to cut into the letter punch?

W1: Exactly. Of course, the counterpunch had to be harder than the letter punch itself. This was accomplished by heat tempering the counterpunch and softening the type punch. Once the punches were read, um, a mold could then be created from the punch by using the punch on a softer metal, like copper, to create a matrix. Then, the type metal, that alloy of lead, antimony, and tin, flowed into the matrix to produce a single piece of type, ready for typesetting. One characteristic of type metal that makes it valuable for this use is that it expands as it cools, filling in any gaps present in the thinner portions of letters. I hope I didn't confuse anyone. Does everyone get this? Great!

Lecture 29~34

29. Ⓑ 30. Ⓑ 31. Ⓐ 32. Ⓑ 33. Ⓒ
34. Ⓓ

5-23

M1: Could I get everyone to place their chairs in a semi-circle? That's it. Thank you. Today, we will discuss, ah, method acting and its importance to theatrical acting. Let me begin by giving you a definition of method acting as well as a little background. Ready? Okay. Method acting is an acting technique in which actors try to replicate in real life the emotional conditions under which the character operates in an effort to create a lifelike, realistic performance. "The Method" typically refers to the practice of actors drawing on their own emotions, memories, and experiences to influence their portrayals of characters.

M2: Isn't the method an American invention?

M1: Not necessarily. "The Method", as we will call it, um, was popularized by Lee Strasberg at the Actors Studio and the Group Theater in New York City in the 1940s and 1950s. But, the method was derived from "the Stanislavski System," after Konstantin Stanislavski, who pioneered similar ideas in his quest for "theatrical truth." This was done through, um, friendships with Russia's leading actors as well as his teachings, writings, and acting at the Moscow Art Theater, founded in 1897. By the way, this is very important. The system is the result of Stanislavski's many years of efforts to determine how a, umm, how should I say this, how a human being can control, in their performance, the most intangible and uncontrollable aspects of human behavior: things such as emotions and artistic inspiration. Geez, that's a mouthful! Question?

M2: Ah, you mean the Stanislavski System encouraged actors to act naturally?

M1: Exactly! But there's more to it than that. The Stanislavski System is a complex method for producing, shall we say, realistic characters, and most of today's actors, on stage, television, and film, owe much to it. By using "The System," an actor is required to, um, deeply analyze his or her character's motivations. Stanislavski and his system are frequently misunderstood. For instance, often the system is confused with the method.

W2: So, let me get this straight. The method is an offshoot of the system, correct?

M1: Yes, correct. But there is more to it. The method is also an outgrowth of the American theater scene of the 1930s and 40s. This is when actors and directors such as, let's see, Elia Kazan and Lee Strasberg, for example, came across Stanislavski's ideas through theatrical teachers like Stella Adler.

She showed Strasberg Stanislavski's system ideas, and within two years, Strasberg was artistic director of the Actors Studio and the Group Theater, teaching his version of the Stanislavski System or the Method. Actors under his tutelage there included Al Pacino, Marilyn Monroe, and Robert De Niro, just to name a few of many. I hope that's clear for everyone.

M2: Got it! By the way, that's a pretty impressive list of actors!

M1: Absolutely! And since all of the above mentioned actors are method actors, we can see the importance of method acting as related to theater and movies.

W2: Well, I don't get it. What makes a method actor more important or better than an actor who hasn't studied Strasberg's method?

M1: Well, maybe a little more insight into the method is needed here. In general, method acting combines a careful consideration of the, um, psychological motives of the character and some sort of personal identification with and, in some cases, possibly the reproduction of the character's emotional state in a realistic way. This process can include, ah, various ideologies and practices such as "as if," "substitution," "emotional memory," and "preparation." So, the difference between a method actor and a non-method actor would probably be the amount of preparation given for a particular part. Most method actors therefore would be considered lead actors.

W2: Okay. But how does the method impact a performance? Can you give us a well known example of an actor who has gone above the call of duty to prepare for a part?

M1: Very well. There are so many examples of method actors who have put their bodies and souls into the characters that they are playing. Let's use Robert de Niro as an example. Praised for his commitment to roles stemming from his background in method acting, De Niro gained 60 pounds and learned how to box for his portrayal of Jake LaMotta in *Raging Bull*, ground his teeth for *Cape Fear*, lived in Sicily for *The Godfather Part II*, and learned to play the saxophone for *New York, New York*. He also put on weight and shaved his hairline to play Al Capone in *The Untouchables*. And how did de Niro's preparation impact his performances? He won two Academy Awards for doing it.

《托福考试官方指南》

（第4版）（含光盘1张）

ETS（美国教育考试服务中心）编著

◎ ETS中国唯一授权版本
◎ 托福考试的必备权威辅导书
◎ 数百道托福考试题目及写作题库

定价：118元 开本：16开 页码：664页

《托福考试全真试题集》

（含光盘1张）

ETS（美国教育考试服务中心）编著

◎ ETS官方独家版本，托福考生必备辅导用书
◎ 5套托福全真考试试题，体验真实考试情境
◎ 提供考题答案详解及全部音频内容，深入、透彻分析托福题目
◎ 提供托福考试备考计划，帮助考生高效科学备考

定价：108元 开本：16开 页码：560页

《新托福考试综合教程》（第二版）

（含互动模考光盘1张 + 9张CD）

Deborah Phillips 著

◎ 8套专项训练题目，全方位强化应试技能
◎ 2套完整的全真模拟试题，帮助考生熟悉真实考试形式

定价：148元 开本：16开 页码：704页

《托福考试备考策略与模拟试题》

（含光盘1张） Nancy Gallagher 著

◎ 35个包含阅读、听力、口语及写作的语言技能训练单元
◎ 4套完整的全真强化试题
◎ 为考生设置了15周的学习计划，提供大量练习资料

定价：108元 开本：16开 页码：720页

《新托福考试全真模考题与精解》

（含MP3和模考盘各1张）

Pamela J. Sharpe 著

◎ 详细说明听说读写四部分的特点及有效的应试策略
◎ 含650分钟录音光盘1张，包含书中所有音频内容
◎ 含模考光盘1张，模拟真实考试情景

定价：118元 开本：16开 页码：832页

《新托福考试冲刺试题》

（含光盘1张） Nancy Gallagher 著

◎ 6套完整全真冲刺试题，600道经典测试题目，体现托福考试的最新特色
◎ 文章题材、出题角度、考题类型以及话题内容等与实际考试一致
◎ 随书配有360分钟录音光盘1张，语境逼真，契合真实考场情景

定价：58元 开本：16开 页码：396页

《TOEFL 官方题库范文精讲》

（附 MP3） Lin Lougheed 编著

◎ 提供TOEFL写作三步法，详解写作技巧和策略
◎ 精编大量练习题目，针对性极强
◎ 10篇综合写作参考例文 + 185篇独立写作题库范文

定价：58元 开本：16开 页码：432页

《新托福考试口语胜经》（附 MP3）

翟少成 编著

◎ 深入剖析各个口语题型，点拨回答技巧
◎ 3份真题详解+4套模拟试题+5个核心章节+6大实用模板 = 实现托福口语高分

定价：49元 开本：16开 页码：320页

《托福主题词汇与阅读》

（附 CD-ROM） 赖水信 编著

◎ 以历年真题为蓝本，精编48个Advanced Test
◎ 每个Advanced Test包含50道词汇题目，全书共计2400道
◎ 全书涉及的主题广泛而多样，充满知识性与趣味性

定价：55元 开本：16开 页码：524页

《新托福考试写作高分速成》

陈向东 著

◎ 详细阐述托福综合写作解答的7大步骤及5大写作原则，给出独立写作3大写作策略和5大解题原则
◎ 深刻剖析写作思路，并提供解题策略及思维训练，解读真题
◎ 精心打造托福写作题型、解答原则与黄金模板

定价：35元 开本：16开 页码：280页

《TOEFL 写作/口语论证论据素材大全》
韦晓亮 编著

◎ 全面性：全面补充TOEFL写作和口语英文论证论据素材

◎ 权威性：汇集世界优秀外文期刊、报纸、书籍、检索数据库和权威新闻网站的英文内容

◎ 指导性：汇集新东方TOEFL考试培训项目数年教学经验和写作、口语教学成果

定价：25元　开本：32开　页码：248页

《新托福考试听力特训》（第二版）
（含光盘1张）

Ji-Yeon Lee 著

◎ 59篇精选听力练习语料，题材广泛，全面满足备考需求

◎ 提供多种练习方式，逐步掌握答题技巧

◎ 特设听力模拟试题，体验真实考试情景

定价：58元　开本：16开　页码：452页

《新托福考试核心语法》
（含光盘1张）　Nancy Gallagher 编著

◎ 全书涵盖20个重要的英语语法点，紧扣新托福考试语法要点

◎ 结合经典的例子，对各个语法点进行精辟深入的讲解

◎ 提供大量模考练习，设有计时测验

定价：50元　开本：16开　页码：308页

《新托福考试写作特训》（第二版）
（含光盘1张）

Ji-Yeon Lee 著

◎ 三个章节精练详解，两种题型各个击破

◎ 提供多种练习方式，逐步掌握写作技巧

◎ 特设仿真写作测试，体验真实考试情境

定价：46元　开本：16开　页码：304页

《新托福考试阅读特训》（第二版）

Ji-Yeon Lee 著

◎ 62篇精选文章，题材广泛，全面满足备考需求

◎ 特设仿真阅读试题，体验真实考试情境

◎ 全书结构编排科学合理，实用性强

定价：55元　开本：16开　页码：472页

《TOEFL 巴朗词表》（附MP3）

Steven J. Matthiesen 编著

◎ 系统研究真题，提炼高频词汇

◎ 收录双语释义，遴选同义派生

◎ 提供经典例句，加深理解记忆

定价：35元　开本：16开　页码：256页

《托福考试口语特训》（第二版）
（附MP3）**Ji-Yeon Lee 著**

◎ 69个单元精练详解，6大题型逐个突破

◎ 提供多种练习方式，逐步掌握答题技巧

◎ 特设口语模拟试题，体验真实考试情景

定价：65元　开本：16开　页码：520页

《托福词组必备》
俞敏洪 编著

◎ 紧扣真题，选词科学

◎ 例句经典，原汁原味

◎ 收录同义词组，扩充词汇量

◎ 幽默插图，巧妙助记

定价：22元　开本：32开　页码：256页

《TOEFL词汇词根＋联想记忆法：45天突破版》

（含光盘1张）　　　　俞敏洪 编著

◎ "词根＋联想记忆法"实用有趣，有效提升词汇量
◎ 甄选重点词汇，紧跟TOEFL考试趋势
◎ 增加单词返记菜单，有助于复习和自测
◎ 再现真题例句，直击TOEFL考试要点

定价：45元　开本：32开　页码：528页

《TOEFL iBT 阅读词汇小伴侣》

张洪伟 蔡青 编著

◎ 针对性强——囊括托福阅读全部话题及学科领域词汇
◎ 实用性佳——精选托福阅读词汇及同义词，在语境中真正融会贯通
◎ 分类清晰——囊括托福阅读基础、核心、高频及次高频分类词汇

定价：15元　开本：32开　页码：204页

《TOEFL iBT 词汇 10000》

（含光盘1张）　　张洪伟 戴云 编著

◎ 源于真题目——收录托福真题的必备词汇与经典例句
◎ 奉献真经典——凝结托福名师的教学感悟与智慧结晶

定价：45元　开本：16开　页码：444页

《托福写作词汇小伴侣》

张洪伟 戴云 编著

◎ 针对性强——浓缩托福独立写作和综合写作最常用词汇
◎ 实用性佳——精选鲜活的托福写作常用短语与习惯搭配

定价：16元　开本：32开　页码：332页

《TOEFL iBT 听力词汇小伴侣》

邱政政 戴懿德 编著

◎ 紧跟TOEFL考试趋势，权威指点
◎ 精选常考核心词汇，针对性强
◎ 分类词汇专业全面，重点突出
◎ 精选TOEFL常用短语与习惯搭配，实用性佳

定价：18元　开本：32开　页码：388页

《词以类记：TOEFL iBT 词汇》

张红岩 编著

◎ TOEFL iBT 最新词汇：覆盖听说读写
◎ 按学科和意群分类：细分至最小同义词区间

定价：35元　开本：32开　页码：424页

《TOEFL iBT 口语词汇小伴侣》

张洪伟 翟少成 编著

◎ 应试导向——紧扣新托福口语考试趋势，给出三类词汇供考生掌握
◎ 科学统计——所涉及学术类专业词汇来自真实词频统计数据

定价：15元　开本：32开　页码：280页

《TOEFL 词汇词根＋联想记忆法》

（附 MP3）　　　　俞敏洪 编著

◎ "GRE红宝书"姊妹篇，"词根＋联想"实用有趣
◎ 500个常考习语短语，打通听力、阅读经脉
◎ 释义精准并配真题例句，直击TOEFL考试要点

定价：28元　开本：32开　页码：424页

《新托福考试专项进阶——初级听力》（附MP3光盘）

定价：42元　开本：16开　页码：288页

《新托福考试专项进阶——中级听力》（附MP3光盘）

定价：45元　开本：16开　页码：344页

《新托福考试专项进阶——高级听力》（附MP3光盘）

定价：45元　开本：16开　页码：348页

《新托福考试专项进阶——阅读模拟试题（上）》

定价：36元　开本：16开　页码：252页

《新托福考试专项进阶——阅读模拟试题（下）》

定价：36元　开本：16开　页码：252页

《新托福考试专项进阶——初级写作》（附MP3光盘）

定价：40元　开本：16开　页码：268页

《新托福考试专项进阶——中级写作》（附MP3光盘）

定价：38元　开本：16开　页码：248页

《新托福考试专项进阶——高级写作》（附MP3光盘）

定价：42元　开本：16开　页码：304页

《新托福考试专项进阶——初级口语》（附MP3光盘）

定价：42元　开本：16开　页码：296页

《新托福考试专项进阶——中级口语》（附MP3光盘）

定价：38元　开本：16开　页码：248页

《新托福考试专项进阶——高级口语》（附MP3光盘）

定价：42元　开本：16开　页码：288页

《新托福考试专项进阶——听力模拟试题（上）》（附MP3光盘）

定价：40元　开本：16开　页码：256页

《新托福考试专项进阶——听力模拟试题（下）》（附MP3光盘）

定价：36元　开本：16开　页码：220页

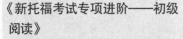

《新托福考试专项进阶——初级阅读》

定价：35元　开本：16开　页码：308页

《新托福考试专项进阶——中级阅读》

定价：38元　开本：16开　页码：344页

《新托福考试专项进阶——高级阅读》

定价：40元　开本：16开　页码：368页

◎　《新托福考试专项进阶》系列丛书从托福考试所考查的听、说、读、写四项技能入手，为考生提供了详尽的考试指导，并将各技能分为初、中、高三级，通过独特的"进阶训练"方式，再辅以大量练习，让考生逐步掌握托福实考的技巧，同时切实提高英语实际运用能力，从而在短期内轻松取得托福高分。本丛书内容编排由易到难，循序渐进，实战性强，是不可多得的托福备考资料。

◎　本丛书引进自韩国多乐园出版社。该社成立于1977年，在韩国英语教育出版领域始终处于领军地位。本丛书被韩国众多学校和培训机构指定为课堂教材，在托福考生中享有较高声誉。

《走进美国顶尖本科大学》

周成刚　杨维新　编著

◎　提供权威、准确、全面的院校信息

◎　展示高等学府优良传统与治学特色

◎　深入剖析院校录取标准

◎　集萃留学生精彩随笔

定价：38 元　开本：16 开　页码：264 页

《留学申请写作模板：个人陈述、推荐信、简历》

包凡一　王薇　编著

◎　一本让莘莘学子实现留学梦想的权威写作指南！

◎　一本由一线留学专家推荐的专业文书写作模板！

◎　一本你不能错过的经典申请文书集萃！

定价：42 元　开本：16 开　页码：336 页

《留美申请白皮书》

许轶　曾舒煜　编著

◎　收集国内和美国名校超过60位各专业精英的真实案例、成功经验以及权威指导

◎　系统地将经济学、统计学、营销学理论运用到申请领域

定价：35 元　开本：16 开　页码：280 页

《留学要趁早》

俞敏洪　张洪伟　周容　编著

◎　读十位优秀学子真实的成长故事，收获感动，尽早立志

◎　看成功者高中毕业即步入哈佛、剑桥等世界顶尖高校，实现梦想，助跑人生

◎　教育专家俞敏洪、张洪伟、"哈佛妈妈"周容倾力打造留学励志宝典

定价：29.8 元　开本：16 开　页码：268 页

《北美名校本科留学申请写作指导及范文》

Adrienne Dowhan, Chris Dowhan, Dan Kaufman 　编著

◎ 甄选50多篇出自北美名校本科申请者之手的精彩范文

◎ 基于多年评审经验，全面总结写作六大步骤

◎ 总结留学申请写作四大成功要素

◎ 专业人员精彩点评范文，结合实例点拨写作技巧

定价：35元　开本：16开　页码：276页

《北美研究生院留学申请写作指导及范文》

何庆权　包凡一　编著

◎ 总结申请北美研究生院的各大步骤与注意事项

◎ 集萃大量文书写作实例，涵盖理、工、文、法、医等专业

◎ 通过个案详细讲解文书写作思路，深入剖析常见写作误区

定价：40元　开本：16开　页码：300页

《北美名校商学院留学申请写作指导及范文》

Adrienne Dowhan, Chris Dowhan, Dan Kaufman 　编著

◎ 荟萃50多篇申请文实例，出自北美名校商学院申请者之手

◎ 基于多年评审经验，全面总结写作五大步骤

◎ 总结留学申请写作四大成功要素

◎ 专业人员精彩点评每篇范文，结合实例点拨写作技巧

定价：35元　开本：16开　页码：288页

《北美名校商学院留学申请论题回答范例》

张咏诚　编著

◎ 近百所名校MBA申请人ESSAY回答范例

◎ 范例搜集了北美近百所大学MBA ESSAY，从哈佛大学、斯坦福大学到伊利诺伊大学芝加哥分校

◎ 详细列举众多欧洲名校的MBA ESSAY，精彩范例，独家呈现

◎ MBA申请人必备的留学申请书籍

定价：32元　开本：16开　页码：206页

《美国签证口语指南》（附 CD-ROM）

邱政政　编著

◎　以面试口语问答分析签证成败之因

◎　知己知彼，了解美国签证官思维表达方式

◎　案例实录与分析助您吸取前人的经验与教训

定价：25 元　开本：32 开　页码：176 页

《美国本科留学指南》

Joyce Slayton Mitchell 编著　冯云　等译

　　本书由美国知名留学咨询专家、教育专家Joyce Slayton Mitchell女士所撰写，帮助中国青少年到美国接受高等教育。全书分为两大部分：第一部分重点讲述申请美国大学的注意事项、文书写作以及相关考试等内容；第二部分重点介绍包括哈佛、耶鲁等知名学府在内的美国150余所大学的基本情况，包括学生比例、专业、奖学金等等。本书从专家的角度对计划申请美国本科的学生给予指导与建议，是中国学生留学美国的一本必备参考书。

定价：30 元　开本：16 开　页码：288 页

《这就是美国》

Olga Mark Landsberg 著　吴春晓　译

◎　美国本土人看自己 + 世界各国人看美国，为您呈现"真实、立体的美国"

◎　广泛的调查研究 + 权威的专家观点，为您提供"专业、可靠的意见参考"

◎　无所不包的预设情境 + 丰富具体的信息指导，给您提供"贴心、实用的服务指南"

◎　细致周详的行前准备 + 行之有效的预案攻略，为您增加"畅行美国的从容与自信"

定价：45 元　开本：16 开　页码：460 页

《澳大利亚留学指南》

陈晴　耿耿　编著

◎　强强联手——两位多年从事澳大利亚留学咨询工作和雅思教学工作的名师共同打造。

◎　覆盖面广——从准备到成行，从学习到生活，从课程介绍到学校特色，一书在手，远赴异国不再难。

◎　权威可靠——权威的参考资料，可靠的信息来源，全力助你赴澳留学！

定价：49 元　开本：16 开　页码：472 页

《出国留学 DIY 全攻略》

钟凌 编著

本书的一大特色是DIY，以详尽的解说引导消费群体，以自助的形式独立申请留学，作科学的规划，享受DIY的挑战与满足。此书对各国留学信息及申请出国的步骤都作了详细的介绍，同时还详细地介绍了国外留学专业分类，并对热门专业及相关职业规划作了详尽的建议，为您设计了最佳的留学申请方案。本书信息量丰富，理论知识与实战经验兼备，是一本不可多得的宝书。

定价：28元　开本：16开　页码：228页

《中文可以这样教——海外汉语辅导通用手册》

邱政政 史中琦 编著

打算远赴重洋求学深造、正在为撰写申请信和个人陈述而绞尽脑汁的同学们，你是否意识到，中文可以为你的简历增添亮丽的一笔？正在海外为学业和工作忙碌、为生活打拼的同胞们，你可曾意识到，中文可以为你打开一扇新的就业之门？立志于中外交流、希望结识更多外国友人的朋友们，你是否想过，中文可以让你在跨文化交际中更具魅力？如果，你还没有意识到中文可能带来的巨大影响，那么，请你跟我走进中文的世界，确切地说，是中文辅导的世界。

定价：22元　开本：32开　页码：208页

《美国名校毕业演说集萃》

许轶 编著

本书收录了美国著名大学的毕业演说。这些站在美国顶级名校毕业典礼讲台上的演说者们，来自政界、商界、学术界、娱乐界……他们在这里"齐聚一堂"，侃侃而谈，以他们的视角、经历和感悟来传道、授业、解惑。

定价：20元　开本：32开　页码：224页

《我的美利坚本科岁月》

马俏 著

本书记述了从高考前的抉择到美国一流名校的留学生涯，从充实、和谐的美国社区见闻到充满冒险及人文关怀的异国游记，从单纯、快乐的校园生活到险象环生的求职之路，全方位展现了一位优秀的80后留学生的奋斗路程，同时，通过作者对生活的细腻观察，从一个女留学生的视角展示了现代美国及美洲国家的生活风貌。

定价：25元　开本：32开　页码：304页